The International Jew

—

Volumes I and II

being

Volume I: The International Jew—The World's Foremost Problem

and

Volume II: Jewish Activities in the United States

By Henry Ford, founder of the
Ford Motor Company, and the
Editors of *The Dearborn Independent*.

Ostara Publications

The International Jew: Volumes I and II
being
Volume I: The International Jew: The World's Foremost Problem
and
Volume II: Jewish Activities in the United States

By Henry Ford, founder of the Ford Motor Company, and the Editors of *The Dearborn Independent*.

First published by *The Dearborn Independent*
as
Volume 1: The International Jew: The World's Foremost Problem (1920)
Volume 2: Jewish Activities in the United States (1921)

This edition (2016) by Ostara Publications
ostarapublications.com

ISBN 978-1-68418-612-9

CONTENTS

Volume 1: The International Jew: The World's Foremost Problem

Preface..1
1. The Jew in Character and Business..3
2. Germany's Reaction against the Jew..16
3. Jewish History in the United States..24
4. The Jewish Question—Fact or Fancy?..33
5. Anti-Semitism—Will It Appear in the U.S.?.......................................43
6. Jewish Question Breaks Into the Magazines......................................55
7. Arthur Brisbane Leaps to the Help of Jewry......................................61
8. Does a Definite Jewish World Program Exist?...................................68
9. The Historic Basis of Jewish Imperialism..78
10. An Introduction to the "Jewish Protocols"......................................89
11. "Jewish" Estimate of Gentile Human Nature..................................96
12. "Jewish Protocols" Claim Partial Fulfillment................................106
13. "Jewish" Plan to Split Society by "Ideas".......................................116
14. Did the Jews Foresee the World War?...126
15. Is the Jewish "Kahal" the Modern "Soviet"?..................................135
16. How the "Jewish Question" Touches the Farm.............................145
17. Does Jewish Power Control the World Press?..............................155
18. Does This Explain Jewish Political Power?...................................167
19. The All-Jewish Mark on "Red Russia"...176
20. Jewish Testimony in Favor of Bolshevism.....................................186

Volume 2: Jewish Activities in the United States

Preface..196
21. How Jews in the U.S. Conceal Their Strength..............................198
22. Jewish Testimony on "Are Jews a Nation?"..................................208
23. Jew Versus Non-Jew in New York Finance...................................217
24. The High and Low of Jewish Money Power..................................227
25. "Disraeli of America"—A Jew of Super-Power..............................237
26. The Scope of Jewish Dictatorship in the U.S................................247
27. Jewish Copper Kings Reap Rich War-Profits................................256

Contents (Continued)

28. Jewish Control of the American Theater.................................267
29. The Rise of the First Jewish Theatrical Trust.........................276
30. How Jews Capitalized a Protest Against Jews........................283
31. The Jewish Aspect of the "Movie" Problem............................291
32. Jewish Supremacy in Motion Picture World..........................300
33. Rule of the Jewish Kehillah Grips New York..........................309
34. The Jewish Demand for "Rights" in America........................319
35. "Jewish Rights" Clash With American Rights........................329
36. "Jewish Rights" to Put Studies Out of Schools......................341
37. Disraeli—British Premier, Portrays the Jews.........................351
38. Taft Once Tried to Resist Jews—and Failed...........................361
39. When Editors Were Independent of the Jews.......................372
40. Why the Jews Dislike the Morgenthau Report......................381
41. Jews Use the Peace Conference to Bind Poland...................391
42. The Present Status of the Jewish Question..........................402

Volume 1: The International Jew: The World's Foremost Problem

Preface

Why discuss the Jewish Question? Because it is here, and because its emergence into American thought should contribute to its solution, and not to a continuance of those bad conditions which surround the Question in other countries.

The Jewish Question has existed in the United States for a long time. Jews themselves have known this, even if Gentiles have not. There have been periods in our own country when it has broken forth with a sullen sort of strength which presaged darker things to come. Many signs portend that it is approaching an acute stage.

Not only does the Jewish Question touch those matters that are of common knowledge, such as financial and commercial control, usurpation of political power, monopoly of necessities, and autocratic direction of the very news that the American people read; but it reaches into cultural regions and so touches the very heart of American life.

This question reaches down into South America and threatens to become an important factor in Pan-American relations. It is interwoven with much of the menace of organized and calculated disorder which troubles the nations today. It is not of recent growth, but its roots go deep, and the long Past of this Problem is counterbalanced by prophetic hopes and programs which involve a very deliberate and creative view of the Future.

This little book is the partial record of an investigation of the Jewish Question. It is printed to enable interested readers to inform themselves on the data published in *The Dearborn Independent* prior to Oct. 1, 1920. The demand for back copies of the paper was so great that the supply was exhausted early, as was also a large edition of a booklet containing the first nine articles of the series. The investigation still proceeds, and the articles will continue to appear as heretofore until the work is done.

The motive of this work is simply a desire to make facts known to the people. Other motives have, of course, been ascribed to it. But the motive of prejudice or any form of antagonism is hardly strong enough to support such an investigation as this. Moreover, had an unworthy motive existed, some sign of it would inevitably appear in the work itself. We confidently call the reader to witness that the tone of these articles is all that it should be. The International Jew and his satellites, as the conscious enemies of all that Anglo-Saxons mean by civilization, are not spared, nor is that unthinking mass which defends anything that a Jew does, simply because it has been taught to believe that what Jewish leaders do is Jewish. Neither do these articles proceed upon a false emotion of brotherhood and apology, as if this stream of doubtful tendency in the world were only accidentally Jewish. We give the facts as we find them; that of itself is sufficient protection against prejudice or passion.

This volume does not complete the case by any means. But it brings the reader along one step. In future compilations of these and subsequent articles the entire scope of the inquiry will more clearly appear.

October, 1920.

"Among the distinguishing mental and moral traits of the Jews may be mentioned: distaste for hard or violent physical labor; a strong family sense and philoprogenitiveness; a marked religious instinct; the courage of the prophet and martyr rather than of the pioneer and soldier; remarkable power to survive in adverse environments, combined with great ability to retain racial solidarity; capacity for exploitation, both individual and social; shrewdness and astuteness in speculation and money matters generally; an Oriental love of display and a full appreciation of the power and pleasure of social position; a very high average of intellectual ability."
— *The New International Encyclopedia.*

1. The Jew in Character and Business

The Jew is again being singled out for critical attention throughout the world. His emergence in the financial, political and social spheres has been so complete and spectacular since the war, that his place, power and purpose in the world are being given a new scrutiny, much of it unfriendly. Persecution is not a new experience to the Jew, but intensive scrutiny of his nature and super-nationality is. He has suffered for more than 2,000 years from what may be called instinctive anti-Semitism of the other races, but this antagonism has never been intelligent nor has it been able to make itself intelligible. Nowadays, however, the Jew is being placed, as it were, under the microscope of economic observation that the reasons for his power, the reasons for his separateness, the reasons for his suffering may be defined and understood.

In Russia he is charged with being the source of Bolshevism, an accusation which is serious or not according to the circle in which it is made; we in America, hearing the fervid eloquence and perceiving the prophetic ardor of young Jewish apostles of social and industrial reform, can calmly estimate how it may be. In Germany he is charged with being the cause of the Empire's collapse and a very considerable literature has sprung up, bearing with it a mass of circumstantial evidence that gives the thinker pause.

In England he is charged with being the real world ruler, who rules as a super-nation over the nations, rules by the power of gold, and who plays nation against nation for his own purposes, remaining himself discreetly in the background. In America it is pointed out to what extent the elder Jews of wealth and the younger Jews of ambition swarmed through the war organizations — principally those departments which dealt with the commercial and industrial business of war, and also the extent to which they have clung to the advantage which their experience as agents of the government gave them.

In simple words, the question of the Jews has come to the fore, but like other questions which lend themselves to prejudice, efforts will be made to hush it up as impolitic for open discussion. If, however, experience has taught us anything it is that questions thus suppressed will sooner or later break out in undesirable and unprofitable forms.

The Jew is the world's enigma. Poor in his masses, he yet controls the world's finances. Scattered abroad without country or government, he yet presents a unity of race continuity which no other people has achieved. Living under legal disabilities in almost every land, he has become the power behind many a throne. There are ancient prophecies to the effect that the Jew will return to his own land and from that center rule the world, though not until he has undergone an assault by the united nations of mankind.

The single description which will include a larger percentage of Jews than members of any other race is this: he is in business. It may be only gathering rags and selling them, but he is in business. From the sale of old clothes to the control of international trade and finance, the Jew is supremely gifted for business. More than any other race he exhibits a decided aversion to industrial employment, which he balances by an equally decided adaptability to trade. The Gentile boy works his way up, taking employment in the productive or technical departments; but the Jewish boy prefers to begin as messenger, salesman or clerk — anything — so long as it is connected with the commercial side of the business. An early Prussian census illustrates this characteristic: of a total population of 269,400, the Jews comprised six per cent or 16,164. Of these, 12,000 were traders and 4,164 were workmen. Of the Gentile population, the other 94 per cent, or 153,236 people, there were only 17,000 traders.

A modern census would show a large professional and literary class added to the traders, but no diminution of the percentage of traders and not much if any increase in the number of wage toilers. In America alone most of the big business, the trusts and the banks, the natural resources and the chief agricultural products, especially tobacco, cotton and sugar, are in the control of Jewish financiers or their agents. Jewish journalists are a large and powerful group here. "Large numbers of department stores are held by Jewish firms," says the *Jewish Encyclopedia*, and many if not most of them are run under Gentile names. Jews are the largest and most numerous landlords of residence property in the country. They are supreme in the theatrical world. They absolutely control the circulation of publications throughout the country. Fewer than any race whose presence among us is noticeable, they receive daily an amount of favorable publicity which would be impossible did they not have the facilities for creating and distributing it themselves. Werner Sombart, in his "Jew and Modern Capitalism" says, "If the conditions in America continue to develop along the same lines as in the last generation, if the immigration statistics and the proportion of births among all the nationalities remain the same, our imagination may picture the United States of fifty or a hundred years hence as a land inhabited only by Slavs, Negroes and Jews, wherein the Jews will naturally occupy the position of economic leadership." Sombart is a pro-Jewish writer.

The question is, If the Jew is in control, how did it happen? This is a free country. The Jew comprises only about three per cent of the population; to every Jew there are 97 Gentiles; to the 3,000,000 Jews in the United States there are 97,000,000 Gentiles. If the Jew is in control, is it because of his superior ability, or is it because of the inferiority and don't-care attitude of the Gentiles?

It would be very simple to answer that the Jews came to America, took their chances like other people and proved more successful in the competitive struggle. But that would not include all the facts. And before a more adequate answer can be given, two points should be made clear. This first is this: all Jews are not rich controllers of wealth.

There are poor Jews aplenty, though most of them even in their poverty are their own masters. While it may be true that the chief financial controllers of the country are Jews, it is not true that every Jew is one of the financial controllers of the country.

The classes must be kept distinct for a reason which will appear when the methods of the rich Jews and the methods of the poor Jews to gain power are differentiated. Secondly; the fact of Jewish solidarity renders it difficult to measure Gentile and Jewish achievements by the same standard. When a great block of wealth in America was made possible by the lavish use of another block of wealth from across the seas; that is to say, when certain Jewish immigrants came to the United States with the financial backing of European Jewry behind them, it would be unfair to explain the rise of that class of immigration by the same rules which account for the rise of, say, the Germans or the Poles who came here with no resource but their ambition and strength.

To be sure, many individual Jews come in that way, too, with no dependence but themselves, but it would not be true to say that the massive control of affairs which is exercised by Jewish wealth was won by individual initiative; it was rather the extension of financial control across the sea.

That, indeed, is where any explanation of Jewish control must begin. Here is a race whose entire period of national history saw them peasants on the land, whose ancient genius was spiritual rather than material, bucolic rather than commercial, yet today, when they have no country, no government, and are persecuted in one way or another everywhere they go, they are declared to be the principal though unofficial rulers of the earth. How does so strange a charge arise, and why do so many circumstances seem to justify it?

Begin at the beginning. During the formative period of their national character the Jews lived under a law which made plutocracy and pauperism equally impossible among them.

Modern reformers who are constructing model social systems on paper would do well to look into the social system under which the early Jews were organized.

The Law of Moses made a "money aristocracy," such as Jewish financiers form today, impossible because it forbade the taking of interest. It made impossible also the continuous enjoyment of profit wrung out of another's distress. Profiteering and sheer speculation were not favored under the Jewish system.

There could be no land-hogging; the land was apportioned among the people, and though it might be lost by debt or sold under stress, it was returned every 50 years to its original family ownership, at which time, called "The Year of Jubilee," there was practically a new social beginning. The rise of great landlords and a moneyed class was impossible under such a system, although the interim of 50 years gave ample scope for individual initiative to assert itself under fair competitive conditions.

If, therefore, the Jews had retained their status as a nation, and had remained in Palestine under the Law of Moses, they would hardly have achieved the financial distinction which they have since won. Jews never got rich out of one another. Even in modern times they have not become rich out of each other but out of the nations among whom they dwelt. Jewish law permitted the Jew to do business with a Gentile on a different basis than that on which he did business with a brother Jew. What is called "the Law of the Stranger" was defined thus: "unto a stranger thou mayest lend upon usury; but unto thy brother thou shalt not lend upon usury."

Being dispersed among the nations, but never merging themselves with the nations and never losing a very distinctive identity, the Jew has had the opportunity to practice "the ethics of the stranger" for many centuries. Being strangers among strangers, and often among cruelly hostile strangers, they have found this law a compensating advantage. Still, this alone would not account for the Jew's preeminence in finance.

The explanation of that must be sought in the Jew himself, his vigor, resourcefulness and special proclivities.

Very early in the Jewish story we discover the tendency of Israel to be a master nation, with other nations as its vassals. Notwithstanding the fact that the whole prophetic purpose with reference to Israel seems to have been the moral enlightenment of the world through its agency, Israel's "will to mastery" apparently hindered that purpose. At least such would seem to be the tone of the Old Testament.

Divinely ordered to drive out the Canaanites that their corrupt ideas might not contaminate Israel, the Jews did not obey, according to the old record. They looked over the Canaanitish people and perceived what great amount of manpower would be wasted if they were expelled, and so Israel enslaved them —

"And it came to pass, when Israel was strong, that they put the Canaanites to tribute, and did not utterly drive them out." It was this form of disobedience, this preference of material mastery over spiritual leadership, that marked the beginning of Israel's age-long disciplinary distress.

The Jews' dispersion among the nations temporarily (that is, for more than 25 centuries now) changed the program which their scriptures declare was divinely planned, and that dispersion continues until today. There are spiritual leaders in modern Judaism who still claim that Israel's mission to the nations is spiritual, but their assertions that Israel is today fulfilling that mission are not as convincing as they might be if accompanied by more evidence.

Israel, throughout the modern centuries is still looking at the Gentile world and estimating what its man-power can be made to yield. But the discipline upon Israel still holds; he is an exile from his own land, condemned to be discriminated against wherever he goes, until the time when exile and homelessness shall end in a reestablished Palestine, and Jerusalem again the moral center of the earth, even as the elder prophets have declared.

Had the Jew become an employe, a worker for other men, his dispersion would not probably have been so wide. But becoming a trader, his instincts drew him round the habitable earth. There were Jews in China at an early date. They appeared as traders in England at the time of the Saxons. Jewish traders were in South America 100 years before the Pilgrim Fathers landed at Plymouth Rock. Jews established the sugar industry in the Island of St. Thomas in 1492. They were well established in Brazil when only a few villages dotted the eastern coast of what is now the United States.

And how far they penetrated when once they came here is indicated by the fact that the first white child born in Georgia was a Jew — Isaac Minis. The Jew's presence round the earth, his clannishness with his own people, made him a nation scattered among the nations, a corporation with agents everywhere.

Another talent, however, contributed greatly to his rise in financial power — his ability to invent new devices for doing business. Until the Jew was pitted against the world, business was very crudely done. And when we trace the origins of many of the business methods which simplify and facilitate trade today, more likely than not we find a Jewish name at the end of the clue. Many of the indispensable instruments of credit and exchange were thought out by Jewish merchants, not only for use between themselves, but to check and hold the Gentiles with whom they dealt. The oldest bill of exchange extant was drawn by a Jew — one Simon Rubens. The promissory note was a Jewish invention, as was also the check "payable to bearer."

An interesting bit of history attaches to the "payable to bearer" instrument. The Jews' enemies were always stripping them of their last ounce of wealth, yet strangely, the Jews recovered very quickly and were soon rich again.

How this sudden recovery from looting and poverty? Their assets were concealed under "bearer" and so a goodly portion was always saved. In an age when it was lawful for any pirate to seize goods consigned to Jews, the Jews were able to protect themselves by consigning goods on policies that bore no names. The influence of the Jew was to center business around goods instead of persons. Previously all claims had been against persons; the Jew knew that the goods were more reliable than the persons with whom he dealt, and so he contrived to have claims laid against goods. Besides, this device enabled him to keep himself out of sight as much as possible.

This introduced an element of hardness into business, inasmuch as it was goods which were being dealt in rather than men being dealt with, and this hardness remains. Another tendency which survives and which is of advantage in veiling the very large control which Jews have attained, is of the same origin as "bearer" bills; it permits a business dominated by Jewish capital to appear under a name that gives no hint of Jewish control.

The Jew is the only and original international capitalist, but as a rule he prefers not to emblazon that fact upon the skies; he prefers to use Gentile banks and trust companies as his agents and instruments. The suggestive term "Gentile front" often appears in connection with this practice.

The invention of the stock exchange is also credited to Jewish financial talent. In Berlin, Paris, London, Frankfort, and Hamburg, Jews were in control of the first stock exchanges, while Venice and Genoa were openly referred to in the talk of the day as "Jew cities" where great trading and banking facilities might be found. The Bank of England was established upon the counsel and assistance of Jewish emigrants from Holland. The Bank of Amsterdam and the Bank of Hamburg both arose through Jewish influence.

There is a curious fact to be noted in connection with the persecution and consequent wanderings of the Jews about Europe and that is: wherever they wandered, the center of business seemed to go with them.

When the Jews were free in Spain, there was the world's gold center. When Spain drove out the Jews, Spain lost financial leadership and has never regained it. Students of the economic history of Europe have always been puzzled to discover why the center of trade should have shifted from Spain, Portugal and Italy, up to the northern countries of Holland, Germany, and England.

They have sought for the cause in many things, but none has proved completely explanatory. When, however, it is known that the change was coincident with the expulsion of the Jews from the South and their flight to the North, when it is known that upon the Jews' arrival the northern countries began a commercial life which has flourished until our day, the explanation does not seem difficult. Time and again it has proved to be the fact that when the Jews were forced to move, the center of the world's precious metals moved with them.

This distribution of the Jews over Europe and the world, each Jewish community linked in a fellowship of blood, faith and suffering with every other group, made it possible for the Jew to be international in the sense that no other race or group of merchants could be at that time. Not only were they everywhere (Americans and Russians are everywhere, too) but they were in touch.

They were organized before the days of conscious international commercial organizations, they were bound together by the sinews of a common life. It was observed by many writers in the Middle Ages that the Jews knew more of what was transpiring in Europe than the governments did. They also had better knowledge of what was likely to occur.

They knew more about conditions than the statesmen did. This information they imparted by letter from group to group, country to country. Indeed, they may be said thus to have originated unconsciously the financial news-letter. Certainly the information they were able to obtain and thus distribute was invaluable to them in their speculative enterprises. Advance knowledge was an immense advantage in the days when news was scarce, slow and unreliable.

This enabled Jewish financiers to become the agents of national loans, a form of business which they encouraged wherever possible. The Jew has always desired to have nations for his customers. National loans were facilitated by the presence of members of the same family of financiers in various countries, thus making an interlocking directorate by which king could be played against king, government against government, and the shrewdest use made of national prejudices and fears, all to the no small profit of the fiscal agent.

One of the charges most commonly made against Jewish financiers today is that they still favor this larger field of finance. Indeed, in all the criticism that is heard regarding the Jew as a business man, there is comparatively little said against him as an individual merchant serving individual customers. Thousands of small Jewish merchants are highly respected by their trade, just as tens of thousands of Jewish families are respected as our neighbors.

The criticism, insofar as it respects the more important financiers, is not racial at all. Unfortunately the element of race, which so easily lends itself to misinterpretation as racial prejudice, is injected into the question by the mere fact that the chain of international finance as it is traced around the world discloses at every link a Jewish capitalist, financial family, or a Jewish-controlled banking system.

Many have professed to see in this circumstance a conscious organization of Jewish power for Gentile control, while others have attributed the circumstance to Jewish racial sympathies, to the continuity of their family affairs down the line of descent, and to the increase of collateral branches. In the old Scriptural phrase, Israel grows as the vine grows, ever shooting out new branches and deepening old roots, but always part of the one vine.

The Jew's aptitude for dealing with governments may also be traced to the years of his persecution. He early learned the power of gold in dealing with mercenary enemies. Wherever he went there followed him like a curse the aroused antipathy of other peoples. The Jew was never popular as a race; even the most fervid Jew will not deny that, howsoever he may explain it. Individuals have been popular, of course; many phases of Jewish nature are found to be very lovable when known; but nevertheless one of the burdens the Jews have had to bear as a race is this burden of racial unpopularity.

Even in modern times, in civilized countries, in conditions which render persecution absolutely impossible, this unpopularity exists. And what is more, the Jew has not seemed to care to cultivate the friendship of the Gentile masses, due perhaps to the failures of experience, but due more likely to his inborn persuasion that he belongs to a superior race.

Whatever the true reason, he has always placed his main dependence on cultivating friendship with kings and nobles. What cared the Jew if the people gnashed their teeth against him, so long as the king and the court were his friends?

Thus there was always, even through most of the severely trying times, "a court Jew," one who had bought by loans and held by the stranglehold of debt an entrance to the king's chamber. The policy of the Jews has always been to "go to headquarters."

They never tried to placate the Russian people, but they did endeavor to enlist the Russian court. They never tried to placate the German people, but they did succeed in permeating the German court. In England they shrug their shoulders at the outspoken anti-Jew reactions of the British populace — what care they?

Have they not all of lorddom at their heels, do they not hold the strings of Britain's purse?

Through this ability of theirs to "go to headquarters" it is possible to account for the stronghold they got upon various governments and nations. Added to this ability was, of course, the ability to produce what the governments wanted. If a government wanted a loan, the Jew at court could arrange it through Jews at other financial centers and political capitals.

If one government wanted to pay another government a debt without risking the precious metal to a mule train through a robber-infested country, the Jew at court arranged that too. He transferred a piece of paper and the debt was paid by the banking house at the foreign capital.

The first time an army was ever fed in the modern commissary way, it was done by a Jew — he had the capital and he had the system; moreover he had the delight of having a nation for his customer.

And this tendency, which served the race so well throughout the troublous centuries, shows no sign of abatement. Certainly, seeing to what an extent a race numerically so unimportant influences the various governments of the world today, the Jew who reflects upon the disparity between his people's numbers and their power may be pardoned if he sees in that fact a proof of their racial superiority. It may be said also that Jewish inventiveness in business devices continues to the present time, as well as Jewish adaptability to changing conditions.

The Jew is credited with being the first to establish branch houses in foreign countries in order that responsible representatives of the home office might be on the ground taking instant advantage of every opening. During the war a great deal was said about the "peaceful penetration" which the "German Government" had effected in the United States by establishing here branch offices and factories of German firms. The fact that there were many German branch houses here is unquestionable.

It should be known, however, that they were not the evidence of German enterprise but of Jewish enterprise. The old German business houses were too conservative to "run after customers" even in the hustling United States, but the Jewish firms were not, and they came straight to America and hustled. In due time the competition forced the more conservative German firms to follow suit.

But the idea was Jewish in its origin, not German.

Another modern business method whose origin is credited to Jewish financiers is that by which related industries are brought together, as for example, if an electrical power company is acquired, then the street railway company using the electricity would be acquired too, one purpose being in this way to conserve all the profit accruing along the line, from the origination of the power down to the delivery of the street car ride; but perhaps the main purpose being that, by the control of the power house the price of current could be increased to the car company, and by the control of the car company the cost of a ride could be increased to the public, the controllers thus receiving an additional profit all down the line.

There is much of this going on in the world today, and in the United States particularly. The portion of the business immediately next to the ultimate consumer explains that its costs have risen, but it does not explain that the costs were increased by the owners and not by outsiders who were forced to do so by economic pressure.

There is apparently in the world today a central financial force which is playing a vast and closely organized game, with the world for its table and universal control for its stakes. The people of civilized countries have lost all confidence in the explanation that "economic conditions" are responsible for all the changes that occur. Under the camouflage of "economic law" a great many phenomena have been accounted for which were not due to any law whatever except the law of the selfish human will as operated by a few men who have the purpose and the power to work on a wide scale with nations as their vassals.

Whatever else may be national, no one today believes that finance is national. Finance is international. Nobody today believes that international finance is in any way competitive. There are some independent banking houses, but few strong independent ones. The great masters, the few whose minds see clearly the entire play of the plan, control numerous banking houses and trust companies, and one is used for this while another is used for that, but there is no disharmony between them, no correction of each other's methods, no competition in the interests of the business world.

There is as much unity of policy between the principal banking houses of every country as there is between the various branches of the United States Post Office — and for the same reason, namely, they are all operated from the same source and for the same purpose.

Just before the war Germany bought very heavily in American cotton and had huge quantities of it tied up here for export. When war came, the ownership of that mountainous mass of cotton wealth changed in one night from Jewish names in Hamburg to Jewish names in London. At this writing cotton is selling in England for less than it is selling in the United States, and the effect of that is to lower the American price. When the price lowers sufficiently, the market is cleared of cotton by buyers previously prepared, and then the price soars to high figures again.

In the meantime, the same powers that have engineered the apparently causeless strengthening and weakening of the cotton market, have seized upon stricken Germany to be the sweatshop of the world. Certain groups control the cotton, lend it to Germany to be manufactured, leave a pittance of it there in payment for the labor that was used, and then profiteer the length and breadth of the world on the lie that "cotton is scarce."

And when, tracing all these anti-social and colossally unfair methods to their source, it is found that the responsible parties all have a common characteristic, is it any wonder that the warning which comes across the sea — "Wait until America becomes awake to the Jew!" — has a new meaning?

Certainly, economic reasons no longer explain the condition in which the world finds itself today. Neither does the ordinary explanation of "the heartlessness of capital." Capital has endeavored as never before to meet the demands of labor, and labor has gone to extremes in leading capital to new concessions — but what has it advantaged either of them?

Labor has heretofore thought that capital was the sky over it, and it made the sky yield, but behold, there was yet an higher sky which neither capital nor labor had seen in their struggles one with another. That sky is so far unyielding.

That which we call capital here in America is usually money used in production, and we mistakenly refer to the manufacturer, the manager of work, the provider of tools and jobs — we refer to him as the "capitalist." Oh, no. He is not the capitalist in the real sense. Why, he himself must go to capitalists for the money with which to finance his plans.

There is a power yet above him — a power which treats him far more callously and holds him in a more ruthless hand than he would ever dare display to labor. That, indeed, is one of the tragedies of these times, that "labor" and "capital" are fighting each other, when the conditions against which each one of them protests, and from which each one of them suffers, is not within their power to remedy at all, unless they find a way to wrest world control from that group of international financiers who create and control both these conditions.

There is a super-capitalism which is supported wholly by the fiction that gold is wealth. There is a super-government which is allied to no government, which is free from them all, and yet which has its hand in them all.

There is a race, a part of humanity, which has never yet been received as a welcome part, and which has succeeded in raising itself to a power that the proudest Gentile race has never claimed — not even Rome in the days of her proudest power. It is becoming more and more the conviction of men all over the world that the labor question, the wage question, the land question cannot be settled until first of all this matter of an international super-capitalistic government is settled.

"To the victor belongs the spoils" is an old saying. And in a sense it is true that if all this power of control has been gained and held by a few men of a long-despised race, then either they are super-men whom it is powerless to resist, or they are ordinary men whom the rest of the world has permitted to obtain an undue and unsafe degree of power.

Unless the Jews are super-men, the Gentiles will have themselves to blame for what has transpired, and they can look for rectification in a new scrutiny of the situation and a candid examination of the experiences of other countries.

The Dearborn Independent, May 22, 1920

2. Germany's Reaction against the Jew

Humanity has become wise enough to discuss those forms of physical sickness over which it formerly drew the veil of shame and secrecy, but political hygiene is not so far advanced. The main source of the sickness of the German national body is charged to be the influence of the Jews, and although this was apparent to acute minds years ago, it is now said to have gone so far as to be apparent to the least observing.

The eruption has broken out on the surface of the body politic, and no further concealment of this fact is possible. It is the belief of all classes of the German people that the collapse which has come since the armistice, and the revolution from which they are being prevented a recovery, are the result of Jewish intrigue and purpose. They declare it with assurance; they offer a mass of facts to confirm it; they believe that history will provide the fullest proof.

The Jew in Germany is regarded as only a guest of the people; he has offended by trying to turn himself into the host. There are no stronger contrasts in the world than the pure Germanic and pure Semitic races; therefore, there has been no harmony between the two in Germany; the German has regarded the Jew strictly as a guest, while the Jew, indignant at not being given the privileges of the nation-family, has cherished animosity against his host.

In other countries the Jew is permitted to mix more readily with the people, he can amass his control unchallenged; but in Germany the case was different.

Therefore, the Jew hated the German people; therefore, the countries of the world which were most dominated by the Jews showed the greatest hatred of Germany during the recent regrettable war. Jewish hands were in almost exclusive control of the engines of publicity by which public opinion concerning the German people was molded. The sole winners of the war were Jews.

But assertion is not enough; proof is wanted; therefore, consider the evidence. What occurred immediately upon the change from the old regime to the new? The cabinet composed of six men, which substituted the Minister of State, was dominated by the Jews Haase and Landsberg.

Haase had control of foreign affairs; his assistant was the Jew Kautsky, a Czech, who in 1918 was not even a German citizen. Also associated with Haase were the Jews Cohn and Herzfeld. The Jew Schiffer was Financial Minister of State, assisted by the Jew Bernstein. The Secretary of the Interior was the Jew Preuss, with the Jew Dr. Freund for his assistant. The Jew Fritz Max Cohen, who was correspondent of the Frankfurter Zeitung in Copenhagen, was made government publicity agent.

The kingdom of Prussia duplicated this condition of affairs. The Jews Hirsch and Rosenfeld dominated the cabinet, with Rosenfeld controlling the Department of Justice, and Hirsch in the Department of the Interior. The Jew Simon was in charge of the Treasury Department. The Prussian Department of Justice was wholly manned and operated by Jews. The Director of Education was the Jew Furtran with the assistance of the Jew Arndt. The Director of the Colonial Office was the Jew Meyer-Gerhard. The Jew Kastenberg was the director of the Department of Art.

The War Food Supply Department was directed by the Jew Wurm, while in the State Food Department were the Jews Prof. Dr. Hirsch and the Geheimrat Dr. Stadthagen. The Soldiers' and Workmen's Committee was directed by the Jew Cohen, with the Jews Stern, Herz, Lowenberg, Frankel, Israelowicz, Laubenheim, Seligsohn, Katzenstein, Laufenberg, Heimann, Schlesinger, Merz and Weyl having control of various activities of that committee.

The Jew Ernst is chief of police at Berlin; in the same office at Frankfurt is the Jew Sinzheimer; in Munich the Jew Steiner; in Essen the Jew Levy. It will be remembered that the Jew Eisner was President of Bavaria, his financial minister being the Jew Jaffe. Bavaria's trade, commerce and industry were in control of the half-Jew Brentano. The Jews Lipsinsky and Schwarz were active in the government of Saxony; the Jews Thalheimer and Heiman in Wurtemberg; the Jew Fulda in Hessen.

Two delegates sent to the Peace Conference were Jews and a third was notoriously the tool of Jewish purposes. In addition Jews swarmed through the German delegation as experts and advisors — Max Warburg, Dr. Von Strauss, Merton, Oskar Oppenheimer, Dr. Jaffe, Deutsch, Brentano, Bernstein, Struck, Rathenau, Wassermann, and Mendelsohn-Bartholdi.

As to the part which Jews from other countries had in the Peace Conference, German observers declare that any candid student may discover by reading the accounts of impartial non-Jewish recorders of that event. Only the non-Jewish historians seem to have been struck by the fact; the multitude of Jewish writers apparently judged it wise to conceal it.

Jewish influence in German affairs came strongly to the front during the war. It came with all the directness and attack of a flying wedge, as if previously prepared. The Jews of Germany were not German patriots during the war, and although this will not appear a crime in the eyes of the nations who were opposed to Germany, it may throw some light on the Jew's assertion of patriotic loyalty to the land where he lives. Thoughtful Germans hold that it is impossible for a Jew to be a patriot, for reasons which will presently be given.

The point to be considered is the general claim that the persons already named would not have obtained the positions in which they were found had it not been for the Revolution, and the Revolution would not have come had not they brought it. It is true that there were unsatisfactory conditions in Germany, but they could and would have been adjusted by the people themselves; the conditions which destroyed the people's morale and were made impossible of reform were in control of the Jews.

The principal Jewish influences which are charged with bringing about the downfall of German order may be named under three heads: (a) the spirit of Bolshevism which masqueraded under the name of German Socialism; (b) Jewish ownership and control of the Press; (c) Jewish control of the food supply and the industrial machinery of the country. There was a fourth, "higher up," but these worked upon the German people directly.

As it is possible that German conclusions upon this matter may be received doubtfully by people whose public opinion has been shaped by Jewish influence, it may help to quote George Pitter-Wilson, of the London Globe, who wrote early in April, 1919, "Bolshevism is the dispossession of the Christian nations of the world to such an extent that no capital will remain in the hands of the Christians, that all Jews may jointly hold the world in their hands and reign wherever they choose." As early as the second year of the war, German Jews were preaching that Germany's defeat was necessary to the rise of the proletariat, at which time Strobel declared, "I openly admit that a full victory of the country would not be in the interest of the Social Democrats." Everywhere it was preached that "the exaltation of the proletariat after a won victory is an impossibility." These instances, out of many, are cited not to reopen the military question but to show how the so-called German Jew forgot loyalty to the country in which he lived and joined the outside Jews in accomplishing the collapse of Germany, and not merely, as we shall see, to rid Germany of militarism, which every thoughtful German desired, but to throw the country into such confusion as to permit them to seize control.

The press of Germany echoed this plan of the Jewish spokesmen, at first faintly, then boldly. The Berliner Tageblatt and the Munchner Neuester Nachrichten were during the whole war official and semi-official organs of the government. They were owned and controlled by Jews, as was also the Frankfurter Zeitung and a host of smaller papers that were their spiritual dependents. These papers, it is charged, were really German editions of the Jew-controlled press of the Allied countries, and their purpose was the same. One of the great pieces of research that ought to be undertaken for the purpose of showing the world how its thought is manufactured for it every day, and for what ulterior purposes, is this union of the Jewish press, which passes for the Public Press, throughout the world.

The food and supplies of the people quickly passed into Jewish hands as soon as the war emergency came, and then began a period of dishonesty which destroyed the confidence of the bravest. Like all other patriotic people, the German people knew that war meant sacrifice and suffering, and like other people they were willing to share the common lot. But they found themselves preyed upon by a class of Jews who had prepared everything to make profit out of the common distress. Immediately Jews appeared in banks, war companies, distribution societies, and the ministries of supplies — wherever the life of the people could be speculated in or taxed. Articles that were plentiful disappeared, only to reappear again at high prices. The war companies were exclusively Jewish, and although the government attempted to regulate the outgo of food in the interests of all the people, it became notorious that those with money could get all of anything they wanted, regardless of the food cards. The Jews simply trebled the price of the goods they let go without the cards, and so kept a stream of the nation's gold flowing into their private treasuries. None of the government's estimates of the food stocks could be depended on, because of the hidden hoards on which these speculators drew. This began to disturb the morale of the people, and complaints were made and prosecutions started; but as soon as the cases came up it was discovered that the prosecutor appointed to charge and the commissioner appointed to judge were also Jews, and so the cases usually wore themselves out without results. When, however, a German merchant was caught, great noise was made about it, and the penalty placed upon him was equal to what all the others should have had. Go the length and breadth of Germany today, say the reports, study the temper of the people, and you will discover that the abuse of power by the Jews has burned across Germany's memory like a hot iron.

While these influences were undermining the mass of the people, higher influences of Jewish origin were operating upon the government. The advisors of the Bethmann-Hollweg government were the great ship magnate Ballin, a Jew; Theodor Wolff, of the Berliner Tageblatt and member of the Pan-Jewish press; Von Gwinner, director of the German Bank who is connected by marriage with the great Jew bankers, the Speyers; and Rathenau, the leader of Jewish Industrial-financial activities. These men were at the source of things and were bending the government as the other influences were bending the people.

The rich German Jew could buy the recognition he desired by acquiring financial power over those interests which most directly affected the ruling class of Germany, but how was the poor Jew to gain the recognition he desired? — for all Jews are actuated by the same desire; it is in them; they feel the spur to mastery. Having explored the conquest of the higher circles by Jewish money-power, there is yet to explore the conquest of the body of the nation by Jews who had no money except what they could seize in the disorder which they caused. The analysis that is given, follows:

The Jew is not an anarchist. He is not a destructionist. All this is true, notwithstanding he is the world's Bolshevist and preeminently Germany's revolutionist. His anarchy is not ingrain, it is a device which he uses for a purpose.

The rich Jew is not an anarchist, because he can achieve what he desires by more subtle methods. The poor Jew has no other recourse. But rich and poor go jointly for a long stretch; the bond of sympathy between them never breaks; for, if the anarchy is successful, then the poor Jew shall take his place with the rich Jew; and if the anarchy is not successful, it has nevertheless served to break up new fields in which the rich Jew may operate.

In Germany it was possible for the poor Jew to thrust himself up through the wall of Germanism above him only by breaking it up. In Russia the same was true. The social system had encrusted around the Jew, keeping him in a position where, as the nations knew by experience, he would be less harmful. As nature encysts the harmful foreign element in the flesh, building a wall around it, so nations have found it expedient to do with the Jew. In modern times, however, the Jew has found a means of knocking down the walls and throwing the whole national house into confusion, and in the darkness and riot that follows, seize the place he has long coveted. When Russia broke, who came first to light? Kerensky, who is a Jew. But his plans were not radical enough, and then came Trotsky, another Jew. Trotsky found the system too strong for him to break in America — he broke through the weak spot in Russia and would extend that weakness round the world. Every commissar in Russia today is a Jew.

Publicists are accustomed to speak of Russia as if it were in disorder. It may be that Russia is, but the Jewish government of Russia is not. From a mass of underlings, the Jews of Russia came up a perfect phalanx, a flying wedge through the superinduced disorder, as if every man's place had been previously prepared for him.

That also is the way it was in Germany. The German ceiling had to be broken, as it were, before the poor Jews could realize their ambition. When the break was made they swarmed through and settled in places of control above the nation.

This may explain why Jews the world over supply the energy of disruptive movements. It is understood that the young Jews of the United States are propagandists of an ideal that would practically abolish the United States.

The attack is aimed, of course, against "capitalism," which means the present government of the world by the Gentile. The true capitalists of the world are Jews, who are capitalists for capital's sake. It is hard to believe that they wish to destroy capital; they wish to obtain sole control of it, and their wish has long been in fair way to fulfillment.

In Germany, therefore, as in Russia, distinction is made between the methods of the rich and of the poor Jews, because one method affects the government and the other the morale of the people, but both converge on the same objective. It is not only desire to escape oppression that actuates the lower classes of Jews, but desire to gain control — for the spirit of mastery pulses strong within them.

German convictions on this question have reached the place where they may be expressed thus: Revolution is the expression of the Jews' will to power. Parties such as the socialists, democrats, and freethinkers are but tools for the Jewish plan to power. The so-called "dictatorship of the proletariat" is really and practically the dictatorship of Jews.

So suddenly have German eyes been opened, so stormfully wrathful has been the reaction, that the word has gone out through German Judaism to retire to the second trench. There has been a sudden and concerted abandonment of office wherever the office made direct contact with the public; there has, however, been no abandonment of power. What will happen in Germany is not now known. Some regrettable things have already happened. But the Germans will doubtless prove themselves equal to the situation by devising methods of control at once unobjectionable and effective. But as to Russia, it is hardly doubtful any longer what will happen there. When Russia, turns, a shudder will run through the earth.

How Gentile Germany and Russia look at the entire question may be summarized as follows:

Judaism is the most closely organized power on earth, even more than the British Empire. It forms a State whose citizens are unconditionally loyal wherever they may be and whether rich or poor.

The name which is given in Germany to this State which circulates among all the states is "All-Judaan." The means of power of the State of All-Judaan are capital and journalism, or money and propaganda.

All-Judaan is the only State that exercises world government; all the other States can and may exercise national government only.

The principal culture of All-Judaan is journalistic; the technical, scientific, literary performances of the modern Jew are throughout journalistic performances. They are due to the marvelous talent of the Jews for receptivity of others' ideas. Capital and Journalism are joined in the Press to create a political and spiritual medium of Jewish power.

The government of this state of All-Judaan is wonderfully organized. Paris was its first seat, but has now been moved to third place. Before the war London was its first, and New York its second capital. It remains to be seen whether New York will now supplant London — the drift is toward America.

As All-Judaan is not in a position to have a standing army and navy, other states supply these for it. Its fleet is the British fleet, which guards from hindrance the progress of all-Jewish world economy, or that part of it which depends on the sea. In return, All-Judaan assures Britain an undisturbed political and territorial world rule. All-Judaan has added Palestine to British control. Wherever there was an All-Judaan land force (whatever national uniform it might wear), it worked with the British navy.

All-Judaan is willing to entrust the government of various strips of the world to the nationalistic governments; it only asks to control the governments. Judaism is passionately in favor of perpetuating nationalistic divisions for the Gentile world. For themselves, Jews never become assimilated with any nation. They are a separate people, always were and always will be.

All-Judaan's only quarrel with any nation occurs when that nation makes it impossible for All-Judaan to control that nation's industrial and financial profits.

It can make war, it can make peace; it can command anarchy in stubborn cases, it can restore order. It holds the sinews of world power in its hand and it apportions them among the nations in such ways as will best support All-Judaan's plan.

Controlling the world's sources of news, All-Judaan can always prepare the minds of the people for its next move. The greatest exposure yet to be made is the way that news is manufactured and the way in which the mind of whole nations is molded for a purpose. When the powerful Jew is at last traced and his hand revealed, then comes the ready cry of persecution and it echoes through the world press. The real causes of the persecution (which is the oppression of the people by the financial practices of the Jews) are never given publicity.

Alljudaan has its vice-governments in London and New York. Having wreaked its revenge on Germany it will now go forth to conquer other nations. Britain it already has. Russia it is struggling for, but the chances are against it. The United States, with its good-natured tolerance of all races, offers a promising field. The scene of operations changes, but the Jew is the same throughout the centuries.

The Dearborn Independent, May 29, 1920

"At first sight it would seem as if the economic system of North America was the very one that developed independently of the Jews . . . . Nevertheless I uphold my assertion that the United States (perhaps more than any other land) are filled to the brim with the Jewish spirit. This is recognized in many quarters, above all in those best capable of forming a judgment on the subject . . . .
"In the face of this fact, is there not some justification for the opinion that the United States owe their very existence to the Jews? And if this be so, how much more can it be asserted that Jewish influence made the United States just what they are — that is, American? For what we call Americanism is nothing else, if we may say so, than the Jewish spirit distilled."
— Werner Sombart, *The Jews and Modern Capital*, pp. 38, 43

3. Jewish History in the United States

The story of the Jews in America begins with Christopher Columbus. On August 2, 1492, more than 300,000 Jews were expelled from Spain, with which event Spain's prestige began its long decline, and on August 3, the next day, Columbus set sail for the West, taking a group of Jews with him. They were not, however, refugees, for the prophetic navigator's plans had aroused the sympathy of influential Jews for a long period previously. Columbus himself tells us that he consorted much with Jews. The first letter he wrote detailing his discoveries was to a Jew. Indeed, the eventful voyage itself which added to men's knowledge and wealth "the other half of the earth" was made possible by Jews.

The pleasant story that it was Queen Isabella's jewels which financed the voyage has disappeared under cool research. There were three Maranos or "secret Jews" who wielded great influence at the Spanish court: Luis de Santagel, who was an important merchant of Valencia and who was "farmer" of the royal taxes; his relative, Gabriel Sanchez, who was the royal treasurer; and their friend, the royal chamberlain, Juan Cabrero.

These worked unceasingly on Queen Isabella's imagination, picturing to her the depletion of the royal treasury and the likelihood of Columbus discovering the fabulous gold of the Indies, until the Queen was ready to offer her jewels in pawn for the funds. But Santagel craved permission to advance the money himself, which he did, 17,000 ducats in all, about $20,000, perhaps equal to $160,000 today. It is probable that the loan exceeded the expedition's cost. Associated with Columbus in the voyage were at least five Jews: Luis de Torres, interpreter; Marco, the surgeon; Bernal, the physician; Alonzo de la Calle, and Gabriel Sanchez. The astronomical instruments and maps which the navigators used were of Jewish origin. Luis de Torres was the first man ashore, the first to discover the use of tobacco; he settled in Cuba and may be said to be the father of Jewish control of the tobacco business as it exists today.

Columbus' old patrons, Luis de Santagel and Gabriel Sanchez, received many privileges for the part they played in the work, but Columbus himself became the victim of a conspiracy fostered by Bernal, the ship's doctor, and suffered injustice and imprisonment as his reward.

From that beginning, Jews looked more and more to America as a fruitful field, and immigration set in strongly toward South America, principally Brazil. But because of military participation in a disagreement between the Brazilians and the Dutch, the Jews of Brazil found it necessary to emigrate, which they did in the direction of the Dutch colony of what is now New York. Peter Stuyvesant, the Dutch governor, did not entirely approve of their settling among his people and ordered them to leave, but the Jews had evidently taken the precaution to assure their being received even if not welcomed, because upon revoking the order of Stuyvesant, the Directors gave as one of the reasons for the Jews being received, "the large amount of capital which they have invested in the shares of the Company." Nevertheless they were forbidden to enter public service and to open retail shops, which had the effect of driving them into foreign trade in which they were soon exercising all but a monopoly because of their European connections.

This is only one of the thousand illustrations which can be given of the resourcefulness of the Jew. Forbid him in one direction, he will excel in another. When he was forbidden to deal in new clothes, he sold old clothes—that was the beginning of the organized traffic in secondhand clothing. When he was forbidden to deal in merchandise, he dealt in waste—the Jew is the originator of the waste product business of the world; he was the originator of the salvage system; he found wealth in the debris of civilization. He taught people how to use old rags, how to clean old feathers, how to use gall nuts and rabbit skins. He has always had a taste for the furrier trade, which he now controls, and to him is due the multitude of common skins which now pass under various alluring trade names as furs of high origin. The idea of renovation gained commercial value through the Jew. In the "rag men" who blow tin horns through our cities and save the old iron, old bottles, old paper and old fabrics, we have the commercial descendants of those earlier Jews who turned adversity into success by converting the rubbish of the earth into material of value.

Unwittingly, old Peter Stuyvesant compelled the Jew to make New York the principal port of America, and though a majority of New York Jews had fled to Philadelphia at the time of the American Revolution, most of them returned to New York at the earliest opportunity, instinct seeming to make them aware that in New York was to be their principal paradise of gain. And so it has proved. New York is the greatest center of Jewish population in the world.

It is the gateway where the bulk of American imports and exports are taxed, and where practically all the business done in America pays tribute to the masters of money. The very land of the city is practically the holdings of the Jews. A list of the property owners of the metropolis reveals only at rare intervals a Gentile name. No wonder that Jewish writers, viewing this unprecedented prosperity, this unchecked growth in wealth and power, exclaim enthusiastically that the United States is the Promised Land foretold by the prophets, and New York the New Jerusalem. Some have gone even further and described the peaks of the Rockies as "the mountains of Zion," and with reason, too, if the mining and coastal wealth of the Jews is considered.

The new waterways proposal, which will make an ocean port of practically every great city on the Great Lakes and take from New York the prestige she has maintained by being the gateway toward which the principal railways narrowed, is being strongly protested at this time. And the strongest motive in opposing this most obvious betterment is that so much wealth counted in New York is not wealth at all, but fictitious values depending solely on New York remaining New York. When anything comes which will make New York merely a city on the coast, and not the city where the great taxers sit to levy their tribute, much Jewish wealth will decrease. It was fabulous before the war. What it is now the statisticians will hardly undertake to say.

In fifty years the increase in the Jewish population of the United States has been from 50,000 to more than 3,300,000. In the British Isles there are only 300,000, in Palestine only 100,000. It is fortunate for the Jew himself that in Great Britain his numbers are not greater, for the large and evident control he exercises in great matters would sometimes make it inconvenient for the poorer Jew, if he were abroad in England in large numbers. An unusually well-informed Briton says that anti-Semitism is always ready to break out in England upon sufficient cause, but it cannot break out against the inaccessible rich Jews who control in politics and international finance.

It us probably true that the commonest real cause of anti-Semitism is the action of the international Jew who is often unknown and always secure, but the innocent victim of it is the poor Jew. Anti-Semitism, however, will be considered in the next article.

The figures representing Jewish population in Great Britain and the United States indicate that the colossal power wielded by international Jewish financiers is neither consequent nor dependent upon their number. The arresting fact about the Jew is his world-wide unchallenged power, coupled with comparative numerical inferiority. There are only about 14,000,000 Jews in the world; they are about as numerous as the Koreans. This comparison of their numbers with the Koreans will illustrate still more vividly the phenomenon of their power.

In the time of George Washington there were about 4,000 Jews in the country, most of them well-to-do traders. For the most part they favored the American side. Haym Salomon helped the Colonies out with the loan of his entire fortune at a critical moment. But they never assimilated, they did not take up the usual employments nor farming, they never seemed to care for the worry of manufacturing things, but only for the selling of them after they were made.

It is only of recent years the Jew has shown any capacity for manufacturing, and most of what he now engages in has grown up as an adjunct to his merchandising plans. By manufacturing, he saves a profit. The result has not been a decrease in cost to the public, but an increase.

It is characteristic of Jewish business methods that economies are for the sake of the business, not for the sake of the public. The commodities in which there have been the most inexcusable and exorbitant increases in prices to the public, and the lines of business which have been most quickly frightened into lower prices without any explanatory change in the general situation, have been those lines in which Jews exercise the widest control.

Business to the Jewish mind is money; what the successful Jew may do with the money after he gets it is another matter, but in the getting of it he never permits "idealistic slush" to interfere with the dollar. His dollar of profit is never "clipped" by any of the voluntary reforms by which a few men are trying to ameliorate the condition of the workers.

This is not by any means due to the hardness of the Jewish heart, but to the hardness of the Jewish view of business. Business is to it a matter of goods and money, not of people.

If you are in distress and suffering, the Jewish heart would have sympathy for you; but if your house were involved in the matter, you and your house would be two separate entities; the Jew would naturally find it difficult, in his theory of business, to humanize the house; he would deal with it after a manner which other people would call "hard," but he would not feel the charge to be just; he would say that it was only "business."

It is probably this way that the Jewish "sweatshops" of New York may be explained. When the susceptible people of the nation commiserated the poor Jews of the New York sweatshops, they for the most part did not know that the inventors and operators of the "sweatshop" method were themselves Jews. Indeed, while it is the boast of our country that no race or color or creed is persecuted here, but liberty is insured to all, still it is a fact which every special investigator has noted that the only heartless treatment ever accorded the Jew in the United States came from his own people, his overseers and masters. And yet there is no evidence that either the "sweater" or the "sweated" ever thought of it as inhumanity or as "heartless."

It was "business." The "sweated" lived in the hope of having a roomful of people sewing for him or her some day.

Their endlessly vital interest in "business" and their unflagging ambition to get further up the ladder and become masters in their own sweatshop, enabled them to work without the slightest sense of oppression or injustice which, after all, is the sorest thing about poverty. The Jews never regard work as a calamity, but neither do they regard subordinate positions as permanently theirs. Thus, they spend their energies in getting up and out rather than in lamenting the inconveniences of the place where they are and trying to improve it.

All this is individually excellent but socially harmful. The result is that, until recently, the lower ranges of employment were wholly unsupervised, and the higher circles never felt the necessity of devising industrial reforms and benefits. The record of the great Jews in charity is very noble; their record in industrial reforms is nil. With commendable sympathy toward their own people, they will donate a part of their profits to rectify some of the human need resulting from the method by which they made their profits, but as for reforming the method by which they get their profits in order that the resulting need might be diminished or prevented, apparently it has never occurred to them. At least, while there are many charitable names among the wealthier Jews, there are no names that stand for an actual, practical humanizing of industry, its methods and its returns.

This, of course, is unfortunate; but it is intelligible; more than that, it is explanatory of many things for which the Jew is blamed by those who do not understand his nature. The Jew will go part way in sharing the results of his prosperity; he has not gone any length, save upon outer compulsion, in sharing the processes, or sharing wealth in the making. And while the social effect is the same as if this were done out of cruel insensibility and inhumanity, still it must be said that mostly it is done not out of such feelings, but out of the Jew's ingrain conception of the game of business. Some proposals of industrial reform appear as crazy to him as would a proposal to credit one baseball batter's hit to his opponent's score, just as a matter of humanity.

The American Jew does not assimilate.

This is stated, not to blame him, but merely as a fact. The Jew could merge with the people of America if he desired, but he doesn't. If there is any prejudice existing against him in America, aside from the sense of inquiry which his colossal success engenders, it is because of his aloofness. The Jew is not objectionable in his person, creed, or race. His spiritual ideals are shared by the world.

But still he does not assimilate; he cultivates by his exclusiveness the feeling that he does not "belong." This is his privilege, and from one point of view it may indicate excellent judgement, but he must not make it one of the grounds of his complaint against Gentiles in general, as he has a tendency to do.

It is better that he should make it clear to Gentiles once and for all where true Jews stand in the matter, as when a young Jew said—"There is all the difference in the world between an American Jew and a Jewish American. A Jewish American is a mere amateur Gentile, doomed to be a parasite forever."

The ghetto is not an American product but the Jews' own importation. They have separated themselves into a distinct community. Speaking of this matter the *Jewish Encyclopedia* says: "The social organization of the Jews resident in America has differed little from that in other countries . . . in the main, and without any compulsion, Jews preferred to live in close proximity to one another, a peculiarity which still prevails."

To make a list of the lines of business controlled by the Jews of the United States would be to touch most of the vital industries of the country—those which are really vital, and those which cultivated habit has made to seem vital.

The theatrical business, of course, as everyone knows, is exclusively Jewish. Play-producing, booking, theater operation are all in the hands of Jews. This perhaps accounts for the fact that in almost every production today can be detected propaganda, sometimes glaringly commercial advertisement, which does not originate with playwrights, but with producers.

The motion picture industry.
The sugar industry.
The tobacco industry.
Fifty per cent or more of the meat packing industry.
Upward of 60 per cent of the shoemaking industry.
Men's and women's ready-made clothing.
Most of the musical purveying done in the country.
Jewelry.
Grain.
More recently, cotton.
The Colorado smelting industry.
Magazine authorship.
News distribution.
The liquor business.
The loan business.

These, only to name the industries with national and international sweep, are in control of the Jews of the United States, either alone or in association with Jews overseas.

The American people would be vastly surprised if they could see a line-up of some of the "American business men" who hold up our commercial prestige overseas.

They are mostly Jews. They have a keen sense of the value of the American name, and when in a foreign port you stroll up to the office which bears the sign, "American Importing Company," or "American Commercial Company," or other similarly noncommittal names, hoping to find a countryman, an American, you usually find a Jew whose sojourn in America appears to have been all too brief. This may throw a sidelight on the regard in which "American business methods" are held in some parts of the world.

When 30 or 40 different races of people can carry on business under the name "American," and do it legally, too, it is not surprising that Americans do not recognize some of the descriptions of American methods which appear in the foreign press. The Germans long ago complained that the rest of the world was judging them by the German-speaking Jewish commercial traveler.

Instances of Jewish prosperity in the United States are commonplace, but prosperity, the just reward of foresight and application, is not to be confounded with control.

The prosperity of the Jews can be had by anyone who is willing to pay the price which the Jews pay for it a very, very high price, as a rule, all things considered—but it would be impossible for any Gentile coalition under similar circumstances to attain the control which the Jews have won, for the reason that there is lacking in the Gentile a certain quality of working-togetherness, a certain conspiracy of objective, and the adhesiveness of intense raciality, which characterizes the Jew.

It is nothing to a Gentile that another man is a Gentile; it is next to everything to a Jew that the man at his door is another Jew. So, if instances of Jewish prosperity were needed, the case of the Temple Emmanu-el, New York, might be cited, which in 1846 could scarcely raise $1,520 for its budget, but in 1868, following the Civil War, raised $708,755 from the rental of 231 pews. And the rise of the Jewish clothing monopoly as one of the results of the same Civil War might be cited as an instance of prosperity plus national and international control.

Indeed, it might be said that the Jew has succeeded in everything he has attempted in the United States, except farming. The explanation usually made in Jewish publications is that ordinary farming is far too simple to engage the Jew's intellect and therefore he is not enough interested in it to succeed, but that in dairy and cattle farming where the "brain" is more necessary he has made a success.

Numerous attempts have been made in various parts of the United States to start Jewish farming colonies, but their story is a series of failures. Some have blamed the failures on the Jew's lack of knowledge of scientific farming, others on his distaste for manual labor, others on the lack of the speculative element in agriculture.

In any case, he stands higher in the non-productive employments than in this basically productive one. Some students of the question state that the Jew never was a man of the land, but always a trader, for which assertion one of the proofs offered is the Jews' selection of Palestine as their country, that strip of land which formed a gateway between East and West and over which the overland traffic of the world passed.

The Dearborn Independent, June 5, 1920

"The Jewish Question still exists. It would be useless to deny it . . . . The Jewish Question exists wherever Jews live in perceptible numbers. Where it does not exist, it is carried by Jews in the course of their migrations. We naturally move to those places where we are not persecuted, and there our presence produces persecution . . . . The unfortunate Jews are now carrying anti-Semitism into England; they have already introduced it into America."
—Theodore Herzl, *A Jewish State*, p. 4.

4. The Jewish Question—Fact or Fancy?

The chief difficulty in writing about the Jewish Question is the supersensitiveness of Jews and non-Jews concerning the whole matter. There is a vague feeling that even to openly use the word "Jew," or to expose it nakedly to print, is somehow improper. Polite evasions like "Hebrew" and "Semite," both of which are subject to the criticism of inaccuracy, are timidly essayed, and people pick their way gingerly as if the whole subject were forbidden, until some courageous Jewish thinker comes straight out with the good old word "Jew," and then the constraint is relieved and the air cleared. The word "Jew" is not an epithet; it is a name, ancient and honorable, with significance for every period of human history, past, present and to come.

There is extreme sensitiveness about the public discussion of the Jewish Question on the part of Gentiles. They would prefer to keep it in the hazy borderlands of their thought, shrouded in silence. Their heritage of tolerance has something to do with their attitude, but perhaps their instinctive sense of the difficulty involved has more to do with it.

The principal public Gentile pronouncements upon the Jewish Question are in the manner of the truckling politician or the pleasant after-dinner speaker; the great Jewish names in philosophy, medicine, literature, music and finance are named over, the energy, ability and thrift of the race are dwelt upon, and everyone goes home feeling that a difficult place has been rather neatly negotiated. But nothing is changed thereby. The Jew is not changed. The Gentile is not changed. The Jew still remains the enigma of the world.

Gentile sensitiveness on this point is best expressed by the desire for silence—"Why discuss it at all?" is the attitude. Such an attitude is itself a proof that there is a problem which we would evade if we could. "Why discuss it at all?"—the keen thinker clearly sees in the implications of such a question, the existence of a problem whose discussion or suppression will not always be within the choice of easy-going minds.

Is there a Jewish Question in Russia? Unquestionably, in its most virulent form. Is it necessary to meet that Question in Russia? Undoubtedly, meet it from every angle along which light and healing may come.

Well, the percentage of the Jewish population of Russia is just one per cent more than it is in the United States. The majority of the Jews themselves are not less well-behaved in Russia than they are here; they lived under restrictions which do not exist here; yet in Russia their genius has enabled them to attain a degree of power which has completely baffled the Russian mind. Whether you go to Rumania, Russia, Austria or Germany, or anywhere else that the Jewish Question has come to the forefront as a vital issue, you will discover that the principal cause is the outworking of the Jewish genius to achieve the power of control.

Here in the United States it is the fact of this remarkable minority—a sparse Jewish ingredient of three per cent in a nation of 110,000,000—attaining in 50 years a degree of control that would be impossible to a ten times larger group of any other race, that creates the Jewish Question here.

Three per cent of any other people would scarcely occasion comment, because we could not meet with a representative of them wherever we went in high places—in the innermost secrecy of the councils of the Big Four at Versailles; in the supreme court; in the councils of the White House; in the vast dispositions of world finance—wherever there is power to get or use. Yet we meet the Jew everywhere in the upper circles, literally everywhere there is power. He has the brains, the initiative, the penetrative vision which almost automatically project him to the top, and as a consequence he is more marked than any other race.

And that is where the Jewish Question begins. It begins in very simple terms—How does the Jew so habitually and so resistlessly gravitate to the highest places? What puts him there? Why is he put there? What does he do there? What does the fact of his being there mean to the world?

That is the Jewish Question in its origin. From these points it goes on to others, and whether the trend becomes pro-Jewish or anti-Semitic depends on the amount of prejudice brought to the inquiry, and whether it becomes pro-Humanity depends on the amount of insight and intelligence.

The Jewish Question—Fact or Fancy?

The use of the word Humanity in connection with the word Jew usually throws a side-meaning which may not be intended. In this connection it is usually understood that the humanity ought to be shown toward the Jew. There is just as great an obligation upon the Jew to show his humanity toward the whole race. The Jew has been too long accustomed to think of himself as exclusively the claimant on the humanitarianism of society; society has a large claim against him that he cease his exclusiveness, that he cease exploiting the world, that he cease making Jewish groups the end and all of his gains, and that he begin to fulfill, in a sense his exclusiveness has never yet enabled him to fulfill, the ancient prophecy that through him all the nations of the earth should be blessed.

The Jew cannot go on forever filling the role of suppliant for the world's humanitarianism; he must himself show that quality to a society which seriously suspects his higher and more powerful groups of exploiting it with a pitiless rapacity which in its wide-flung and long drawn-out distress may be described as an economic pogrom against a rather helpless humanity. For it is true that society is as helpless before the well-organized extortions of certain financial groups, as huddled groups of Russian Jews were helpless against the anti-Semitic mob. And as in Russia, so in America, it is the poor Jew who suffers for the delinquencies of the rich exploiter of his race.

This series of articles is already being met by an organized barrage by mail and wire and voice, every single item of which carries the wail of persecution. One would think that a heartless and horrible attack were being made on a most pitiable and helpless people—until one looks at the letterheads of the magnates who write, and at the financial ratings of those who protest, and at the membership of the organizations whose responsible heads hysterically demand retraction. And always in the background there is the threat of boycott, a threat which has practically sealed up the columns of every publication in America against even the mildest discussion of the Jewish Question.

The Jewish Question in America cannot be concealed forever by threats against publications, nor by the propagandist publication of matter extremely and invariably favorable to everything Jewish. It is here and it cannot be twisted into something else by the adroit use of propaganda, nor can it be forever silenced by threats. The Jews of the United States can best serve themselves and their fellow-Jews all over the world by letting drop their far too ready cry of "anti-Semitism," by adopting a franker tone than that which befits a helpless victim, and by seeing what the Jewish Question is and how it behooves every Jew who loves his people to help solve it.

There has been used in this series the term "International Jew." It is susceptible of two interpretations: one, the Jew wherever he may be; the other, the Jew who exercises international control. The real contention of the world is with the latter and his satellites, whether Jew or Gentile.

Now, this international type of Jew, this grasper after world-control, this actual possessor and wielder of world-control is a very unfortunate connection for his race to have. The most unfortunate thing about the international Jew, from the standpoint of the ordinary Jew, is that the international type is also a Jew.

And the significance of this is that the type does not grow anywhere else than on a Jewish stem. There is no other racial nor national type which puts forth this kind of person. It is not merely that there are a few Jews among international financial controllers; it is that these world controllers are exclusively Jews. That is the phenomenon which creates an unfortunate situation for those Jews who are not and never shall be world-controllers, who are the plain people of the Jewish race.

If world-control were mixed, like the control, say, of the biscuit business, then the occasional Jews we might find in those higher financial altitudes would not constitute the problem at all; the problem would then be limited to the existence of world-control in the hands of a few men, of whatever race or lineage they might be. But since world-control is an ambition which has only been achieved by Jews, and not by any of the methods usually adopted by would-be world conquerors, it becomes inevitable that the question should center in that remarkable race.

This brings another difficulty: in discussing this group of world-controllers under the name of Jews (and they are Jews), it is not always possible to stop and distinguish the group of Jews that is meant. The candid reader can usually determine that, but the Jew who is in a state of mind to be injured is sometimes pained by reading as a charge against himself what was intended for the upper group.

"Then why not discuss the upper group as financiers and not as Jews?" may be asked. Because they are Jews. It is not to the point to insist that in any list of rich men there are more Gentiles than Jews; we are not talking about merely rich men who have, many of them, gained their riches by serving a System, we are talking about those who Control—

and it is perfectly apparent that merely to be rich is not to control. The world-controlling Jew has riches, but he also has something much more powerful than that.

The international Jew, as already defined, rules not because he is rich, but because in a most marked degree he possesses the commercial and masterful genius of his race, and avails himself of a racial loyalty and solidarity the like of which exists in no other human group. In other words, transfer today the world-control of the international Jew to the hands of the highest commercially talented group of Gentiles, and the whole fabric of world-control would eventually fall to pieces, because the Gentile lacks a certain quality, be it human or divine, be it natural or acquired, that the Jew possesses.

This, of course, the modern Jew denies. There is a new position taken by the modernists among the Jews which constitutes a denial that the Jew differs from any other man except in the matter of religion. "Jew" they say is not a racial designation, but a religious designation like "Episcopalian," "Catholic," "Presbyterian." This is the argument used in newspaper offices in the Jews' protests against giving the Jewish designation to those of their people who are implicated in crime—"You don't give the religious classification of other people who are arrested," the editor is told, "why should you do it with Jews?" The appeal to religious tolerance always wins, and is sometimes useful in diverting attention from other things.

Well, if the Jews are only religiously differentiated from the rest of the world, the phenomenon grows stranger still. For the rest of the world is interested less in the Jew's religion than in anything else that concerns him. There is really nothing in his religion to differentiate the Jew from the rest of mankind, as far as the moral content of that religion is concerned, and if there were he would have overcome that by the fact that his Jewish religion supplies the moral structure for both of the other great religions. Moreover, it is stated that there are among English speaking nations 2,000,000 Jews who acknowledge their race and not their religion, while 1,000,000 are classed as agnostic—are these any less Jews than the others? The world does not think so. The authoritative students of human differences do not think so. An Irishman who grows indifferent to the Church is still an Irishman, and it would seem to be equally true that a Jew who grows indifferent to the Synagogue is still a Jew. He at least feels that he is, and so does the non-Jew. A still more serious challenge would arise if this contention of the modernists were true, for it would necessitate the explanation of these world-controlling Jews by their religion. We should have to say, "They excel through their religion," and then the problem would turn on the religion whose practice should bring such power and prosperity to its devotees.

But another fact would intervene, namely, that these world-controlling Jews are not notably religious; and still another fact would hammer for recognition, namely, the most devout believers and most obedient followers of the Jewish religion are the poorest among the Jews. If you want Jewish orthodoxy, the bracing morality of the Old Testament, you will find it, not among the successful Jews, who have Unitarianized their religion to the same extent that the Unitarians have Judaized their Christianity, but among the poor in the side streets who still sacrifice the Saturday business for their Sabbath keeping. Certainly their religion has not given them world-control; instead, they have made their own sacrifices to keep it inviolate against modernism.

Of course, if the Jew differs from the rest of mankind only when he is in full accord with his religion, the question becomes very simple. Any criticism of the Jew becomes sheer religious bigotry and nothing else! And that would be intolerable. But it would be the consensus of thoughtful opinion that the Jew differs less in his religion than in anything else. There is more difference between the two great branches of Christianity, more conscious difference, than between any branch of Christianity and Judaism.

So that, the contention of certain modernists notwithstanding, the world will go on thinking of the Jew as a member of a race, a race whose persistence has defeated the utmost efforts made for its extermination, a race that has preserved itself in virility and power by the observance of those natural laws the violation of which has mongrelized so many nations, a race which has come up out of the past with the two great moral values which may be reckoned on monotheism and monogamy, a race which today is before us as the visible sign of an antiquity to which all our spiritual wealth harks back. Nay, the Jew will go on thinking of himself as the member of a people, a nation, a race. And all the mixture and intermixture of thought or faith or custom cannot make it otherwise. A Jew is a Jew and as long as he remains within his perfectly unassailable traditions, he will remain a Jew. And he will always have the right to feel that to be a Jew is to belong to a superior race.

These world-controlling Jews at the top of affairs, then, are there by virtue of, among other things, certain qualities which are inherent in their

The Jewish Question—Fact or Fancy?

Jewish natures. Every Jew has these qualities even if not in the supreme sense, just as every Englishman has Shakespeare's tongue but not in Shakespeare's degree. And thus it is impracticable, if not impossible, to consider the international Jew without laying the foundations broadly upon Jewish character and psychology.

We may discount at once the too common libel that this greater form of Jewish success is built upon dishonesty. It is impossible to indict the Jewish people or any other people on a wholesale charge. No one knows better than the Jew how widespread is the notion that Jewish methods of business are all unscrupulous. There is no doubt a possibility of a great deal of unscrupulousness existing without actual legal dishonesty, but it is altogether possible that the reputation the Jewish people have long borne in this respect may have had other sources than actual and persistent dishonesty.

We may indicate one of these possible sources. The Jew at a trade is naturally quicker than most other men. They say there are other races which are as nimble at a trade as is the Jew, but the Jew does not live much among them. In this connection one may remember the famous joke about the Jew who went to Scotland.

Now, it is human nature for the slower man to believe that the quicker man is too deft by far, and to become suspicious of his deftness. Everybody suspects the "sharper" even though his sharpness be entirely honest. The slower mind is likely to conceive that the man who sees so many legitimate twists and turns to a trade, may also see and use a convenient number of illegitimate twists and turns. Moreover, there is always the ready suspicion that the one who gets "the best of the bargain" gets it by trickery which is not above board. Slow, honest, plain-spoken and straight-dealing people always have their doubts of the man who gets the better of it.

The Jews, as the records for centuries show, were a keen people in trade. They were so keen that many regarded them as crooked. And so the Jew became disliked for business reasons, not all of which were creditable to the intelligence or initiative of his enemies. Take for example, the persecution which Jew merchants once suffered in England. In older England the merchant class had many easygoing traditions. One tradition was that a respectable tradesman would never seek business but wait for it to come to him. Another tradition was that to decorate one's store window with lights or colors, or to display one's stock of goods attractively in the view of the public, was a contemptible and underhanded method of tempting a brother tradesman's customers away from him. Still another tradition was that it was strictly unethical and unbusinesslike to handle more than one line of goods. If one sold tea, it was the best reason in the world why he should not sell teaspoons. As for advertising, the thing would have been so brazen and bold that public opinion would have put the advertiser out of business. The proper demeanor for a merchant was to seem reluctant to part with his goods.

One may readily imagine what happened when the Jewish merchant bustled into the midst of this jungle of traditions. He simply broke them all. In those days tradition had all the force of a divinely promulgated moral law and in consequence of his initiative the Jew was regarded as a great offender. A man who would break those trade traditions would stop at nothing! The Jew was anxious to sell. If he could not sell one article to a customer, he had another on hand to offer him. The Jews' stores became bazaars, forerunners of our modern department stores, and the old English custom of one store for one line of goods was broken up. The Jew went after trade, pursued it, persuaded it. He was the originator of "a quick turnover and small profits." He originated the installment plan. The one state of affairs he could not endure was business at a standstill, and to start it moving he would do anything. He was the first advertiser—in a day when even to announce in the public prints the location of your store was to intimate to the public that you were in financial difficulties, were about to go to the wall and were trying the last desperate expedient to which no self-respecting merchant would stoop.

It was as easy as child's play to connect this energy with dishonesty. The Jew was not playing the game, at least so the staid English merchant thought. As a matter of fact he was playing the game to get it all in his own hands—which he has practically done.

The Jew has shown that same ability ever since. His power of analyzing the money currents amounts to an instinct. His establishment in one country represented another base from which the members of his race could operate. Whether by the natural outworking of innate gifts, or the deliberate plan of race unity and loyalty, all Jewish trading communities had relations, and as those trading communities increased in wealth, prestige and power, as they formed relations with governments and great interests in the countries where they operated, they simply put more power into the central community wherever it might be located, now in Spain, now in Holland, now in England. Whether by intention or not,

The Jewish Question—Fact or Fancy?

they became more closely allied than the branches of one business could be, because the cement of racial unity, the bond of racial brotherhood cannot in the very nature of things exist among the Gentiles as it exists among the Jews. Gentiles never think of themselves as Gentiles, and never feel that they owe anything to another Gentile as such. Thus they have been convenient agents of Jewish schemes at times and in places when it was not expedient that the Jewish controllers should be publicly known; but they have never been successful competitors of the Jew in the field of world-control.

From these separated Jewish communities went power to the central community where the master bankers and the master analysts of conditions lived. And back from the central community flowed information of an invaluable character and assistance wherever needed. It is not difficult to understand how, under such a condition, the nation that did not deal kindly with the Jews was made to suffer, and the nation that yielded to them their fullest desire was favored by them. And it is credibly stated that they have made certain nations feel the power of their displeasure.

This system, if it ever existed, exists in greater power today. It is today, however, threatened as it has never been. Fifty years ago, international banking, which was mostly in control of the Jews as the money brokers of the world, was on top of business. It exercised the supercontrol of governments and finance everywhere. Then came that new thing, Industry, which expanded to a degree unguessed by the shrewdest prophets and analysts.

As Industry gathered strength and power it became a powerful money magnet, drawing the wealth of the world in its train, not, however, merely for the sake of possessing the money, but of making it work. Production and profit on production, instead of loans and interest on loans, became the master method for a time. The war came, in which the former broker-masters of the world had undoubtedly their large part. And now the two forces, Industry and Finance, are in a struggle to see whether Finance is again to become the master, or creative Industry. This is one of the elements which is bringing the Jewish Question to the bar of public opinion.

To state this and to prove it may be nothing more than to establish the superiority of Jewish ability. Certainly it is not a tenable position to say that the Jew is extraordinarily successful and therefore must be curbed. It would be equally aside from the truth to say that the co-ordination of

Jewish activity has been, on the whole, a harmful thing for the world. It may be possible to show that up to this point it has been useful. Success cannot be attacked nor condemned. If any moral question arises at all, it must concern the use made of the success which has been attained. The whole matter centers there, after the previous fact is established. May the Jew go on as he has gone, or does his duty to the world require another use of his success?

This inquiry obviously leads to further discussion, as well as a gathering up of the remaining threads of the present discussion, which future articles will attempt to do.

The Dearborn Independent, June 12, 1920

"To this end we must organize. Organize, in the first place, so that the world may have proof of the extent and the intensity of our desire for liberty. Organize, in the second place, so that our resources may become known and be made available . . . .
"Organize, organize, organize, until every Jew must stand up and be counted—counted with us, or prove himself, wittingly or unwittingly, of the few who are against their own people."
—Louis D. Brandeis, Justice of the United States Supreme Court, *Zionism*, pp. 113, 114.

5. Anti-Semitism—Will It Appear in the U.S.?

Anyone who essays to discuss the Jewish Question in the United States or anywhere else must be fully prepared to be regarded as an Anti-Semite, in high-brow language, or in low-brow language, a Jew-baiter. Nor need encouragement be looked for from people or from press.

The people who are awake to the subject at all prefer to wait and see how it all turns out; while there is probably not a newspaper in America, and certainly none of the advertising mediums which are called magazines, which would have the temerity even to breathe seriously the fact that such a Question exists. The press in general is open at this time to fulsome editorials in favor of everything Jewish (specimens of the same being obtainable almost anywhere), while the Jewish press, which is fairly numerous in the United States, takes care of the vituperative end.

Of course, the only acceptable explanation of any public discussion at present of the Jewish Question is that some one—writer, or publisher, or a related interest—is a Jew-hater.

That idea seems to be fixed; it is fixed in the Jew by inheritance; it is sought to be fixed in the Gentile by propaganda, that any writing which does not simply cloy and drip in syrupy sweetness toward things Jewish is born of prejudice and hatred. It is, therefore, full of lies, insult, insinuation, and constitutes an instigation to massacre. These terms are culled at random from Jewish editorial utterances at hand. It would seem to be necessary for our Jewish citizens to enlarge their classification of Gentiles to include the class which recognizes the existence of a Jewish Question and still is not anti-Semitic. There are four distinct parties traceable among the Jews themselves. First, those whose passionate purpose is to keep Jewish faith and life alive at the cost of any sacrifice of popularity or success; second, those who are willing to make whatever sacrifice may be needed to preserve Jewish religion, but are not so particular about the traditional customs of Jewish life; third, those who have no very strong convictions either way, but are opportunists, and will always swerve in the direction of success; and, fourth, those who believe and preach that the only solution of the differences between the Jew and other men is the complete absorption of the Jewish race by the other races. The fourth is the weakest, most unpopular and least to be considered of all the parties.

With the Gentiles there are only two classes, as far as this special question is concerned: those who dislike Jews, they cannot tell why; and those who are disposed to fairness, in spite of the accident of congeniality or uncongeniality, and who recognize the Jewish Question as, at least, a problem. Both these attitudes, whenever they become apparent, are subject to the charge of "anti-Semitism."

Anti-Semitism is a term which is bandied about too loosely. It ought to be reserved to denote the real anti-Jewish temper of violent prejudice. If used indiscriminately about all who attempt to discuss Jewish characteristics and Jewish world-power, it may in time arrive at the estate of respectability and honor.

Anti-Semitism in almost every form is bound to come to the United States; indeed, it may be said that it is here now, and has been here for a long time. If it be mislabeled now, the United States will not be able to work within it the transformation which has been effected upon so many other ideas that have arrived here in their journey round the globe.

I.

It may be a serviceable clearing of the ground to define what anti-Semitism is not:.

1. It is not recognition of the Jewish Question. If it were, then it could be set down that the bulk of the American people are destined to become anti-Semites, for they are beginning to recognize the existence of a Jewish Question and will steadily do so in increasing numbers as the Question is forced upon them from the various practical angles of their lives. The Question is here. We may be honestly blind to it. We may be timidly silent about it. We may even make dishonest denial of

Anti-Semitism—Will It Appear in the U.S.?

it. But it is here. In time all will have to recognize it. In time the polite "hush, hush" of oversensitive or intimidated circles will not be powerful enough to suppress it. But to recognize it will not mean that we have gone over to a campaign of hatred and enmity against the Jews. It will only mean that a stream of tendency which has been flowing through our civilization has at last accumulated bulk and power enough to challenge attention, to call for some decision with regard to it, to call for the adoption of a policy which will not repeat the mistakes of the past and yet will forestall any possible social menace of the future.

2. Again, the public discussion of the Jewish Question is not anti-Semitism. Publicity is sanitary. The publicity given the Jewish Question, or certain aspects of it, in this country has been very misleading. It has been discussed more fully in the Jewish press than elsewhere, but not with candor or breadth of vision. The two dominant notes—they are sounded over and over again with monotonous regularity in the Jewish press—are Gentile unfairness and Christian prejudice.

These apparently are the two chief aspects of life which impress Jewish publicists when they look over the line of their own race. It is said in all soberness that it is fortunate for Jews generally that the Jewish press does not circulate very widely among Gentiles, for it is probably the one established agency in the United States which, without altering its program in the least, could stir up anti-Jewish sentiment by the simple expedient of a general reading among non-Jews.

Jewish writers writing for Jewish readers present unusual material for the study of race consciousness and its accompaniment of contempt for other races. It is true that in the publications referred to, America is constantly praised, but not America as the land of the American people; America, rather, as the land of the Jews' opportunity.

On the side of the daily press, there has been no serious discussion at all. This is neither surprising nor reprehensible. The daily press deals with matters that have reached the overheated stage.

When it mentions the Jews at all, it has stock phrases for the purpose; the effort includes a list of the famous Jews of history, and usually closes with complimentary references to certain local Jews of commendable qualities, whose advertisements are not infrequently found in another part of the paper.

Summing up, it may be said that the publicity given the question in this country consists in misrepresentative criticism of the Gentiles by the Jewish press and misrepresentative praise of the Jews by the non-

Jewish press. An independent effort to give a constructive publicity cannot, therefore, be laid to anti-Semitism, even when some of the statements which are made in the course of it arouse the resentment of Jewish readers.

3. Nor is it anti-Semitism to say that the suspicion is abroad in every capital of civilization and the certainty is held by a number of important men that there is active in the world a plan to control the world, not by territorial acquisition, not by military aggression, nor by governmental subjection, not even by economic control in the scientific sense, but by control of the machinery of commerce and exchange. It is not anti-Semitism to say that, nor to present the evidence which supports that, nor to bring the proof of that. Those who could best disprove it if it were not true are the international Jews themselves, but they have not disproved it.

Those who could best prove it would be those Jews whose ideals include the good of the whole of humanity on an equality and not the good of one race only, but they have not proved it. Some day a prophetic Jew may arise who will see that the promises bestowed upon the Ancient People are not to be fulfilled by Rothschild methods, and that the promise that all the nations were to be blessed through Israel is not to be fulfilled by making the nations the economic vassals of Israel; and when that time comes we may hope for a redirection of Jewish energy into channels that will drain the present sources of the Jewish Question. In the meantime, it is not anti-Semitism, it may even be found to be a world service to the Jew, to throw light on what purpose motivates certain higher circles.

If the above propositions are true, then the term "anti-Semitic," so freely bestowed on this series of articles, betrays a worse spirit in the critics than in the author. But enough of that. There is much yet to do, and what is done must stand on what merit remains after friend and foe alike are through with praise and blame.

II.

Anti-Semitism has unquestionably swayed large sections of humanity at various times, warping the vision, twisting the characters and staining the hands of its victims, but the most amazing statement that can be made of it is that it has never accomplished anything in behalf of those who used it, and it has never taught anything to the Jews against whom it was used.

The grades of anti-Semitism are fairly numerous, and a few of them may be cited here:

1. There is first that degree of anti-Semitism, if it may be so described, which consists in plain dislike of the Jew as a person, no matter whom he may be. This is often found in people of all grades. It is found mostly, however, in those whose contact with Jews has been very limited. It begins sometimes in childhood with an instinctive dislike for the word "Jew." It is encouraged by the misuse of the word "Jew" as an epithet, or as an adjective generally descriptive of unpopular practices. The feeling is not different from that which exists toward Gentiles, concerning whom the same notions are held, but it differs in that it is extended to the race of unknown individual Jews instead of being restricted to known individuals who may justify such a feeling.

Congeniality is not within our choice, but control of the sentiment of uncongeniality is. Every fair-minded person is compelled at times to reflect that it is not impossible that the person for whom he feels a dislike may be as good and possibly a better person than he. Our dislike merely registers the result of attraction and repulsion as they operate between another person and oneself; it does not indicate that the disliked person is unworthy. Of course, wherever intelligence is joined with this instinctive withdrawal from social contact with members of the Jewish race, prejudice is forestalled, except, of course, in those persons who hold that there are no individuals among the Jews worthy of respect. This is an extreme attitude and is composed of other elements beside natural dislike. It is possible for people to dislike Jews and not be anti-Semitic. Indeed, it is not at all uncommon, it grows more and more common, that intelligent and refined Jews themselves do not relish the society of their own people except in cases of exceptional refinement.

This reality calls for some comment on the manners and characteristics of the ordinary member of the Jewish race, the accidents of behavior which stand out most obnoxiously and of which Jews themselves are often the most unsparing critics, but these comments must fall into place later.

2. A second stage of the spirit of anti-Semitism may be designated as hatred and enmity. It should be noted that the antipathy referred to immediately above was not hatred. Dislike is not hatred, nor is it necessarily enmity. One may dislike sugar in his tea without troubling to hate sugar. But undoubtedly there are people who because they have let their dislikes deepen into prejudice, and perhaps also because

of unpleasant experiences with members of the Jewish race (probably a million Americans have been brought to the verge of becoming Jew-haters this winter because of contact with Jewish merchants and landlords) may be classified as, at least, incipient anti-Semites. This is most of all unfortunate for the persons who harbor these emotions. It is unfortunate in that it unfits the mind to consider intelligently the facts which constitute the Jewish Question, and also unfits it to deal with them in a fair and constructive way. For one's own sake, whatever the provocation otherwise, it is better not to let passion deflect the needle of one's mind.

Hatred at the wheel means hazard on the course. Enmity lives in the vicinity of the Jews more than of any other race, and the reason for this is one of the puzzles of the ages. The Jewish nature itself, as shown in ancient and modern history, is not without its own share of enmity, and it either evokes or provokes enmity where it comes in contact with those Aryan races which follow their natural impulses unchecked by cultural and ethical influences. This age-long conflict of the Jew has puzzled the minds of students for generations.

Some explain it Biblically as the curse of Jehovah upon His Chosen People for their disobedience to the discipline by which He would have made them the Prophet Nation of the world. If this offense must come, if it is part of the Jew's heritage, an old saying—Christian and Scriptural, by the way—would still remain true: "It must needs be that offenses come, but woe to that man by whom the offense cometh."

3. In some parts of the world at various times this feeling of hatred has broken into murderous violence, which has roused, as wholesale physical outrage always does, the horror and resentment of humanity. This is the extreme form in which anti-Semitism has exhibited itself, and it is the charge of intending to stimulate it here and elsewhere which every public discussion of the Jewish Question has to bear. There is, of course, no excuse for these outbreaks, but there is sufficient explanation of them.

The Jews usually explain them as expressions of religious prejudice, and the Gentiles as rebellion against an economic yoke which the Jews have woven for the people. It is an astonishing fact that, to take one country, the parts of Russia where anti-Semitic violence has been most marked are the most prosperous parts, so prosperous indeed and with a prosperity so unquestionably due to Jewish enterprise that the Jews have openly declared that they have the power to throw those parts of Russia back into commercial lethargy again by simply withdrawing. It is utterly idle to throw denials at this statement. It is confirmed time and time again by men who have gone to Russia full of resentment against the attitude of the Russians toward the Jews, as that attitude is represented in the Anglo-Saxon press, and who have come home with a new light on the cause of these outbreaks, though not excusing their character. Impartial observers have also found that some of the outbreaks have been precipitated by the Jews themselves.

A correspondent, known the world over for his trenchant defense of the Jews under Russian persecution, was always bitterly attacked by the Jews themselves whenever he stated the truth about this, notwithstanding his protest to them that if he did not tell the truth when they were in the wrong the world would not be ready to believe him when he said they were blameless.

To this day, in every country, the Jews are slow to admit blameworthiness for anything. They must be excused, whoever else may be accused. It is a trait which will have to be disciplined before they can be brought to assist, if ever they can, the removal of those characteristics which arouse the antagonism of other peoples. Elsewhere in the world, it may be said that out-and-out enmity to the Jews has an economic basis. This, of course, leads to the question whether the Jew shall have to become a deliberate failure, or deny his genius, and forego his just meed of prosperity before he can win the approval of the other races—a question which will arise for discussion later.

As to the religious prejudice which the Jews are, as a rule, readiest to affirm, it is safe to say that it does not exist in the United States. Yet it is charged up to Americans by Jewish writers just as freely as it is charged up to Russians.

Each non-Jew reader is competent to settle this for himself. He can easily do so by asking himself whether in all his life he has ever felt a moment's resentment against the Jew on account of his religion. In an address recently delivered in a Jewish lodge and reported in the Jewish press, the speaker, a Jew, stated that if 100 non-Jews on the street were approached at random and casually asked what a Jew is, the reply of the majority would be, "He is a Christ-killer." One of the best known and most highly respected rabbis in the United States said recently in a sermon that children in Christian Sunday schools were taught to regard the Jew as a Christ-killer. He repeated it in a conversation several weeks later.

It would probably be the testimony of Christians generally that they never heard this term until they heard it in a Jewish complaint, and certainly themselves never used it. The charge is absurd. Let the 20,000,000 now in the Christian Sunday schools of Canada and the United States testify as to the instruction given. There is no hesitation in stating that there is no prejudice whatever in the Christian churches against the Jew on account of his religion. On the contrary, there is not only a deep sense of indebtedness, but a feeling of sharing with the Jew in his religion. The Sunday schools of the Christian churches of the world are spending six months of this year studying the International Lessons which are appointed for the Books of the Judges, Ruth, First and Second Samuel and the Books of the Kings, and every year is devoted in part to the Old Testament.

Here, however, is something for Jewish religious leaders to consider: there is more downright bitterness of religious prejudice on the part of the Jews against Christianity than could ever be possible in the Christian churches of America. Simply take the church press of America and compare it with the Jewish press in this regard, and there is no answer. No Christian editor would think it either Christian or intelligent to attack the Jewish religion, yet any six months' survey of the Jewish press would yield a mass of attack and prejudice on the other side. Moreover, no religious bitterness in America attains within infinite distances to that bitterness visited upon the Jew who becomes a Christian in his faith. It amounts almost to a holy vendetta. A Christian may become a Jewish proselyte and his motives be respected; it is never so when a Jew becomes a Christian. These statements are true of both the orthodox and liberal wings of Judaism. It is not his religion that gives prominence to the Jew today; it is something else. And yet, with undeviating monotony, it is repeated wherever the Jew takes cognizance of the feeling toward him that it is on account of three things, first and most prominent of which is his religion. It may be comforting to him to think that he is suffering for his faith, but it is not true. Every intelligent Jew must know it.

Every Jew ought to know also that in every Christian church where the ancient prophecies are received and studied, there is a great revival of interest in the future of the Ancient People. It is not forgotten that certain Promises were made to them regarding their position in the world, and it is held that these prophecies will be fulfilled. The future of the Jew, as prophetically outlined, is intimately bound up with the future of this planet, and the Christian church in large part—at least by the evangelical wing, which the Jews most condemn—sees a Restoration of the Chosen People yet to come. If the mass of the Jews knew how understandingly and sympathetically all the prophecies concerning them are being studied in the Church, and the faith that exists that these prophecies will find fulfillment and that they will result in great Jewish service to society at large, they would probably regard the Church with another mind. They would at least know that the Church does not believe that it will be the instrument in the conversion of the Jews—a point on which Jewish leaders are tragically misled and which evokes more bitterness than anything else—but that it depends on quite other instruments and conditions, which it is not the function of this article to point out except to say that it will be the Jews' very own Messiah which will accomplish it and not the "wild olive," or the Gentile.

Curiously enough, there is a phase of anti-Semitism having to do with religion, but not in the way here discussed. There are those, very few in number and of atheistical tendencies, who assert that all religion is a sham, being the invention of Jews for the purpose of enslaving the minds of the people of the world to an enervating superstition. This position, however, has had no effect on the main issue. It is a far extreme.

III.

Now, which of these exhibitions of anti-Semitism will show itself in America? If certain tendencies continue, as they are certain to do, what form will the feeling toward the Jew take? Not that of mass violence, we may be sure.

The only mass action visible now is that of the Jewish agencies themselves against any person or institution that dares bring the Jewish Question to public attention.

1. Anti-Semitism will come to America because of the habit which emotions and ideas apparently have of making their way westward around the world. North of Palestine, where the Jews have been longest settled and where they are now in great numbers, anti-Semitism is acute and well-defined. Westward, in Germany, it is clearly defined but, until the seizure of German revolutionary agencies, was devoid of violence.

Still farther westward, in Great Britain, it is defined, but because of the comparatively small number of Jews in the British Isles and their coalition with the ruling class, it is more a feeling than a movement. In the United States it is not so definite, but shows itself in a restlessness, a questioning, a sensible friction between the traditional tendency of the American to fair-mindedness and his respect for the cold facts.

Because the Question will assume more and more pressure in America it behooves everyone of foresight to disregard the shortsighted protests of the Jews themselves and see to it that the Question shall not present itself among us as it has done among other people, in its most distressing and confusing forms.

It is a public duty to seize this problem at its beginning and train it up, so to speak; that is, so prepare for it that it may be handled here in a manner which will form a model for all other countries, which will indeed supply all other countries with the essential materials for a permanent solution. And this can be done only by exposing and recognizing and treating with the serum of publicity the conditions before which, heretofore, the nations have helplessly floundered because they lacked either the desire or the means to get at the great root of the difficulty.

2. Another cause of the Question appearing here will be the great influx of Jews which is planned for America. There will probably be a million Jews enter the country this year, increasing our Jewish population to nearly 4,500,000. This does not mean merely an immigration of persons, but an immigration of ideas.

No Jewish writer has ever told us, in systematic fashion, just what is the Jews' idea of non-Jews, how they regard the Gentiles in their private minds. But there are indications of it, although one would not attempt to reconstruct the Jewish attitude toward Gentiles.

A Jew ought to do this for us, but he would probably be cast out by his own people if he discharged his task with rigorous jealousy for the exact fact.

These people are coming here regarding the Gentile as an hereditary enemy, as perhaps they have good ground for doing, and so believing they are going to model their behavior in a manner that will show it. Nor will these Jews be so helpless as they appear. In stricken Poland, where the Jews are represented as having been stripped of everything during the war, there are hundreds daily appearing before the consulate to arrange their passage here. The fact is significant. In spite of their reputed suffering and poverty, they are able to travel a great distance and to insist on coming. No other people are financially able to travel in such numbers. But the Jews are. It will readily be seen that they are not objects of charity. They have been able to keep afloat in a storm that has wrecked the other people. They know it and they joy in it, as is natural. And they will bring here the same thoughts toward the majority which they have harbored in their present lands of domicile. They may hail America; they will have their own thoughts about the majority of the American people. They may be in the lists as Russians or Poles or what not, but they will be Jews with the full Jewish consciousness, and they will make themselves felt.

All this is bound to have its effect. And it is not race prejudice to prepare for it, and to invite American Jews themselves to consider the fact and contribute to the solution of the problem which it presents.

3. Every idea which has ruled Europe has met with transformation when it was transplanted in America. It was so with the idea of Liberty, the idea of Government, the idea of War. It will be so with the idea of anti-Semitism. The whole problem will center here and if we are wise and do not shirk it, it will find its solution here. A recent Jewish writer has said: "Jewry today largely means American Jewry . . . . all former Jewish centers were demolished during the war and were shifted to America." The problem will be ours, whether we choose it or not.

And what course will it take? Much depends on what can be accomplished before it becomes very strong. It may be said, however, that the first element to appear will be a show of resentment against certain Jewish commercial successes, more particularly against the united action by which they are attained. Our people see the spectacle of a people in the midst of a people, in a sense which the Mormons never were, and they will not like it. The Mormons made an Exodus; Israel is going back into Egypt to subjugate it.

The second element which will undoubtedly appear is prejudice and its incitement. The majority may always be right, but they are not always initially reasonable.

That prejudice which exists now, and which is freely admitted by both Jew and Gentile, may become more marked, to the distress of both parties, for neither the subject nor the object of prejudice can attain that freedom of mind which is happiness.

Then we may most confidently look for a reaction of Justice. It is here that the whole matter will begin to bend to the genius of Americanism. The innate justice of the American mind has come to the aid of every object that ever roused American resentment. The natural reaction with us is of very brief duration; the intellectual and ethical reaction swiftly follows.

The American mind will never rest with merely resenting certain individuals. It will probe deeper. Already this deeper probe has been begun in Great Britain and America. We characteristically do not stop with persons when principles are in sight.

And upon this there will be an investigation of materials, part of which may yet be presented in this series and which may possibly be disregarded for a time, but which at a future date will be found to be the clue to the maze. Upon this, the root of all the trouble will be bared to the light, to die as all roots do when deprived of their concealment of darkness, and then the Jewish people themselves may be expected to begin an adjustment to the new order of things, not to lose their identity or to curtail their energy or to dim their brilliance, but to turn all into more worthy channels for the benefit of all races, which alone can justify their claim to superiority. A race that can achieve in the material realm what the Jews have achieved while asserting themselves to be spiritually superior, can achieve in a less sordid, a less society-defying realm also.

The Jews will not be destroyed; neither will they be permitted to maintain the yoke which they have been so skillful in fastening upon society. They are the beneficiaries of a system which itself will change and force them to other and higher devices to justify their proper place in the world.

The Dearborn Independent, June 19, 1920

"We must force the Gentile governments to adopt measures which will promote our broadly conceived plan already approaching its triumphal goal by bringing to bear the pressure of stimulated public opinion which has in reality been organized by us with the help of the so-called 'great power' of the Press. With few exceptions, not worth considering, it has already fallen into our hands."
—The Seventh Protocol.

6. Jewish Question Breaks into the Magazines

Once upon a time an American faculty member of an American university went to Russia on business. He was expert in a very important department of applied science and a keen observer. He entered Russia with the average American's feeling about the treatment which the government of that people accorded the Jew.

He lived there three years, came home for a year, and went back again for a similar period, and upon his second return to America he thought it was time to give the American public accurate information about the Jewish Question in Russia. He prepared a most careful article and sent it to the editor of a magazine of the first class in the Eastern United States. The editor sent for him, spent most of two days with him, and was deeply impressed with all he learned but he said he could not print the article. The same interest and examination occurred with several other magazine editors of the first rank.

It was not because the professor could not write—these editors gladly bought anything he would write on other subjects. But it was impossible for him to get his article on the Jews accepted or printed in New York. The Jewish Question, however, has at last broken into a New York magazine. Rather it is a fragment of a shell hurled from the Jewish camp at the Jewish Question to demolish, if possible, the Question and thus make good the assertion that there is no such thing.

Incidentally it is the only kind of article on the Jewish Question that the big magazines, whose mazes of financial controllers make most interesting rummaging, would care to print. Yet, the general public may learn much about the Question even from the type of article whose purpose is to prove that the Question doesn't exist.

Mr. William Hard, in the Metropolitan for June, has done as well as could be expected, considering the use he was supposed to make of such material as he had at hand. And doubtless the telegraph and letter brigades, which keep watch over all printed references to the Jews, have duly congratulated the good editors of the Metropolitan for their assistance in soothing the public to further sleep.

It is to be hoped, for the sake of the Question, that Mr. Hard's effort will have a wide reading, for there is very much to be learned from it—much more than it was anybody's intention should be learned from it.

It may be learned, first, that the Jewish Question exists. Mr. Hard says it is discussed in the drawing-rooms of London and Paris. Whether the mention of drawing-rooms was a writer's device to intimate that the matter was unimportant and frivolous, or merely represented the extent of Mr. Hard's contact with the Question is not clear. He adds, however, that a document relating to the Question has "travelled a good bit in certain official circles in Washington." He also mentions a cable dispatch to the New York World, concerning the same Question, which that paper published. His article was probably published too early to note the review which the London Times made of the first document referred to. But he has told the reader who is looking for the objective facts in the article that there is a Jewish Question, and that it does not exist among the riff-raff either but principally in those circles where the evidence of Jewish power and control is most abundant. Moreover, the Question is being discussed. Mr. Hard tells us that much. If he does not go further and tell us that it is being discussed with great seriousness in high places and among men of national and international importance, it is probably because of one of two things, either he does not know, or he does not consider it consonant with the purpose of the article to tell.

However, Mr. Hard has already made it clear that there is a Jewish Question, that it is being discussed, that it is being discussed by people who are best situated to observe the matter they are talking about.

The reading of Mr. Hard's article makes it clear also that the Question always comes to the fore on the note of conspiracy. Of course, Mr. Hard says he does not believe in conspiracies which involve a large number of people, and it is with the utmost ease that his avowal of unbelief is accepted, for there is nothing more ridiculous to the Gentile mind than a mass conspiracy, because there is nothing more impossible to the Gentile himself. Mr. Hard, we take it, is of non-Jewish extraction, and he knows how impossible it would be to band Gentiles together in any considerable number for any length of time in even the noblest conspiracy. Gentiles are not built for it. Their conspiracy, whatever it might be, would fall like a rope of sand. Gentiles have not the basis either in blood or interest that the Jews have to stand together. The Gentile does not naturally suspect conspiracy; he will indeed hardly bring himself to the verge of believing it without the fullest proof.

It is therefore quite easy to understand Mr. Hard's difficulty with conspiracy; the point is that to write his article at all, he is forced to recognize at almost every step that whenever the Jewish Question is discussed, the idea of conspiracy occupies a large part in it. As a matter of fact, it is the central idea in Mr. Hard's article, and it completely monopolizes the heading—"Great Jewish Conspiracy."

The search for basic facts in Mr. Hard's article will disclose the additional information that there are certain documents in existence which purport to contain the details of the conspiracy, or—to drop a word that is unpleasant and may be misleading and which has not been used in this series—the tendency of Jewish power to achieve complete control. That is about all that the reader learns from Mr. Hard about the documents, except that he describes one as "strange and horrible." Here is indeed a regrettable gap in the story, for it is to discredit a certain document that Mr. Hard writes, and yet he tells next to nothing about it. Discreditable documents usually discredit themselves. But this document is not permitted to do that. The reader of the article is left to take Mr. Hard's word for it.

The serious student or critic will feel, of course, that the documents themselves would have formed a better basis for an intelligent judgement. But laying that matter aside, Mr. Hard has made public the fact that there are documents.

And then Mr. Hard does another thing, as well as he can with the materials at hand, the purpose of the article being what it was, and that is to show how little the Jews have to do with the control of affairs by showing who are the Jews that do control certain selected groups of affairs. The names are all brought forward by Mr. Hard and he alone is responsible for them, our purpose in referring to them being merely to show what can be learned from him.

Mr. Hard leans heavily on Russian affairs. Sometimes it would almost seem as if the Jewish Question were conceived as the Soviet Question, which it is not, as Mr. Hard very well knows, and although the two have their plain connections, it is nothing less than well-defined propaganda to set up Bolshevist fiction and knock it down by Jewish fact for the purpose of the latter. However, what Mr. Hard offers as fact is very instructive, quite apart from the conclusion which he draws from it.

Now, take his Russian line-up first. He says that in the cabinet of Soviet Russia there is only one Jew. But he is Trotsky. There are others in the government, of course, but Mr. Hard is speaking about the cabinet now. He is not speaking about the commissars, who are the real rulers of Russia, nor about the executive troops, who are the real strength of the Trotsky-Lenin régime.

No, just the cabinet. Of course, there was only one Jew prominent in Hungary, too, but he was Bela Kun. Mr. Hard does not ask us to believe, however, that it is simply because of Trotsky and Kun that all Europe believes that Bolshevism has a strong Jewish element. Else the stupid credibility of the Gentiles would be more impossible of conception than the idea of a Jewish conspiracy is to Mr. Hard's mind. Why should it be easier to believe that Gentiles are dunces than that Jews are clever? However, it is not too much to say that Trotsky is way up at the top, sharing the utmost summit of Bolshevism with Lenin, and Trotsky is a Jew—nobody ever denied that, not even Mr. Braunstein himself (the latter being Trotsky's St. Louis, U.S.A., name).

But then, says Mr. Hard, the Mensheviks are led by Jews, too! That is a fact worth putting down beside the others. Trotsky at the head of the Bolsheviks; at the head of the Mensheviks during their opposition of the Bolsheviks were Leiber, Martov and Dan—"all Jews," says Mr. Hard.

There is, however, a middle party between these extremes, the Cadets, which, Mr. Hard says, are or were the strongest bourgeois political party in Russia. "They now have their headquarters in Paris. Their chairman is Vinaver—a Jew."

There are the facts as stated by Mr. Hard. He says that Jews, whose names he gives, head the three great divisions of political opinion in Russia. And then he cries, look how the Jews are divided! How can there be conspiracy among people who thus fight themselves?

But another, looking at the same situation may say, look how the Jews control every phase of political opinion in Russia! Doesn't there seem to be some ground for the feeling that they are desirous of ruling everywhere? The facts are there. What significance does it bring to the average mind that the three great parties of Russia are led by Jews?

But that does not exhaust the information which the matter-of-fact reader may find in Mr. Hard's article. He turns to the United States and makes several interesting statements.

"There is Otto Kahn," he says. Well, sometimes Otto Kahn is there, and sometimes he is in Paris on important international matters, and

Jewish Question Breaks into the Magazines

sometimes he is in London advocating certain alliances between British and American capital which have to do in a large way with European political conditions. Mr. Kahn is rated as a conservative, and that may mean anything. A man is conservative or not according to the angle from which he is viewed.

The most conservative men in America are really the most radical; their motives and methods go to the very roots of certain matters; they are radicals in their own field. The men who controlled the last Republican Convention—if not the last, the most recent—are styled conservatives by those whose vision is circumscribed by certain limited economic interests; but they are the most radical of radicals, they have passed the red stage and are white with it.

If it were known what is in the back of Mr. Kahn's mind, if he should display a chart of what he is doing and aiming to do, the term which would then most aptly describe him might be quite different. Anyway, we have it from Mr. Hard, "There is Mr. Kahn."

"On the other hand," says Mr. Hard, "there is Rose Pastor Stokes." He adds the name of Morris Hillquit. They are, in Mr. Hard's classification, radicals. And to offset these names he adds the names of two Gentiles, Eugene V. Debs and Bill Haywood and intimates that they are much more powerful leaders than the first two. Students of modern influences, of which Mr. Hard has long appeared as one, do not think so. Neither Debs nor Haywood ever generated in all their lives a fraction of the intellectual power which Mrs. Stokes and Mr. Hillquit have generated. Both Debs and Haywood live by the others.

To every informed person, as to Mr. Hard in this article, come the Jewish names to mind when the social tendencies of the United States are passed under reflection.

This is most instructive indeed, that in naming the leaders of so-called conservatism and radicalism, Mr. Hard is driven to use Jewish names. On his showing the reader is entitled to say that Jews lead both divisions here in the United States.

But Mr. Hard is not through. "The man who does more than any other man—the man who does more than any regiment of other men to keep American labor anti-radical is a Jew—Samuel Gompers." That is a fact which the reader will place in his list—American labor is led by a Jew. Well, then, "the strongest anti-Gompers trade union in the country—The Amalgamated Clothing Workers—and very strong indeed, and very large—is led by a Jew—Sidney Hillman."

It is the Russian situation over again. Both ends of the movements, and the movement which operate within the movement, are under the leadership of Jews. This, whatever the construction put upon it, is a fact which Mr. Hard is compelled by the very nature of his task to acknowledge.

And the middle movement, "the Liberal Middle" as Mr. Hard calls it, which catches all between, produces in this article the names of Mr. Justice Brandeis, Judge Mack and Felix Frankfurter, gentlemen whose activities since Armistice Day would make a very interesting story.

For good measure, Mr. Hard produces two other names, "Baron Gunzberg—a Jew" who is "a faithful official" of the Russian Embassy of Ambassador Bakhmetev, a repesentative of the modified old regime, while the Russian Information Bureau, whose literary output appears in many of our newspapers is conducted by another Jew, so Mr. Hard calls him, whose name is familiar to newspaper readers, Mr. A. J. Sack.

It is not a complete list by any means, but it is quite impressive. It seems to reflect importance on the documents which Mr. Hard endeavors to minimize to a position of ridiculous unimportance. And it leads to the thought that perhaps the documents are scrutinized as carefully as they are because the readers of them have observed not only the facts which Mr. Hard admits but other and more astonishing ones, and have discovered that the documents confirm and explain the observations. Other readers who have not had the privilege of learning all that the documents contain are entitled to have satisfaction given to the interest thus aroused.

The documents did not create the Jewish Question. If there were nothing but the documents, Mr. Hard would not have written nor would the Metropolitan Magazine have printed the article here discussed.

What Mr. Hard has done is to bring confirmation in a most unexpected place that the Question exists and is pressing for discussion. Someone felt the pressure when "The Great Jewish Conspiracy" was ordered and written.

The Dearborn Independent, June 26, 1920

"What are you prating about? As long as we do not have the Press of the whole world in our hands, everything you may do is vain. We must control or influence the papers of the whole world in order to blind and deceive the people." —Baron Montefiore.

7. Arthur Brisbane Leaps to the Help of Jewry

Once more the current of this series on the Modern Jewish Question is interrupted to give notice of the appearance of the Question in another quarter, the appearance this time consisting of a more than two-column "Today" editorial in the Hearst papers of Sunday, June 20, from the pen of Arthur Brisbane. It would be too much to say that Mr. Brisbane is the most influential writer in the country, but perhaps he is among the dozen most widely read. It is, therefore, a confirmation of the statement that the Question is assuming importance in this country, that a writer of Mr. Brisbane's prominence should openly discuss it.

Of course, Mr. Brisbane has not studied the Question. He would probably admit in private conversation—though such an admission would hardly be in harmony with the tone of certainty he publicly adopts—that he really knows nothing about it. He knows, however, as a good newspaper man, how to handle it when the exigencies of the newspaper day throw it up to him for offhand treatment. Every editorial writer knows how to do that. There is something good in every race, or there have been some notable individuals in it, or it has played a picturesque part in history that is enough for a very readable editorial upon any class of people who may happen to be represented in the community.

The Question, whatever it may be, need not be studied at all; a certain group of people may be salved for a few paragraphs, and the job need never be tackled again. Every newspaper man knows that.

And yet, having lived in New York for a long time, having had financial dealings of a large and obligating nature with certain interests in this country, having seen no doubt more or less of the inner workings of the great trust and banking groups, and being constantly surrounded by assistants and advisors who are members of the Jewish race, Mr. Brisbane must have had his thoughts. It is, however, no part of a newspaper man's business to expose his thoughts about the racial groups of his community, any more than it is a showman's business to express his opinion of the patrons of his show. The kinds of offense a newspaper will give, and the occasions on which it will feel justified in giving it, are very limited.

So, assuming that Mr. Brisbane had to write at all, it could have been told beforehand what he would write. The only wonder is that he felt he had to write. Did he really feel that the Jews are being "persecuted" when an attempt is made to uncover the extent and causes of their control in the United States and elsewhere? Did he feel, with good editorial shrewdness, that here was an opportunity to win the attention and regard of the most influential group in New York and the nation? Or—and this seems within the probabilities—was he inclined simply to pass it over, until secretarial suggestions reached him for a Sunday editorial, or until some of the bondholders made their wishes known? This is not at all to impugn Mr. Brisbane's motives, but merely to indicate on what slender strings such an editorial may depend.

But what is more important—does Mr. Brisbane consider that, having disposed of the Sunday editorial, he is through with the Question, or that the Question itself is solved? That is the worst of daily editorializing; having come safely and inoffensively through with one editorial, the matter is at an end as far as that particular writer is concerned—that is, as a usual thing.

It is to be hoped that Mr. Brisbane is not through. He ought not to leave a big question without contributing something to it, and in his Sunday editorial he did not contribute anything. He even made mistakes which he ought to correct by further study. "What about the Phoenicians?" he asks. He should have looked that up while his mind was opened receptively toward the subject, and he would not have made so miserable a blunder as to connect them so closely with the Jews. He would never find a Jew doing that. It is permissible, however, in Jewish propaganda intended for Gentile consumption. The Phoenicians themselves certainly never thought they were connected in any way with the Jews, and the Jews were equally without light on the subject. If in nothing else, they differed in their attitude toward the sea. The Phoenicians not only built boats but manned them; the Jew would rather risk his investment in a boat than himself. In everything else the differences between the two peoples were deep and distinct. Mr. Brisbane should have turned up the *Jewish Encyclopedia* at that point in his dictation. It is to be hoped he will resume his study and when he has found something that is not printed in "simply written" Jewish books will give the world the benefit of it. It is hardly like the question

Arthur Brisbane Leaps to the Help of Jewry

of the rotundity of the earth; this Question is not settled and it will be discussed.

Mr. Brisbane is in a position to pursue some investigations of his own on this subject. He has a large staff, and it is presumed that some of its members are Gentiles of unbiased minds; he has a world-wide organization; since his own modification of speech and views following upon his adventure in the money-making world, he has a "look-in" upon certain groups of men and certain tendencies of power—why does he not take the Question as a world problem and go after the facts and the solution?

It is a task worthy of any newspaper organization. It will assist America to make the contribution which she must make if this Question is ever to be turned from the bugbear it has been through all the centuries. All the talk on earth about "loving our fellow men" will not serve in lieu of an investigation, because it is asking men to love those who are rapidly and insidiously gaining the mastery of them. "What's wrong with the Jew?" is the first question, and then, "What's wrong with the Gentile to make it possible?"

As in the case of every Gentile writer who appears as the Jew's good-natured defender, Mr. Brisbane is compelled to state a number of facts which comprise a part of the very Question whose existence is denied.

"Every other successful name you see in a great city is a Jewish name," says Mr. Brisbane. In his own city the ratio is even higher than that. "Jews numbering less than one per cent of the earth's population possess by conquest, enterprise, industry and intelligence 50 per cent of the world's commercial success," says Mr. Brisbane.

Does it mean anything to Mr. Brisbane? Has he ever thought how it will all turn out? Is he willing to absolve that "success" from every quality which humanity has a right to challenge? Is he entirely satisfied with the way that "success" is used where it is supreme? Would he be willing to undertake to prove that it is due to those commendable qualities he has named and nothing less commendable? Speaking of the Jew-financed Harriman railroad campaign, is Mr. Brisbane ready to write his endorsement upon that? Did he ever hear of Jewish money backing railroads that were built for railroad purposes and nothing else?

It would be very easy to suggest to Mr. Brisbane, as editor, a series of articles which would be most enlightening, both to himself and his readers, if he would only put unbiased men at work gathering the facts for them.

One of the articles might be entitled "The Jews at the Peace Conference." His men should be instructed to learn who were the most prominent figures at the Peace Conference; who came and went most constantly and most busily; who were given freest access to the most important persons and chambers; which race provided the bulk of the private secretaries to the important personages there; which race provided most of the sentinels through whom engagements had to be made with men of note; which race went furthest in the endeavor to turn the whole proceeding into a festival rout by dances and lavish entertainment; which civilians of prominence oftenest dined the leading conferees in private session.

If Mr. Brisbane, with the genius for reporting which his organization deservedly has, will turn his men loose on that assignment, and then print what they bring him, he will have a story that will make a mark even in his remarkable career as an editor.

He might even run a second story on the Peace Conference, entitled, "Which Program Won at the Peace Conference?" He might instruct his men to inquire as to the business which brought the Jews in such quality and quantity to Paris, and how it was put through. Particularly should they inquire whether any jot or tittle of the Jews' world program was refused or modified by the Peace Conference. It should also be carefully inquired whether, after getting what they went after, they did not ask for still more and get that, too, even though it constituted a discrimination against the rest of the world. Mr. Brisbane would doubtless be surprised to learn that of all the programs submitted to that Conference, not excepting the great program on which humanity hung so many pathetic hopes, the only program to go through was the Jews' program. And yet he could learn just that if he inquired. The question is, having obtained that information, what would Mr. Brisbane do with it?

There are any number of lines of investigation Mr. Brisbane might enter, and in any one of them his knowledge of his country and of its relation to this particular Question would be greatly enlarged.

Does Mr. Brisbane know who owns Alaska? He may have been under the impression, in common with the rest of us until we learned better, that it was owned by the United States. No, it is owned by the same people who are coming rapidly to own the United States.

Is Mr. Brisbane, from the vantage point afforded by his position in national journalism, even dimly aware that there are elements in our industrial unrest which neither "capital" nor "labor" accurately define?

Has he ever caught a glimpse of another power which is neither "labor" nor "capital" in the productive sense, whose purpose and interest it is to keep labor and capital as far apart as possible, now by provoking labor, now by provoking capital? In his study of the industrial situation and its perfectly baffling mystery, Mr. Brisbane must have caught a flash of something behind the backmost scene. It would be good journalistic enterprise to find out what it is.

Has Mr. Brisbane ever printed the name of the men who control the sugar supply of the United States—does he know them—would he like to know them?

Has he ever looked into the woolen situation in this country, from the change of ownership in cotton lands, and the deliberate sabotage of cotton production by banking threats, right on through to the change in the price of cloth and clothing? And has he ever noted the names of the men he found on that piece of investigation? Would he like to know how it is done, and who does it? Mr. Brisbane could find all these things and give them to the public by using his efficient staff of investigators and writers on this Question.

Whether Mr. Brisbane would feel free to do this, he himself best knows. There may be reasons why he would not, private reasons, prudential reasons.

However that may be, there are no reasons why he should not make a complete study of the Question—a real study, not a superficial glance at it with an eye to its "news value"—and arrive at his own considered conclusion.

There would be no intolerance about that. As it is now, Mr. Brisbane is not qualified to take a stand on either side of the Question; he simply brushes it aside as troublesome, as the old planters used brush aside the anti-slavery moralists; and for that reason the recent defense of the Jew is not a defense at all. It is more like a bid for favor.

Mr. Brisbane's chief aversion, apparently, is toward what he calls race prejudice and race hatred. Of course, if any man should fear that the study of an economic situation would plunge him into these serious aberrations of mind, he should be advised to avoid that line of study. There is something wrong either with the investigation or with the investigator when prejudice and hatred are the result. It is a mighty poor excuse, however, for an intelligent man to put forward either on his own behalf or on behalf of those whose minds he has had the privilege of molding over a course of years.

Prejudice and hatred are the very conditions which a scientific study of the Jewish Question will forestall and prevent. We prejudge what we do not know, and we hate what we do not understand; the study of the Jewish Question will bring knowledge and insight, and not to the Gentile only, but also to the Jew.

The Jew needs this as much, even more than the Gentile. For if the Jew can be made to see, understand, and deal with certain matters, then a large part of the Question vanishes in the solution of ideal common sense. Awaking the Gentile to the facts about the Jew is only part of the work; awaking the Jew to the facts about the Question is an indispensable part. The big initial victory to be achieved is to transform Gentiles from being mere attackers and to transform Jews from being mere defenders, both of them special pleaders for partisan views, and to turn them both into investigators. The investigation will show both Gentile and Jew at fault, and the road will then be clear for wisdom to work out a result, if there should perchance be that much wisdom left in the race.

There is a serious snare in all this plea for tolerance. Tolerance is first a tolerance of the truth. Tolerance is urged today for the sake of suppression. There can be no tolerance until there is first a full understanding of what is tolerated. Ignorance, suppression, silence, collusion—these are not tolerance. The Jew never has been really tolerated in the higher sense because he has never been understood. Mr. Brisbane does not assist the understanding of this people by reading a "simply written" book and flinging a few Jewish names about in a sea of type. He owes it to his own mind to get into the Question, whether he makes newspaper use of his discoveries or not.

As to the newspaper angle, it is impossible to report the world even superficially without coming everywhere against the fact of the Jews, and the Press gets around that fact by referring to them as Russians, Letts, Germans, and Englishmen. This mask of names is one of the most confusing elements in the whole problem. Names that actually name, statements that actually define are needed for the clarification of the world's mind.

Mr. Brisbane should study this question for the light such a study would throw on other matters with which he is concerned. It would be a help to that study if from time to time he would publish some of his findings, because such publication would put him in touch with a phase of Judaism which mere complimentary editorials could not. No doubt Mr. Brisbane has been deluged by communications which praise him for what he has written; the real eye-opener would come if he could get several bushels of the other kind. Nothing that has ever come to him could compare with what would come to him if he should publish even one of the facts he could discover by an independent investigation.

Having written about the Jews, Mr. Brisbane will probably have a readier eye henceforth for other men's pronouncements on the same subject. In his casual reading he will find more references to the Jew than he has ever noticed before. Some of them will probably appear in isolated sentences and paragraphs of his own papers. Sooner or later, every competent investigator and every honest writer strikes a trail that leads toward Jewish power in the world. *The Dearborn Independent* is only doing with system and detail what other publications have done or are doing piecemeal.

There is a real fear of the Jew upon the publicity sources of the United States—a fear which is felt and which ought to be analyzed. Unless it is a very great mistake, Mr. Brisbane himself has felt this fear, though it is quite possible he has not scrutinized it. It is not the fear of doing injustice to a race of people—all of us ought to have that honorable fear—it is the fear of doing anything at all with reference to them except unstintedly praising them. An independent investigation would convince Mr. Brisbane that a considerable modification of praise in favor of discriminate criticism is a course that is pressing upon American journalism.

The Dearborn Independent, July 3, 1920

8. Does a Definite Jewish World Program Exist?

In all the explanations of anti-Jewish feeling which modern Jewish spokesmen make, these three alleged causes are commonly given—these three and no more: religious prejudice, economic jealousy, social antipathy. Whether the Jew knows it or not, every Gentile knows that on his side of the Jewish Question no religious prejudice exists. Economic jealousy may exist, at least to this extent, that his uniform success has exposed the Jew to much scrutiny. A few Jewish spokesmen seek to turn this scrutiny by denying that the Jew is pre-eminent in finance, but this is loyalty in extremity. The finances of the world are in control of Jews; their decisions and their devices are themselves our economic law. But because a people excels us in finance is no sufficient reason for calling them to the bar of public judgement. If they are more intellectually able, more persistently industrious than we are, if they are endowed with faculties which have been denied us as an inferior or slower race, that is no reason for our requiring them to give an account of themselves. Economic jealousy may explain some of the anti-Jewish feeling; it cannot account for the presence of the Jewish Question except as the hidden causes of Jewish financial success may become a minor element of the larger problem. And as for social antipathy—there are many more undesirable Gentiles in the world than there are undesirable Jews, for the simple reason that there are more Gentiles.

None of the Jewish spokesmen today mention the political cause, or if they come within suggestive distance of it, they limit and localize it. It is not a question of the patriotism of the Jew, though this too is very widely questioned in all the countries. You hear it in England, in France, in Germany, in Poland, in Russia, in Rumania—and, with a shock, you hear it in the United States. Books have been written, reports published and scattered abroad, statistics skillfully set forth for the purpose of showing that the Jew does his part for the country in which he resides; and yet the fact remains that in spite of these most zealous and highly sponsored campaigns, the opposite assertion is stronger and lives longer. The Jews who did their duty in the armies of Liberty, and did it

Does a Definite Jewish World Program Exist?

doubtless from true-hearted love and allegiance, have not been able to overcome the impression made upon officers and men and civilians by those who did not.

But that is not what is here meant as the political element in the Jewish Question. To understand why the Jew should think less of the nationalities of the world than do those who comprise them is not difficult.

The Jew's history is one of wandering among them all. Considering living individuals only, there is no race of people now upon the planet who have lived in so many places, among so many peoples as have the Jewish masses. They have a clearer world-sense than any other people, because the world has been their path. And they think in world terms more than any nationally cloistered people could. The Jew can be absolved if he does not enter into national loyalties and prejudices with the same intensity as the natives; the Jew has been for centuries a cosmopolitan. While under a flag he may be correct in the conduct required of him as a citizen or resident, inevitably he has a view of flags which can hardly be shared by the man who has known but one flag.

The political element inheres in the fact that the Jews form a nation in the midst of the nations. Some of their spokesmen, particularly in America, deny that, but the genius of the Jew himself has always put these spokesmen's zeal to shame. And why this fact of nationhood should be so strenuously denied is not always clear. It may be that when Israel is brought to see that her mission in the world is not to be achieved by means of the Golden Calf, her very cosmopolitanism with regard to the world and her inescapable nationalistic integrity with regard to herself will together prove a great and serviceable factor in bringing about human unity, which the total Jewish tendency at the present time is doing much to prevent. It is not the fact that the Jews remain a nation in the midst of the nations; it is the use made of that inescapable status, which the world has found reprehensible. The nations have tried to reduce the Jew to unity with themselves; attempts toward the same end have been made by the Jews themselves; but destiny seems to have marked them out to continuous nationhood. Both the Jews and the World will have to accept that fact, find the good prophecy in it, and seek the channels for its fulfillment.

Theodor Herzl, one of the greatest of the Jews, was perhaps the farthest-seeing public exponent of the philosophy of Jewish existence that modern generations have known. And he was never in doubt of the existence of the Jewish nation. Indeed, he proclaimed its existence on every occasion. He said, "We are a people—One people."

He clearly saw that what he called the Jewish Question was political. In his introduction to "The Jewish State" he says, "I believe that I understand anti-Semitism, which is really a highly complex movement. I consider it from a Jewish standpoint, yet without fear or hatred. I believe that I can see what elements there are in it of vulgar sport, of common trade jealousy, of inherited prejudice, of religious intolerance and also of pretended self-defense.

"I think the Jewish Question is no more a social than a religious one, notwithstanding that it sometimes takes these and other forms. It is a national question, which can only be solved by making it a political world-question to be discussed and controlled by the civilized nations of the world in council."

Not only did Herzl declare that the Jews formed a nation, but when questioned by Major Evans Gordon before the British Royal Commission on Alien Immigration in August, 1902, Dr. Herzl said: "I will give you my definition of a nation, and you can add the adjective 'Jewish.'

A nation is, in my mind, an historical group of men of a recognizable cohesion held together by a common enemy. That is in my view a nation. Then if you add to that the word 'Jewish' you have what I understand to be the Jewish nation."

Also, in relating the action of this Jewish nation to the world, Dr. Herzl wrote—"When we sink, we become a revolutionary proletariat, the subordinate officers of the revolutionary party; when we rise, there rises also our terrible power of the purse."

This view, which appears to be the true view in that it is the view which has been longest sustained in Jewish thought, is brought out also by Lord Eustace Percy, and re-published, apparently with approval, by the Canadian *Jewish Chronicle*. It will repay a careful reading:

"Liberalism and Nationalism, with a flourish of trumpets, threw open the doors of the ghetto and offered equal citizenship to the Jew. The Jew passed out into the Western World, saw the power and the glory of it, used it and enjoyed it, laid his hand indeed upon the nerve centers of its civilization, guided, directed and exploited it, and then—refused the offer . . .

"Moreover—and this is a remarkable thing—the Europe of nationalism and liberalism, of scientific government and democratic equality is more intolerable to him than the old oppressions and persecutions of despotism . . . In the increasing consolidation of the western nations, it is no longer possible to reckon on complete toleration. . .

"In a world of completely organized territorial sovereignties he (the Jew) has only two possible cities of refuge: he must either pull down the pillars of the whole national state system or he must create a territorial sovereignty of his own. In this perhaps lies the explanation both of Jewish Bolshevism and of Zionism, for at this moment Eastern Jewry seems to hover uncertainly between the two.

"In Eastern Europe Bolshevism and Zionism often seem to grow side by side, just as Jewish influence molded Republican and Socialist thought throughout the nineteenth century, down to the Young Turk revolution in Constantinople hardly more than a decade ago—not because the Jew cares for the positive side of radical philosophy, not because he desires to be a partaker in Gentile nationalism or Gentile democracy, but because no existing Gentile system of government is ever anything but distasteful to him."

All that is true, and Jewish thinkers of the more fearless type always recognize it as true. The Jew is against the Gentile scheme of things. He is, when he gives his tendencies full sway, a Republican as against the monarchy, a Socialist as against the republic, and a Bolshevist as against Socialism.

What are the causes of this disruptive activity? First, his essential lack of democracy. Jewish nature is autocratic. Democracy is all right for the rest of the world, but the Jew wherever he is found forms an aristocracy of one sort or another. Democracy is merely a tool of a word which Jewish agitators use to raise themselves to the ordinary level in places where they are oppressed below it; but having reached the common level they immediately make efforts for special privileges, as being entitled to them—a process of which the late Peace Conference will remain the most startling example. The Jews today are the only people whose special and extraordinary privileges are written into the world's Treaty of Peace. But more of that at another time.

No one now pretends to deny, except a few spokesmen who really do not rule the thought of the Jews but are set forth for the sole benefit of influencing Gentile thought, that the socially and economically disruptive elements abroad in the world today are not only manned but also moneyed by Jewish interests. For a long time this fact was held in suspense owing to the vigorous denial of the Jews and the lack of information on the part of those agencies of publicity to which the public had looked for its information. But now the facts are coming forth. Herzl's words are being proved to be true—"when we sink, we become a revolutionary proletariat, the subordinate officers of the revolutionary party"—and these words were first published in English in 1896, or 24 years ago.

Just now these tendencies are working in two directions, one for the tearing down of the Gentile states all over the world, and the other for the establishment of a Jewish state in Palestine. The latter project has the best wishes of the whole world, but it is far from having the best wishes of the whole, or even the larger part, of Jewry.

The Zionist party makes a great deal of noise, but it is really an unrepresentative minority. It can scarcely be designated as more than an unusually ambitious colonization scheme.

It is doubtless serving, however, as a very useful public screen for the carrying on of secret activities. International Jews, the controllers of the world's governmental and financial power, may meet anywhere, at any time, in war time or peace time, and by giving out that they are only considering the ways and means of opening up Palestine to the Jews, they easily escape the suspicion of being together on any other business. The Allies and enemies of the Gentile nations at war thus met and were not molested.

It was at a Zionist conference—the sixth, held in 1903—that the recent war was exactly predicted, its progress and outcome indicated, and the relation of the Jews to the Peace Treaty outlined. That is to say, though Jewish nationalism exists, its enshrinement in a state to be set up in Palestine is not the project that is engaging the whole Jewish nation now.

The Jews will not move to Palestine just yet; it may be said that they will not move at all merely because of the Zionist movement. Quite another motive will be the cause of the exodus out of the Gentile nations, when the time for that exodus fully comes.

As Donald A. Cameron, late British Consul-General at Alexandria, a man fully in sympathy with Zionism and much quoted in the Jewish press, says: "The Jewish immigrants (into Palestine) will tire of taking in one another's washing at three per cent, of winning one another's money in the family, and their sons will hasten by train and steamer to win 10 per cent in Egypt . . . The Jew by himself in Palestine will eat his head off; he will kick his stable to pieces." Undoubtedly the time for the exodus—at least the motive for the exodus—is not yet here.

Does a Definite Jewish World Program Exist?

The political aspect of the Jewish Question which is now engaging at least three of the great nations—France, Great Britain and the United States—has to do with matters of the present organization of the Jewish nation. Must it wait until it reaches Palestine to have a State, or is it an organized State now? Does Jewry know what it is doing? Has it a "foreign policy" with regard to the Gentiles? Has it a department which is executing that foreign policy? Has this Jewish State, visible or invisible, if it exists, a head? Has it a Council of State? And if any of these things is so, who is aware of it?

The first impulsive answer of the Gentile mind would be "No" to all these questions—it is a Gentile habit to answer impulsively. Never having been trained in secrets or invisible unity, the Gentile immediately concludes that such things cannot be, if for no other reason than that they have not crossed his path and advertised themselves.

The questions, however, answered thus, require some explanation of the circumstances which are visible to all men. If there is no deliberate combination of Jews in the world, then the control which they have achieved and the uniformity of the policies which they follow must be the simple result, not of deliberate decisions, but of a similar nature in all of them working out the same way. Thus, we might say that as a love for adventure on the water drove the Britisher forth, so it made him the world's greatest colonist. Not that he deliberately sat down with himself and in formal manner resolved that he would become a colonizer, but the natural outworking of his genius resulted that way. But would this be a sufficient account of the British Empire?

Doubtless the Jews have the genius to do, wherever they go, the things in which we see them excel. But does this account for the relations which exist between the Jews of every country, for their world councils, for their amazing foreknowledge of stupendous events which break with shattering surprise on the rest of the world, for the smoothness and preparedness with which they appear, at a given time in Paris, with a world program on which they all agree?

The world has long suspected—at first only a few, then the secret departments of the governments, next the intellectuals among the people, now more and more the common people themselves—that not only are the Jews a nation distinct from all the other nations and mysteriously unable to sink their nationality by any means they or the world may adopt to this end, but that they also constitute a state; that they are nationally conscious, not only, but consciously united for a common defense and for a common purpose. Revert to Theodor Herzl's definition of the Jewish nation, as held together by a common enemy, and then reflect that this common enemy is the Gentile world.

Does this people which knows itself to be a nation remain loosely unorganized in the face of that fact? It would hardly be like Jewish astuteness in other fields. When you see how closely the Jews are united by various organizations in the United States, and when you see how with practiced hand they bring those organizations to bear as if with tried confidence in their pressure, it is at least not inconceivable that what can be done within a country can be done, or has been done, between all the countries where the Jews live.

At any rate, in the American Hebrew of June 25, 1920, Herman Bernstein writes thus: "About a year ago a representative of the Department of Justice submitted to me a copy of the manuscript of 'The Jewish Peril' by Professor Nilus, and asked for my opinion of the work. He said that the manuscript was a translation of a Russian book published in 1905 which was later suppressed.

The manuscript was supposed to contain 'protocols' of the Wise Men of Zion and was supposed to have been read by Dr. Herzl at a secret conference of the Zionist Congress at Basle. He expressed the opinion that the work was probably that of Dr. Theodor Herzl. . . . . He said that some American Senators who had seen the manuscript were amazed to find that so many years ago a scheme had been elaborated by the Jews which is now being carried out, and that Bolshevism had been planned years ago by Jews who sought to destroy the world."

This quotation is made merely to put on record the fact that it was a representative of the Department of Justice of the United States Government, who introduced this document to Mr. Bernstein, and expressed a certain opinion upon it, namely, "that the work was probably that of Theodor Herzl."

Also that "some American Senators" were amazed to note the comparison between what a publication of the year 1905 proposed and what the year 1920 revealed.

The incident is all the more preoccupying because it occurred by action of the representative of a government who today is very largely in the hands of, or under the influence of, Jewish interests. It is more than probable that as soon as the activity became known, the investigator was stopped. But it is equally probable that whatever orders may have been given and apparently obeyed, the investigation may not have stopped.

Does a Definite Jewish World Program Exist?

The United States Government was a little late in the matter, however. At least four other world powers had preceded it, some by many years. A copy of the Protocols was deposited in the British Museum and bears on it the stamp of that institution, "August 10, 1906." The notes themselves probably date from 1896, or the year of the utterances previously quoted from Dr. Herzl. The first Zionist Congress convened in 1897.

The document was published in England recently under auspices that challenged attention for it, in spite of the unfortunate title under which it appeared. Eyre and Spottiswoode are the appointed printers to the British Government, and it was they who brought out the pamphlet. It was as if the Government Printing Office at Washington should issue them in this country. While there was the usual outcry by the Jewish press, the London Times in a review pronounced all the Jewish counterattacks as "unsatisfactory."

The Times noticed what will probably be the case in this country also that the Jewish defenders leave the text of the protocols alone, while they lay heavy emphasis on the fact of their anonymity. When they refer to the substance of the document at all there is one form of words which recurs very often—"it is the work of a criminal or a madman."

The protocols, without name attached, appearing for the most part in manuscripts here and there, laboriously copied out from hand to hand, being sponsored by no authority that was willing to stand behind it, assiduously studied in the secret departments of the governments and passed from one to another among higher officials, have lived on and on, increasing in power and prestige by the sheer force of their contents. A marvelous achievement for either a criminal or a madman! The only evidence it has is that which it carries within it, and that internal evidence is, as the London Times points out, the point on which attention is to be focused. and the very point from which Jewish effort has been expended to draw us away.

The interest of the Protocols at this time is their bearing on the questions: Have the Jews an organized world system? What is its policy? How is it being worked? These questions all receive full attention in the Protocols. Whosoever was the mind that conceived them possessed a knowledge of human nature, of history and of statecraft which is dazzling in its brilliant completeness, and terrible in the objects to which it turns its powers. Neither a madman nor an intentional criminal, but more likely a super-mind mastered by devotion to a people and a faith could be the author, if indeed one mind alone conceived them. It is too terribly real for fiction, too well-sustained for speculation, too deep in its knowledge of the secret springs of life for forgery.

Jewish attacks upon it thus far make much of the fact that it came out of Russia. That is hardly true. It came by way of Russia. It was incorporated in a Russian book published about 1905 by a Professor Nilus, who attempted to interpret the Protocols by events then going forward in Russia.

This publication and interpretation gave it a Russian tinge which has been useful to Jewish propagandists in this country and England, because these same propagandists have been very successful in establishing in Anglo-Saxon mentalities a certain atmosphere of thought surrounding the idea of Russia and Russians. One of the biggest humbugs ever foisted on the world has been that foisted by Jewish propagandists, principally on the American public, with regard to the temper and genius of the truly Russian people. So, to intimate that the Protocols are Russian, is partially to discredit them.

The internal evidence makes it clear that the Protocols were not written by a Russian, nor originally in the Russian language, nor under the influence of Russian conditions. But they found their way to Russia and were first published there. They have been found by diplomatic officers in manuscript in all parts of the world. Wherever Jewish power is able to do so, it has suppressed them, sometimes under the supreme penalty.

Their persistence is a fact which challenges the mind. Jewish apologists may explain that persistence on the ground that the Protocols feed the anti-Semitic temper, and therefore are preserved for that service. Certainly there was no wide nor deep anti-Semitic temper in the United States to be fed or that felt the greed for agreeable lies to keep itself alive.

The progress of the Protocols in the United States can only be explained on the ground that they supply light and give meaning to certain previously observed facts, and that this light and meaning is so startling as to give a certain standing and importance to these otherwise unaccredited documents. Sheer lies do not live long, their power soon dies. These Protocols are more alive than ever. They have penetrated higher places than ever before. They have compelled a more serious attitude to them than ever before.

The Protocols would not be more worthy of study if they bore, say, the name of Theodor Herzl. Their anonymity does not decrease their power any more than the omission of a painter's signature detracts from the art value of a painting. Indeed, the Protocols are better without a known source. For if it were definitely known that in France or Switzerland in the year 1896, or thereabouts, a group of International Jews, assembled in conference, drew up a program of world conquest it would still have to be shown that such a program was more than a mere vagary, that it was confirmed at large by efforts to fulfill it. The Protocols are a World Program—there is no doubt anywhere of that. Whose program, is stated within the articles themselves. But as for outer confirmation, which would be the more valuable—a signature, or six signatures, or twenty signatures, or a 25-year unbroken line of effort fulfilling that program?

The point of interest for this and other countries is not that a "criminal or a madman" conceived such a program, but that, when conceived, this program found means of getting itself fulfilled in its most important particulars. The document is comparatively unimportant; the conditions to which it calls attention are of a very high degree of importance.

The Dearborn Independent, July 10, 1920

"We are a people—One people.... When we sink, we become a revolutionary proletariat, the subordinate officers of a revolutionary party; when we rise, there rises also our terrible power of the purse."
—Theodore Herzl, *A Jewish State,* pp. 5, 23.

9. The Historic Basis of Jewish Imperialism

A great unloosening of speech with reference to the Jewish Question and the Jewish program for world power has occurred in this country since the beginning of this series of articles. It is now possible to pronounce the word "Jew" in a perfectly serious discussion, without timidity, or without intimidation. Heretofore that has been regarded as the special prerogative of the Jewish publicists themselves and they have used the name exclusively in well-organized and favorable propaganda. They can oust portions of Shakespeare from the public schools on the ground that the Jews are offended; they can demand the removal of one of Sargent's paintings from the Boston Library because it represents the Synagogue in a decline.

But when anything emanates from the Gentile side which indicates that the Gentile is also conscious of the Jew, then the charge of prejudice is instantly and strongly made. The effect of that in this country has been a ban on speech which has had few parallels in our history.

Recently at a banquet a speaker used the term "Jews" in reference to the actions of a group of Jewish bankers. A Jewish guest leaped to his feet demanding to know if the speaker considered it "American" to single out a race that way. The speaker replied, "I do, sir," and received the approval of the audience. In that particular part of the country, business men's tongues had been tied for years by the unwritten law that Jews must never by singled out as Jews.

No one would have predicted a year ago that a newspaper like the *Chicago Tribune* could have convinced itself that it was good newspaper policy to print in the first column of its first page a copyrighted article on the Jewish program for world rule, printing the word "Jew" in large letters in its headline, and abstaining from editorial retouching of the word "Jew" in the body of the article.

The usual plan is to do what an eastern newspaper did when dealing with the same subject: wherever the term "international Jew" occurred in the article which it printed, it was retouched to "financiers." The *Chicago Tribune,* however, on Saturday, June 19, 1920, printed in the

The Historic Basis of Jewish Imperialism

first column of the first page a cable dispatch from John Clayton, its special correspondent, under the heading: "Trotsky Leads Jew-Radicals to World Rule. Bolshevism Only a Tool for His Scheme."

The first paragraph reads as follows:

"For the last two years army intelligence officers, members of the various secret service organizations of the Entente, have been bringing in reports of a world revolutionary movement other than Bolshevism. At first these reports confused the two, but latterly the lines they have taken have begun to be more and more clear."

As previously stated in *The Dearborn Independent*, our own secret service is one of these, though there is reason to believe that because of the influence of Jews upon the government these investigations were not pursued with the persistency that might otherwise have been given them. However, we know from Jewish sources, not to mention any other, that the Department of Justice of the United States was at one time interested enough to make inquiries.

What the *Tribune* writer does in the above paragraph is to show that this interest has been sustained for two years by officials of the Entente, a fact which ought to be borne in mind by those who declare that the whole matter is of German instigation.

The emergence of the Jewish Question into American thought was immediately met by a statement from Jewish sources that it was a German importation, and that the anti-Semitism which flowed over Germany and resulted in cleaning out the overwhelming Jewish revolutionary influences from the new German Government, was only a trick to throw the blame for the defeat of Germany on the Jews.

American rabbis are even now unitedly preaching that history shows that every great war is followed by a new "attack" on the Jews. It is undoubtedly a fact that every war newly opens the people's eyes to the power which international Jewish financiers exert with reference to war—and it would seem that such a fact is worthy of a better explanation than that of "prejudice."

However, as the *Tribune* article shows, and as all the facts confirm, the interest is not confined to the German side; indeed, it is not even strongest there. It is "the various secret service organizations of the Entente" that have been most active in the matter.

The second paragraph further distinguishes between Bolshevism and Jewish imperialism: "Bolshevism aims at the overthrow of existing society and the establishment of an international brotherhood of men who work with their hands as rulers of the world. The second movement aims for the establishment of a new racial domination of the world. So far as the British, French and our own department's inquiry have been able to trace, the moving spirits in the second scheme are Jewish radicals."

Other statements in the article are:

"Within the ranks of communism is a group of this party, but it does not stop there. To its leaders, communism is only an incident."

(This will recall the statement of Lord Eustace Percy, quoted last week from the Canadian *Jewish Chronicle*—"Not because the Jew cares for the positive side of radical philosophy, not because he desires to be a partaker in Gentile nationalism or Gentile democracy, but because no existing Gentile system of government is anything but distasteful to him.")

"They are ready to use the Islamic revolt, hatred by the central empires for England, Japan's designs on India, and commercial rivalry between America and Japan."

"As any movement of world revolution must be, this is primarily anti-Anglo-Saxon."

"The organization of the world Jewish-radical movement has been perfected in almost every land."

"The aims of the Jewish-radical party have nothing of altruism behind them beyond liberation of their own race."

It will be conceded that these are rather startling statements. If they were found in a propagandist publication of no responsibility, the average reader might pass them by as preposterous, so little does the average reader know of the secret influences which shape his life and frame his problems. But appearing in a great newspaper, they must receive a different evaluation. Nor did the *Tribune* stop at the news article. On June 21, 1920, an editorial appeared entitled "World Mischief." The editorial is evidently an effort to prevent possible misunderstanding of what the news article was driving at.

"The Jewish phase of the movement, he asserts, aims at a new racial domination of the world . . ."

The *Tribune* also says that while it is perhaps natural for the Jews of other countries to be engaged in this "world mischief," the Jews of England and the United States "are loyal nationalists and conservative upholders of the national traditions." It were well if this were true. Perhaps it is true of tens of thousands of Jews as individuals; it certainly is not true of those

The Historic Basis of Jewish Imperialism

internationalists who pull the strings of all the governments and who during the last six tragic years have been meddling with world affairs in a way which must soon be plainly told. The unfortunate circumstance is that all the American and English Jews must for a time feel a distress which no one desires them to feel, which everyone would do much to save them from, but which seems inevitable until the whole story is told and until the mass of the Jews themselves cut off from their name and support some who now receive their deepest homage.

It is worth while observing the contrasts and similarities between the Gentile and Jewish reaction to this alleged movement to establish a Jewish imperialism over the world. Jewish publicists first deny it without qualification. It is all false, all a lie, all hatched up by enemies of the Jews in order to stir up hatred and murder. As the evidence accumulates, the Jewish tone changes: "Well, suppose it is true," the publicists say; "is it any wonder that the poor oppressed Jews, driven to madness through their sufferings, should dream dreams of overthrowing their enemies and placing themselves in the seat of authority?"

The Gentile mind, confronted with the statement, says: "Yes, but they are Russian Jews. Don't mind them. American Jews are all right. They would never be taken in by anything like that." Going a little deeper into the subject, the Gentile mind is forced to admit the existence of some kind of a subversive world movement, the power of which has shaken even this country, and that the moving spirits in it are revolutionary Jews. And then the tendency from that point forward is either to fall in with the theory that the movement is really Jewish in its origin, agitation, execution and purpose, or to set up the theory that it is a "world movement" undoubtedly, but only incidentally Jewish. The end of both Jewish and Gentile reaction is an admission that something answering to the movement charged actually exists. For example, the *Christian Science Monitor*, whose standard as a newspaper no one will question, has this to say in a lengthy editorial on the subject:

"In spite of this, it would be a tremendous mistake to conclude that the Jewish peril, given another name and atmosphere, does not exist. It might, indeed, be renamed, out of one of the grandest of the books of the Old Testament, 'the terror by night,' for it is, essentially, the Psalmist's concept of the forces of mental evil at which, consciously or unconsciously, Professor Nilus is aiming. In other words, that a secret international political organization exists, working unremittingly by means of its Bureau of Psychology, though the world which should be awake to it is entirely asleep to it, is, to the man who can read the signs of the times, a thing unquestionable."

The Monitor gives warning against prejudice and disregard of the laws of evidence which is exceedingly timely and is, indeed, the desire of anyone who has ever undertaken to deal with this subject, but too often it is a disregard of facts and not of evidence that makes the difficulty.

It is safe to say that most of the prejudice today is against the facts, it has not been caused by them.

There are two preconceptions to be guarded against in making an approach to this question. One is that the Jewish imperialistic program, if such a thing exists, is of recent origin. Upon the mere mention of such a program, Gentiles are likely to think that it was formulated last week, or last year, or within recent time. That need not be the case at all, and in Jewish matters it is very likely not to be the case. It is very easy to see how, if the program were to be formulated today, it would be wholly different from the one which is to be considered. The kind of program that would be made today indeed exists too, but it is not to be compared in extent and profundity with that which has existed for a very long time. Perfect constitutions of invisible governments are not the creations of secret conventions; they are the accumulated thought and experience of centuries. Moreover, no matter how prone a modern generation may be to disregard such things, the mere fact that they may have existed as a secret racial ideal for centuries is a powerful argument for their respectable acceptance, if not active execution, by the generation that now is. There is no idea deeper in Judaism than that Jews constitute a Chosen People and that their future is to be more glorious than their past. A large part of the Christian world accepts that, too, and it may well be true, but in a moral universe it cannot come to pass by the methods which have been and are being used.

But to mention the ancient lineage of the idea of the Chosen People is merely to suggest that of all the programs that may have gathered round it to assist its full historical realization, it is not strange that there should be one very old one to which the wisest minds of Israel have contributed their best of mind and heart to insure its success. That there is such a plan has been the belief of many deep delvers in the hidden things of the world, and that such a plan has at times had its dress rehearsals, so to speak, on a limited stage, as if in preparation for its grand finale on the universal stage, is another belief held by men at whose knowledge it is impossible to cavil.

The Historic Basis of Jewish Imperialism

So, then, it may be that we are dealing with something for which present-day Jews, even the more important internationalists, are not originally responsible. It may have come to them as part of their ancient Jewish inheritance. Certainly, if it were a mere modern thing, hastily conceived and thrown together after the modern fashion, it could be expected to disappear in the same era which saw it born.

Another preconception to be guarded against is that every Jew one meets has secret knowledge of this program. That is not the case.

With the general idea of the ultimate triumph of Israel every Jew who has retained contact with his people is familiar, but with the special plans which for centuries have existed in formulated form for the attainment of that triumph, the average Jew is no more familiar than anyone else— no more so than was the average German with the secret plans of the Pan-Germanic party whose ideas started and guided the recent war. The average Jew enters into the plans of the secret group just to this extent, except in specially selected cases: It is perfectly understood that the consummation of the Jewish triumph will not be distasteful to any Jew, and if the methods to be used toward the end are a bit violent, every Jew can be depended upon to see in that violence a very insufficient retribution visited upon the Gentile world for the sufferings which it has caused the sons of Judah throughout the centuries.

Still, with even these preconceptions guarded against, there is no escape from the conclusion that if such a program of Jewish world imperialism exists today, it must exist with the cognizance and active support of certain individuals, and that these groups of individuals must have somewhere an official head.

This is, perhaps, the one point at which more investigators stop than at any other. The idea of a Jewish autocrat is too strange for the mind which has not been much in contact with the main question. And yet there is no race which more instinctively supports autocracy than does the Jewish race, no race which more craves and respects position. It is their sense of the value of position that explains the main course their activities take. The Jew is primarily a money-maker for the reason that up to this time money is the only means he knows by which to gain position. The Jews who have gained position for any other reason are comparatively few. This is not a Gentile gibe; it is the position of a famous AngloJewish physician, Dr. Barnard Von Oven, who wrote: "All other means of distinction are denied him; he must rise by wealth, or not at all. And if, as he well knows, to insure wealth will be to insure rank, respect and attention in society, does the blame rest with him who endeavors to acquire wealth for the distinction which it will purchase, or with that society which so readily bows down to the shrine of Mammon?"

The Jew is not averse to kings, only to the state of things which prevents a Jewish king. The future autocrat of the world is to be a Jewish king, sitting upon the throne of David, so ancient prophecies and the documents of the imperialistic program agree.

Is such a king in the world now? If not, the men who could choose a king are in the world. There has been no king of the Jews since before the Christian Era, but until about the eleventh century there were Princes of the Exile, those who represented the headship of the Jews who were dispersed through the nations. They were and still are called "exilarchs," or Princes of the Exile.

They were attended by the wise men of Israel, they held court, they gave the law to their people. They lived abroad wherever their circumstances or convenience dictated, in Christian or Mohammedan countries. Whether the office was discontinued with the last publicly known exilarch or merely disappeared from the surface of history, whether today it is entirely abandoned or exists in another form, are questions which must wait.

That there are offices of world jurisdiction held by Jews is well known. That there are world organizations of Jews—organizations, that is, within the very strong solidarity of the Jewish nation itself—is well known. That there is world unity on certain Jewish activities, defensive and offensive, is well known. There is nothing in the condition or thought of the Jews which would render the existence today of an exilarch distasteful to them; indeed, the thought would be very comfortable.

The *Jewish Encyclopedia* remarks: "Curiously enough, the exilarchs are still mentioned in the Sabbath services of the Ashkenazim ritual . . . The Jews of the Sephardic ritual have not preserved this anachronism, nor was it retained in most of the Reform synagogues of the nineteenth century."

Is there, then, a Jewish Sanhedrin?—a governing or counseling body of Jews who take oversight of the affairs of their people throughout the world? The Jewish Sanhedrin was a most interesting institution. Its origin and method of constitution are obscure. It consisted of 71 members, with the president, and performed the functions of a political senate. There is nothing to show whence the Sanhedrin derived its authority. It was not an elective body. It was not democratic. It was not representative. It was not responsible to the people. In these qualities, it was typically Jewish. The Sanhedrin was chosen by the prince or priest, not with the purpose of safeguarding the people's interest, but to assist the ruler in the work of administration. It was thus assembled by call, or it was self-perpetuating, calling its own members. The arrangement seems to have been that well-known device by which an aristocracy can maintain itself in power whatever the political construction of the nation may be. The *Jewish Encyclopedia* says: "The Sanhedrin, which was entirely aristocratic in character, probably assumed its own authority, since it was composed of members of the most influential families of the nobility and priesthood."

This body was flanked by a similar body, which governed the religious interests of the nation, the members being drawn apparently from classes nearer the common people.

The Sanhedrin exercised authority not only over the Jews of Palestine, but wherever they were scattered throughout the world. As a senate exercising direct political authority, it ceased with the downfall of the Jewish State in the year 70, but there are indications of its continuance as an advisory body down to the fourth century.

In 1806, in order to satisfy the mind of Napoleon upon some questions which had arisen concerning the Jews, an Assembly of Notables was called, whose membership consisted of prominent Jews of France. They, in turn, to bring the sanction of all Jewry to the answers which they should give Napoleon, convoked the Sanhedrin. The Sanhedrin assembled in Paris on February 9, 1807.

It followed the prescribed ancient forms; it was comprised of Jews from all parts of Europe; it was assembled to put the whole authority of Jewry behind any compact the French Jews may have been able to make with Napoleon.

In putting forth its decisions, this Sanhedrin of 1807 declared that it was in all respects like the ancient Sanhedrin, "a legal assembly vested with power of passing ordinances in order to promote the welfare of Israel."

The significance of these facts is this: Whatever the leaders of the Jews may do today in the way of maintaining the policy and constitution of Israel, would not constitute a new departure. It would not signify a new attitude. It would not be evidence of a new plan.

It would be entirely natural, Jewish solidarity being what it is, that the Sanhedrin should still be continued. The ancient Sanhedrin appears to have had a group of ten who were somewhat exalted in importance above the rest; it would be perfectly natural if the leaders of the Jews were today divided into committees, by countries or by objects.

There are always being held, year by year, world meetings of the principal Jews of all lands. They come together whenever called, to the disregard of everything else. Great judges from the high courts of the various countries, international financiers, Jewish orators of the "liberal type" who have the ear of the Gentiles, political maneuverers from all the parties represented in the world, they assemble wherever they will, and the subjects of their deliberations are made known only to the extent they will. It is not to be supposed that all of the attendants on these conventions are members of the inner circle. The list of delegates will show scores of persons with whom no one would associate Lord Reading and Judge Brandeis.

If the modern Sanhedrin meets, and it would be the most natural thing in the world if it should, we may be sure it meets within the closed circle of those persons which the Jewish aristocracy of money, intellect and power approves.

The machinery of a Jewish world government exists ready-made. The Jew is convinced that he has the best religion, the best morality, the best method of education, the best social standards, the best ideal of government. He would not have to go outside the circle of that which he considers best to get anything which he may need to advance the welfare of his people, or to execute any program which may have to do with the outside world.

It is the ancient machinery that the international Jew uses in all those activities which he permits the world to see in part. There are gatherings of the financial, political and intellectual chief rulers of the Jews. These gatherings are announced for one or another thing sometimes. Sometimes there is a gathering of Jews in a world capital, with no announced purpose. They all appear in one city, confer and depart.

Whether there is a recognized head to all of this is yet to be disclosed. There can be little doubt, however, as to the existence of what may be called a "foreign policy," that is, a definite point of view and plan of action with reference to the Gentile world. The Jew feels that he is in the midst of enemies, but he also feels that he is a member of a people—"one people."

He must have some policy with regard to the outer world. He cannot help but consider present conditions, he cannot consider them without being stirred to speculate upon what the outcome must be, and he cannot speculate on the outcome without in some manner endeavoring to make it as he would like it to be.

The invisible government of the Jews, its attitude toward the Gentile world, its policy with regard to the future, are not, then, the abnormal things that some would make them appear. Given the Jewish position, they are of all things most natural. Jewish existence in this world is not such as woos the Jew into sleepy contentment; it is such as stirs him into organization against future contingencies and into programs which may shape those contingencies to the benefit of his race. That there should be a Sanhedrin of the Jews, a world body of the leading men of all countries; that there should even be an exilarch, a visible and recognized head of the Sanhedrin, mystically foreshadowing the autocrat to come; that there should even be a world program, just as every government has its foreign policy, are not strange, uncanny suppositions. They grow normally out of the situation itself.

And it is also natural that not every Jew should know this. The Sanhedrin always was the aristocracy, and would be today. When rabbis cry from their pulpits that they know nothing about this thing, they are doubtless telling the truth. What the international Jew depends upon is the likelihood of every Jew approving that which brings power and prestige to his people. At any rate, it is well enough known that however little the ordinary Jewish leader may have been told about world programs, he regards with the greatest respect and confidence the very men who must put these programs through, if these exist at all.

The twenty-fourth Protocol of the Learned Elders of Zion has this to say:

"Now I will discuss the manner in which the roots of the house of King David will penetrate to the deepest strata of the earth. This dynasty, even to this day, has given the power of controlling world affairs to our wise men, the educational directors of all human thought."

This would indicate, if reliable, that, as the Protocol goes on to recite, the Autocrat himself has not appeared, but the dynasty, or the Davidic line in which he must appear, have entrusted the work of preparing for him to the Wise Men of Zion. These wise men are represented not only as preparing those who exercise rulership over Judaism's affairs, but also as framing and influencing the world's thought toward ends which shall be propitious to these plans. Whatever may be hidden in the program, it is certain that its execution or the effects of its execution cannot be hidden. Therefore, it may be possible to find in the outer world the clues which, traced back to their source, reveal the existence of a program, whose promise for the world, good or bad, ought to be widely known.

The Dearborn Independent, July 17, 1920

10. An Introduction to the "Jewish Protocols"

The documents most frequently mentioned by those who are interested in the theory of Jewish World Power rather than in the actual operation of that power in the world today, are those 24 documents known as "The Protocols of the Learned Elders of Zion."

The Protocols have attracted much attention in Europe, having become the center of an important storm of opinion in England only recently, but discussion of them in the United States has been limited. These are the documents concerning which the Department of Justice was making inquiries more than a year ago, and which were given publication in London by Eyre and Spottiswoode, the official printers to the British Government.

Who it was that first entitled these documents with the name of the "Elders of Zion" is not known. It would be possible without serious mutilation of the documents to remove all hint of Jewish authorship, and yet retain all the main points of the most comprehensive program for world subjugation that has ever come to public knowledge.

Yet it must be said that thus to eliminate all hint of Jewish authorship would be to bring out a number of contradictions which do not exist in the Protocols in their present form. The purpose of the plan revealed in the Protocols is to undermine all authority in order that a new authority in the form of autocracy may be set up. Such a plan could not emanate from a ruling class which already possessed authority, although it might emanate from anarchists.

But anarchists do not avow autocracy as the ultimate condition they seek. The authors might be conceived as a company of French Subversives such as existed at the time of the French Revolution and had the infamous Duc d'Orleans as their leader, but this would involve a contradiction between the fact that those Subversives have passed away, and the fact that the program announced in these Protocols is being steadily carried out, not only in France, but throughout Europe and very noticeably in the United States. In their present form which bears evidence of being their original form, there is no contradiction. The allegation of Jewish authorship seems essential to the consistency of the plan. If these documents were the forgeries which Jewish apologists claim them to be, the forgers would probably have taken pains to make Jewish authorship so clear that their anti-Semitic purpose could easily have been detected. But only twice is the term "Jew" used in them. After one has read much further than the average reader usually cares to go into such matters, one comes upon the plans for the establishment of the World Autocrat, and only then it is made clear of what lineage he is to be.

But all through the documents there is left no doubt as to the people against whom the plan is aimed. It is not aimed against aristocracy as such. It is not aimed against capital as such. It is not aimed against government as such. Very definite provisions are made for the enlistment of aristocracy, capital and government for the execution of the plan. It is aimed against the people of the world who are called "Gentiles." It is the frequent mention of "Gentiles" that really decides the purpose of the documents.

Most of the destructive type of "liberal" plans aim at the enlistment of the people as helpers; this plan aims at the degeneration of the people in order that they may be reduced to confusion of mind and thus manipulated.

Popular movements of a "liberal" kind are to be encouraged, all the disruptive philosophies in religion, economics, politics and domestic life are to be sown and watered, for the purpose of so disintegrating social solidarity that a definite plan, herein set forth, may be put through without notice, and the people then molded to it when the fallacy of these philosophies is shown.

The formula of speech is not, "We Jews will do this," but "The Gentiles will be made to think and do these things." With the exception of a few instances in the closing Protocols, the only distinctive racial term used is "Gentiles."

To illustrate: the first indication of this kind comes in the first Protocol in this way:

"The great qualities of the people—honesty and frankness—are essentially vices in politics, because they dethrone more surely and more certainly than does the strongest enemy. These qualities are attributes of Gentile rule; we certainly must not be guided by them."

And again:

"On the ruins of the hereditary aristocracy of the Gentiles we have set up the aristocracy of our educated class, and over all the aristocracy

An Introduction to the "Jewish Protocols"

of money. We have established the basis of this new aristocracy on the basis of riches, which we control, and on the science guided by our wise men."

Again:

"We will force up wages, which however will be of no benefit to workers, for we at the same time will cause a rise in the prices of prime necessities, pretending that this is due to the decline of agriculture and of cattle raising. We will also artfully and deeply undermine the sources of production by instilling in the workmen ideas of anarchy and encourage them in the use of alcohol, at the same time taking measures to drive all the intellectual forces of the Gentiles from the land."

(A forger with anti-Semitic malice might have written this any time within the last five years, but these words were in print at least 14 years ago according to British evidence, a copy having been in the British Museum since 1906, and they were circulated in Russia a number of years prior.)

The above point continues: "That the true situation shall not be noticed by the Gentiles prematurely we will mask it by a pretended effort to serve the working classes and promote great economic principles, for which an active propaganda will be carried on through our economic theories."

These quotations will illustrate the style of the Protocols in making reference to the parties involved. It is "we" for the writers, and "Gentiles" for those who are being written about. This is brought out very clearly in the Fourteenth Protocol:

"In this divergence between Gentiles and ourselves in ability to think and reason is to be seen clearly the seal of our election as the chosen people, as higher human beings, in contrast with the Gentiles who have merely instinctive and animal minds. They observe, but they do not foresee, and they invent nothing (except perhaps material things). It is clear from this that nature herself predestined us to rule and guide the world."

This, of course, has been the Jewish method of dividing humanity from the earliest times. The world was only Jew and Gentile; all that was not Jew was Gentile.

The use of the word Jew in the Protocol may be illustrated by this passage in the eighth section:

"For the time being, until it will be safe to give responsible government positions to our brother Jews, we shall entrust them to people whose past and whose characters are such that there is an abyss between them and the people."

This is the practice known as using "Gentile fronts" which is extensively practiced in the financial world today in order to cover up the evidences of Jewish control. How much progress has been made since these words were written is indicated by the occurrence at the San Francisco convention when the name of Judge Brandeis was proposed for President. It is reasonably to be expected that the public mind will be made more and more familiar with the idea of Jewish occupancy—which will be really a short step from the present degree of influence which the Jews exercise—of the highest office in the government. There is no function of the American Presidency in which the Jews have not already secretly assisted in a very important degree. Actual occupancy of the office is not necessary to enhance their power, but to promote certain things which parallel very closely the plans outlined in the Protocols now before us.

Another point which the reader of the Protocols will notice is that the tone of exhortation is entirely absent from these documents. They are not propaganda. They are not efforts to stimulate the ambitions or activity of those to whom they are addressed. They are as cool as a legal paper and as matter-of-fact as a table of statistics. There is none of the "Let us rise, my brothers" stuff about them. There is no "Down with the Gentiles" hysteria. These Protocols, if indeed they were made by Jews and confided to Jews, or if they do contain certain principles of a Jewish World Program, were certainly not intended for the firebrands but for the carefully prepared and tested initiates of the higher groups.

Jewish apologists have asked, "Is it conceivable that if there were such a world program on the part of the Jews, they would reduce it to writing and publish it?" But there is no evidence that these Protocols were ever uttered otherwise than in spoken words by those who put them forth.

The Protocols as we have them are apparently the notes of lectures which were made by someone who heard them. Some of them are lengthy; some of them are brief.

The assertion which has always been made in connection with the Protocols since they have become known is that they are the notes of lectures delivered to Jewish students presumably somewhere in France or Switzerland. The attempt to make them appear to be of Russian origin is absolutely forestalled by the point of view, the reference to the times and certain grammatical indications.

An Introduction to the "Jewish Protocols"

The tone certainly fits the supposition that they were originally lectures given to students, for their purpose is clearly not to get a program accepted but to give information concerning a program which is represented as being already in process of fulfillment. There is no invitation to join forces or to offer opinions. Indeed it is specifically announced that neither discussion nor opinions are desired. ("While preaching liberalism to the Gentiles, we shall hold our own people and our own agents in unquestioning obedience." "The scheme of administration must emanate from a single brain... Therefore, we may know the plan of action, but we must not discuss it, lest we destroy its unique character... The inspired work of our leader therefore must not be thrown before a crowd to be torn to pieces, or even before a limited group.")

Moreover, taking the Protocols at their face value, it is evident that the program outlined in these lecture notes was not a new one at the time the lectures were given. There is no evidence of its being of recent arrangement. There is almost the tone of a tradition, or a religion, in it all, as if it had been handed down from generation to generation through the medium of specially trusted and initiated men. There is no note of new discovery or fresh enthusiasm in it, but the certitude and calmness of facts long known and policies long confirmed by experiment.

This point of the age of the program is touched upon at least twice in the Protocols themselves. In the First Protocol this paragraph occurs:

"Already in ancient times we were the first to shout the words, 'Liberty, Equality, Fraternity,' among the people. These words have been repeated many times by unconscious poll-parrots, flocking from all sides to this bait, with which they have ruined the prosperity of the world and true personal freedom... The presumably clever and intellectual Gentiles did not understand the symbolism of the uttered words; did not observe their contradiction in meaning; did not notice that in nature there is no equality..."

The other reference to the program's finality is found in the Thirteenth Protocol:

"Questions of policy, however, are permitted to no one except those who have originated the policy and have directed it for many centuries." Can this be a reference to a secret Jewish Sanhedrin, self-perpetuating within a certain Jewish caste from generation to generation? Again, it must be said that the originators and directors here referred to cannot be at present any ruling caste, for all that the program contemplates is directly opposed to the interests of such a caste. It cannot refer to any national aristocratic group, like the Junkers of Germany, for the methods which are proposed are the very ones which would render powerless such a group. It cannot refer to any but a people who have no government, who have everything to gain and nothing to lose, and who can keep themselves intact amid a crumbling world. There is only one group that answers that description.

Again, a reading of the Protocols makes it clear that the speaker himself was not seeking for honor. There is a complete absence of personal ambition throughout the document. All plans and purposes and expectations are merged in the future of Israel, which future, it would seem, can only be secured by the subtle breaking down of certain world ideas held by the Gentiles. The Protocols speak of what has been done, what was being done at the time these words were given, and what remained to be done.

Nothing like them in completeness of detail, in breadth of plan and in deep grasp of the hidden springs of human action has ever been known. They are verily terrible in their mastery of the secrets of life, equally terrible in their consciousness of that mastery. Truly they would merit the opinion which Jews have recently cast upon them, that they were the work of an inspired madman, were it not that what is written in the Protocols in words is also written upon the life of today in deeds and tendencies.

The criticisms which these Protocols pass upon the Gentiles for their stupidity are just. It is impossible to disagree with a single item in the Protocols' description of Gentile mentality and veniality. Even the most astute of the Gentile thinkers have been fooled into receiving as the motions of progress what has only been insinuated into the common human mind by the most insidious systems of propaganda.

It is true that here and there a thinker has arisen to say that science so-called was not science at all. It is true that here and there a thinker has arisen to say that the so-called economic laws both of conservatives and radicals were not laws at all, but artificial inventions. It is true that occasionally a keen observer has asserted that the recent debauch of luxury and extravagance was not due to the natural impulses of the people at all, but was systematically stimulated, foisted upon them by design. It is true that a few have discerned that more than half of what passes for "public opinion" is mere hired applause and booing and has never impressed the public mind.

An Introduction to the "Jewish Protocols"

But even with these clues here and there, for the most part disregarded, there has never been enough continuity and collaboration between those who were awake, to follow all the clues to their source. The chief explanation of the hold which the Protocols have had on many of the leading statesmen of the world for several decades is that they explain whence all these false influences come and what their purpose is. They give a clue to the modern maze. It is now time for the people to know. And whether the Protocols are judged as proving anything concerning the Jews or not, they constitute an education in the way the masses are turned about like sheep by influences which they do not understand. It is almost certain that once the principles of the Protocols are known widely and understood by the people, the criticism which they now rightly make of the Gentile mind will no longer hold good.

It is the purpose of future articles in this series to study these documents and to answer out of their contents all the questions that may arise concerning them.

Before that work is begun, one question should be answered—"Is there likelihood of the program of the Protocols being carried through to success?" The program is successful already. In many of its most important phases it is already a reality. But this need not cause alarm, for the chief weapon to be used against such a program, both in its completed and uncompleted parts, is clear publicity. Let the people know. Arousing the people, alarming the people, appealing to the passions of the people is the method of the plan outlined in the Protocols. The antidote is merely enlightening the people.

That is the only purpose of these articles. Enlightenment dispels prejudice. It is as desirable to dispel the prejudice of the Jew as of the Gentile. Jewish writers too frequently assume that the prejudice is all on one side. The Protocols themselves ought to have the widest circulation among the Jewish people, in order that they may check those things which are bringing suspicion upon their name.

The Dearborn Independent, July 24, 1920

"In all that I have discussed with you hitherto, I have endeavored to indicate carefully the secrets of past and future events and of those momentous occurrences of the near future toward which we are rushing in a stream of great crises, anticipating the hidden principles of future relationships with the Gentiles and of our financial operations."—Protocol 22.

"Upon completing this program of our present and future actions, I will read to you the principles of these theories."—Protocol 16.

11. "Jewish" Estimate of Gentile Human Nature

The Protocols, which profess themselves to be an outline of the Jewish World Program, are found upon analysis to contain four main divisions. These, however, are not marked in the structure of the documents, but in the thought. There is a fifth, if the object of it all is included, but this object is assumed throughout the Protocols, being only here and there defined in terms. And the four main divisions are great trunks from which there are numerous branches.

There is first what is alleged to be the Jewish conception of human nature, by which is meant Gentile nature. It is inconceivable that such a plan as that which the Protocols set forth could have been evolved by a mind that had not previously based the probability of success on a certain estimate of the ignobility and corruptibility of human nature—which all through the Protocols is referred to as Gentile nature.

Then, secondly, there is the account of what has already been accomplished in the realization of the program—things actually done.

Thirdly, there is a complete instruction in the methods to be used to get the program still further fulfilled—methods which would themselves supply the estimate of human nature upon which the whole fabric is based, if there were nothing else to indicate it.

Fourth, the Protocols contain in detail some of the achievements which, at the time these words were uttered, were yet to be made. Some of these desired things have been achieved in the meantime, for it should be borne in mind that between the year 1905 and the year 1920 there has been time to set many influences in motion and attain many ends. As the second quotation at the head of this article would indicate, the speaker knew that events were "rushing in a stream of great crises," a knowledge which is amply attested by Jewish sources outside the Protocols.

"Jewish" Estimate of Gentile Human Nature

If this series of articles represented a special pleading upon the Jewish Question, the present article would seek to win the reader's confidence by presenting first the set of facts which are described under "secondly" in the above list of main divisions. To begin with the estimate of human nature here disclosed is to court alienation of the reader's interest, especially if the reader be a Gentile. We know from abundant sources what the Jewish estimate of human nature is, and it tallies in all respects with what is disclosed in the Protocols, but it has always been one of the fallacies of Gentile thought that human nature is, now, full of dignity and nobility. There is little question, when the subject is considered in all its lights, that the Jewish conception is right. And so far as these Protocols are concerned, their low estimate of mankind, though harsh to human pride and conceit, are very largely true.

Just to run through the Protocols and select the salient passages in which this view is expressed is to find a pretty complete philosophy of the motives and qualities of human beings.

Take these words from the First Protocol:

"It should be noted that people with evil instincts are more numerous than those with good ones; therefore, the best results in governing them are attained by intimidation and violence, and not by academic argument. Every man aims for power; everyone desires to be a dictator, if possible; moreover, few would not sacrifice the good of others to attain their own ends."

"People in masses and people of the masses are guided by exceptionally shallow passions, beliefs, customs, traditions and sentimental theories and are inclined toward party divisions, a fact which prevents any form of agreement, even when this is founded on a thoroughly logical basis. Every decision of the mob depends upon an accidental or prearranged majority, which, owing to its ignorance of the mysteries of political secrets, gives expression to absurd decisions that introduce anarchy into government."

"In working out an expedient plan of action, it is necessary to take into consideration the meanness, the vacillation, the changeability of the crowd . . . It is necessary to realize that the force of the masses is blind, unreasoning and unintelligent, prone to listen now to the right, and now to the left . . . "

"Our triumph has also been made easier because, in our relations with the people necessary to us, we have always played upon the most sensitive strings of the human mind—on calculation, greed, and the insatiable material desires of men. Each of these human weaknesses, taken separately, is capable of paralyzing initiative and placing the will of the people at the disposal of the purchaser of their activities."

In the Fifth Protocol, this shrewd observation on human nature is to be found:

"In all times, nations as well as individuals, accepted words for acts. They have been satisfied by what is shown them, rarely noticing whether the promise has been followed by fulfillment. For this reason we will organize 'show' institutions which will conspicuously display their devotion to progress."

And this from the Eleventh Protocol:

"The Gentiles are like a flock of sheep . . . They will close their eyes to everything because we will promise them to return all the liberties taken away, after the enemies of peace have been subjugated and all the parties pacified. Is it worth while to speak of how long they will have to wait? For what have we conceived all this program and instilled its measures into the minds of the Gentiles without giving them the possibility of examining its underside, if it is not for the purpose of attaining by circuitous methods that which is unattainable to our scattered race by a direct route?"

Notice also this very shrewd observation upon the "joiners" of secret societies—this estimate being made by the Protocols to indicate how easily these societies may be used to further the plan:

"Usually it is the climbers, careerists and people, generally speaking, who are not serious, who most readily join secret societies, and we shall find them easy to handle and through them operate the mechanism of our projected machine."

The remarks under this head are curtailed by the present writer, because the Protocols make reference to a very important secret order, the mention of whose name in this connection might lead to misunderstanding, and which is therefore reserved for future and fuller attention. It will, however, be of interest to the members of that order to see what the Protocols have to say of it, and then check up the facts and see how far they correspond with the words.

To continue: "The Gentiles join lodges out of curiosity or in the hope that through them they may worm their way into social distinction . . . We therefore give them this success so that we can take advantage of the self-conceit to which it gives birth and because of which people unconsciously accept our suggestions without examination . . . You cannot imagine to what an extent the most intelligent Gentiles may be brought to a state of unconscious naivete under conditions of self-deceit, and how easy it is to discourage them by the least failure, even the stopping of applause, or to bring them into a state of servile subjection for the sake of regaining it. The Gentiles are as ready to sacrifice their plans for the sake of popular success as our people are to ignore success for the sake of carrying out our plans. This psychology of theirs facilitates the task of directing them."

These are a few of the passages in which this estimate of human or Gentile nature is made out in words. But even if it were not so baldly stated, it could be easily inferred from various items in the program which was depended upon to break up Gentile solidarity and strength.

The method is one of disintegration. Break up the people into parties and sects. Sow abroad the most promising and utopian of ideas and you will do two things: you will always find a group to cling to each idea you throw out; and you will find this partisanship dividing and estranging the various groups. The authors of the Protocols show in detail how this is to be done. Not one idea, but a mass of ideas are to be thrown out, and there is to be no unity among them. The purpose is not to get the people thinking one thing, but to think so diversely about so many different things that there will be no unity among them. The result of this will be vast disunity, vast unrest—and that is the result aimed for.

When once the solidarity of the Gentile society is broken up and the name, "Gentile society" is perfectly correct, for human society is overwhelmingly Gentile—then this solid wedge of another idea which is not at all affected by the prevailing confusion can make its way unsuspectedly to the place of control. It is well enough known that a body of 20 trained police or soldiers can accomplish more than a disordered mob of a thousand persons. So the minority initiated into the plan can do more with a nation or a world broken into a thousand antagonistic parties, than any of the parties could do. "Divide and rule" is the motto of the Protocols.

The division of society is perfectly easy, according to the estimate of human nature made in these documents. It is human nature to take promises for acts. No one who considered the list of dreams and vagaries and theories that have swayed the people through the centuries can doubt this. The more utopian, the more butterfly-like the theory, the more it commands public adherence. Just as the Protocols say, Gentile society does not scrutinize the origin or the consequences of the theories it adopts. When a theory makes its appeal to the mind, the tendency is to believe that the mind which receives it always had it in essence, and therefore the experience has all the glow of original discovery.

In this manner, theory after theory has been exploited among the masses, theory after theory has been found to be impracticable and has been discarded, but the result is precisely that which the program of the Protocols aims for—with the discarding of each theory, society is a little more broken than it was before. It is a little more helpless before its exploiters. It is a little more confused as to where to look for leadership. As a consequence society falls an easy victim again to a theory which promises it the good it seeks, and the failure of this theory leaves it still more broken. There is no longer any such thing as public opinion. Distrust and division are everywhere. And in the midst of the confusion everyone is dimly aware that there is a higher group that is not divided at all, but is getting exactly what it wants by means of the confusion that obtains all around. It will be shown, as claimed by the Protocols, that most of the disruptive theories abroad in the world today are of Jewish origin; it will also be shown that the one solid unbroken group in the world today, the group that knows where it wants to go and is going there regardless of the condition of society, is the Jewish group.

The most dangerous theory of all is that which explains the rise of theories and the social break-up which follows them. These are all "symptoms of progress" we are told. If so, then "progress" is toward dissolution.

No one can predicate the fact of "progress" on the ground that, whereas our fathers made wheels to go round with the blowing wind or the running water, we make them go round by successive small explosions of gasoline. The question of "progress" is, Where are the wheels taking us? Was windmill and water wheel society better or worse than the present society? Was it more unified in its morality? Did it more highly respect law, did it produce a higher and sturdier type of character?

The modern theory of "ferment," that out of all the unrest and change and transvaluation of values a new and better mankind is to be evolved is not borne out by any fact on the horizon. It is palpably a theory whose purpose is to make a seeming good out of that which is undeniable evil.

The theories which cause the disruption and the theory which explains the disruption as good, come from the same source. The whole science of economics, conservative and radical, capitalistic and anarchistic, is of Jewish origin. This is another of the announcements of the Protocols which the facts confirm. Now, all this is accomplished, not by acts, but by words.

The word-brokers of the world, those who wish words to do duty for things, in their dealings with the world outside their class, are undoubtedly the Jewish group—the international Jews with which these articles deal and their philosophy and practice are precisely set forth in the Protocols.

Take for illustration these passages: The first is from the First Protocol:

"Political freedom is an idea, not a fact. It is necessary to know how to apply this idea when there is need of a clever bait to gain the support of the people for one's party, if such a party has undertaken to defeat another party already in power.

"This task is made easier if the opponent has himself been infected by principles of freedom or so-called liberalism, and for the sake of the idea will yield some of his own power."

Or consider this from the Fifth Protocol:

"To obtain control over public opinion, it is first necessary to confuse it by the expression from various sides of so many conflicting opinions that the Gentiles will lose themselves in the labyrinth and come to understand that it is best to have no opinion on political questions, which it is not given to society at large to understand but only to the ruler who directs society. This is the first secret.

"The second secret consists in so increasing and intensifying the shortcomings of the people in their habits, passions and mode of living that no one will be able to collect himself in the chaos, and, consequently, people will lose all their mutual understanding.

"This measure will serve us also in breeding disagreement in all parties, in disintegrating all those collective forces which are still unwilling to submit to us and in discouraging all personal initiative which can in any way interfere with our undertaking."

And this from the Thirteenth Protocol:

"... and you may also notice that we seek approval, not for our acts, but for our words uttered in regard to one or another question. We always announce publicly that we are guided in all our measures by the hope and the conviction that we are serving the general good.

"To divert over-restless people from discussing political questions, we shall now bring forward new problems apparently connected with the people—problems of industry. In these, let them lose themselves as much as they like. Under such conditions we shall make them think that the new questions have also a political bearing."

(It is to be hoped that the reader, as his eye passes over these details of the Program, is also permitting his mind to pass over the trend of events, to see if he may detect for himself these very developments in the life and thought of the past few years.)

"To prevent them from really thinking out anything themselves, we shall deflect their attention to amusements, games, pastimes, excitements and people's palaces. Such interests will distract their minds completely from questions on which we might be obliged to struggle with them. Becoming less and less accustomed to independent thinking, people will express themselves in unison with us because we alone offer new lines of thought—of course, through persons whom they do not consider as in any way connected with us."

In this same Protocol it is plainly stated what is the purpose of the output of "liberal" theories, of which Jewish writers, poets, rabbis, societies and influences are the most prolific sources:

"The role of the liberal Utopians will be completely played out when our government is recognized. Until that time they will perform good service. For that reason we will continue to direct thought into all the intricacies of fantastic theories, new and supposedly progressive. Surely we have been completely successful in turning the witless heads of the Gentiles by the word 'progress.'"

Here is the whole program of confusing, enervating, and trivializing the mind of the world. And it would be the most outlandish thought to put into words, were it not possible to show that this is just what has been done, and is still being done, by agencies which are highly lauded and easy to be identified among us.

A recent writer in a prominent magazine has pointed out what he calls the impossibility of the Jewish ruling group being allied in one common World Program because, as he showed, there were Jews acting as leading minds in all the divisions of present-day opinion. There were Jews at the head of the capitalists, Jews at the head of the labor unions, and Jews at the head of those more radical organizations which find even the labor unions too tame. There is a Jew at the head of the judiciary of England and a Jew at the head of Sovietism in Russia. How can you say, he asked, that they are united, when they represent so many points of view?

The common unity, the possible common purpose of it all, is thus expressed in the Ninth Protocol:

"Jewish" Estimate of Gentile Human Nature

"People of all opinions and of all doctrines are at our service, restorers of monarchy, demagogues, Socialists, communists and other Utopians. We have put them all to work. Every one of them from his point of view is undermining the last remnant of authority, is trying to overthrow all existing order. All the governments have been tormented by these actions. But we will not give them peace until they recognize our super-government."

The function of the idea is referred to in the Tenth Protocol also:

"When we introduced the poison of liberalism into the government organism, its entire political complexion changed."

The whole outlook of these Protocols upon the world is that the idea may be made a most potent poison. The authors of these documents do not believe in liberalism, they do not believe in democracy, but they lay plans for the constant preaching of these ideas because of their power to break up society, to divide it into groups, to destroy the power of collective opinion through a variety of convictions. The poison of an idea is their most relied-on weapon.

The plan of thus using ideas extends to education:

"We have misled, stupefied and demoralized the youth of the Gentiles by means of education in principles and theories, patently false to us, but which we have inspired."—Protocol 9.

It extends also to family life:

"Having in this way inspired everybody with the thought of his own importance, we will break down the influence of family life among the Gentiles, and its educational importance."—Protocol 10.

And in a passage which might well provide the material for long examination and contemplation by the thoughtful reader, this is said:

"Until the time is ripe, let them amuse themselves... Let those theories of life which we have induced them to regard as the dictates of science play the most important role for them. To this end we shall endeavor to inspire blind confidence in these theories by means of our Press...

"Note the successes we have arranged in Darwinism, Marxism, and Nietzscheism. The demoralizing effect of these doctrines upon the minds of the Gentiles should be evident at least to us."—Protocol 2.

That this disintegration and division of Gentile society was proceeding at a favorable rate when the Protocols were uttered is evident from every line of them. For it must be remembered that the Protocols are not bidding for support for a proposed program, but are announcing progress on a program which has been in process of fulfillment for "centuries" and "from ancient times." They contain a series of statements regarding things accomplished, as well as a forelook at things yet to be accomplished. The split of Gentile society was very satisfactorily proceeding in 1896, or thereabouts, when these oracles were uttered.

It is to be noticed that the purpose is nowhere stated to be the extermination of the Gentiles, but their subjugation, at first under the invisible rule which is proposed in these documents, at length under the rule of one whom the invisible forces would be able to put in control of the world through political changes which would create an office of World President or Autocrat. The Gentiles are to be subdued, first intellectually, as here shown, and then economically. Nowhere is it hinted that they are to be deprived of the earth, but only of their independence of those whom the Protocols represent to be Jews.

How far the division of society had proceeded when these Protocols were given may be gathered from the Fifth Protocol:

"A world coalition of Gentiles could cope with us temporarily, but we are assured against this by roots of dissension among them so deep that they cannot be torn out. We have created antagonism between the personal and national interests of the Gentiles by arousing religious and race hatreds which we have nourished in their hearts for twenty centuries."

As far as that concerns the dissensions of the Gentiles or Christian world, it is absolutely true. And we have seen in our own nation how "the antagonism between personal and national interests" have rested on "religious and race hatreds." But whoever suspected a common source for these?

More amazing still, who would expect any man or group to avow themselves the source? Yet it is thus written in the Protocols—"we have created the antagonism—we thus assure ourselves against the possibility of a Gentile coalition against us." And whether these Protocols are of Jewish origin or not, whether they represent Jewish interests or not, this is exactly the state of the world, of the Gentile world, today.

But a still deeper division is aimed for, and there are signs of even this coming to pass.

Indeed, in Russia it has already come to pass, the spectacle of a Gentile lower class led by Jewish leaders against a Gentile upper class! In the First Protocol, describing the effects of a speculative industrial system upon the people, it is said that this sort of economic folly—". . . has already created and will continue to create a society which is disillusioned, cold and heartless. Such a society is completely estranged from politics and religion. Lust of gold will be the only guide of the people . . . THEN, not for the sake of good, nor even for the sake of riches, but solely on account of their hatred of the privileged classes, the lower classes of the Gentiles will follow us in the struggle against our rivals for power, the Gentiles of the intellectual classes."

"The lower classes of the Gentiles will follow us . . . against . . . the Gentiles of the intellectual classes."

If that struggle were to occur today, the leaders of the Gentile insurgents against Gentile society would be Jewish leaders. They are in the leader's place now—not only in Russia, but also in the United States.

The Dearborn Independent, July 31, 1920

"There is all the difference in the world," said a young Jewish philosopher, "between an American Jew and a Jewish American. A Jewish American is a mere amateur Gentile, doomed to be a parasite forever." —"The Conquering Jew," p. 91.

"With the present instability of all authority, our power will be more unassailable than any other, because it will be invisible until it has gained such strength that no cunning can undermine it."—Protocol 1.

"It is indispensable for our purposes that, as far as possible, wars should bring no territorial advantages. This will shift war to an economic footing.... Such a condition of affairs will place both sides under the control of our international agents with their million eyes, whose vision is unhampered by any frontiers. Then, our international rights will eliminate national rights in the narrow sense, and will govern the governments as they govern their subjects."—Protocol 2.

12. "Jewish Protocols" Claim Partial Fulfillment

As a mere literary curiosity, these documents which are called "The Protocols of the Learned Elders of Zion" would exercise a fascination by reason of the terrible completeness of the World Plan which they disclose. But they discourage at every turn the view that they are literature; they purport to be statesmanship, and they provide within their own lines the clue by which their status may be determined. Besides the things they look forward to doing, they announce the things they have done and are doing. If, in looking about the world, it is possible to see both the established conditions and the strong tendencies to which these Protocols allude, it will not be strange if interest in a mere literary curiosity gives way to something like alertness, and it may be alarm.

A few general quotations will serve to illustrate the element of present achievement in the assertions of these documents, and in order that the point may be made clear to the reader the key words will be emphasized.

Take this from Protocol Nine:

"In reality there are no obstacles before us. Our super-government has such an extra-legal status that it may be called by the energetic and strong word—dictatorship. I can conscientiously say that, at the present time, we are the lawmakers. We create courts and jurisprudence. We rule with a strong will because we hold in our hands the remains of a once strong party, now subjugated by us."

And this from the Eighth Protocol:

"Jewish Protocols" Claim Partial Fulfillment

"We will surround our government with a whole world of economists. It is for this reason that the science of economics is the chief subject of instruction taught by the Jews. We shall be surrounded by a whole galaxy of bankers, industrialists, capitalists, and especially by millionaires because, actually, everything will be decided by an appeal to figures."

These are strong claims, but not too strong for the facts that can be marshaled to illustrate them. They are, however, but an introduction to further claims that are made and equally paralleled by the facts. All through the Protocols, as in this quotation from the Eighth, the preeminence of the Jews in the teaching of political economy is insisted upon, and the facts bear that out. They are the chief authors of those vagaries which lead the mob after economic impossibilities, and they are also the chief teachers of political economy in our universities, the chief authors of those popular textbooks in the subject, which hold the conservative classes to the fiction that economic theories are economic laws. The idea, the theory, as instruments of social disintegration are common to both the university Jew and the Bolshevik Jew. When all this is shown in detail, public opinion upon the importance of academic and radical economics may undergo a change.

And, as claimed in the quotation just given from the Ninth Protocol, the Jewish world power does today constitute a super-government. It is the Protocol's own word, and none is more fitting. No nation can get all that it wants, but the Jewish World Power can get all that it wants, even though its demands exceed Gentile equality. "We are the lawmakers," say the Protocols, and Jewish influences have been lawmakers in a greater degree than any but the specialists realize. In the past ten years Jewish international rule, or the power of the group of International Jews has quite dominated the world. More than that, it has been powerful enough to prevent the passage of salutary laws, and where one law may have slipped through to a place on the statute books, it has been powerful enough to get it interpreted in a sense that rendered it useless for its purpose. This, too, can be illustrated by a large collection of facts.

Moreover, the method by which this is done was outlined long ago in the program of which the Protocols purport to be an outline. "We create courts," continues the quotation, and it is followed in other Protocols by numerous references to "our judges." There is a Jewish court sitting in a public building in the city of New York every week, and other courts, for the sole advantage and use of this people whose spokesmen deny that they are a "separate people," are in formation everywhere.

The Zionist plan has already been used in some of the smaller European countries to confer an extra-citizenship upon Jews who already enjoy citizenship in the lands of their residence, and in addition to that a degree of self-rule under the very governments which they demand to protect them. Wherever Jewish tendencies are permitted to work unhindered, the result is not "Americanization," or "Anglicization" nor any other distinctive nationalism, but a strong and ruling reversion back to essential "Judaization."

The "agents" referred to in the first quotation will receive attention in another article. To resume the claims of the Protocols: This from the Seventeenth Protocol:

"We have taken good care long ago to discredit the Gentile clergy and thereby to destroy their mission, which at present might hamper us considerably. Their influence over the people diminishes daily.

"Freedom of conscience has been proclaimed everywhere. Consequently it is only a question of time when the complete crash of the Christian religion will occur. It will be easier to handle the other religions, but it is too early to discuss this phase of the subject."

This will be of considerable interest, perhaps, to those clergymen who are laboring with Jewish rabbis to bring about some kind of religious union. Such a union would of necessity dispose of Christ as a well-meaning but wholly mistaken Jewish prophet, and thus distinctive Christianity would cease to exist insofar as the "union" was effective. The principal religious aversion of the Protocols, however, so far as it is expressed, is against the Catholic church in general and the pontifical office in particular.

A curious paragraph in this Protocol claims for the Jewish race a particular skill in the art of insult:

"Our contemporary press will expose governmental and religious affairs and the incapacity of the Gentiles, always using expressions so derogatory as to approach insult, the faculty of employing which is so well known to our race."

This from the Fifth Protocol:

"Under our influence the execution of the laws of the Gentiles is reduced to a minimum. Respect for the law is undermined by the liberal interpretation we have introduced in this sphere. The courts decide as we dictate, even in the most important cases in which are involved fundamental principles or political issues, viewing them in the light in which we present them to the Gentile administration through agents with whom we have apparently nothing in common, through newspaper opinion and other avenues. "In Gentile society where we have planted discord and protestantism . . . "

The word "protestantism" is evidently not used in the religious or sectarian sense, but to denote a temper of querulous fault-finding destructive of harmonious collective opinion.

This from the Fourteenth Protocol:

"In countries called advanced, we have created a senseless, filthy and disgusting literature. For a short time after our entrance into power we shall encourage its existence so that it may show in greater relief the contrast between it and the written and spoken announcements which will emanate from us."

Discussing in the Twelfth Protocol the control of the Press—a subject which must be treated more extensively in another article—the claim is made:

"We have attained this at the present time to the extent that all news is received through several agencies in which it is centralized from all parts of the world. These agencies will then be to all intents and purposes our own institutions and will publish only that which we permit."

This from the Seventh Protocol bears on the same subject:

"We must force the Gentile governments to adopt measures which will promote our broadly conceived plan, already approaching its triumphant goal, by bringing to bear the pressure of stimulated public opinion, which has been organized by us with the help of the so-called 'great power' of the press. With a few exceptions not worth considering, it is already in our hands."

To resume the Twelfth Protocol:

"If we have already managed to dominate the mind of Gentile society to such a point that almost all see world affairs through the colored lenses of the spectacles which we place before their eyes, and if now there is not one government with barriers erected against our access to that which by Gentile stupidity is called state secrets, what then will it be when we are the recognized masters of the world in the person of our universal ruler?"

The Jewish nation is the only nation that possesses the secrets of all the rest. No nation long protects a secret which directly concerns another nation, but even so, no nation has all the secrets of all the other nations. Yet it is not too much to say that the International Jews have this knowledge. Much of it, of course, amounts to nothing and their possession of it does not materially add to their power, but the fact that they have the access, that they can get whatever they want when they want it is the important point—as many a secret paper could testify if it could talk, and many a custodian of secret papers could tell if he would. The real secret diplomacy of the world is that which hands over the world's so-called secrets to a few men who are members of one race. The surface of diplomacy, those activities which get written down in the memoirs of comfortably aging statesmen, those coups and treaties which are given high-sounding fame as if they really were important— that is incomparable with the diplomacy of Judah, and its matchless enginery for worming out the hidden knowledge of every ruling group. The United States is included in all these statements. Perhaps there is no government in the world so completely at their service as our own at present, their control having been gained during the past five or six years.

The Protocols do not regard the dispersal of the Jews abroad upon the face of the earth as a calamity, but as a providential arrangement by which the World Plan can be more certainly executed, as see these words of the Eleventh Protocol:

"God gave to us, His Chosen People, as a blessing, the dispersal, and this which has appeared to all to be our weakness has been our whole strength. It has now brought us to the threshold of universal rule."

The claims to accomplishment which are put forth in the Ninth Protocol would be too massive for words were they too massive for concrete realization, but there is a point where the word and the actuality meet and tally.

"In order not to destroy prematurely the Gentile institutions, we have laid our efficient hands on them, and rasped the springs of their mechanism. They were formerly in strict and just order, but we have replaced them with a liberal disorganized and arbitrary administration. We have tampered with jurisprudence, the franchise, the press, freedom of the person, and, most important of all, education and culture, the corner stone of free existence.

"We have misled, stupefied and demoralized the youth of the Gentiles by means of education in principles and theories patently false to us, but which we have inspired.

"Above existing laws, without actual change but by distorting them through contradictory interpretations, we have created something stupendous in the way of results."

"Jewish Protocols" Claim Partial Fulfillment

Everyone knows that, in spite of the fact that the air was never so full of theories of liberty and wild declarations of "rights," there has been a steady curtailment of "personal freedom." Instead of being socialized, the people, under a cover of socialistic phrases, are being brought under an unaccustomed bondage to the state. The Public Health is one plea. Various forms of Public Safety are other pleas. Children are hardly free to play nowadays except under play-masters appointed by the State, among whom, curiously enough, an astonishing proportion of Jews manage to find a place.

The streets are no longer as free as they were; laws of every kind are hedging upon the harmless liberties of the people. A steady tendency toward systemization, every phase of the tendency based upon some very learnedly stated "principle," has set in, and curiously enough, when the investigator pursues his way to the authoritative center of these movements for the regulation of people's life, he finds Jews in power. Children are being lured away from the "social center" of the home for other "centers"; they are being led away (and we are speaking of Gentile children—no Gentiles are ever allowed to regulate the lives of Jewish children) from their natural leaders in home, church and school, to institutionalized "centers" and scientific "play spots," under "trained leaders" whose whole effect, consciously or unconsciously, is to lead the modern child to look to the State, instead of its natural environment, for leadership. All this focuses up to the World Plan for the subjugation of the Gentiles, and if it is not the Jewish World Plan it would be interesting to know why the material for it is so largely Gentile children and the leaders of it so often of the Jewish race.

Jewish liberties are the best safeguarded in the United States. Gentiles take their chance with public matters, but every Jewish community is surrounded by special protectors who gain special recognition by various devices—political and business threats not the least of them. No public spirited Gentiles are welcomed to the task of regulating the lives of Jewish children.

The Jewish community in every city is all-sufficient in itself as far as such activities go. The most secret of all parochial schools are the Jewish schools, whose very locations are not all known to the officials of large cities. The Jew is almost anxious in his efforts to mold the Gentile mind; he insists on being permitted to tell the Gentile what to think, especially about the Jew; he is not averse to influencing general Gentile thought in a manner which, though it come about by wide circles, works ultimately into the Jewish scheme of things. The anxiety and the insistence, so well known to all who have observed them, are only reflections of the Jew's conviction that his is the superior race and is capable of directing the inferior race—of which there is but one, including the whole non-Jewish world.

Every influence that leads to lightness and looseness in Gentile youth today heads up in a Jewish source. Did the young people of the world devise the "sport clothes" which have had so deleterious an effect on the youth of the times that every publicist has thought it worthy of mention? Those styles come out of Jewish clothing concerns, where certainly art is not the rule nor moral influence the main consideration. The moving picture is an interesting development of photography allied with the show business, but whose is the responsibility for its development along such lines as make it a menace to the minds of millions—so serious a menace that it has not escaped observation and condemnation everywhere? Who are the masters of musical jazz in the world? Who direct all the cheap jewelry houses, the bridge-head show parks, the "coney islands," the centers of nervous thrills and looseness? It is possible to take the showy young man and woman of trivial outlook and loose sense of responsibility, and tag them outwardly and inwardly from their clothing and ornaments to their hectic ideas and hopes, with the same tag, "Made, introduced and exploited by a Jew."

There is, therefore, something most sinister in the light which events cast upon that paragraph:

"We have misled, stupefied, and demoralized the youth of the Gentiles by means of education in principles and theories, patently false to us but which we have inspired."

"Principles and theories" do not necessarily imply lofty or even modest intellectual qualities. The youngster who spends his noon hours and evenings at the movies is getting his "principles and theories" just as the more intellectual youngster from a higher grade of society who listens to a Jewish "liberal" expound "sex liberty" and the "control of population" is getting his. The looseness which inheres in these "principles and theories" does not emanate from the Gentile home, or the Gentile church, or from any line of money-making which is filled principally with Gentiles, but from theories, movements and lines of money-making mostly fancied by Jews. This line of accusation could be run much deeper, but it is preferred to restrict it to what is observable by decent eyes everywhere.

"Jewish Protocols" Claim Partial Fulfillment

And that "the youth of the Gentiles" are the principal victims, and not the youth of the Jews, is also observable. While a certain percentage of Jewish youth itself is overcome by this social poison, the percentage is almost nothing compared with the results among the youth of the Gentiles.

It is a significant fact that Jews who link this process of enervation of Gentiles with large profits are not themselves, nor are their sons and daughters, the victims of this enervation. Jewish youth comes through more proudly and more cleanly than the mass of Gentile youth.

Many a father and mother, many a sound-minded, uncorrupted young person, and thousands of teachers and publicists have cried out against luxury. Many a financier, observing the manner in which the people earned and flung away their money, has warned against luxury. Many an economist, knowing that the nonessential industries were consuming men and materials that were necessary to the stabilizing of essential industries; knowing that men are making knick-knacks who should be making steel; knowing that men are engaged in making gew-gaws who should be working on the farm; that materials are going into articles that are made only to sell and never to use, and that materials are thus diverted from the industries that support the people's life—every observer knowing this crazy insistence on luxurious nonessentials has lifted up a strong voice against it.

But, according to these Protocols, we have been starting at the wrong end. The people, it is true, buy these senseless nonessentials which are called luxuries. But the people do not devise them. And the people grow tired of them one by one.

But the stream of varieties continues always something else being thrust at the people, dangled before their eyes, set bobbing down the avenue on enough manikins to give the impression that it is "style"; newspaper print and newspaper pictures; movie pictures; stage costumes enough to force the new thing into "fashion" with a kind of force and compulsion which no really worthy essential thing can command.

Where does it come from? What power exists whose long experience and deliberate intent enable it to frivolize the people's minds and tastes and compel them to pay most of their money for it too?

Why this spasm of luxury and extravagance through which we have just passed? How did it occur that before luxury and extravagance were apparent, all the material to provoke and inflame them had been prepared beforehand and shipped beforehand, ready for the stampede which also had been prepared? If the people of the United States would stop to consider, when the useless and expensive thing is offered them—if they would trace its origin, trace the course of the enormous profits made out of it, trace the whole movement to flood the market with uselessness and extravagance and thus demoralize the Gentile public financially, intellectually, and socially—if, in short, it could be made clear to them that Jewish financial interests are not only pandering to the loosest elements in human nature, but actually engaged in a calculated effort to render them loose in the first place and keep them loose—it would do more than anything else to stop this sixfold waste—the waste of material, the waste of labor, the waste of Gentile money, the waste of Gentile mind, the waste of Jewish talent, and the worse than waste of Israel's real usefulness to the world.

We say the Gentile public is the victim of this stimulated trade in useless luxuries. Did you ever see Jewish people so victimized? They might wear very noticeable clothing, but its price and its quality agree. They might wear rather large diamonds, but they are diamonds. The Jew is not the victim of the Jew, the craze for luxuries is just like the "Coney island" crowd to him; he knows what attracts them and the worthlessness of it.

And it is not so much the financial loss that is to be mourned, nor yet the atrocities committed upon good taste, but the fact that the silly Gentile crowds walk into the net willingly, even gaily, supposing the change of the fashion to be as inevitable as the coming of spring, supposing the new demand on their earnings to be as necessary and as natural as taxes. The crowds think that somehow they have part in it, when their only part is to pay, and then pay again for the new extravagance when the present one palls. There are men in this country who know two years ahead what the frivolities and extravagances of the people will be, because they decree what they shall be. These things are strictly business, demoralizing to the Gentile majority, enriching to the Jewish minority.

Look at the Sixth Protocol for a sidelight on all this:

This is an excerpt from a longer passage dealing with the plans by which the people's interest could be swung from political to industrial questions, how industry could be made insecure and unfair by the introduction of speculation into its management, and finally how against this condition the people could be rendered restless and helpless. Luxury was to be the instrument:

"Jewish Protocols" Claim Partial Fulfillment

"To destroy Gentile industry, we shall, as an incentive to this speculation, encourage among the Gentiles a strong demand for luxuries all enticing luxuries."

And in the First Protocol:

"Surely we cannot allow our own people to come to this. The people of the Gentiles are stupefied with spirituous liquors . . ."

—incidentally, the profits of spirituous liquors flow in large amounts to Jewish pockets. The history of the whiskey ring in this country will show this. Historically, the whole prohibition movement may be described as a contest between Gentile and Jewish capital, and in this instance, thanks to the Gentile majority, the Gentiles won.

The amusement, gambling, jazz song, scarlet fiction, side show, cheap-dear fashions, flashy jewelry, and every other activity that lived by reason of an invisible pressure upon the people, and that exchanged the most useless of commodities for the prices that would just exhaust the people's money surplus and no more—every such activity has been under the mastery of the Jews.

They may not be conscious of their participation in any wholesale demoralization of the people. They may only be conscious of "easy money." They may sometimes yield to surprise as they contrast the silly Gentiles with their own money-wise and fabric-wise and metal-wise Jews. But however this may be, there is the conception of a program by which a people may be deliberately devastated materially and spiritually, and yet kept pleasant all the time and there also is the same program translated into terms of daily transactions and for the most part, perhaps altogether under control of the members of one race.

The Dearborn Independent, August 7, 1920

13. "Jewish" Plan to Split Society by "Ideas"

The method by which the Protocols work for the breakdown of society should now be fairly evident to readers of these articles. An understanding of the method is necessary if one is to find the meaning of the currents and cross-currents which make so hopeless a hodgepodge of the present times. People who are confused and discouraged by the various voices and discordant theories of today, each seeming to be plausible and promising, may find a clear clue to the value of the voices and the meaning of the theories if they understand that their confusion and discouragement comprise the very objective which is sought. The uncertainty, hesitation, hopelessness, fear; the eagerness with which every promising plan and offered solution is grasped—these are the very reactions which the program outlined in the Protocols aims to produce. The condition is proof of the efficacy of the program.

It is a method that takes time, and the Protocols declare that it has taken time, indeed, centuries. Students of the matter find the identical program of the Protocols, announced and operated by the Jewish race, from the first century onward.

It has taken 1900 years to bring Europe to its present degree of subjugation—violent subjugation in some countries, political subjugation in some, economic subjugation in all—but in America the same program, with almost the same degree of success, has required about 50 years. Certain mistaken ideas of liberalism, certain flabby ideas of tolerance, all of them originating at European sources which the Protocolists had completely polluted, were transported to America, and here under cover of the blindness and innocence of a false liberalism and tolerance, together with modern appliances for the swift acceleration of opinion, there has been worked a subjugation of our institutions and public thought which is the amazement of European observers. It is a fact that some of the important students of the Jewish Question, whom Jewish publicists are pleased to damn with the term "Anti-Semites," have been awakened to the existence of the Question not by what they have observed in Europe, but by what they have seen in the swift and distinct "close-up" which has been afforded in American affairs.

"Jewish" Plan to Split Society by "Ideas"

The center of Jewish power, the principal sponsors of the Jewish program, are resident in America, and the leverage which was used at the Peace Conference to fasten Jewish power more securely upon Europe, was American leverage exercised at the behest of the strong Jewish pressure which was brought from the United States for that purpose. And these activities did not end with the Peace Conference.

The whole method of the Protocols may be described in one word, Disintegration. The undoing of what has been done, the creation of a long and hopeless interim in which attempts at reconstruction shall be baffled, and the gradual wearing down of public opinion and public confidence, until those who stand outside the created chaos shall insert their strong calm hand to seize control—that is the whole method of procedure.

Putting together the estimate of human nature which obtains in these Protocols, and their claims to a rather definite though as yet incomplete fulfillment of the World Program (these two comprising the themes of the previous two articles), some of the aspects of this propaganda of disintegration have become clear. But not all of them. There are yet other aspects of these methods, which will be dealt with in the present article, and there are yet future reaches of the program which will be considered later.

The first point of attack is Collective Opinion, that body of ideas which through men's agreement with them, holds large groups together in political, racial, religious, or social unity. Sometimes we call them "standards," sometimes we call them "ideals"; whatever they may be called, they are the invisible bonds of unity, they are the common faith, they are the great overarching reason for group unity and loyalty.

The Protocols assert that here the first attack has been made. The history of Jewish propaganda in the world shows that also.

The first wave of attack is to corrupt Collective Opinion. Now, to "corrupt" in the real sense does not mean anything unsavory or unclean. The whole power of every heresy is its attractiveness to the good mind. The whole explanation of the strong hold which untruth has gained upon the world of our day, is that the untruth is reasonable, inspiring and apparently good. It is only after a long discipline in false ideals—which are reasonable, inspiring and good—that the evil fruits appear in acts and conditions which are unreasonable, destructive and wholly evil. If you will trace the idea of Liberty as it has appeared in Russian history, from its philosophic beginning (a Jewish beginning, by the way) to its present ending (a Jewish ending also), you will see the process.

The Protocols claim that the Gentiles are not thinkers, that attractive ideas have been thrown at them so strategically and persistently that the power of thought is almost destroyed out of them. Fortunately this is a matter on which any Gentile may apply his own test. If he will segregate his ruling ideas, especially those that center round the thought of "democracy," he will discover that he is being ruled in his mind by a whole company of ideas into whose authority over him he has not inquired at all.

He is ruled by "say so" whose origin he has not traced. And when, pursuing those ideas, he finds that they are not practicable, he is received by the explanation that "we are not yet sufficiently advanced." Yet when he does see men who are sufficiently "advanced" to put these very ideas into operation, he recoils from what he sees them do, because he knows that "advancement" such as that is deterioration—a form of disintegration. Yet every one of the ideas were "good," "reasonable," "inspiring," "humane," to begin with. And, if this Gentile will observe a little further, he will see that they are the most persistently preached ideas in the world; he will also see who the preachers are.

The Protocols distinctly declare that it is by means of the set of ideals which cluster around "democracy," that their first victory over public opinion was obtained.

The idea is the weapon. And to be a weapon it must be an idea at variance with the natural trend of life. It must indeed be a theory opposed to the facts of life. And no theory so opposed can be expected to take root and become the ruling factor, unless it appeals to the mind as reasonable, inspiring and good. The Truth frequently seems unreasonable; the Truth frequently is depressing; the Truth sometimes seems to be evil; but it has this eternal advantage, it is the Truth, and what is built thereon neither brings nor yields to confusion.

This first step does not give the control of public opinion, but leads up to it. It is worthy of note that it is the sowing of "the poison of liberalism," as the Protocols name it, which comes first in order in those documents. Then, following upon that, the Protocols say:

"To obtain control over public opinion it is first necessary to confuse it."

Truth is one and cannot be confused, but this false, appealing liberalism which has been sown broadcast, and which is ripening faster under Jewish nurture in America than ever it did in Europe, is easily confused because it is not truth. It is error, and error has a thousand forms. Take a nation, a party, a city, an association in which "the poison of liberalism" has been sown, and you can split that up into as many factions as there are individuals simply by throwing among them certain modifications of the original idea. This is a piece of strategy well known to the forces that invisibly control mass-thought. Theodor Herzl, the arch-Jew, a man whose vision was wider than any statesman's and whose program paralleled the Protocols, knew this many years ago when he said that the Zionist (cryptic for "Jewish") state would come before the Socialist state could come; he knew with what endless divisions the "liberalism" which he and his predecessors had planted would be shackled and crippled. The process of which all Gentiles have been the victims, but never the Jews—never the Jews!—is just this

First, to create an ideal of "broad-mindedness." That is the phrase which appears in every Jewish remonstrance against public mention of the Jew and his alleged World Program: "We thought you were too broadminded a man to express such thoughts;" "we thought Mr. So-and-So was too broad-minded a man to suspect the Jews of this;" "we thought the daily or weekly or monthly such-and-such a paper was too broadminded editorially to consider such material." It is a sort of keyword, indicative of the state of mind in which it is desired that the Gentles be kept. It is a state of flabby tolerance. A state of mind which mouths meaningless phrases about Liberty, phrases which act as an opiate on the mind and conscience and which allow all sorts of things to be done under cover. The phrase, the slogan, is a very dependable Jewish weapon. ("In all times people have accepted words for acts."—Protocol 5.) The reality behind the phrase the Protocols frankly admit to be non-existent.

Nothing has served to create "broad-mindedness," a state of mind whose breadth indicates its lack of depth, so much as the ideas of liberalism which the Jews are constantly teaching to Gentiles and on which they never themselves act. We need a new sort of allegiance to the reality of life, to the facts as they are, which will enable us to stand up under all cajoling to "broad-mindness" and assert a new intolerance of everything but truth. The terms "narrow" and "broad" as they are used today represent lies. The liberal man ought to believe more, he ought to be deep and wide in his beliefs in order to merit that name; but as a usual thing he believes nothing. He is not liberal at all. When you seek belief, belief with a foundation, belief with vitality, you must seek it among men who are sneered at, under this false Jewish-propagated notion of liberality, as "narrow men." Jewish propaganda, in common with the Protocols, is against men who have dug down to the rock; they want "broad-minded men" who can easily be shifted about the surface and thus serve the invisible scheme in any manner desired. This type of men, on their part, never imagine but that their "broad-mindedness" is a mark of their superiority and independence.

Now, see what follows. Men are born believers. For a time they may believe in "broad-mindedness" and under the terrific social pressure that has been set up in its favor they will openly espouse it. But it is too shallow to satisfy any growing roots of life. They must believe, deeply, something. For proof of this, notice the undeniable strength of the negative beliefs which are held by men who fancy that they believe nothing. Therefore, some who are highly endowed with independence of spirit, root down into those prohibited matters which at some point touch Jewish concerns—these are the "narrow" men. But others find it more convenient to cultivate those departments which promise a highway whereon there shall be no clashes of vital opinion, no chance of the charge of "intolerance"; in short they transfer all their contemplative powers to the active life, even as it is written in the Protocols—

"To divert Gentile thought and observation, interest must be deflected to industry and commerce."

It is amazing to look around and see the number of men who have been actually browbeaten into committing their whole lives to these secondary or even tertiary things, while they look with great timidity and aversion at the vital things which really rule the world and upon the issue of which the world really depends.

But it is just this deflection to the materialistic base that offers the Protocolists, and similarly Jewish propagandists, their best hold. "Broad-mindedness" today consists in leaving vital matters severely alone. It descends quickly to material-mindedness. Within this lower sphere all the discord which distresses the world today is to be found.

First, there is the ruin of the upper circles of industry and commerce:

"To make it possible for liberty definitely to disintegrate and ruin Gentile society, industry must be placed on a speculative basis."

No one needs to be told what this means. It means, as everything about us shouts, the prostitution of service to profits and the eventual disappearance of the profits. It means that the high art of management degenerates into exploitation. It means reckless confusion among the

"Jewish" Plan to Split Society by "Ideas"

managers and dangerous unrest among the workmen. But it means something worse; it means the splitting up of Gentile society. Not a division between "Capital" and "Labor," but the division between the Gentiles at both ends of the working scheme.

Gentile managers and manufacturers are not the "capitalists" of the United States. Most of them have to go to the "capitalists" for the funds with which they work—and the "capitalists" are Jewish, International Jews.

But with Jewish capital at one end of the Gentile working scheme putting the screws on the manufacturers, and with Jewish agitators and disruptionists and subversives at the other end of the Gentile working scheme putting the screws on the workmen, we have a condition at which the world-managers of the Protocol program must be immensely satisfied.

"We might fear the combined strength of the Gentiles of vision with the blind strength of the masses, but we have taken all measures against such a possible contingency by raising a wall of mutual antagonism between these two forces. Thus, the blind force of the masses remains our support. We, and we alone, shall serve as their leaders. Naturally, we will direct their energy to achieve our end."—Protocol 9.

The indication that they are highly satisfied is that they are not only not doing anything to relieve the situation, but are apparently willing to have it made worse, and if it be at all possible for them to do so they would like to see this coming winter, and the privations which are scheduled for it (unless Gentile flabbiness before the Jewish power, high and low, receives a new backbone), bring the United States to the verge of, if not across the very line of Bolshevism. They know the whole method of artificial scarcity and high prices. It was practiced in the French Revolution and in Russia. All the signs of it are in this country too. Industrial problems for their mental food and light amusement for their leisure hours, these are the Protocols' method with regard to the Gentile mind, and under cover of these the work is to be done—the work which is best expressed by the motto, "Divide and Rule."

Read this:

"To divert over-restless people from discussing political questions, we shall now bring forward new problems apparently connected with them—problems of industry."—Protocol 13.

Has not everyone been struck by the divorcement which exists in this country between the mass-thought which is almost exclusively devoted to industrial questions, and the party-thought which is endeavoring to keep the field of pure politics? And is it not a fact that our friends, the Jews, are strongly entrenched in both fields—in politics to keep it reactionary, and in industrial circles to keep it radical—and so widen the split? And what is this split but a split of the Gentiles?—for society is Gentile, and the disruptive influences are Jewish.

Read this:

"We have included in the constitution rights for the people that are fictitious and not actual rights. All those so-called 'rights of the people' can only exist in the abstract and can never be realized in practice . . . The proletarian gains no more from the constitution than the miserable crumbs thrown from our table in return for his votes to elect our agents and pass our measures. Republican rights are a bitter irony to the poor man, for the pressure of daily labor prevents him from using them, and at the same time, deprives him of the guaranty of a permanent and certain livelihood by making him dependent upon strikes, organized either by his employers or his comrades."—Protocol 3.

This remark about strikes is not at all puzzling to anyone who has studied the different types of strikes in this country. The number fomented from above the working class is astoundingly large.

Read this also: "We will force up wages, which, however, will be of no benefit to the workers, for we will at the same time cause a rise in the prices of necessities, pretending that this is due to the decline of agriculture and of cattle raising. We will also artfully and deeply undermine the sources of production by instilling in the workmen ideas of anarchy."—Protocol 6.

And this:

"We will represent ourselves as the saviours of the working class who have come to liberate them from this oppression by suggesting that they join our army of socialists, anarchists, communists, to whom we always extend our help under the guise of the fraternal principles of universal human solidarity."—Protocol 3.

"Broad-mindedness" again! In this connection it is always well to remember the words of Sir Eustace Percy, heretofore quoted, words which are sponsored by Jews themselves—"Not because the Jew cares for the positive side of radical philosophy, not because he desires to be a partaker in Gentile nationalism or Gentile democracy, but because no existing Gentile system of government is ever anything but distasteful to him."

"Jewish" Plan to Split Society by "Ideas"

Or, as the author of "The Conquering Jew" says: "He is democratic in his sentiments, but not in his nature. When he proclaims the common brotherhood of man, he is asking that the social gate now closed against him in so many quarters shall be open to him; not because he wants equality, but because he desires to be master in the social world, as he is showing himself in so may other spheres. Many an honorable Jew will, I doubt not, dispute the accuracy of this distinction; but if he does it will be because he has lived so long in the atmosphere of the West that he is unconscious of what is bred in the bone of his Eastern race."

It is not difficult, therefore, to see the genealogy of the Jewish ideas of liberalism from their origin to their latest effects upon Gentile life. The confusion aimed for is here. There is not a reader of these lines who has not felt in his own life the burden of it. Bewilderment characterizes the whole mental climate of the people today. They do not know what to believe. First one set of facts is given to them, then another. First one explanation of conditions is given to them, and then another.

The fact-shortage is acute. There is a whole market-full of explanations that explain nothing, but only deepen the confusion. The government itself seems to be hampered, and whenever it starts on a line of investigation finds itself mysteriously tangled up so that procedure is difficult. This governmental aspect is also set forth in the Protocols.

Add to this the onslaught on the human tendency toward religion, which is usually the last barrier to fall before violence and robbery unashamed stalk forth. In order to bring the condition about at which this World Program aims, the Fourth Protocol says:

"It is for this reason that we must undermine faith, eradicate from the minds of the Gentiles the very principles of God and Soul, and replace these conceptions by mathematical calculations and material desires."

"When we deprived the masses of their belief in God, ruling authority was thrown into the gutter, where it became public property, and we seized it."—Protocol 5.

"We have taken good care long ago to discredit the Gentile clergy."—Protocol 17.

"When we become rulers we shall regard as undesirable the existence of any religion except our own, proclaiming One God with Whom our fate is tied as The Chosen People, and by Whom our fate has been made one with the fate of the world. For this reason we must destroy all other religions. If thereby should emerge contemporary atheists, then, as a transition step, this will not interfere with our aims."—Protocol 14.

This will probably offer matter for reflection by the "broadminded."

It is curious to note how this religious program has worked out in Russia where Trotsky (as loudly heralded in the American Jewish Press) is said to have no religion, and where Jewish commissars tell dying Russians who ask for priests, "We have abolished the Almighty." Miss Katherine Dokoochief is reported, under a Philadelphia date, to have told the Near East Relief that Russian Christian churches have been subjected to the vilest indignities by the Bolsheviki, details of which she gives; but "the synagogues remain untouched, meeting with no damage."

All these lines of attack, whose object is the destruction of the natural rallying points of Gentile thought, and the substitution of other rallying points of an unwholesome and destructive nature, are assisted, as we saw in the last article, by the propaganda for luxury. Luxury is recognizedly one of the most enervating influences. Its course runs from ease, through softness, to flabbiness, to degeneracy, mental, physical and moral. Its beginnings are attractive, its end is lasciviousness in some form, testifying to the complete breakdown of all the strong fiber of the life. It may make a theme for a more complete study some day, this lure to lasciviousness through luxury, and the identity of the forces that set the lure.

But now, to conclude this general view of the method, rather this part of the method, the confusion itself, which all these influences converge to produce, is expected to produce another more deeply helpless state. And that state is, Exhaustion.

It needs no imagination to see what this means. Exhaustion is today one of the conditions that menace the people. The recent political conventions and their effect upon the public fully illustrate it. Nobody seemed to care. Parties might make their declarations and candidates their promises—nobody cared. The war and its strain began the exhaustion; the "peace" and its confusion have about completed it. The people believe little and expect less. Confidence is gone. Initiative is nearly gone. The failure of movements falsely heralded as "people's movements" has gone far to make the people think that no people's movement is possible.

So say the Protocols:

"To wear everyone out by dissensions, animosities, feuds, famine, inoculation of diseases, want, until the Gentiles see no other way of escape except an appeal to our money and power."—Protocol 10.

"Jewish" Plan to Split Society by "Ideas"

"We will so wear out and exhaust the Gentiles by all this that they will be compelled to offer us an international authority, which by its position will enable us to absorb without disturbance all the governmental forces of the world and thus form a super-government.

"We must so direct the education of Gentile society that its hands will drop in the weakness of discouragement in the face of any undertaking where initiative is needed."—Protocol 5.

The Jews have never been worn out or exhausted. They have never been nonplussed. This is the true psychic characteristic of those who have a clue to the maze. It is the unknown that exhausts the mind, the constant wandering around among tendencies and influences whose source is not known and whose purpose is not understood. Walking in the dark is wearing work. The Gentiles have been doing it for centuries. The others, having a pretty accurate idea what it was all about, have not succumbed. Even persecution is endurable if it is understandable, and the Jews of the world have always known just where it fitted in the scheme of things. Gentiles have suffered from Jewish persecutions than have the Jews, for after the persecutions were over, the Gentile was as much in the dark as ever; whereas Judaism simply took up again its century-long march toward a goal in which it implicitly believes, and which, some say who have deep knowledge of Jewish roots in the world and who too may be touched with exhaustion, they will achieve. However this may be, the revolution which would be necessary to unfasten the International Jewish system from its grip on the world, would probably have to be just as radical as any attempts the Jews have made to attain that grip. There are those who express serious doubts that the Gentiles are competent to do it at all. Maybe not. Let them at least know who their conquerors are.

The Dearborn Independent, August 14, 1920

14. Did the Jews Foresee the World War?

Before proceeding to a more detailed study of the connection between the written program of the documents which are called "The Protocols of the Learned Elders of Zion," and the actual program as it can be traced in real life, we shall now view those plans which were future when the Protocols were uttered. It must be borne in mind, however, that what was future in 1896 and 1905, may be past today, that what was plan then may be fulfillment now. To bear this in mind will be in exact accord with the expression of Protocol 22—"I have endeavored to indicate carefully the secrets of past and future events, and of those momentous occurrences of the near future toward which we are rushing in a stream of great crises." Some of those "momentous occurrences" have come to pass, and with them a brighter light on the Question which we are studying.

An illustration of this which is fresh in the minds of all was furnished by the Great War. Jewish comment on this series of articles has made much of the fact that one of the articles was devoted to the then prominence of the Jewish Question in Germany, and it was sought to mislead the people to think that this series was really a part of subtle German after-the-war propaganda. The fact is that articles on the Question in a number of countries were set aside in order to bring the Question itself prominently before the minds of Americans with the least delay. The postponed articles will appear in due season, though out of their order. Germany is today, with perhaps the possible exception of the United States, the most Jew-controlled country in the world—controlled within and from without—and a much stronger set of facts could be presented now than was presented in the original article (the facts of which were at first denied and later admitted by the Jewish spokesmen in the United States). For, since that article was written, public sentiment in Germany has swept the Jews largely out of public office. German public opinion exerted itself to the utmost to put German political administration back into German hands. But did that liberate Germany from the Jews? Not at all. For their entrenchments stretched further and deeper than mere display of official power. Their hold on the basic industries, the finances,

Did the Jews Foresee the World War?

the future of Germany has not been loosened in the least. It is there, unmovable. In what that hold consists, the reader will be told at some convenient time.

Germany is mentioned now, in connection with the Jews, for this purpose: It will be remembered that it was from Germany that the first cry of "annexations" came, and it came at a time when all German war activities and war sentiment were admittedly in Jewish control. "Annexations" was the cry that flashed across the world one day. And back across the world, from the United States, a nation that was not even a party to the war at that time, the word flashed back, "No Annexations." Thus by a dramatic play the whole question was thrust before the world.

Soon the people of all countries had forgotten the blood of battle, the war profiteers and every other vital point, and were discussing a matter which belonged to the end of the war and not the beginning, the question of "annexations." Now, when it is known who were controlling the formulation of war-aims in Germany and who were the chief counselors of the foreign policy of the United States at the same time, the projection of this question of "annexations" into the world's mind becomes interesting; interesting but not wholly intelligible.

Not until you read the Protocols do you get a full light on this and this report of the Protocols which is now given the world probably dates from 1896; there is absolutely ironclad proof of the date 1905.

The Second Protocol begins on the note of war, and its opening words are these:

"It is indispensable for our purpose that as far as possible, wars should bring no territorial advantages. This will shift war to an economic footing, and nations will perceive the strength of our superiority in the aid we render."

Who was thinking, between 1896 and 1905, of the new "no annexations" rule to be applied to war? Were you? Do you know of any statesman who was? We know that military men were concerned about the appliances and operations of any future war that might occur. We know that statesmen, of the more responsible sort, were working to consolidate a balance of interests that would make war extremely improbable. Who had outdistanced them all in foresight and planning sufficiently to lay down a definite program of "no annexations?"

Fortunately the clue to the answer is supplied to us by unquestionable Jewish sources. The American Jewish News of September 19, 1919, had an advertisement on its front page which read thus:

"WHEN PROPHETS SPEAK
By Litman Rosenthal
Many years ago Nordau prophesied the Balfour Declaration. Litman Rosenthal, his intimate friend, relates this incident in a fascinating memoir."

The article, on page 464, begins: "It was on Saturday, the day after the closing of the Sixth Congress, when I received a telephone message from Dr. Herzl asking me to call on him."

This fixes the time. The Sixth Zionist Congress was held at Basle in August, 1903.

The memoir continues: "On entering the lobby of the hotel I met Herzl's mother who welcomed me with her usual gracious friendliness and asked me whether the feelings of the Russian Zionists were now calmer.

"'Why just the Russian Zionists, Frau Herzl?' I asked. 'Why do you only inquire about these?'

"'Because my son,' she explained, 'is mostly interested in the Russian Zionists. He considers them the quintessence, the most vital part of the Jewish people.'"

At this Sixth Congress the British Government ("Herzl and his agents had kept in contact with the English Government"—*Jewish Encyclopedia*, Vol. 12, page 678) had offered the Jews a colony in Uganda, East Africa. Herzl was in favor of taking it, not as a substitute for Palestine, but as a step toward it. It was this which formed the chief topic of conversation between Herzl and Litman Rosenthal in that Basle hotel. Herzl said to Rosenthal, as reported in this article: "There is a difference between the final aim and the ways we have to go to achieve this aim."

Suddenly Max Nordau, who seems at the conference held last month in London to have become Herzl's successor, entered the room, and the Rosenthal interview was ended.

Let the reader now follow attentively the important part of this Rosenthal story:—(the italics are ours)

"About a month later I went on a business trip to France. On my way to Lyons I stopped in Paris, and there I visited, as usual, our Zionist friends. One of them told me that this very same evening Dr. Nordau was scheduled to speak about the Sixth Congress, and I, naturally, interrupted my journey to be present at this meeting and to hear Dr. Nordau's report. When we reached the hall in the evening we found it filled to overflowing and all were waiting impatiently for the great master, Nordau, who, on entering, received a tremendous ovation. But Nordau, without paying heed to the applause showered upon him, began his speech immediately, and said:

"'You all came here with a question burning in your hearts and trembling on your lips, and the question is, indeed, a great one, and of vital importance. I am willing to answer it. What you want to ask is: How could I—I who was one of those who formulated the Basle program how could I dare to speak in favor of the English proposition concerning Uganda, how could Herzl as well as I betray our ideal of Palestine, because you surely think that we have betrayed it and forgotten it. Yet listen to what I have to say to you. I spoke in favor of Uganda after long and careful consideration; deliberately I advised the Congress to consider and to accept the proposal of the English Government, a proposal made to the Jewish nation through the Zionist Congress, and my reasons—but instead of my reasons let me tell you a political story as a kind of allegory. "'I want to speak of a time which is now almost forgotten, a time when the European powers had decided to send a fleet against the fortress of Sebastopol. At this time Italy, the United Kingdom of Italy, did not exist. Italy was in reality only a little principality of Sardinia, and the great, free and united Italy was but a dream, a fervent wish, a far ideal of all Italian patriots. The leaders of Sardinia, who were fighting for and planning this free and united Italy, were the three great popular heroes: Garibaldi, Mazzini, and Cavour.

"'The European powers invited Sardinia to join in the demonstration at Sebastopol and to send also a fleet to help in the siege of this fortress, and this proposal gave rise to a dissension among the leaders of Sardinia. Garibaldi and Mazzini did not want to send a fleet to the help of England and France and they said: "Our program, the work to which we are pledged, is a free and united Italy. What have we to do with Sebastopol? Sebastopol is nothing to us, and we should concentrate all our energies on our original program so that we may realize our ideal as soon as possible."

"'But Cavour, who even at this time was the most prominent, the most able, and the most far-sighted statesman of Sardinia, insisted that his country should send a fleet and beleaguer with the other powers Sebastopol, and, at last, he carried his point. Perhaps it will interest you to know that the right hand of Cavour, his friend and adviser, was his secretary, Hartum, a Jew, and in those circles, which were in opposition to the government, one spoke fulminantly of Jewish treason. And once at an assembly of Italian patriots one called wildly for Cavour's secretary, Hartum, and demanded of him to defend his dangerous and treasonable political actions. And this is what he said: "Our dream, our fight, our ideal, an ideal for which we have paid already in blood and tears, in sorrow and despair, with the life of our sons and the anguish of our mothers, our one wish and one aim is a free and united Italy. All means are sacred if they lead to this great and glorious goal. Cavour knows full well that after the fight before Sebastopol sooner or later a peace conference will have to be held, and at this peace conference those powers will participate who have joined in the fight. True, Sardinia has no immediate concern, no direct interest in Sebastopol, but if we will help now with our fleet, we will sit at the future peace conference, enjoying equal rights with the other powers, and at this peace conference Cavour, as the representative of Sardinia, will proclaim the free and independent, united Italy. Thus our dream for which we have suffered and died, will become, at last, a wonderful and happy reality. And if you now ask me again, what has Sardinia to do at Sebastopol, then let me tell you the following words, like the steps of a ladder: Cavour, Sardinia, the siege of Sebastopol, the future European peace conference, the proclamation of a free and united Italy.'"

"The whole assembly was under the spell of Nordau's beautiful, truly poetic and exalted diction, and his exquisite, musical French delighted the hearers with an almost sensual pleasure. For a few seconds the speaker paused, and the public, absolutely intoxicated by his splendid oratory, applauded frantically. But soon Nordau asked for silence and continued: "'Now this great progressive world power, England, has after the pogroms of Kishineff, in token of her sympathy with our poor people, offered through the Zionist Congress the autonomous colony of Uganda to the Jewish nation. Of course, Uganda is in Africa, and Africa is not Zion and never will be Zion, to quote Herzl's own words. But Herzl knows full well that nothing is so valuable to the cause of Zionism as amicable political relations with such a power as England is, and so much more valuable as England's main interest is concentrated in the Orient. Nowhere else is precedent as powerful as in England, and so it is most important to accept a colony out of the hands of England and create thus a precedent in our favor. Sooner or later the Oriental question will have to be solved, and the Oriental question means, naturally, also the question of Palestine. England, who had addressed a formal, political

Did the Jews Foresee the World War?

note to the Zionist Congress—the Zionist Congress which is pledged to the Basle program, England will have the deciding voice in the final solution of the Oriental question, and Herzl has considered it his duty to maintain valuable relations with this great and progressive power. Herzl knows that we stand before a tremendous upheaval of the whole world. Soon, perhaps, some kind of a world-congress will have to be called, and England, the great, free and powerful England, will then continue the work it has begun with its generous offer to the Sixth Congress. And if you ask me now what has Israel to do in Uganda, then let me tell you as the answer the words of the statesmen of Sardinia, only applied to our case and given in our version; let me tell you the following words as if I were showing you the rungs of a ladder leading upward and upward: Herzl, The Zionist Congress, the English Uganda proposition, the future world war, the peace conference where with the help of England a free and Jewish Palestine will be created.'

"Like a mighty thunder these last words came to us, and we all were trembling and awestruck as if we had seen a vision of old. And in my ears were sounding the words of our great brother Achad Haam, who said of Nordau's address at the First Congress:

"'I felt that one of the great old prophets was speaking to us, that his voice came down from the free hills of Judea, and our hearts were burning in us when we heard his words, filled with wonder, wisdom and vision.'"

The amazing thing is that this article by Litman Rosenthal should ever have been permitted to see print. But it did not see print until the Balfour Declaration about Palestine, and it never would have seen print had not the Jews believed that one part of their program had been accomplished.

The Jew never betrays himself until he believes that what he seeks has been won, then he lets himself go. It was only to Jews that the 1903 "program of the Ladder"—the future world war—the peace conference—the Jewish program—was communicated. When the ascent of that ladder seemed to be complete, then came the public talk.

A similar illustration of this is to be found in the fall of the Czar. When that event transpired it was an occasion of great rejoicing in New York, and a Gentile of world-wide fame made a speech in which he lauded an American Jew of national reputation for having begun the downfall of the Czar by providing the money with which propaganda had been made among Russian prisoners in Japan during the Russo-Japanese war.

The story came out only after the success of the plot. It is not at all out of keeping that the last men to see the last act of the plot carried out, the actual murder of Nicholas Romanovitch, his wife, his young daughters and his invalid boy, were "five Soviet deputies, the latter five all Jews." What began with the assistance of an American financier, finished with Soviet deputies.

Did International Jews in 1903 foresee the war? This Rosenthal confession is but one bit of evidence that they did. And did they do nothing but foresee it? It were well if the facts stopped at foresight and did not run on to provocation.

For the present the reader is invited to retain in his mind two points in this Rosenthal article: "Perhaps it will interest you to know that the right hand of Cavour, his friend and adviser, was his secretary, Hartum, a Jew." This is the way the Jewish press speaks of its own. If this paper, or a Chicago paper, or a New York paper should go through the list of the secretaries of the men of power in the world today and make the note after the names—"His secretary, a Jew," the Anti-Defamation Society would send letters of protest. There is one rule for the Gentile and one for the Jew, in the Jewish mind. Writing in the public prints about Hartum, he would be described as an "Italian."

Were the Jewish secretaries who abounded before the war, during the war and throughout the Peace Conference of less brilliance than Hartum? Were there not Hartums in England, France, Germany, yes and in Russia too (in the United States there were many) who saw the "program of the Ladder"? Did Max Nordau who saw it so clearly in 1903 forget it in 1914 and 1918?

We know this: the Jews in their Congress at Basle in 1903 foresaw

"the future world war." How did they know it was to be a "world war"? We know this also: the Protocols, perhaps as early as 1896,

certainly not later than 1905, foresaw the policy of "no annexations." The World War came to pass.

"No annexations" came to pass. What was then future in the Jewish world program, is now past.

In the Protocols there are two forms of declaration. One is, "we have." The other is, "we shall." If somewhere in the world this summer the high secret spokesman of the World Program is addressing his class of International Initiates, he will have to say "we have" in many places where this spokesman of 1896 said "we shall." Things have been accomplished.

"We will represent ourselves as the saviors of the laboring classes." That has been and is being done. "We will deflect the thoughts of the Gentiles to industry and commerce." That has been done. "We will create a strongly centralized administration so as to grasp all the social forces strongly in our hands." That has been done. "We will adopt for ourselves the liberal side of all parties and all movements and provide orators." That has been done. "We will force up wages." That has been done. "We will at the same time cause a rise in the price of prime necessities." That has been done. "We will also undermine the sources of production by instilling in the workmen ideas of anarchy." That has been done.

"To demonstrate our enslavement of the Gentile governments of Europe, we shall show our power to one by crimes of violence, that is, by a reign of terror."—Protocol 7.

Who that sees Russia and beholds the attitude of the premiers of England, France, and Italy toward the Soviets, the "enslavement" of statesmanship by a condition that tangles more gnarledly the more it is dealt with—who that sees the prostration of Europe before a wound that is deliberately kept from healing, can forbear to say: That too has been done!

"Our plans will not upset contemporary institutions immediately. Their management will only be altered and consequently the whole procedure of their activity will thus be directed according to plans laid down by us." That has been done.

"We shall saddle the press and keep a tight reign upon it." That has been done. The rein is being strongly pulled in the United States at this moment, as many an editor can testify.

"Even if there should be those who desire to write against us, no one will print their writings." In large part, that has been done. It has been done completely with the profit-making press.

"We shall, as an incentive to speculation, encourage among the Gentiles a strong demand for luxuries—all-enticing luxuries." That has been done.

"To each act of opposition we must be in a position to respond by bringing on war through the neighbors of any country that dares to oppose us, and if these neighbors should plan to stand collectively against us, we must let loose a world war." (Protocol 7). The term "world war" is the same as that used by Rosenthal and Nordau. "Herzl knows," said Nordau in 1903, "that we stand before a tremendous upheaval of the whole world."

"We must create unrest, dissension and mutual animosities throughout Europe and, with the help of her relationships, on other continents." This has been done. This passage continues: "There is a double advantage in this. First, we shall command the respect of all countries by this method, for they will realize that we have the power to create disorder or establish order at will." This too has been done.

Truly did the spokesman of 1896 speak of "those momentous occurrences of the near future toward which we are rushing in a stream of great crises."

Not only was "no annexations" achieved "as far as possible," just as the Protocols outlined it, but a host of other plans have matured in achievement along with it. "No annexations" as a matter of political morality is one thing; and "no annexations" for the reason that "this will shift war to an economic footing and nations will perceive the strength of our superiority in the aid we render" is quite another thing. The world was with the "no annexations" program as a matter of political morality; the other program, which used this morality as its vehicle, was hidden.

There are still other matters in this group which must receive attention, but another article will be necessary to do it. In the meantime, it is natural to wonder whether, with the program as outlined in this report of the Protocols having received fulfillment in so many particulars, a new Protocol, or a further unfolding of the Ladder has been made by the Wise Men to their Initiates; and whether any additional unveiling will ever come to the knowledge of the world. It would seem that a proper estimate of the knowledge now available would lead to such an awakening as to nullify the present program and make all future ones impossible. But Gentiles like their ease, and Judah is beckoned on by a bright star.

The Dearborn Independent, August 21, 1920

15. Is the Jewish "Kahal" the Modern "Soviet"?

The Soviet is not a Russian but a Jewish institution. Nor is it the invention of Russian Jews of the present time, a new political device which has been set up as a vehicle of the ideas of Lenin and Trotsky; it is of ancient Jewish origin, a device which the Jews themselves invented to maintain their distinctive racial and national life after the conquest of Palestine by the Romans.

Modern Bolshevism, which is now known to be merely the outer cloak of a long-planned coup to establish the domination of a race, immediately set up the Soviet form of government because the Jews of all countries who contributed to Russian Bolshevism had long been schooled in the nature and structure of the Soviet.

The Soviet appears in the "Protocols of the Learned Elders of Zion" under the ancient name of KAHAL. In the Seventeenth Protocol this passage occurs:

"Even now our brothers are under obligation to denounce apostates of their own family or any person known to be opposed to the Kahal. When our kingdom comes, it will be necessary for all subjects to serve the state in a similar manner."

Anyone who is acquainted with contemporary Jewish life knows what this denunciation of apostates means. The bitterness of the persecution which falls upon a convert to Christianity or upon the Jewish son or daughter of an orthodox family who chooses to marry a Gentile, is without parallel among men. Very recently in a western state a fine Jewish girl chose to marry a Gentile, who was a newspaperman. From the time of her announcement of intention, the girl was treated as an apostate. Had she died a most wretched death, had she descended to a status of most ignominious shame, the feelings which her fate would have aroused could not have been more terrible. A darkly solemn funeral service was held for her, and on her bridal day she was declared to be dead to her people.

The case is very far from being unusual. Perhaps one of the most moving descriptions of it is to be found in the life of Spinoza, the great philosopher whom modern Jews are fond of holding up for exhibition as a great ornament of their people. Spinoza's studies led him to question many of the dogmas the rabbis taught, those "commandments of men" of which the New Testament speaks, and as Spinoza was already a person of influence the very common Jewish tactic of bribery was tried upon him.

There would be some hesitation in using the words just set down—"the very common Jewish tactic of bribery"—if they were not known to be true. There is no desire to cast aspersions which grow out of malice. But Jewish history as written by Jews provides mountains of proof that bribery was, while present knowledge amply testifies that it still is, the favorite and most dependable weapon of the Jews. A Jewish writer, Jacob Israel De Haan, a Dutch lawyer resident in Jerusalem, has recently stated that one hope of a settlement of the Arab agitation in Palestine is the ease with which the Arab press can be bribed. His words are: "There is a strong agitation here among the Arabs against what they call the Zionist peril. But the Arabs, especially the Arabian papers, are open to bribe. This weakness will cause them, in the long run, to lose out against us."

So, young Spinoza was offered an annual stipend of 1,000 florins if he would be silent upon his convictions and from time to time show himself at the synagogue. This he refused with high-minded scorn. He made ready to earn his bread by polishing lenses for optical instruments. Upon this, he was excommunicated, a proceeding which is thus described:

"The day of excommunication at length arrived, and a vast concourse assembled to witness the awful ceremony. It began by the silent and solemn lighting of a quantity of black wax candles and by opening the tabernacle wherein were deposited the books of the Law of Moses. Thus were the imaginations of the faithful prepared for all the horror of the scene. The chief rabbi, the ancient friend and master, now the fiercest enemy, of the condemned, was to order the execution. He stood there pained, but implacable; the people fixed their eager eyes upon him. High above, the chanter rose and chanted forth in loud lugubrious tones the words of execration; while from the opposite side another mingled with these curses the thrilling sounds of the trumpet. And now the black candles were reversed and were made to melt drop by drop into a huge tub filled with blood." (Lewes: Biographical History of Philosophy.)

Then came the final anathema. "'With the judgment of the angels and of the saints, we excommunicate, cut off, curse and anathematize

Is the Jewish "Kahal" the Modern "Soviet"?

Baruch de Espinoza, with the consent of the elders and all this holy congregation, in the presence of the holy books: by the 613 precepts which are written therein, with the anathema wherewith Joshua cursed Jericho, with the curse which Elisha laid upon the children, and with all the curses which are written in the law. Cursed be he by day, and cursed be he by night. Cursed be he in sleeping, and cursed be he in waking, cursed in going out, and cursed in coming in. The Lord shall not pardon him, the wrath and the fury of the Lord shall henceforth be kindled against this man, and shall lay upon him all the curses written in the Book of the Law. The Lord shall destroy his name under the sun, and cut him off for his undoing from all the tribes of Israel, with all the curses of the firmament which are written in the Law . . . And we warn you that none may speak with him by word of mouth nor by writing, nor show any favor unto him, nor be under one roof with him, nor come within four cubits of him, nor read any paper composed by him.'" (Pollock: Life of Spinoza.)

"As the blasting words were uttered, the lights were all suddenly immersed in the blood, a cry of religious horror and execration burst from all; and in that solemn darkness, and to those solemn curses, they shouted Amen, Amen!" (Professor J. K. Hosmer: The Jews.)

That is a commentary on the decree of denunciation. It also throws a very strong light on the pressure which is brought against many Jews who would cry out against the anti-social ideas of their people, but who dare not because of the penalties it would bring.

This denunciation, as Protocol Seventeen orders, is to be made against anyone who is "known to be opposed to the Kahal" or ancient Soviet system of the Jews.

After the destruction of the Jewish state by the Romans, the Jews maintained a center in the Patriarch; and after the dispersion of the Jews out of Palestine this center of nationality was preserved in the Prince of the Exile, or Exilarch, an office which is believed to persist to the present time, and which some believe to be held now by an American Jew. In spite of all assertions to the contrary, the Jews have never ceased to be "a people"; that is, a consciously united racial group, different from all others, and with purposes and ideals which are strictly of the Jews, by the Jews, and for the Jews in distinction from the rest of the world. That they constitute a nation within the nations, the most responsible Jewish thinkers not only declare but insist upon. And this is wholly in accord with the facts as observed. The Jew not only desires to live apart from other people, but he works with his own people as against others, and he desires as much as possible to live under his own laws. In the city of New York today, the Jews have succeeded in establishing their own court for the settlement of their own questions according to their own laws. And that is precisely the principle of the Soviet-Kahal.

From the first century forward, as any reader can see by consulting the *Jewish Encyclopedia*, the "community," "assembly" or "Kahal" has been the center of Jewish life. It was so earlier, in the time of the Babylonian captivity. And the last official appearance of it was at the Peace Conference, where the Jews, in accordance with their World Program, the only program that passed successfully and unchanged through the Peace Conference, secured for themselves the right to the Kahal for administrative and cultural purposes in addition to many other privileges in countries where their activities had been a matter of protest. The Polish question is purely a Jewish question, and Paderewski's failure as a statesmen was entirely due to his domination by Jewish influences. The Rumanian question is likewise a Jewish question, and all Rumanians speak of the United States as "The Jews' Country" because they know through their statesmen the terrific pressure which was exerted by American Jews against their country, a pressure extending to the very necessities of life, and which compelled Rumania to sign agreements which are as humiliating as those that Austria asked of Serbia, out of which the World War grew. The Jewish Question is written all over the forces that provoked the war, and over all the hindrances to peace which the world has since seen.

Under the Kahal or ancient Soviet, the Jews lived by themselves and governed themselves, doing business with the government solely through their representatives. It was communism in a more drastic form than has been seen anywhere in the world outside Russia. Education, health, taxes, domestic affairs, all were under the absolute control of a few men who constituted the ruling board. This board, as the present-day Jewish hierarchy is supposed to be, was self- perpetuating, the office often passing in an unbroken line of hereditary succession through many generations. All property was in common, which however did not prevent the leaders becoming rich. These Kahals or Soviets existed in Rome, France, Holland, Germany, Austria, Russia, Denmark, Italy, Rumania, Turkey and England. In the United States the idea has developed around the synagogue and around national and international secret societies of Jews, of which more will be said in succeeding articles.

Is the Jewish "Kahal" the Modern "Soviet"?

The Kahal is the traditional Jewish political institution during the dispersal of the race among the nations. Its international aspect is to be seen in the higher councils. These councils enlarged as the Jews spread over the world. The *Jewish Encyclopedia* cites the Council of Three Lands, the Council of Four Lands, and the Council of Five Lands, showing an international relationship in earlier years. But like all such records, public view of them is not easily accessible so far as they relate to modern times. The recent Zionist Congress in London, where doubtless much business was done that pertained to the Jewish people throughout the world, though not in public halls by any means, may be called the Council of Thirty-Seven Lands, for the delegates to that congress came from all parts of the world, from points remote as Lapland and South Africa, Persia and New Zealand. The purpose of these World Councils was the unification of the Jews, and the records of their assemblages run back through the centuries.

It is therefore no new thing that has arisen in Russia. It is the imposition by the Jewish revolutionists upon Gentile Russia of a form of control in which Judaism has been schooled from the earliest times of its contact with the world. Soviet Russia could not have been possible had not 90 per cent of the commissars been Jewish. Soviet Hungary could not have been possible had not Bela Kun, the chief Red, been a Jew, and had not 18 of his 24 commissars been Jews. The Jews are the only group schooled in the erection and administration of the Kahal.

An Associated Press dispatch under date of August 12 throws a light on the congeniality of the Soviet system and the Jewish mind. Speaking of the Polish towns and villages occupied by Bolshevik forces in their recent drive, the dispatch says:

"The local Jewish parish populations already are said to be setting up Soviet and Communist governments."

Of course. Yet this is in strange contrast with what we are constantly told through the press of the sufferings of the Jews under the Soviet form and of their abhorrence of the Reds. However, most of what we read concerning this in the public press is Jewish propaganda, pure and simple, and the reports of men on the spot contradict it all. One relief worker testifies that relief work in Poland is frequently "hung up because some Jew landlord asks an exorbitant rent for his premises," while another testifies that though railroad fares in the supposedly famine-stricken districts have gone up 1,000 per cent, the best and highest-fare trains are "exclusively occupied by Jews." He adds, of his trip through Hungary, "The Hungarians have no money any more, but the Jews have."

"But American Jews abhor Trotsky and Sovietism" is the plea sometimes made.

Do they?

On page 9 of the *American Jewish World*, of July 30, a letter signed "Mrs. Samuel Rush" appears. It is headed: "Are We Really Ashamed of Trotsky?" Read a few excerpts from it:

"I have read of late several laments from editors of Jewish publications that the Jew is now libeled as a radical.

"It is true that many Jews are radicals. It is also true that some of the radical leaders are Jews.

"But before weeping over the downfall of the race, let's think a bit.

"Trotsky himself has never been represented as anything but a cultured man, a student of world economics, a powerful and efficient leader and thinker who will surely go down in history as one of the great men our race has given the world.

". . . Very few of us doubt any longer that behind the absurdities written about Russia is the great truth that Russia is in that unsettled state which attends reconstruction. There is a plan behind this seeming disorder, and out of the upheaval will come order. It will not be utopia, but as good a government as the undoubtedly high-minded practical idealists who are building for Russia can build with the necessarily imperfect materials—human beings—with which they must work.

"And one of the leaders is Leon Trotsky!

"Are we really ashamed of Trotsky?"

The lady is evidently not ashamed of Trotsky, or Mr. Braunstein, as his real name is.

Or take Judge Harry Fisher, of Chicago. While drawing a salary for work in the court, Judge Fisher went abroad on Jewish relief work. His plans were changed somewhat after his departure and he landed in Russia. He asserts in several interviews that he was permitted to arrive in Russia on condition that he leave political matters alone. There has been no such restriction placed upon him since his return to the United States, for he appears as an open advocate of full trade relations with the Soviet Government of Russia.

The *Chicago Tribune* thus quotes him:

"'We must leave Russia alone' he said in summarizing his views. 'We should resume trade with the Soviet. The Bolshevist Government is

Is the Jewish "Kahal" the Modern "Soviet"?

permanent.... While there are only 700,000 members of the Communist party, the peasants, who represent almost 100,000,000 people, are solidly back of the Lenin regime.'"

Among the Soviet devices which the 100,000,000 peasants of Russia are said to be "solidly back of," is the following (it is particularly interesting in view of the fact that Judge Fisher is judge of the Morals Court of Chicago):

"'Some time ago, it was published that the women of Russia had become national property,' he said. 'That is untrue, but the ease with which marriage and divorce may be effected makes for rapid changes. Everyone wanting to marry goes to what we would call the city hall and registers.

"'Inducements to marry are great. When people are hard pressed for clothes and food they sometimes make a pact to wed for a day.

"'The next day they go down to the city hall and register again. This time their names are put side by side in the divorce book. That is all that is necessary to be divorced, and they have had a good feed in the bargain.'"

Judge Harry Fisher, of Chicago, who has returned from Jewish relief work abroad, evidently is one with the others in not being ashamed of Trotsky.

Also Max Pine, for many years secretary of the United Hebrew Trades of New York, had been abroad in Soviet Russia as "a labor delegate." He too had many good things to say of the Soviets, among other things the strange contradiction that the Jews are doing very well in Russia but are not pro-Bolshevik!

Here are three persons from widely different spheres of life, yet each one of them indicates a natural liking for the Kahal or Soviet, an admiration of its methods, and a distinct good feeling towards its rulers. For Sovietism is the rankest form of autocracy, and the marriage laws of Soviet Russia are in full harmony with the program stated in the Protocols—

"We will break down the influence of family life among the Gentiles."

Whether the Soviet-Kahals of Russia will succeed in completely undermining Russian family life is extremely doubtful. The weakness of Soviet rule is the same as that of the Protocols—a moral weakness that must eat like a cancer until it destroys the institutions which it infests.

Russia today, viewed in the light of the Protocols, does not represent the Judaic state, but it represents the Gentile state seized by Jewish forces. There are three degrees of action set forth in the Protocols. There is first the secret process of breaking up the integrity of society by the admixture of alluring but disruptive ideas. This is a work in which Gentile agitators are used. When the ideas have worked sufficiently to break up society and explode in a crisis, then as in Germany, the forces that have worked in secret swiftly come to the front to take the reins and guide the riot.

In Germany this immediately occurred upon the collapse which followed the armistice, but the Germans were wise enough to know the meaning of the influx of Jews into all the official positions of the former empire, and it was not long before they were politically ousted. In Russia, however, the Jews sprang immediately into official positions and have succeeded in remaining there. It began with Kerensky compelling the Czar to lay aside his crown; it continues with Trotsky and his armies at the throat of Europe.

But this seizure of a country, as was attempted in Germany, and as was not only attempted but succeeded in Russia, is not the end of the Program. It is only the beginning of its open or public phase. The SovietKahal makes for the complete breaking up of society, the entire cutting off of co-operation and communication, the ruling of each little section in the way desired, until the whole country lies helpless in isolated bits. The process includes, of course, the disintegration of industry also, the massing of Gentiles into an army, and a general destruction of morality and order. It is the Protocol program in its last stage before the reconstruction begins which shall make the conquered country a Jewish state.

The world has not seen that last stage yet. It has not come, even in Russia. If the Russian people waken from the daze into which they have been thrust, it will not come. Jewish voices loudly proclaim that Soviet Russia has come to stay. The only authoritative voice on that subject is the voice of Russia, and Russia has not yet spoken. Today the world is trembling on the very verge of Real Russia's awakening, and with it a retribution most terrible upon the Sovietists.

The program of the Protocols once came near succeeding in the French Revolution, but its essential immorality overreached itself. It has come a step nearer success in Russia, but there too its defiance of the moral law will be its undoing. The Jewish Question of today is being fought out in Russia and Poland, and the strength of the Jewish forces is largely and mostly supplied from the United States of America. No

Is the Jewish "Kahal" the Modern "Soviet"?

wonder those small East European independencies which are fighting for their lives refer to our country as "The Land of the Jews."

"We will show our power to one," say the Protocols. "In order to demonstrate our enslavement of the Gentile governments of Europe, we shall show our power to one of them by crimes of violence, that is, by a reign of terror." (Protocol Seven.)

One by one the Gentile nations of Europe have been compelled to withdraw their troops from Russia. One by one the premiers of Europe have submitted to heavy shackling of their official hands with regard to the Russian question. And today the world looks on while little Poland, apparently the second country on the list of Soviet victims, is made to feel heavy vengeance for her daring to be independent of Jewish power. Russia has been made to pay for her attempted independence of the Jew; Poland is now being made to pay. It is a flame, the Jews of Eastern Europe hope, and many Jews of America also, which will sweep round the world.

If the ruling Jews of the world wished the Russian people freed, if they wished the flames of Bolshevism to be quenched, if they wished Jewish participation in revolutionary movements to be withdrawn, they could accomplish it in a week. What is going on today is going on by permission of the Jewish world powers.

There is apparently no desire to curtail a movement which largely originated in American Jewry. This is the program of "showing our power to one," and the program will be followed out. The "showing," however, is twofold; it is a showing of power, but it is also a showing of the people who wield the power, and in the end it might have been just as well had the power never been coveted, attained, or used.

Anyone who desires to test the exactitude of the Protocols' estimate of human nature may do so by observing his own reactions to the Russian Bolshevist situation. It is undeniable that there exists among all classes of Gentiles in America a kind of admiration for the coup which Lenin and Trotsky have managed on such a massive scale. The audacity of it, the ability to stay afloat thus long in defiance of so many laws, have conspired to draw out unwilling applause.

Consider then this passage from the Tenth Protocol:

"The people feel an especial love and respect toward the genius who wields political power, and they say of all his high-handed actions: 'It is base, but clever! It is a trick, but how he played it! So majestic! So impudent!'

The International Jew Volumes I and II

"We count on attracting all nations to the constructive work of laying the foundations for the structure planned by us. It is necessary for us first of all to acquire the services of bold and fearless agents, who will overcome all obstacles in our pathway.

"When we accomplish our governmental coup d'etat, we will say to the people: 'Everything has gone badly, all have suffered. We will eliminate the cause of your sufferings—nationality, frontiers and diversity of coinage. Of course you are free to pronounce sentence upon us, but that can scarcely be just if you do so before giving a trial to that which we offer you.'"

This is very well conceived, and this is the way in which, up to this time, it has worked out. But there will be a strong reaction set in. False promises like chickens come home to roost. The real originators, the real purpose of the movement hidden behind Bolshevism will become evident. And then the world will crush out again the World Program which at times has seemed so near success.

There will probably be more light upon this World Program as a result of the Russian Kahal-Soviet system than from any other attempt to realize it. For five generations the world has lived in a false light supposed to be shed by the French Revolution. It is now known that that revolution was not the Revolution of the French People, but the disorders of a minority who sought to impose upon the French People the very Plan which is now being considered. It was the French People who ultimately put down the so-called French Revolution. And France, as a result of that upheaval of a well-organized minority, has been bound by Jewish control ever since.

The Russian Revolution will go down in history with no such false halo of romance around it. The world now knows it for what it is. The world will soon know whose was the money and whose were the brains that fostered it, and from what part of the world the principal impetus came. The Russian upheaval is racial, not political nor economic. It conceals beneath all its false socialism and its empty mouthings of "human brotherhood" a clear-cut plan of racial imperialism, which is not Russian, and which the common sense and interest of the world will speedily stamp out.

The Dearborn Independent, August 28, 1920

16. How the "Jewish Question" Touches the Farm

The real estate speculations of the Jews are familiar to all, but unfortunately do not constitute their entire land program. Many American cities have changed their characters entirely during the past 15 years by reason of Jewish speculation in residence property, and it is a fact established in the larger eastern cities that the recent exorbitant and extortionate rise in rents was largely a matter of the Jewish landlord. The governor of one of the most important of our commonwealths was loath to sign a bill regulating rents. His hesitancy was encouraged by very heavy pressure brought to bear upon him by the weightiest Jewish financial interests in his own and neighboring states. He finally decided that he would sign the bill and give the law effect, and the fact that decided him was his personal investigation and the investigation of his personal agents into hundreds of cases of abuse where he discovered that it was a common practice among Jewish landlords to transfer the same piece of property round and round to every member of the family in turn, each "transfer" being the excuse for a new increase in the rent. Men have their eyes opened to the Jewish Question in various ways: this was the way a governor had his eyes opened.

That, however, is not the peculiarity of Jewish landlords alone; Gentile landlords have played the same trick. But landlordism is peculiarly a Jewish ambition and distinction; the Jew is the Landlord of America. Any group of tenants almost anywhere in America, except the West, could testify to this.

Nor is landlordism itself reprehensible, things being what they are, unless it is anti-social and anti-American. And just here is where it gets point. Some of the oldest and most sacred shrines of Americanism in the East have entirely lost their character as such by the invasion—not of "foreigners"—but of Jews.

The more one sees of the invasion, the more one utterly distrusts the statistics given out by Jews as to the Jewish population of the United States. Do you know that the one nationality on which the Government of the United States is estopped from asking questions, either for immigration or census statistics, is the Jewish? Do you know that when the Government of the United States wants to know anything about the Jews it must go to statisticians which the Jews themselves support?

If a nation claims that it is no nation with respect to the United States Government, as the Jews claim, and has no national statistics which it will permit to government to collect in the official way, why should it treat itself as a nation and keep its own records?

The Jews of the United States, like the Jews of every European country, are a nation among themselves, with their own government, their own policy, their own records; and the United States Government does business with the Jewish Government in America through chosen Jews no doubt of that.

It is, however, a digression. The matter of Jewish statistics will come up again. In the meantime a glance at the rapid changing of so many American cities in all parts of the land leads to the belief that the Jewish statistics furnished by the Jews for Gentile consumption entirely misstate the facts, and this belief is strengthened by the knowledge that the statistics given by the Jews for Jewish consumption are very different from those supplied for the outside world.

Landlordism may be explained by the inclination of the Jew toward speculation, and we know that real estate has been made one of the most speculative of occupations, disgracefully, almost disastrously so. The Jew cannot be condemned for becoming a landlord, for becoming the most conspicuous landlord in America; he cannot be condemned apart from his Gentile co-offenders for the abuse he has made of his advantage as landlord. But it is a matter for American concern that the cities to which, in the schoolbooks, our children are taught to look as the birthplaces of liberty and as still the spokesmen of Americanism, should become Semite cities, financially and politically, and the recruiting grounds of the world's Bolshevism.

Until recently, however, the Jew in America has not cared for the land. It is a characteristic. The Jew is not an agriculturist. Lavish fortunes have been expended to make him so, but the productive work of farming has not had, and does not now have, any appeal to him. His choice in land is this: land that produces gold from the mine, and land that produces rents. Land that produces mere potatoes and wheat has not directly interested him.

It is true, of course, that the land question has been distinctly Jewish in countries like Poland and Rumania. No law against Jews owning land

How the "Jewish Question" Touches the Farm ?

in those countries has ever been effective in preventing their control of whole provinces. Not that the Jews demanded the right to farm the land, their choice was to farm the farmers. By devious methods and the use of "Gentile fronts" they could always secure control of the land, and thus dominating the peasants they could create almost any condition they wished. That is what they actually did. That is the Jewish Question in those parts of the world. Not for farming purposes, it must be understood, but for the purpose of controlling the main source of wealth in agricultural countries and for taking the control of people away from their natural Gentile leaders.

These two things always go together in countries where there is intellectual or landed aristocracy to which the people look for leadership: the Jewish program is to destroy that leadership by gaining control of the land. It is profitable, of course, but when you survey the outworking of the plan you always see something other than profits involved. The consummate perfection of the Jewish plan for World Control is that it does not involve sacrifice as have other plans, it is immensely profitable at every stage, and the greater the profitableness the more surely the purpose is being achieved.

In America there was no aristocracy to be cut under by the gaining of land control. Jewish activity in the United States until recently has confined itself to the control of land products after they have been produced: that is, so to say, Jewish interests do not engage in trapping, but they control the fur trade.

Speaking of furs, it is very funny to see how some affairs turn out. During the war there was a great to-do made about the German control of the American fur trade. It was true that the fur trade was controlled from Germany, but not by Germans—by Jews! And then a great to-do was made about seizing, confiscating and absolutely selling out that "German" fur business to Americans, and the "Americans" who bought it were—Jews! The actual control has never changed; the profits still find their way to the "International" purse.

But furs is just an example. Jewish interests do not engage in raising grain, but control the grain that others produce. The need of the United States is a "Who's Who of Jewish Financiers" that the people may identify the men about whom they read as having made this "corner" or sprung that "coup." These interests, which have simply grabbed American-produced wealth and made American consumers pay and pay and pay, have been able to operate almost openly because of the sheer blindness of the American people as they read their newspapers. And, of course, while the American newspaper will gladly inform you that this man is an Italian and that man a Pole and the other man a Briton, it will never tell you that the fourth man is a Jew. There is a Jewish organization in every city, large and small, to prevent it—and they prevent it by methods that are violent and wholly subversive of the American ideal of liberty.

So, until recently, the plan in the United States has been to seize the commodity at just that point in its passage from the producer to the consumer where the heaviest weight of profit can be extracted from it— at the neck of the bottle, so to speak—and control it there. It is not service that the people pay for; they pay for seizure.

But a new movement has begun in the United States. Jewish millions are now being used to secure immense tracts of American lands. Formerly it was enough to control the cotton, as the bread was controlled, but now the movement is toward controlling the cotton lands. The operations are carefully guarded; "Gentile fronts" are used almost exclusively; but follow the trail through all the "blinds" and "false scents," and you come at last to the International Jew, whose throne is set up in London.

Many Jews have written *The Dearborn Independent* saying that they do not know about these racial plans for world control. It may well be believed that they do not. One purpose of these articles is to tell them about it. But this every Jew rejoices in—the movement of his people toward power. And it is this sentiment that the International Jew implicitly trusts, and because this sentiment exists the International Program secures a maximum of success at a minimum risk of exposure. Jewry is not a democracy but an autocracy. Of course the ordinary Jew does not know! The question is, Why should he revile the Gentile who tries to tell him? If a Jew will not seal his mind against the statements made in these articles, he will find in his own knowledge sufficient corroboration of their principal features, and he will be in a better position to assist in the solution of the Jewish Question.

It is with amazement at certain men's conception of editorial honesty that *The Dearborn Independent* has read some of the reports made of these articles. Under cover, principally of the Yiddish, alleged translations of these articles have been flung broadcast among non-English speaking Jews, translations which not only bear no resemblance to the original, but actually insert whole paragraphs of matter which never appeared in the original at all. Is there a fear of permitting the average Jew to read this series? Nothing is more desired by those whose

How the "Jewish Question" Touches the Farm ?

purpose is to lay foundations for the solution of the Jewish Question in America than that every Jew in the United States should know exactly what is being printed here week by week. The Jew has been deceived by his leaders long enough.

The fact is, then, that there is a definite and already well forwarded movement toward the control of the cotton lands of the United States. The first step was to depreciate the market value of these lands as much as possible. Pressure was brought through certain banks to limit the cotton farmers' efforts. They were told that if they planted more acreage to cotton than they were told to, they would not be financed. Cotton production was to go down while cotton prices were to go up, and the profits were not the farmers' but those who controlled the course of cotton from the first market to the wearer. Cotton farming was to be made less profitable, while cotton speculation was to become more profitable.

The public was being compelled to supply the money by which the Jewish controllers were to buy the land. In brief, it was to be made more profitable to sell cotton lands than to sell cotton.

These statements are being deliberately restricted to the traffic in cotton lands. Jewish financiers in New York and London know these things, even if Jewish editors and rabbis do not.

This movement has been within the knowledge of certain classes of business men for a long time, indeed some have been forced by what used to be called "the pressure of circumstances," to serve the movement. But they were not able to interpret its meaning. It is only recently that the more important Gentile business men of the United States have been able to interpret certain things. The war was a potent eye-opener.

Those wonderful documents known as the "Protocols," with their strong grasp of every element of life, have not overlooked Land. The Land Program found in the Sixth Protocol, which is one of the briefest of these documents and may be quoted in full to show now the relation it bears to certain excerpts made in previous articles:

Protocol VI.

"We shall soon begin to establish huge monopolies, colossal reservoirs of wealth, upon which even the big Gentile properties will be dependent to such an extent that they will all fall together with the government credit on the day following the political catastrophe. The economists here present must carefully weigh the significance of this combination. We must develop by every means the importance of our super-government, representing it as the protector and benefactor of all who voluntarily submit to us.

"The aristocracy of the Gentiles as a political force has passed away. We need not take them into consideration. But, as owners of the land, they are harmful to us in that they are independent in their sources of livelihood. Therefore, at all costs, we must deprive them of their land.

"The best means to attain this is to increase the taxes and mortgage indebtedness. These measures will keep land ownership in a state of unconditional subordination. Unable to satisfy their needs by small inheritances, the aristocrats among the Gentiles will burn themselves out rapidly.

"At the same time it is necessary to encourage trade and industry vigorously and especially speculation, the function of which is to act as a counterpoise to industry. Without speculation, industry will cause private capital to increase and tend to improve the condition of Agriculture *by freeing the land from indebtedness for loans* by the land banks. It is necessary for industry to deplete the land both of laborers and capital, and, through speculations, transfer all the money of the world into our hands, thereby throwing the Gentiles into the ranks of the proletariat. The Gentiles will then bow before us to obtain the right to existence.

"To destroy Gentile industry, we shall, as an incentive to this speculation, encourage among the Gentiles a strong demand for luxuries, all-enticing luxuries.

"We will force up wages, which however, will be of no benefit to workers, for we will at the same time cause a rise in the prices of prime necessities, pretending that this is due to the decline of agriculture and of cattle raising. We will also artfully and deeply undermine the sources of production by instilling in the workmen ideas of anarchy, and encourage them in the use of alcohol, at the same time taking measures to drive all the intellectual forces of the Gentiles from the land.

"That the true situation shall not be noticed by the Gentiles prematurely, we will mask it by a pretended effort to serve the working classes and promote great economic principles, for which an active propaganda will be carried on through our economic theories."

The local and passing element in this is "the aristocracy of the Gentiles." That is to say, the program is not entirely fulfilled by the passing of aristocrats. Jewry goes on just the same. Its program stretches far. Jewry will retain such kings as it desires as long as it desires them. Probably

How the "Jewish Question" Touches the Farm?

the last throne to be vacated will be the British throne because what to the British mind is the honor of being Jewry's protector and therefore the inheritor of the blessing which that attitude brings, is to the Jewish mind the good fortune of being able to use a world-wide empire for the furtherance of Jewry's purpose. Each has served the other and the partnership will probably last until Jewry gets ready to throw Britain over, which Jewry can do at almost any time. There are indications that it has already started in this last task.

But the permanent elements in the Protocol are the Land, the Jews, and the Gentiles. A word of explanation may be necessary on this inclusion of the Gentiles as permanent: the Protocols do not contemplate the extermination of the Gentiles, nor the making of this world a completely Jewish populated world. The Protocols contemplate a Gentile world ruled by the Jews—the Jews as masters, the Gentiles as hewers of wood and drawers of water, a policy which every Old Testament reader knows to be typically Jewish and the source of divine judgement upon Israel time and again. Now, look at this whole Program as it concerns the Land. "Owners of the land ... are harmful to us in that they are independent in their sources of livelihood."

That is a foundation principle of the Protocols. It matters not whether the owners are the "Gentile aristocracy," the peasants of Poland, or the farmers of the United States—land ownership makes the owners, "independent in their sources of livelihood." And any form of independence is fatal to the success of the World Program which is written so comprehensively in the Protocols and which is advancing so comprehensively under Jewish guidance in the world of actual affairs today.

Not "tillers" of the land, not "dwellers" on the land, not "tenants," not an "agricultural peasantry," but "owners of the land"—this is the class singled out for attention in this Sixth Protocol, BECAUSE they are "independent in their sources of livelihood."

Now, there has been no time in the history of the United States when apparently it was more easy for the farmer to own his land than now. Mortgages should be a thing of the past. Everywhere the propaganda of the question tells us that the farmers are growing "rich." And yet there were never so many abandoned farms!

"Therefore, at all costs we must deprive them of their land."

How? "The best means to attain this is to increase land taxes and mortgage indebtedness." High taxes to keep the land at all, borrowed money to finance the tilling of it. "These measures will keep land ownership in a state of unconditional subordination."

We will leave it to the farmers of the United States to say whether this is working out or not.

And in a future reference to this subject we will show that whenever an attempt is made to enable farmers to borrow money at decent rates, whenever it is proposed to lighten the burden of "mortgage indebtedness" on the farm, Jewish financial influence in the United States steps in to prevent it, or failing to prevent it, mess it all up in the operation.

By increasing the farmer's financial disability on the one hand, and by increasing industrial allurements on the other, a very great deal is accomplished. The Protocol says: "It is necessary for industry to deplete the Land both of laborers and capital."

Has that been done? Have the farms of the United States been depleted both of laborers and capital? Certainly. Money is harder for the farmer to get than it is for any other man; and as for labor, he cannot get it on any terms.

What is the result of these two influences, the one working on the farm, and the other in the cities? It is precisely what the Protocol says it will be: Increased wages that buy less of the materials of life—"We will at the same time cause a rise in the prices of prime necessities, pretending that this is due to the decline of agriculture and cattle raising."

The Jew who set these Protocols in order was a financier, economist and philosopher of the first order. He knew what he was talking about. His operations in the ordinary world of business always indicated that he knew exactly what he was doing. How well this Sixth Protocol has worked and is still working out in human affairs is before the eyes of everyone to see.

Here in the United States one of the most important movements toward real independence of the financial powers has been begun by the farmers. The farmer's strong advantage is that, owning the land, he is independent in his sources of livelihood. The land will feed him whether he pleases International Jewish Financiers or not. His position is impregnable as long as the sun shines and the seasons roll. It was therefore necessary to do something to hinder this budding independence. He was placed under a greater disadvantage than any other business man in borrowing capital. He was placed more ruthlessly than any other producer between the upper and nether stones of a

How the "Jewish Question" Touches the Farm ?

thievish distribution system. Labor was drawn away from the farm. The Jew-controlled melodrama made the farmer a "rube," and Jew-made fiction presented him as a "hick," causing his sons to be ashamed of farm life. The grain syndicates which operate against the farmer are Jew-controlled. There is no longer any possibility of doubting, when the facts of actual affairs are put alongside the written Program, that the farmer of the United States has an interest in this Question.

What would this World Program gain if the wage-workers were enslaved and the farmers were allowed to go scot-free? Therefore the program of agricultural interference which has been only partially outlined here.

But this is not all.

Any writer who attempts fully to inform the Gentile mind on the Jewish Question must often feel that the extent of the Protocols' Conspiracy is so great as to stagger the Gentile mind. Gentiles are not conspirators. They cannot follow a clue through long and devious and darkened channels. The elaborate completeness of the Jewish Program, the perfect co-ordination of its mass of details wearies the Gentile mind. This, really more than the daring of the Program itself, constitutes the principal danger of Program being fulfilled. Gentile mental laziness is the most powerful ally the World Program has.

For example: after citing the perfectly obvious coincidence and most probable connection between the Protocols and the observable facts with reference to the farm situation, the writer is compelled to say, as above, "But this is not all." And it is a peculiarity of Gentile psychology that the Gentile reader will feel that it ought to be all because it is so complete. This is where the Jewish mind out-maneuvers the Gentile mind.

Gentiles may do a thing for one reason: the Jew often does the same thing for three or four reasons. The Gentile can understand thus far why Jewish financiers should seek control of the land in order to prevent widespread Agricultural Independence which, as Protocol Six says, would be "harmful to us." That reason is perfectly clear.

But there is another. It is found in the Twelfth Protocol. It contemplates nothing less than the playing of City against Country in the great game now being exposed. Complete control over the City by the industrial leverage, and over the Country by the debt leverage, will enable the Hidden Players to move first the Country by saying that the City demands certain things, and then move the City by saying that the

Country demands certain things, thus splitting Citizens and Farmers apart and using them against one another.

Look at the plainness and the boldness, yet the calm assurance, with which this plan is broached:

"Our calculations reach out, especially into the country districts. There we must necessarily arouse those interests and ambitions which we can always turn against the city, representing them to the cities as dreams and ambitions for independence on the part of the provinces. It is clear that the source of all this will be precisely the same, and that it will come from us. It will be necessary for us before we have attained full power to so arrange matters that, from time to time, the cities shall come under the influence of opinion in the country districts, that is, of the majority prearranged by our agents . . . "

The preliminaries of the game are here set forth—to jockey City and Farm against each other, that in the end the Conspirators may use whichever proves the stronger in putting the Plan over. In Russia, both schemes have been worked. The old regime, established in the Cities, was persuaded to lay down power because it was made to believe that the peasants of Russia requested it. Then, when the Bolshevists seized power, they ruled the peasantry on the ground that the Cities wanted it. The Cities listened to the Country, now the Country is listening to the Cities.

If you see any attempt made to divide City and Farm into antagonistic camps, remember this paragraph from the Twelfth Protocol. Already the poison is working. Have you never heard that Prohibition was something which the backwoods districts forced upon the cities? Have you never heard that the High Cost of Living was due to extravagant profits of the farmer?—profits which he doesn't get.

One big dent in this Program of World Control could be made if the Citizen and the Farmer could learn each other's mind, not through self-appointed spokesmen, but directly from each other. City and Farm are drifting apart because of misrepresentation of outsiders, and in the widening rift the sinister shadow of the World Program appears.

Let the Farmers look past the "Gentile fronts" in their villages or principal trading points, past them to the real controllers who are hidden.

The Dearborn Independent, September 4, 1920

17. Does Jewish Power Control the World Press?

The purpose of this article is twofold: to set forth what the Protocols have to say about the relation of the Press to the World Program, and to make an introduction to a study of Jewish influence on the Press.

The Jewish race has always been aware of the advantages to be derived from news. This was one of the factors in its control of European commerce from the earliest Christian times. To be informed beforehand, to know what was coming before the Gentiles among whom they lived knew it, was a special privilege of the Jews, made possible by the close communication in which widely separated Jewish groups kept themselves. From the first they were inveterate correspondents. They were the inventors of the news-letter.

This does not imply, however, that the Jews were the forerunners or even the sponsors of the modern Press. It was no part of their purpose to distribute news among the people, but to keep it for themselves as a secret advantage. The political, economic and commercial news which sped with really remarkable facility throughout Europe, from Jewish community to Jewish community, was in reality the official budget by which each community informed all the others of what was transpiring, as to war, trade currents, rising emergencies, or whatever the matter may have been. For centuries the Jews were the best informed people on the continent; from their secret sources in courts and chancellories, from privileged Jews who were placed in every position of vantage, the whole race was informed of the state of the world.

Scouts were kept in motion everywhere. Far down in South America, before the British or Dutch colonies in North America had hardly secured a foothold, there were Jews who served as outposts for European trade interests. The world was spied out in the interests of their race, just as today the entire planet is under the watchful eyes of Jewish agents— mostly Gentiles, it must be said—for any hint of new gold discoveries.

An interesting and historic illustration of the Jews' appreciation of news is to be found in the career of Nathan Rothschild. Rothschild had laid all his plans on the assumption that the Emperor Napoleon, then banished to Elba, was finally eliminated from European affairs.

Napoleon unexpectedly returned, and in the "Hundred Days" it seemed as if the Rothschild financial edifice might collapse. Feverishly the financier aided both Prussia and England, and as the Battle of Waterloo approached, no one was more interested in the outcome than he.

Rothschild was a man who shrank from the sight of blood; he was physically a coward, and any sign of violence unnerved him; but so intense was his interest in the battle on which his whole fortune seemed to depend, that he hastened to France, followed the British Army, and when the battle began he hid himself in "some shot-proof nook near Hougomont" where he watched all day the ebb and flow of battle. Just before Napoleon ordered the last desperate charge Rothschild had made up his mind. He said afterward that his exclamation at this point was, "The House of Rothschild has won the battle."

He hurried from the field, galloped wildly to Brussels, communicating not a word of what he knew to the anxious people he met by the way. Hiring a carriage at an exorbitant price, he galloped away to Ostend. Here a fierce storm was raging on the ocean and no sailor was willing to set out for England, about 20 miles away. Rothschild himself, always afraid of danger, forgot his fear in his visions of the stock market. He offered 500, 800, and at length 1,000 francs to the man who would take him across. But no one dared. Finally one sailor proposed that if Rothschild would pay 2,000 francs into his wife's hands, he would attempt it.

Half dead the two men reached the English coast, but without rest Rothschild ordered express post and hurried away to London. Whip and spur were not spared on that journey.

There were no telegrams in those days, no swift communication. England was anxious. The rumors were bad. And on the morning of June 20, 1815, when Nathan Rothschild appeared in his usual place at the Stock Exchange and leaned against the column, England knew nothing of what he knew. He was pale and broken. The sight of his face led the other financiers to believe that he had received bad news from the front. Then it was seen that he was quietly selling his securities. What? Rothschild unloading? The market dropped disastrously, a very panic seized the financiers, the market was flooded with consols offered for sale—and all that was offered, Rothschild's agents bought!

So it went on, all day the 20th, and all day the 21st. At the close of business the second day, Rothschild's heavy chests were crammed with securities. Then in the evening a courier galloped into London with the news that Wellington had won and Napoleon was a fugitive. But Nathan Rothschild had made $10,000,000 and the men he did business with had lost that much—all as an affair of news!

There was a little incident in Washington during the war—a "leak" of news, it was called. The wise men of Wall Street sometimes whisper that even between 1914-1918 there were men of Rothschild's race who showed his same appreciation of "news," with the same profitable results. And not only the men of "Rothschild's race," but some of their "Gentile fronts," also.

There were times during the war when no Gentile knew what was going on in certain countries. The Jewish leaders always knew. Some very interesting testimony can be presented on that point.

Aside from its own interest, this Rothschild narrative fully illustrates the statement that while the Jews were very early news-gatherers, they were not publicists. They used the news for their own benefit; they did not disseminate it.

If it had depended on their influence, there would have been no public Press at all. It was in France, which had no newspapers outside the capital, that the French Revolution was possible. There being no reliable exchange of news and opinion, the people were kept in ignorance. Paris itself did not know that the Bastille had fallen until next day. Where there is no Press, minorities easily gain control—as the Jewish-Bolshevist revolution in Russia illustrates.

One of the most dangerous developments of the time is public distrust of the Press. If the day ever comes when swift, reliable and authoritative communication with the entire people shall be necessary for public action in the interests of public safety, the nation may find itself sadly crippled unless a new confidence in the daily Press can be built up. If for no other reason than that the free press is a safeguard against minority seizure of control, such laws as the zone laws, or any restrictions on the freest and fullest communication between various parts of the country, should be absolutely abolished.

But, the Press being in existence, and being largely an Anglo-Saxon creation, it is a force not to be treated lightly, and that is the point where the World Program and Jewish Control come in contact with it.

The Protocols, which overlook nothing, propose a very definite plan with regard to the Press. As in the multitude of other matters with which these remarkable documents deal, there are the two phases—"what we have done," and "what we will do."

As early as the Second Protocol, the Press comes in for attention. It is significant that it makes its appearance in the same Protocol in which the "No Annexations" program was announced 20 years before the World War, in the same Protocol in which it is announced that Gentile rulers will be allowed to appear before the people for a short period, while Jewish influences were organizing themselves behind the seats of power, and in the same Protocol where Darwinism, Marxism and Nietzscheism are claimed among the most "demoralizing" doctrines which Jewish influence has disseminated. These are very curious statements, but not stranger than the actuality that has come to pass.

Says the Second Protocol:

"There is one great force in the hands of modern governments which creates thought movements among the people, that is, the Press. The presumed role of the Press is to indicate supposedly indispensable needs, to register popular complaints, and to create discontent. The triumph of 'free speech' (babbling) rests in the Press. But governments are unable to profit by this power, and it has fallen into our hands. Through it we have attained influence while remaining in the shadow. Thanks to it, we have amassed gold, though it has cost us torrents of blood and tears."

In the same Protocol, "our Press" is spoken of as the agency through which are disseminated "those theories of life which we have induced them (the Gentiles) to regard as the dictates of science."

"To this end we shall certainly endeavor to inspire blind confidence in these theories by means of our Press."

Then follows the claim made concerning the three most revolutionary theories in the physical, economic and moral realms, namely Darwinism, Marxism and Nietzscheism.

In the Third Protocol the claim is made that this control of the Press is being used to break down respect for authority:

"Daring journalists and audacious pamphleteers make daily attack upon the personnel of the administration. This abuse of authority is definitely preparing the downfall of all institutions, and everything will be overturned by blows coming from the infuriated populace."

Again, in the Seventh Protocol, discussing the progress which the World Program has already made, the part played by the Press is indicated:

"We must force the Gentile governments to adopt measures which will promote our broadly conceived plan already approaching its triumphal goal, by bringing to bear the pressure of stimulated public opinion, which has in reality been organized by us with the help of the so-called 'great power' of the Press. With few exceptions not worth considering, it is already in our hands."

Thus twice is the claim made to control of the Press. "It has fallen into our hands," says the Second Protocol. "It is already in our hands," says the Seventh. In the Second Protocol the Press is represented as furthering revolutionary physical, economic and moral philosophies; while in the Seventh it is used to create the "pressure of stimulated public opinion" for the purpose of "forcing Gentile governments to adopt measures which will promote our broadly conceived plan, already approaching its triumphal goal."

A word of comment may be made here upon the claim of the Second Protocol that "thanks to it (the Press), we have amassed gold, though it has cost us torrents of blood and tears."

This is a statement which can be illustrated in many ways. "Though it has cost us torrents of blood and tears" is an admission upon which the Protocols throw light, a light which also shines upon the Jewish argument regarding responsibility for the recent war, namely, that Jewish World Financial Power could not have willed the war seeing that Jews suffered so heavily in Eastern Europe. The Protocols frankly recognize the possibility of Jews suffering during the establishment of the World Program, but it consoles them with the thought that they fall as soldiers for the good of Israel. The death of a Jew, we are told in the Protocols, is more precious in the sight of God than the death of a thousand "seed of cattle," which is one of the delicate names applied to the Gentiles.

The reference to the amassment of gold is very clear. It does not apply to ownership of publications and a share in their profits only, but also the use that may be made of them through silence or outcry to promote International Jewish Financiers' schemes. The Rothschilds bought editors as they bought legislators. It was a preliminary of nearly every scheme they floated to first "fix" the newspapers, either for silence or claque boosting. In matters of war and peace; in the removal of administrations inimical to Jewish financial or political plans; in the elimination by public exposure of "Gentile fronts" whom their Jewish masters wished to be rid of; in the gradual building up of reputation and influence for "rising men" who had been chosen for work in the future in these and like matters the Press very greatly aided the International Cabal in attaining its end.

All the details of the foregoing paragraph can be illustrated at length by instances which have occurred in the United States within the past 15 years.

There was once a Senator of the United States who—but that story illustrates another point also, and will be reserved until that point is reached in this series of discussions.

The Twelfth Protocol, however, contains the entire plan of Control of the Press, reaching from the present time into the future when the Jewish World Government shall be established. The reader is invited to read carefully and thoughtfully the deep and wide outreaching of this plan.

Keep also in mind the boast that has been made for generations that no publication that has handled the Jewish Question in a manner distasteful to the Jewish powers has been allowed to live.

"What role is played at present by the Press? It serves to inflame the passions of selfish partisanship which our interests require. It is shallow, lying and unfair, the most people do not understand what end it serves."

In that quotation we have the same low estimate which was noted when we studied "the estimate of human nature" which the Protocols contain.

Now, for the Plan of Press Control: We separate the points for convenience:

"We shall handle the Press in the following manner:

1. "We shall saddle it and keep tight rein upon it. We shall do the same also with other printed matter, for of what use is it to rid ourselves of attacks in the Press, if we remain exposed to criticism through pamphlets and books?"

2. "Not one announcement will reach the people save under our supervision. We have attained this at the present time to the extent that all news is received through several agencies in which it is centralized from all parts of the world."

A sidelight on the first sentence above may be had from the Jewish statement regarding the British Declaration relating to Palestine: "This Declaration was sent from the Foreign Office to Lord Walter Rothschild. . . . It came perhaps as a surprise to large sections of the Jewish people . . . But to those who were active in Zionist circles, the declaration was no surprise. . . . The wording of it came from the British Foreign Office, but the text had been revised in the Zionist offices in America as well as in England. The British Declaration was made in the form in which

Does Jewish Power Control the World Press?

the Zionists desired it. . . . " pp. 85–86, "Guide to Zionism," by Jessie E. Sampter, published by the Zionist Organization of America.

3. "Literature and journalism are two most important educational forces, and consequently our government will become the owner of most of the journals. . . . If we permit ten private journals, we shall organize thirty of our own, and so on. This must not be suspected by the public, for which reason all the journals published by us will be *externally* of the most contrary opinions and tendencies thus evoking confidence in them and attracting our unsuspecting opponents, who thus will be caught in our trap and rendered harmless."

This is most interesting in view of the defense now being made for so many Jewish journals. "Look at the newspapers owned and controlled by Jews," they say; "see how they differ in policy! See how they disagree with each other!" Certainly, "externally," as Protocol 12 says, but the underlying unity is never hard to find.

Besides, one way of discovering who are the people that have knowledge of the Jewish World problem, of who can be convinced of it, or who will write about it is just to start a paper which "externally" seems to be independent of the Jewish Question. So deeply is this thought shared by even uneducated Jews that a rumor is today widespread in the United States that the reason for the present series of articles in *The Dearborn Independent* is the desire of its owner to forward the Jewish World Program! Unfortunately, this scheme of starting a fake opposition in order to discover where the real opposing force is, is not confined to the Jewish Internationalists, although there is every indication that it was learned from them.

This idea of a misrepresentative front for certain secret purposes is expressed at length not only with reference to the Press, but throughout the Protocols in other relations. But in Protocol 12 it is fully developed with regard to the Press, as the following quotations show.

(a) In order to force writers into such long productions that no one will read them, a tax on writing is proposed—"on books of less than 30 pages a double tax." Small articles are most feared. Therefore doubly tax the pamphlets of less than 30 pages. The longer articles fewer will read, so the Protocols argue, and the double tax will thus "force writers into such long productions that they will be little read, especially as they will be expensive."

But—"That which we ourselves shall publish for directing the public mind will be cheap and widely read. The tax will discourage mere literary ambition, whereas the fear of punishment will make the writers subservient to us. Even if there should be those who may desire to write against us, no one will publish their writings." (How many American writers know this!)

"Before accepting any work for printing, the publisher or printer must obtain permission from the authorities. Thus we will know in advance what attacks are being prepared against us and shall be able to counteract them by coming out beforehand with explanations on the subject."

That is largely the situation today. They do know in advance what is being done, and they do seek to disarm it beforehand.

(b) Here are the Three Degrees of Jewish Journalism, which are not only stated in the Protocols but are observable in the everyday world of the present.

"The leading place will be held by organs of an official character. They will always stand guard over our interests and consequently their influence will be comparatively small.

"The second place will be held by semi-official organs whose aim it will be to attract the indifferent and lukewarm.

"In the third category we shall place organs of apparent opposition. At least one will be extremely antagonistic. Our true opponents will mistake this seeming opposition as belonging to their own group and will thus show us their cards.

"I beg you to notice that among those who attack us there will be organs founded by us, and they will attack exclusively those points which we plan to change or eliminate.

"All our papers will support most diverse opinions: aristocratic, republican, even anarchist, so long of course as the Constitution lives. * * These fools who believe they are repeating the opinions expressed by their party newspapers will be repeating our opinions or those things which we wish them to think.

"By always discussing and contradicting our writings superficially, and without touching upon their essence, our press will keep up a blank fire against the official newspapers, only to give us opportunity to express ourselves in greater detail than we could in our first declaration. This will be done when useful to us.

"These attacks will also convince the people of the full freedom of the press, and it will give our agents the opportunity of declaring that the papers opposing us are mere wind-bags, since they cannot find any real arguments to oppose our orders."

Undoubtedly that would be the case were all the papers controlled. In the case of the present series of articles, however, the tables appear to be turned. It is the Jewish Press which has so signally failed to bring forward disproof either by fact or argument.

"When necessary, we shall promulgate ideas in the third section of our Press as feelers, and then refute them vigorously in the semiofficial press.

"We shall overcome our opponents without fail because they will not have organs of the Press at their disposal.

"The pretext for suppressing a publication will be that it stirs up the public mind without basis of reason"—a pretext which has already been urged time and again, but without the legal power to effect suppression, although without legal power the Jewish interests in the United States have effected a pretty complete suppression of everything they do not desire.

How far does Jewish influence control the Newspapers of the United States?

In so far as the use of the word "Jew" is concerned, the Press is almost completely dominated. The editor who uses it is certain to hear from it. He will be visited and told—contrary to everything the Jew is told—that the word "Jew" denotes a member of a religious denomination and not a member of a race, and that its use with reference to any person spoken of in the public prints is as reprehensible as if "Baptist," "Catholic," or "Episcopalian" were used.

The Jew is always told by his leaders that regardless of religion or country of birth, he is a Jew, the member of a race by virtue of blood. Pages of this paper could be filled with the most authoritative Jewish statements on this point. But what the Jew is told by his leaders, and what the Gentile editor is told by the Jewish committee are two different and antagonistic things. A Jewish paper may shriek to the skies that Professor So-and-So, or Judge So-and-So, or Senator So-and-So is a Jew, but the secular newspaper that should do that would be visited by an indignant committee bearing threats.

A certain newspaper, as a mere matter of news, published an excerpt from one of *The Dearborn Independent* articles. Next day a number of advertising accounts dropped for lack of copy. Inquiry developed the fact that the reticent advertisers were all Jewish firms and the cause of their action was the really unimportant excerpt which the paper published. It developed also that the advertising agent who handled all the advertising for those Jewish firms was himself a Jew who also held an office in a Jewish secret society, which office was concerned exclusively with the control of newspapers in the matter of Jewish publicity. It was this man who dealt with the editor. A lame editorial retraction followed which faintly praised the Jews. The advertising was returned to the paper, and it is just a question whether that editor was rightly handled or not. Certainly he has been made to feel the power. But the diplomacy of it was bad. The editor, along with hundreds of others, has only been given the proper background for estimating the Jewish power in its wider reaches.

This is not to say that every editor should enter upon a campaign to expose the secret power. That is a matter for personal decision. Every editor, however, is so situated that he can see certain things, and he ought to see them, note them, and inwardly digest them.

Jewish publicity in response to these articles is very easy to get in almost any newspaper. Some have fallen most lamentably for lying statements. Others have opened their columns to propaganda sent out from Jewish sources. That is all very well. But the Gentile interest in the question has been largely ignored, even in cases where the editors are awake to the whole Question. This too affords a vantage from which the average editor can view what is transpiring in this country.

If a list of the Jewish owners, bondholders and other interests in our newspapers should be published the list would be impressive. But it would not account for the widespread control of the Press as observed in this country. Indeed, it would be unfair in such a connection as this to list some of the Jewish-owned newspapers of the United States, because their owners are fair and public-spirited servants of the people.

Actual ownership does not often account for much in a newspaper. Ownership in the newspaper business in not always synonymous with control.

If you wish to know the control of the newspaper, look to its attorney and the interests he serves; look to the social connections of its chief editors; look to the advertising agents who handle the bulk of Jewish advertising; and then look to the matter of the paper's partisanship or independence in politics.

Newspaper control of the Press by the Jews is not a matter of money. It is a matter of keeping certain things out of the public mind and putting certain things into it. One absolute condition insisted upon with the daily Press is that it shall not identify the Jew, mention him, or in any but the most favorable way call the public's attention to his existence.

The first plea for this is based on "fairness," on the false statement that a Jew is not a Jew but a church member. This is the same statement which Jewish agents in the United States Government have used for years to prevent the United States Government from listing the Jews in any racial statistics. It is in direct contradiction to what the Jews themselves are told. A flabby "fairness," a sloppy "broad-mindedness," a cry of "religious prejudice," is the first plea. The second is a sudden cessation of Jewish patronage. The third is withdrawal of patronage by every Gentile concern that is under the grip of Jewish financiers. It is a mere matter of brutal bludgeoning. And the fourth act, in a community thoroughly blinded to the Jewish Question, is the collapse of the offending publication.

Read the *Jewish Encyclopedia* for a list of some of the papers which dared open up the Question, and ceased!

When old Baron Moses Montefiore said at Krakau:

"What are you prating about? As long as we do not have the press of the whole world in our hands, everything you may do is vain. We must control or influence the papers of the whole world in order to blind and deceive the people."—he knew what he was saying. By "blinding" the people he only meant that they should not see the Jew, and by "deceiving" them he only meant that the people should think certain world movements meant one thing when they really meant another. The people may be told what happens: they may not be told what was behind it. The people do not yet know why certain occurrences which have affected their whole lives, should have occurred at all. But the "why" of it is very definitely known in certain circles whose news service never sees print, and sometimes not even writing.

Statistics as to the space given the Jews by newspapers concerning things they want to get into print would also be an eye-opener. A minority nation, they get more publicity than any ten of the important minor nations of Europe—of the kind of publicity they want!

The number of Jewish contributors to the Press of the United States makes another interesting statistical bit. It would be sheer prejudice to make objectionable mention of many Jewish journalists and writers, and they come within the scope of this study only as they have shown themselves to be the watchful agents and active servants of the System. This is what many of them are. Not the ambitious young Jewish reporter who runs around the streets gathering news, perhaps, but the journalist at the seat of the news and at the necks of those two or three important international runways through which the news of the world flows.

The whole matter, as far as extent of control is concerned, could be visualized on a map of the United States, by means of colored pins showing the number of Jewish-owned, provably Jewish-controlled papers, and the number of Jewish writers who are directing the majority thought of the various sections of the country.

The Jewish journalist who panders to unrest, whose literary ambition is to maintain a ferment in his readers, whose humor is sordid and whose philosophy is one of negation; as well as the Jewish novelist who extols his or her own people even while the story sows subtle seeds of disruption in Gentile social or economic life must be listed as the agents of that World Program which would break down society through the agency of "ideas." And it is very striking how many there are, and how skillfully they conceal their propaganda in their work.

Here and there in the United States it is now becoming possible to print the word "Jew" in the headlines of an article, and tell the Jewish committee which calls the next day that this is yet a free country. Quietly a number of newspapers have tested the strength of this assumed control in their communities, and have discounted it.

There is no reason for fear on the part of the editor who has his facts. But the editor who backs down will more and more feel the pressure upon him. The man who courageously and fairly holds his ground will soon learn another thing that is not so generally known, namely, that with all the brilliance there is a lot of bluff, and that the chain of control once broken is felt throughout the whole system as a blow.

There is nothing that the International Jew fears so much as the truth, or any hint of the truth about himself or his plans. And, after all, the rock of refuge and defense, the foundation of endurance for Jew or Gentile must be the Truth.

The Dearborn Independent, September 11, 1920

18. Does This Explain Jewish Political Power?

Little has yet been said in this commentary on the Protocols about the political program contained in them. It is desirable that the points be taken separately in order that when our study turns to actual conditions in this country, the reader may be in a position to judge whether the written program agrees with the acted program as it may be seen all about us. The World Program as outlined in these strange documents turns upon many points, some of which have already been discussed. Its success is sought (a) by securing financial control of the world, this having already been secured by the overwhelming indebtedness of every nation through wars, and by the capitalistic (not the manufacturing or managerial) control of industry; (b) by securing political control, which is easily illustrated by the condition of every civilized country today; (c) by securing control of education, a control which has been steadily won under the blinded eyes of the people; (d) by trivializing the public mind through a most complete system of allurement which has just brought us into a period which requires the new word "jazz" to describe it; and (e) by the sowing of seeds of disruption everywhere—not the seeds of progress, but of economic fallacies and revolutionary temper. All of these main objectives entail various avenues of action, none of which has been overlooked by the Protocols.

In leading up to what the Protocols have to say about the selection and control of Presidents, it will be enlightening to take the views which these documents express about other phases of politics.

It may be very interesting to those Jewish apologists, who in all their pronouncements never discuss the contents of the Protocols, to know that so far from their being a plea for monarchy, they are a plea for the most drastic and irresponsible liberalism in government. The powers behind the Protocols appear to have absolute confidence in what they can do with the people once the people are made to believe that popular government has really arrived.

The Protocols believe in frequent change. They like elections; they approve frequent revisions of constitutions; they counsel the people to change their representatives often.

Take this from the First Protocol:

"The abstract conception of Liberty made it possible for us to convince the crowd that government is only the management for the owner of the country, the people, and that the steward can be changed like a pair of worn-out gloves. The possibility of changing the representatives of the people has placed them at our disposal and, as it were, has placed them in our power as creatures of our purposes." Note also how this Use of Change is buried in this paragraph from the Fourth Protocol, which describes the evolution of a Republic:

"Every republic passes through several stages. The first is that of senseless ravings, resembling those of a blind man throwing himself from right to left. The second is that of demagogy, which breeds anarchy and inevitably leads to despotism, not of a legal, open and consequently responsible character, but an unseen and unknown despotism, felt none the less because exercised by a secret organization. Such a despotism acts with even less scruple because it is hidden under cover and works behind the backs of various agents, the shifting and changing of which will not harm its secret power, but serve it, since such changes will relieve the organization from the necessity of expending its resources on rewards for long service."

This "changing" of servants is not unknown in the United States.

A former Senator of the United States could easily testify to this if he only knew who did the "changing." Time was when he was the tool of every Jewish lobbyist in the Senate. His glib tongue lent charm and plausibility to every argument they wished to advance against the government's intentions.

Secretly, however, the Senator was receiving "favors" from a very high source, "favors" of a financial character. The time came when it was desirable to "detach" the Senator. The written record of his "favors" was abstracted from its place of supposed secrecy, a newspaper system that has always been the ready organ of American Jewry made the exposure, and an indignant public did the rest.

It could not have been done had not the man been compromised first; it could not have been done without certain newspaper connivance; it would never have been done had not the Senator's masters wished it. However, it was done.

In the Fourteenth Protocol, which begins "When we become rulers," it is pictured how hopeless the Gentile peoples will have become of any betterment of conditions through changes of government, and therefore will accept the promise of stability which the Protocolists of that time will be prepared to offer:

"The masses will become so satiated with the endless changes of administration which we instigated among the Gentiles when we were undermining their governmental institutions, that they will tolerate anything from us . . . "

The official who is changed most quickly in this country is the man who questions certain matters which come from Jewish sources.

There must be a small army of such men in the United States today. Some of them do not know even now how it happened. Some are still wondering why perfectly legitimate and patriotic information should have been lost in an icy silence when they sent it in, and why they should have lost favor for sending it.

Protocol Nine is full of the most amazing claims, of which these may serve as illustration:

"At the present time, if any government raises a protest against us, it is only for the sake of form, it is under our control, and it is done by our direction, for their anti-Semitism is necessary for keeping in order our lesser brothers. I will not explain this further as already it has been the subject of numerous discussions between us."

This doctrine of the usefulness of anti-Semitism and the desirability of creating it where it does not exist are found in the words of Jewish leaders, ancient and modern.

"In reality there are no obstacles before us. Our super-government has such an extra-legal status that it may be called by the energetic and strong word—dictatorship. I can conscientiously say that at the present time we are the lawmakers."

In that Protocol this claim is made:

"De facto, we have already eliminated every government except our own, although de jure there are still many others left."

That is simple: the governments still exist, under their own names, having authority over their own people; but the super-government has unchallenged influence over all of them in matters pertaining to the Jewish Nation and particularly in matters pertaining to the purpose of The International Jew.

The Eighth Protocol shows how this can be:

"For the time being, until it will be safe to give responsible government positions to our brother Jews, we shall entrust them to people whose past and whose character are such that there is an abyss between them and the people; to people, for whom, in case of disobedience to our orders, there will remain only trial or exile (from public life), thus forcing them to protect our interest to their last breath."

In the Ninth Protocol again is this reference to party funds:

"The division into parties has placed them all at our disposal, inasmuch as in order to carry on a party struggle it is necessary to have money, and we have it all."

There have been many investigations of campaign funds. None has ever yet gone deep enough to inquire into the "international" sources of these funds.

Now, in the United States during the last five years we have seen an almost complete Judaized administration in control of all the war activities of the American people. The function of the regularly organized United States Government during that time was practically confined to the voting of money. But the administration of the business end of the war was in charge of a government within a government, and this inner, extra government was Jewish.

It is, of course, often asked why this was so. The first answer given is that the Jews who were immediately placed in charge of the business administration of the war were competent men, the most competent men who could be found.

This was actually the answer given to an inquiry as to the reason for so large a part of the foreign policy of the United States depending on the counsel of a certain group of Jews they were the men who knew, no one else knew so much, the officials chosen by the people had a right to select the most efficient and able counsel they could find.

Very well, let that stand. Let the explanation be that in all the United States, Jews were the only persons to be found who could handle the emergency with masterly ease. We shall see more of this phase of the matter at another time. The war is not under discussion in this article, merely the fact that in an emergency the government became distinctly Jewish. But the Second Protocol would appear to throw a little light on the matter.

"The administrators chosen by us from the masses for their servility will not be persons trained for government, and consequently they will easily become pawns in our game, played by our learned and talented counsellors, specialists educated from early childhood to administer world affairs. As we know, our specialists have been acquiring the necessary knowledge for governing...."

Does This Explain Jewish Political Power?

The language is a trifle raw, as it usually is when Gentiles are under discussion. But the same fact, namely, that Jewish specialists have come to the aid of Gentile administrators in an emergency, when uttered for the consideration of the general public, may be very beautifully phrased.

The untrained Gentile administrator must have help; his unpreparedness makes it necessary. And who knows it better than those who have the help to offer? The Gentile public has been taught to suspect the man who has had experience in politics or government. This, of course, makes the whole situation doubly easy for those whose speciality it is to give "aid." Just what interests they aid most will give, when discovered, a strong light upon their zeal.

But in all that the Protocols have to say about the political angle of the World Program, nothing is of so great interest as that which concerns the selection and control of Presidents. The whole plan is outlined in the Tenth Protocol. The fact that the President of France seems to have been in mind is a localism; the plan is applicable elsewhere; indeed has elsewhere its most perfect illustration.

This Tenth Protocol, then, leads gradually up to the subject, tracing the evolution of rulers from Autocrat to President, and of nations from Monarchies to Republics.

The language of this passage is particularly objectionable, but no more so than can be found in current Jewish literature where boasting of power is indulged in. Unpleasant as the whole attitude is, it is valuable as showing in just what light the supporters of the Protocol Program view the Gentiles and their dignities. It must be born in mind that the Jewish ideal is not a President, but a Prince and a King. The Jewish students of Russia marched the streets in 1918 singing this hymn—

"We have given you a God;

Now we will give you a King."

The new flag of Palestine, now permitted to fly without hindrance, bears insignia, as does every synagogue, of a Jewish King. The Jewish hope is that the Throne of David shall be set up again, as doubtless it will be. None of these things is to be decried in the least, nor to be regarded with anything but a decent respect, but they should be borne in mind as a side light on the expressed contempt for Gentile Presidents and Legislatures.

The Tenth Protocol reaches the theme of President thus:

"Then the rise of the republican era became possible, and then in the place of a sovereign we substituted a caricature of him, a President picked from the crowd ... Such was the foundation of the mine we laid underneath the Gentile people, or more accurately, the Gentile peoples."

It is with something of a shock that one reads that men with a "past" are specially favored for the presidential office. Men with a "past" have become President in various countries, including the United States, there is no doubt of that. In some instances, the particular scandal that constituted the "past" has been publicly known; in other cases it has been hushed up and lost in a maze of rumor. In at least one case it was made the special property of a syndicate of men who, while protecting the official from public knowledge, compelled him to pay rather stiffly for their service. Men with a "past" are not uncommon, and it is not always the "past" but the concealment of it that concerns them most, and in this lack of frankness, this distrust of the understanding and mercy of the people, they usually fall into another slavery, namely, the slavery of political or financial blackmail.

"We will manipulate the election of Presidents whose past contains some undisclosed dark affair, some 'Panama,' then they will be faithful executors of our orders from fear of exposure and from the natural desire of every man who has attained a position of authority to retain the privileges, emoluments and the dignity associated with the position of President."

The use of the word "Panama" here refers to the various scandals which arose in French political circles over the original efforts to construct the Panama Canal. If the present form of the Protocols had been written at a later date they might have referred to the "Marconi wireless" scandals in England—though on second thought, they would not have done so because certain men were involved who were not Gentiles. Herzl, the great Jewish Zionist leader, uses the expression in "The Jewish State." Speaking of the management of the business of Palestine he says that the Society of the Jews "will see to it that the enterprise does not become a Panama but a Suez." That the same expression should occur in Herzl and in the Protocols is significant; it has also another significance, which will be described at another time. It must be clear to the reader, however, that no one writing for the general public at this day would refer to a "Panama" in a man's past. The reference would not be understood.

It is this practice of holding a man under obligation which makes it needful on the part of the true publicist to tell the truth and the whole truth about aspirants for public office. It is not enough to say of a candidate that he "began as a poor boy" and then became "successful."

Does This Explain Jewish Political Power?

How did he become successful? How explain the "rise" of his fortunes? Sometimes the clue leads deep into the domestic life of the candidate. It may be told of a man, for example, that he helped another out of a scrape by marrying the woman involved, and received a sum of money for doing so. It may be told of another that he was implicated by his too friendly relations with another's wife, but was relieved of his predicament by the astute diplomacy of powerful friends, to whom thereafter he felt himself in debt of honor. It is strange that, in American affairs at least, the woman-note is predominant. In our higher offices that has more frequently occurred than any other, oftener than the money-note.

In European countries, however, where the fact of a man's being entangled illegitimately with a woman does not carry so heavy a stamp of shame with it, the controlled men have been found to have "pasts" of another character.

The whole subject is extremely distasteful, but truth has its surgical duties to perform, and this is one of them. When, for example, a pivotal assemblage like that of the Peace Conference is studied, and the men who are most subject to the Jewish influence are isolated, and their past history is carefully traced, there is almost no difficulty whatever in determining the precise moment when they passed over into that fateful condition which, while it did not hinder them of public honors for one hour, made them unchangeably the servants of a power the public did not see.

The puzzling spectacle which the observer sees of the great leaders of Anglo-Saxon races closely surrounded and continuously counseled by the princes of the Semitic race, is explained only by knowledge of those leaders' "past" and those words of the Protocols—"We will manipulate the election of Presidents whose past contains some undisclosed dark affair." And where this Jewish domination of officials is glaringly apparent, it may be safely assumed that the custody of the secret is almost entirely with that race. When necessity arises, it may be a public service for those in possession of the facts to make them public—not for the purpose of destroying reputations, but for the purpose of damning for all time a most cowardly practice.

Politically, so the Jewish publicists tell us, Jews do not vote as a group. Because of this so we are told, they have no political influence. Moreover, we are told, they are so divided among themselves that they cannot be led in one direction. It may be true that when it is a question of being for anything, the Jewish community may show a majority and minority opinion—a small minority, it is likely to be. But when it becomes a question of being against anything, the Jewish community is always a unit.

These are facts to which any ward politician can testify. Any man in political life can test it for himself by announcing that he will not permit himself to be dominated by Jews or anybody else. Just let him mention Jews in that manner; he will no longer have to read about Jewish solidarity; he will have felt it. Not that, in a vote, the Jewish solidarity can accomplish anything it wishes; the Jew's political strength is not in his vote, but in the "pull" of, say, seven men at the seat of government. The Jews, a political minority so far as votes are concerned, were a political majority so far as influence was concerned, during the last five years. They ruled. They boast that they ruled. The mark of their rule is everywhere.

The note which everyone observes in politics, as in the Press, is the fear of the Jews. This fear is such that nowhere are the Jews discussed as are, say, the Armenians, the Germans, the Russians, or the Hindoos. What is this fear but reflection of the knowledge of the Jews' power and their ruthlessness in the use of it? It is possibly true, as many Jewish publicists say, that what is called anti-Semitism is just a panic-fear. It is a dread of the unknown. The uncanny spectacle of an apparently poor people who are richer than all, of a very small minority which is more powerful than all, creates phantoms before the mind.

It is very significant that those who most assume to represent the Jews are quite content that the fear should exist. They wish it to exist. To keep it delicately poised and always there, though not too obtrusively, is an art they practice. But once the balance is threatened, their crudeness instantly appears. Then comes the threat, by which it is hoped to reestablish the fear again. When the threat fails, there comes the wail of anti-Semitism.

How strange this is, that the Jews should not see that the most abject form of anti-Semitism is just this fear which they are willing to have felt toward them by their neighbors. This fear is "Semitophobia" in its worst form. To inspire fear—what is more dreaded by the normal man, and yet what more delights an inferior race?

Now, a great service is done when the people are emancipated from this fear. It is the process of emancipation that Jewish publicists attack. It is this they call anti-Semitism. It is not anti-Semitism at all; it is the only course that can prevent anti-Semitism. The process involves several steps. The extent of the Jewish power must be shown. To this, of course, strong Jewish objection is made, though no strong disproof can be made.

Then the existence of this power must be explained. It can be explained only by the Jewish Will to Power, as it may be called, or by the deliberate program which is followed in the attainment of the power. When the method is explained, half the damage is undone. The Jew is not a superman. He is bright, he is intense, his philosophy of material things leaves him free to do many things from which his neighbor draws back; but, given equal advantages, he is not a superman. The Yankee is more than his equal any time, but the Yankee has an inborn inclination to observe the rules of the game. When the people know by what means this power is gained—when they are informed how, for example, political control is seized, as it has been in the United States, the very method takes all the glamour from the power, and shows it to be a rather sordid thing after all.

This series of articles is attempting to take these orderly steps, and it is believed the complete effort will justify itself to reasonable minds, both Jewish and Gentile. In the present article one important means of power has been described on the authority of the Protocols. Whether the method laid down by the Protocols is worth considering or not depends entirely on whether it can be found in actual affairs today. It can be found. The two tally. The parallel is complete. It were well for the Jew, of course, if no trace of him could be found in either the written or the actual program. But he is there, and it is illogical for him to blame anyone but himself for being there. Certainly, it is small defense against the fact to heap abuse upon the one who discloses the fact. We have agreed that the Jews are clever, but they are not so clever as to be able to cover their work. There is a certain element of weakness in them which reveals the whole matter in the end. And even the revelation would not mean much if the thing revealed were not wrong. But that is the weakness of the Jewish program it is wrong. The Jews have never gained any measure of success so great that the world cannot check it. The world is engaged in a great checking tactic now, and if there are still prophets among the Jews they should lead their people in another path.

The proof and the fruit of any exposure of the World Program is the removal of the element of fear from the peoples among whom the Jews live.

The Dearborn Independent, September 18, 1920

"In a world of completely organized territorial sovereignties he (the Jew) has only two possible cities of refuge; he must either pull down the pillars of the whole national state system, or he must create a territorial sovereignty of his own . . . . In Eastern Europe, Bolshevism and Zionism seem to grow side by side . . . . not because the Jew cares for the positive side of radical philosophy, not because he desires to be a partaker in Gentile nationalism or Gentile democracy, but because no existing Gentile system is ever anything but distasteful to him."

19. The All-Jewish Mark on "Red Russia"

We shall now briefly interrupt the commentary which we have been making on the Protocols to set at rest once and for all certain misstatements which are made for Gentile consumption.

To learn what the Jewish leaders of the United States or any other country think, do not read their addresses to the Gentiles; read their addresses to their own people. On such matters as these—Whether the Jew regards himself as destined to rule the world; whether he regards himself as belonging to a nation and race distinct from every other nation and race; whether he regards the Gentile world as the legitimate field of his exploitation by a lower moral method than is permissible among his own people; whether he knows and shares the principles of the Protocols—on such matters as these, the only safe guide is to be found in the words which Jewish leaders speak to Jews, not in the words they speak to Gentiles.

The notable Jewish names which appear oftenest in the Press do not represent the spokesmen of Judaism at all, but only a selected few who represent the Department of Propaganda Among the Gentiles. Sometimes that propaganda is in the form of donations for Christian charitable organizations; sometimes it is in the form of "liberal" opinion on religious, social and political questions. In whatever form it comes, you may depend upon it that the real activities of the Jewish hierarchy proceed under cover of that which the Gentile is invited to observe and approve.

The statements offered in this series are never made without the strictest and fullest proof, confirmation and corroboration in the utterances of Jewish leaders. This is one of the strange features of the multitude of Jewish attacks on this series: they are attacking what they themselves stand for, and their only reason for the attack must be their belief that this investigation has not been able to penetrate through to that which has been kept hidden from the world.

The most persistent denials have been offered to the statement that Bolshevism everywhere, in Russia or the United States, is Jewish. In these denials we have perhaps one of the most brazen examples of the double intent referred to above. The denial of the Jewish character of Bolshevism is made to the Gentile; but in the confidence and secrecy of Jewish communication, or buried in the Yiddish dialect, or obscurely hidden in the Jewish national press, we find the proud assertion made to their own people!—that Bolshevism is Jewish.

Jewish propaganda has only two straws to grasp in the terrible tale of murder, immorality, robbery, enforced starvation and hideous humanism which make the present Russian situation impossible to describe and all but impossible to comprehend.

One of these straws is that Kerensky, the man who eased in the opening wedge of Bolshevism, is not a Jew. Indeed, one of the strongest indications that Bolshevism is Jewish is that the Jewish press emphasizes so fiercely the alleged Gentilism of a least two of the revolutionary notables. It may be cruel to deny them two among hundreds, but merely saying so cannot change Kerensky's nationality. His name is Adler. His father was a Jew and his mother a Jewess. Adler, the father, died, and the mother married a Russian named Kerensky, whose name the young child took. Among the radicals who employed him as a lawyer, among the forces that put him forward to drive the first nail into Russia's cross, among the soldiers who fought with him, his Jewish descent and character have never been doubted.

"Well, but there is Lenin," our Jewish publicists say—"Lenin the head of it all, the brains of it all, and Lenin is a Gentile! We've got you there—Lenin is a Gentile!"

Perhaps he is, but why do his children speak Yiddish? Why are his proclamations put forth in Yiddish? Why did he abolish the Christian Sunday and establish by law the Jewish Saturday Sabbath?

The explanation of all this may be that he married a Jewess. The fact is that he did. But another explanation may be that he himself is a Jew. Certainly he is not the Russian nobleman he has always claimed to be. The statements he has made about his identity thus far have been lies. The claim that he is a Gentile may be unfounded too.

No one has ever doubted Trotsky's nationality—he is a Jew. His name is Braunstein. Recently the Gentiles were told that Trotsky had said he wasn't much of anything—in religion. That may be. But still he must be something—else why are the Russian Christian churches turned into stables, slaughter houses and dancing halls, while the Jewish synagogues remain untouched? And why are Christian priests and ministers made to work on roads, while Jewish rabbis are left their clerical privileges?

Trotsky may not be much of anything in religion, but he is a Jew nevertheless.

This is not mere Gentile insistence that he shall be considered a Jew whether or no; it is straight Jewish teaching that he is. In a future discussion on "religion or race?" we shall show that even without

Table Showing Jewish Control of Russia			
Body	Number of Members	Number of Jewish Members	Jewish Percentage
The Council of the Commissaries of the People	22	17	77.2%
The Commissariat of War	43	33	76.7%
The Commissariat of Foreign Affairs	16	13	81.2%
The Commissariat of Finance	30	24	80.0%
The Commissariat of Justice	21	20	95.2%
The Commissariat of Public Instruction	53	42	79.2%
The Commissariat of Social Assistance	6	6	100.0%
The Commissariat of Work	8	7	87.5%
Delegates of the Bolshevik Red Cross to Berlin, Vienna, Varsovie, Bucharest, Copenhagen	8	8	100.0%
Commissaries of the Provinces	23	21	91.3%
Journalists	41	41	100.0%

The All-Jewish Mark on "Red Russia"

religion, Trotsky is, and is considered by all Jewish authorities to be, a Jew.

An apology must be made here for repeating well-known facts. Yet, so many people are not even now aware of the true meaning of Bolshevism, that at the risk of monotony, we shall cite a few of the salient facts. The purpose, however, is not alone to explain Russia, but to throw a warning light on conditions in the United States.

The Bolshevik Government, as it stood late this summer when the latest report was smuggled through to certain authorities, shows up the Jewish domination of the whole affair. It has changed very slightly since the beginning. We give only a few items to indicate the proportion. It must not be supposed that the non-Jewish members of the government are Russian.

Very few Russians have anything to say about their own country these days. The so-called "Dictatorship of the Proletariat," in which the proletariat has nothing whatever to say, is Russian only in the sense that it is set up in Russia; it is not Russian in that it springs from or includes the Russian people. It is the international program of the Protocols, which might be "put over" by a minority in any country, and which is being given a dress-rehearsal in Russia.

[The table on the previous page has] enlightening figures. The reader will note that the Jewish percentage is high at all times, never lower than 76 per cent in any case.

(Curiously enough, the lowest percentage of Jews is found in the Commissariat of War.) But in those committees which deal most closely with the mass of the people, as well as in the committees of defense and propaganda, Jews fill literally all the places.

Remember what the Protocols say about Press control: remember what Baron Montefiore said about it, and then look at the Government Journalists. That committee comprises 41 men, and the 41 are Jews. Only Jewish pens are trusted with Bolshevist propaganda.

And then the so-called "Red Cross delegates," which are merely Red Revolutionary delegates to the cities named—of the 8, there are 8 Jews.

The Commissariat of Social Assistance, upon whose word the life and privilege of tens of thousands hang—there are 6 members, and the 6 are Jews. And so on through the list.

Out of the 53 members of the Commissariat of Public Instruction, 11 are noted as non-Jews. But what kind of non-Jews is not stated. They may be "non-Jews like Lenin" whose children speak the Yiddish as their native tongue. Whatever they are, there is a sidelight upon their attitude in the fact that the Bolsheviki immediately took over all the Hebrew schools and continued them as they were and laid down a rule that the ancient Hebrew language should be taught in them. The ancient Hebrew language is the vehicle of the deeper secrets of the World Program.

And for the Gentile Russian children—? "Why," said these gentle Jewish educators, "we will teach them sex knowledge. We will brush out of their minds the cobwebs. They must learn the truth about things!"—with consequences that are too pitiable to narrate. But this can be said: unquestionably there were deaths among innocent Jews when Hungary wrested itself free from the Red Bolshevism of Bela Kun (or Cohen). The Jews may well call it the "White Terror" that followed their failure to re-enact the tragedy of Russia in Hungary. But there are mountains of evidence to show that nothing had so potent an effect in producing the bloodshed of the "White Terror" as the outraged minds of parents whose children had been compulsorily drawn through sloughs of filth during the short time the Jewish Bolsheviki had charge of the schools.

American Jews do not like to hear this. Their shrinking from it would be greatly to their honor did they not immediately return to the defense of the people who do these things. It is well enough known that the chastity of Christians is not so highly regarded by the orthodox male Jew as is the chastity of his own people, but it would be pleasant to be certain that all of them condemn what went on in Russia and Hungary in the matter of education. However, as most of the influences which destroy Gentile youth today—in America—are in the hands of the Jews, and as it is plainly stated in the Protocols that one of the lines of campaign is "to corrupt the youth of the Gentiles," the situation is one that calls for something more than mere hard feelings and angry denials whenever these facts are referred to.

It is not the economic experiment, so-called, that one objects to in Russia; it is not the fallacies, the sad delusion of the people. No. It is the downright dirty immorality, the brutish nastiness of it all; and the line which the immorality and nastiness draws between Jew and Gentile. The horrible cruelty involved we will not deal with, leaving it merely with the explanation which has found utterance in the Jewish press that "it may be that the Jew in Russia is taking an unconscious revenge for his centuries of suffering."

"But," asks some reader, "how may we know that all this is true?"

Bearing in mind that we are speaking of Russia, not for the interest of

The All-Jewish Mark on "Red Russia"

the Russian situation at all, but to indicate the international character of those who are responsible for conditions there, and to identify them for the protection of the United States, we shall look at the evidence.

There is, of course, the evidence brought to light by our own United States Senate and printed in a Report of the Committee on the Judiciary. We do not wish to spend much time on this, because we prefer in these articles to use Jewish testimony instead of Gentile. But we shall pause long enough to show the nature of the testimony brought out by our own government.

Dr. George A. Simons, a clergyman in charge of an American congregation in Petrograd at the time the Bolshevik terror broke out, was a witness. Parts of his testimony are given here:

"'There were hundreds of agitators who followed in the trail of Trotsky-Bronstein, these men having come over from the lower East Side of New York . . . A number of us were impressed by the strange Yiddish element in this thing right from the start, and it soon became evident that more than half the agitators in the so-called Bolshevik movement were Yiddish.'

"Senator Nelson—'Hebrews?'

"Dr. Simons—'They were Hebrews, apostate Jews. I do not want to say anything against the Jews, as such. I am not in sympathy with the anti-Semitic movement, never have been, and do not ever expect to be . . . But I have a firm conviction that this thing is Yiddish, and that one of its bases is found in the East Side of New York.'

"Senator Nelson—'Trotsky came over from New York during that summer, did he not?'

"Dr. Simons—'He did.'

"Later Dr. Simons said: 'In December, 1918 . . . under the presidency of a man known as Apfelbaum . . . out of 388 members, only 16 happened to be real Russians, and all the rest Jews, with the exception possibly of one man, who is a Negro from America, who calls himself Professor Gordon . . . and 265 of this northern commune government that is sitting in the Old Smolny Institute came from the lower East Side of New York—265 of them. . . .

"'I might mention this, that when the Bolsheviki came into power, all over Petrograd we at once had a predominance of Yiddish proclamations, big posters, and everything in Yiddish. It became very evident that now that was to be one of the great languages of Russia; and the real Russians, of course, did not take very kindly to it.'"

William Chapin Huntington, who was commercial attache of the United States Embassy at Petrograd, testified:

"The leaders of the movement, I should say, are about two-thirds Russian Jews... The Bolsheviks are internationalists, and they were not interested in the particular national ideals of Russia."

William W. Welch, an employee of the National City Bank, New York, testified:

"In Russia it is well known that three-fourths of the Bolshevik leaders are Jewish... There were some—not many, but there were some real Russians; and what I mean by real Russians is Russian-born, and not Russian Jews."

Roger E. Simmons, Trade Commissioner connected with the United States Department of Commerce, also testified. An important anonymous witness, whom the committee permitted to withhold his name, told the same things.

The British White Book, Russia, No. 1—"A Collection of Reports on Bolshevism in Russia, presented to Parliament by Command of His Majesty, April, 1919," contains masses of the same testimony from many sources, all of them eyewitnesses.

In that very highly respected magazine Asia for February-March, 1920, is an article which contains, among other important ones, these statements: (the italics are ours)

"In all the Bolshevist institutions the heads are Jews. The Assistant Commissar for Elementary Education, Grunberg, can hardly speak Russian. The Jews are successful in everything and obtain their ends. They know how to command and get complete submission. But they are proud and contemptuous toward everyone, which strongly excites the people against them... At the present time there is a great national religious fervor among the Jews. They believe that the promised time of the rule of God's elect on earth is coming. They have connected Judaism with a universal revolution. They see in the spread of revolution the fulfilling of the Scriptures: 'Though I make an end of all the nations whither I have scattered thee, yet will I not make an end of thee.'"

Now if Gentile proof were wanted, the files of the *The Dearborn Independent* for a whole year would not begin to contain it. But Jewish proof is better.

There has been a strange vacillation in Jewish opinion concerning Bolshevism. At first it was hailed with delight. There was no concealment whatever in the early days of the new regime as to the part which Jewry

The All-Jewish Mark on "Red Russia"

had in it. Public meetings, interviews, special articles poured forth in which very valuable elements of truth were mingled. There was no attempt at concealment of names.

Then the horror of the thing began to take hold upon the world, and for just a breathing space Jewish opinion fell silent. There was a spasmodic denial or two. Then a new burst of glorification. The glorification continues within Judaism itself, but it now carries on the Gentile side of its face a very sad expression labeled "persecution."

We have lived to see the day when to denounce Bolshevism is to "persecute the Jews."

In the American Hebrew, for September 10, 1920, an article appears which not only acknowledges and explains the part which the Jew plays in the present unrest and upheaval, but justifies it—and justifies it, curiously enough, by The Sermon on the Mount.

The writer says that "the Jew evolved organized capitalism with its working instrumentality, the banking system."

This is very refreshing, in view of the numerous Jewish denials of this economic fact.

"One of the impressive phenomena of the impressive time is the revolt of the Jew against the Frankenstein which his own mind conceived and his own hand fashioned . . . " If this is true, why is Jewish "organized capital with its working instrumentality, the banking system" supporting the revolt?

"That achievement (referring to the Russian overthrow), destined to figure in history as the overshadowing result of the World War, was largely the outcome of Jewish thinking, of Jewish discontent, of Jewish effort to reconstruct."

"This rapid emergence of the Russian revolution from the destructive phase and its entrance into the constructive phase is a conspicuous expression of the constructive genius of Jewish discontent."

(This, of course, requires proof that the constructive phase has appeared. The implication here is sheer propaganda. The Protocols, however, have a reconstructive program. We have not reached it as yet in this series of articles, but it is clearly outlined in the Protocols—destroy the Gentile society, and then reconstruct it according to "our" plans.)

Now read carefully:

"What Jewish idealism and Jewish discontent have so powerfully contributed to accomplish in Russia, the same historic qualities of the Jewish mind and heart *are tending to promote in other countries."* Read that again. "What Jewish idealism and Jewish discontent have so powerfully contributed to accomplish in Russia!" Just what was that? And just how did it "powerfully contribute?"

And why are "Jewish idealism" and "Jewish discontent" always linked together? If you read the Protocols it is all very clear. Jewish idealism is the destruction of Gentile society and the erection of Jewish society. Was it not so in Russia?—Yiddish proclamations on the walls, the ancient Hebrew in the schools, Saturday substituted for Sunday, and the rabbis respected while the priests were put to work on the roads! All "powerfully contributed" to by murder, rapine, theft and starvation.

Our author is more candid than he realizes. He calls this linked idealism and discontent "the historic qualities of the Jewish mind." *The Dearborn Independent* is indebted to him for this clear confirmation of what it has been saying for some time.

But even that is not all. "These same historic qualities of the Jewish mind" which "contributed so powerfully to accomplish in Russia" the Red Terror still existing there, are declared by this author to be tending to promote the same sort of thing in other countries. He says so in so many words—"tending to promote in other countries."

But we knew that. The only difference is that when Gentiles said it, they were overwhelmed with the wildest abuse; but now a pro-Jewish writer says it in a leading Jewish publication. And he says it apologetically—listen to him:

"It was natural that . . . discontent in other parts of the world should find expression in overemphasis of issues and overstatement of aims."

What discontent? Jewish discontent, of course. Discontent with what? With any form of Gentile rule. And how did it find expression? "In overemphasis of issues and overstatement of aims." What were these issues and aims? To bring the Bolshevik revolution to the United States.

No, they did not overstate their aims; they exactly stated them they simply selected the wrong country, that's all.

There are Russian Bolshevists in this country now, hawking about the streets of New York the gold cigaret cases which they stole from Russian families, and the family jewels, the wedding and birthday rings, which they filched from Russian women. Bolshevism never got further than the pawnshop and burglar's "fence" idea. The proof of this traffic in stolen property is going to drive some people into hiding before long. It will be a long, long time before America will be taking orders in Yiddish, or American women will be giving up their jewels to "the chosen race."

However, that happens to be only the most recent acknowledgement that has come to hand. It is significant for its confession that "Jewish discontent" was "tending to promote" in "other countries" what it has "so powerfully contributed to accomplish in Russia."

And with such a link between the American Hebrew, Russian Bolshevism and the Protocols, there are still Jewish publicists with the crust to say that only crazy people could see the connection. Only blind people will not see it. But that is only a minor connection. This series of articles does not rest on anything so accidental as the Jewish New Year's apology for Bolshevism in the great Hebrew weekly of the United States.

The Dearborn Independent, September 25, 1920

"Out of the economic chaos, the discontent of the Jew evolved organized capital with its working instrumentality, the banking system . . . . "One of the impressive phenomena of the impressive time is the revolt of the Jew against the Frankenstein which his own mind conceived and his own hand fashioned. . . .

"That achievement (Russian Bolshevik revolution—Ed.), destined to figure in history as the over-shadowing result of the World War, was largely the outcome of Jewish thinking, of Jewish discontent, of Jewish effort to reconstruct . . . .

"What Jewish idealism and Jewish discontent have so powerfully contributed to accomplish in Russia, the same historic qualities of the Jewish mind and heart are tending to promote in other countries . . . .

"Shall America, like the Russia of the Czars, overwhelm the Jew with the bitter and baseless reproach of being a destroyer, and thus put him in the position of an irreconcilable enemy?

"Or shall America avail itself of Jewish genius as it avails itself of the peculiar genius of every other race? . . . .

"That is the question for the American people to answer."
—From an article in *The American Hebrew*, Sept. 10, 1920.

20. Jewish Testimony in Favor of Bolshevism

The American people will answer that question, and their answer will be against the disruptive genius of dissatisfied Jews. It is very well known that "what Jewish idealism and Jewish discontent have so powerfully contributed to accomplish in Russia" is also being attempted in the United States. Why did not the writer in the American Hebrew say the United States, instead of saying "the same historic qualities of the Jewish mind and heart are tending to promote in other countries."

"Jewish idealism and Jewish discontent" are not directed against capital. Capital is enlisted in their service. The only governmental order the Jewish effort is directed against is Gentile governmental order; and the only "capital" it attacks is Gentile capital.

Lord Eustace Percy who, if one may judge by the full and appreciative quotations of his words in the Jewish press, has the sanction of thinkers among the Jews, settles the first point. Discussing the Jewish tendency to revolutionary movements he says:

"In Eastern Europe Bolshevism and Zionism often seem to grow side by side, just as Jewish influence molded Republican and Socialist hought throughout the nineteenth century down to the Young Turk revolution in Constantinople hardly more than a decade ago—not because the Jew cares for the positive side of radical philosophy, not because he desires to be a partaker in Gentile nationalism or Gentile democracy, but because no existing Gentile system of government is ever anything but distasteful to him."

And that analysis is absolutely true. In Russia, the excuse was the czar; in Germany, the kaiser; in England it is the Irish question; in the numerous South American revolutions, where the Jews always had a ruling hand, no particular reason was thought necessary to be given; in the United States it is "the capitalistic class;" but always and everywhere it is, by the confession of their own spokesman, a distaste for any form whatsoever of Gentile government. The Jew believes that the world is his by right; he wants to collect his own, and the speediest way of doing so is the destruction of order by revolution—a destruction which is made possible by a long and clever campaign of loose and destructive ideas.

As to the second point, every reader can verify the fact from his own experience. Let him recall to his mind the capitalists who have been held up to public scorn in the Jew-controlled press of the United States and whom does he find them to be?

Whose forms have you seen caricatured with the dollar-mark in Hearst's papers? Are they Seligman, Kahn, Warburg, Schiff, Kuhn, Loeb & Company, or any of the others? No. These are Jewish bankers. The attack is never made on them. The names made most familiar to you by newspaper denunciation are the names of Gentile industrial and banking leaders—and Gentile leaders only—the principal ones being Morgan and Rockefeller.

It is a well-known fact that during the French Commune when men of wealth suffered severe losses in property, the Jewish Rothschilds were not injured to the extent of one pennyworth. It is also a well-known fact, capable of proof satisfactory to any ordinary mind, that the connections between Jewish financiers and the more dangerous revolutionary elements here in the United States are such that it is most unlikely that the former stand to lose anything in any event.

Under cover of the disorder in Russia at the present time, Jewish financiers are taking advantage of the stress of the people to gain control of all the strategic natural resources and municipal property, by methods which they fully expect to be legalized by Jewish courts when the present "Bolshevik regime" announces that it will give way to a "modified communism." The world hasn't seen the end of Bolshevism yet. Like the World War, Bolshevism cannot be interpreted until it is seen who profits most by it, and the profiteering is in full sway now. The enemy is Gentile capital. Not any other. And "all the wealth of the world is in our hands" is the unspoken slogan of every Jewish outbreak in the world today.

The quotation at the head if this article represents the position which the Jews are now ready to take with reference to the Russian Revolution. They have always been charged with responsibility for what has occurred in that unhappy country, but at first their spokesmen denied it. The denials were most indignant, and were usually accompanied by the typical plaint that the charge was "persecution." But the facts have been so overwhelming, and the government investigations have been so revealing, that denials have been abandoned.

For a while an attempt was made to distract attention from Russia by a tremendously powerful propaganda concerning the Jews in Poland. There are many indications that the Polish propaganda was undertaken as a "cover" for the immense immigration of Jews into the United States. It may be that some of our readers do not know it, but an endless stream of the most undesirable immigrants pours daily into the United States, tens of thousands of the same people whose presence has been the problem and menace of the governments of Europe.

Well, the Polish propaganda and the immigration movement are sailing along smoothly, and the United States Government is assured by the Jewish ring at Washington that everything is quiet along the Potomac (it is quiet there, quiet as the Jewish ring could wish), but still the Russian fact persists in calling for explanation.

And here is the explanation: The Jews created capitalism, we are told. But capitalism has proved itself ill-behaved. So now, the Jewish creators are going to destroy their creation. They have done so in Russia. And now, will the American people be good and let their Jewish benefactors do the same in America?

That is the new explanation, and typically Jewish again, it is coupled with a proposal for the United States—and a threat! If America refuses this particular service of the Jew, we "put him in a position of an irreconcilable enemy." See quotation at the head of this article.

But the Jews have not destroyed capitalism in Russia. When Lenin and Trotsky make their farewell bow and retire under the protective influence of the Jewish capitalists of the world, it will be seen that only

Gentile or Russian capital has been destroyed, and that Jewish capital has been enthroned.

What is the record? Documents printed by the United States Government contain this letter: Please note the date, the Jewish banker and the Jewish names:

"Stockholm, Sept. 21, 1917.

"To Mr. Raphael Scholan:

"Dear Comrade:—The banking house, M. Warburg, opened an account for the enterprise of Comrade Trotsky upon receipt of a telegram from the Chairman of the 'Rhein-Westphalian Syndicate.' A lawyer, probably Mr. Kestroff, obtained ammunition and organized the transportation of same, together with that of the money... to whom the sum demanded by Comrade Trotsky is to be handed.

"Fraternal Greetings!

"Furstenberg."

Long before that, an American Jewish financier was supplying the funds which carried revolutionary propaganda to thousands of Russian prisoners of war in Japanese camps.

It is sometimes said, by way of explaining the Bolshevik movement, that it was financed from Germany, a fact which was seized upon to supply war propaganda. It is true that part of the money came from Germany. It is true that part of the money came from the United States. It is the whole truth that Jewish finance in all the countries was interested in Bolshevism as an All-Jewish investment. For the whole period of the war, the Jewish World Program was cloaked under this or that national name—the blame being laid on the Germans by the Allies, and on the Allies by the Germans, and the people kept in ignorance of who the real personages were.

It was stated by a French official that two millions of money was contributed by one Jewish banker alone.

When Trotsky left the United States to fulfill his appointed task, he was released from arrest at Halifax upon request of the United States, and everyone knows who constituted the War Government of the United States.

The conclusion, when all the facts are considered, is irresistible, that the Bolshevik revolution was a carefully groomed investment on the part of International Jewish Finance.

It is easy to understand, then, why the same forces would like to introduce it to the United States. The real struggle in this country is not between labor and capital; the real struggle is between Jewish capital and Gentile capital, with the I.W.W. leaders, the Socialist leaders, the Red leaders and the labor leaders almost a unit on the side of the Jewish capitalists.

Again recall which financiers these men most attack. You cannot recall a single Jewish name.

The main purpose in these two articles, however, is to introduce the Jewish testimony which exists as to the Jewish nature of Bolshevism.

The *Jewish Chronicle*, of London, said in 1919:

"There is much in the fact of Bolshevism itself, in the fact that so many Jews are Bolsheviks, in the fact that the ideals of Bolshevism at many points are consonant with the finest ideals of Judaism."

In the same paper, of 1920, is a report of an address made by Israel Zangwill, a noted Jewish writer, in which he pronounced glowing praise on "the race which has produced a Beaconsfield, a Reading, a Montagu, a Klotz, a Kurt Eisner, a Trotsky." Mr. Zangwill, in his swelling Semitic enthusiasm, embraced the Jews in the British Government in the same category with the Jews of the Hungarian and Russian Bolshevik governments. What is the difference? They are all Jewish, and all of equal honor and usefulness to "the race."

Rabbi J. L. Magnes, in an address at New York in 1919, is reported to have said:

"When the Jew gives his thought, his devotion, to the cause of the workers and of the dispossessed, of the disinherited of the world, the radical quality within him goes to the roots of things, and in Germany he becomes a Marx and a Lassalle, a Haas and an Edward Bernstein; in Austria he becomes a Victor Adler and a Friedrich Adler; in Russia, a Trotsky. Just take for a moment the present situation in Russia and in Germany. The revolution set creative forces free, and see what a large company of Jews was available for immediate service. Socialist Revolutionaries and Mensheviki, and Bolsheviki, Majority and Minority Socialists—whatever they be called—Jews are to be found among the trusted leaders and the routine workers of all these revolutionary parties."

"See," says the rabbi, "what a large company of Jews are available for immediate service." One ought to see where he points. There are as many Jewish members of revolutionary societies in the United States, as there were in Russia; and here, as there, they are "available for immediate service."

Jewish Testimony in Favor of Bolshevism

Bernard Lazare, a Jewish writer who has published a work on anti-Semitism, says:

"The Jew, therefore, does take a part in revolutions, and he participates in them in so far as he is a Jew, or more correctly, in so far as he remains a Jew."

He says also—"The Jewish spirit is essentially a revolutionary spirit, and consciously or otherwise, the Jew is a revolutionist."

There is hardly any country in the world, except the United States, where denials of this could be made in such a way as to require proof. In every other country the fact is known. Here we have been under such a fear of mentioning the word "Jew" or anything pertaining to it, that the commonest facts have been kept from us—facts which even a superficial knowledge of Jewish writing would have given us. It was almost a pathetic spectacle to see American audiences go to lectures about the Russian situation, and come away from the hall confused and perplexed because the Russian situation is so un-Russian, all because no lecturer thought it politic to mention "Jew" in the United States, for, as some day we shall see, the Jew has contrived to gain control of the platform too.

Not only do the literary lights of Jewry acknowledge the Jew's propensity to revolution generally, and his responsibility for the Russian situation particularly, but the lower lights also have a very clear idea about it. The Jew in the midst of the revolution is conscious that somehow he is advancing the cause of Israel. He may be a "bad Jew" in the synagogue sense, but he is enough of a Jew to be willing to do any thing that would advance the prestige of Israel. Race is stronger than religion in Jewry.

The Russian paper, On to Moscow, in September, 1919, said: "It should not be forgotten that the Jewish people, who for centuries were oppressed by kings and czars, are the real proletariat, the real Internationale, which has no country."

Mr. Cohan, in the newspaper, Communist, in April, 1919, said: "Without exaggeration, it may be said that the great Russian social revolution was indeed accomplished by the hands of the Jews. Would the dark, oppressed masses of the Russian workmen and peasants have been able to throw off the yoke of the bourgeoisie by themselves? No, it was precisely the Jews who led the Russian proletariat to the dawn of the Internationale and not only have led, but are also now leading the Soviet cause which remains in their safe hands. We may be quiet as long as the chief command of the Red Army is in the hands of Comrade Leon Trotsky. It is true that there are no Jews in the ranks of the Red Army as far as privates are concerned, but in the committees and Soviet organizations, as commissars, the Jews are gallantly leading the masses of the Russian proletariat to victory. It is not without reason that during the elections to all Soviet institutions the Jews are winning by an overwhelming majority . . . The symbol of Jewry, which for centuries has struggled against capitalism, has become also the symbol of the Russian proletariat, which can be seen even in the adoption of the Red five-pointed star, which in former times, as it is well known, was the symbol of Zionism and Jewry. With this sign comes victory, with this sign comes the death of the parasites of the bourgeoisie . . . Jewish tears will come out of them in sweat of drops of blood."

This confession, or rather boast, is remarkable for its completeness.

The Jews, says Mr. Cohan, are in control of the Russian masses the Russian masses who have never risen at all, who only know that a minority, like the czar's minority, is in control at the seat of government.

The Jews are not in the Red Army, Mr. Cohan informs us, that is, in the ranks where the actual fighting is done; and this is strictly in line with the Protocols. The strategy of the World Program is to set Gentiles to kill Gentiles. This was the Jewish boast during the various French social disasters, that so many Frenchmen had been set killing each other.

In the World War just passed, there were as many Gentiles killed by Gentiles as there are Jews in the world. It was a great victory for Israel. "Jewish tears will come out of them in sweat of drops of blood."

But the Jews are in the places of control and safety, says Mr. Cohan, and he is absolutely right about it. The wonder is that he was so honest as to say it.

As to the elections, so-called, at which the Jews are so unanimously chosen, the literature of Bolshevism is very explicit. Those who voted against the Jewish candidates were adjudged "enemies of the revolution" and executed. It did not require many executions at a voting place to make all the elections unanimous.

Mr. Cohan is especially instructive on the significance of the Red Star, the five-pointed emblem of Bolshevism. "The symbol of Jewry," he says, "has become also the symbol of the Russian proletariat."

The Star of David, the Jewish national emblem, is a six-pointed Star, formed by two triangles, one standing on its base, the other on its apex. Deprived of their base lines, these triangles approximate the familiar

Masonic emblem of the Square and Compass. It is this Star of David of which a Jewish observer in Palestine remarks that there are so few among the graves of the British solders who won Palestine in the recent war; most of the signs are the familiar wooden Cross. These Crosses are now reported to be objectionable to the new rulers of Palestine, because they are so plainly in view of the visitor who approaches the new Jewish university. As in Soviet Russia, so in Palestine, not many Jews laid down their lives for the cause: there were plenty of Gentiles for that purpose.

As the Jew is a past master in the art of symbolism, it may not be without significance that the Bolshevik Star has one point less than the Star of David. For there is still one point to be fulfilled in the World Program as outlined in the Protocols—and that is the enthronement of "our leader." When he comes, the World Autocrat for whom the whole program is framed, the sixth point may be added.

The Five Points of the Star now apparently assured are the Purse, the Press, the Peerage, Palestine and Proletarianism. The sixth point will be the Prince of Israel.

It is very hard to say, it is hard to believe, but Mr. Cohan has said it, and revolutions especially since the French Revolution confirm it, that "with this sign comes the death of the parasites of the bourgeoisie . . . Jewish tears will come out of them in sweat of drops of blood." The "bourgeoisie," as the Protocols say, are always Gentile.

The common counterargument to the invincible fact of the Jewish character of the Russian revolution—an argument which is destined to disappear now that Jewish acknowledgement is coming thick and fast—is that the Jews in Russia suffer too. "How can we favor a movement which makes our own people suffer?" is the argument put up to the Gentile.

Well, the fact is this: they are favoring that movement. Today, this very moment, the Bolshevik Government is receiving money from Jewish financiers in Europe, and if in Europe, then of course from the International Jewish bankers in America also. That is one fact.

Another fact is this: the Jews of Russia are not suffering to anywhere near the extent we are told by the propagandists. It is now a fact admitted by Jews themselves that upon the first sweep of the Bolshevists across Poland, the Polish Jews were friendly with the invaders and helped them. The fact was explained by American Jews in this manner: since Bolshevism came to Russia, the condition of the Jews there has greatly improved—therefore the Polish Jews were friendly. And it is true the condition of Russian Jews is good. One reason is: they have Russia. Everything there belongs to them.

The other reason is: The Jews of Russia are the only ones receiving help there today.

Did that second statement ever strike you as significant? Only the Jews of Russia have food and money sent to them. It is one form, of course, of the support which the Jewish world is giving Bolshevism. But if the suffering among the Jews is what the propagandists say it is, what must it be among the Russians? Yet no one is sending food or money to them. The probable truth of the whole situation is that Jewish Bolshevism is laying a tax on the world. Any time it may be required, there is plenty of evidence as to the good condition of the Jews in Russia. They have all there is.

Another source of confusion is revealed in the question: "How can Jewish capitalists support Bolshevism when Bolshevism is against capitalism?"

Bolshevism, as before stated, is only against Gentile capitalism. Jewish financiers who remained in Russia are very useful to the Bolsheviki. Read this description by an eyewitness: "A Jew is this Commissary of the Bank, very elegant, with a cravat of the latest style, and a fancy waistcoat. A Jew is this District Commissary, former stockbroker, with a double bourgeois chin. Again a Jew, this inspector of taxes: he understands perfectly how to squeeze the bourgeoisie."

These agents of Jewry are still there. Other agents are among the Russians who fled, getting their lands away from them on mortgage loans. When the curtain lifts, most of the choice real estate will be found to have passed into Jewish control by perfectly "legal" means.

That is one answer to the question, Why the Jewish capitalists support Bolshevism. The Red Revolution is the greatest speculative event of human history. Besides, it is for the exaltation of Israel; it is a colossal revenge, which the Jews always take where they can, for wrongs real or imaginary.

Jewish capitalism knows exactly what it is doing. What are its gains?

1. It has taken a whole rich country, without the cost of war.

2. It has demonstrated the necessity of gold. Jewish power rests on the fiction that gold is wealth. By the premeditated clumsiness of the Bolshevik monetary system, the unthinking world has been made to believe still more strongly that gold is necessary, and this belief gives Jewish capitalism another hold on the Gentile world. If the Bolshevists

had been honest, they could have dealt Jewish capitalism its death blow. No! Gold is still on its throne. Destroy the fiction that gold has value, and you leave the Jewish International Financiers sitting forlorn on heaps of useless metal.

3. It has demonstrated its power to the world. Protocol Seven says: "To demonstrate our enslavement of the Gentile governments of Europe, we will show our power to one of them by crimes of violence, that is, a reign of terror." Has Europe been sufficiently "shown"? Europe has, and is afraid! That is a great gain for Jewish capitalists.

4. Not the least of the gains is the field practice in the art of revolution which Russia has offered. Students of that Red school are coming back to the United States. The technique of revolution has been reduced to a science according to the details laid down in the Protocols. To use Rabbi Magnes's words again: "See what a large company of Jews was available for immediate service." The available company is now much larger.

The Dearborn Independent, October 2, 1920

Volume 2: Jewish Activities in the United States

Preface

A former volume, containing the first twenty articles in the series of Jewish studies which began their appearance in *The Dearborn Independent* of May 22, 1920, dealt largely with the theory of the Jewish World Program. The present volume gives a general view of some of the evidence which illustrates and substantiates that Program. As the first volume brought the subject forward a step, the present volume brings it forward another step. The Question is a very big one, the material is of mountainous proportions, so that it is very desirable that there be simplicity of method. The method therefore has been to lay the observable everyday facts alongside the Program, to see if they agree. It will be time enough to take up the authenticity of the Protocols when the parallel between them and the activities of the Jewish leaders is shown.

The articles thus far printed remain unanswered. They have been denounced and misrepresented, but not answered. A favorite evasion of Jewish editors is to say that the statements made about the Jews could be made about any other race, and that no race could refute the statements with facts.

But these statements have not been made about any other race and could they be? If they were made about, say the Hungarians, Poles, Rumanians, Italians, English, Scotch, Irish, Russian or Syrian in our midst, could they not be met?

Not the mere fact that certain statements are made about the purposes of Jewish leaders, but the fact that people can see wherein the statements agree with actual conditions, is what gives strength to the statements. The same statements made about any other group would fall because the people could find nothing to sustain them. Say-so and hearsay have no weight at all. Neither has abuse or prejudice. If the statements made in these articles are false, they are of a nature which can be refuted with facts. If there is no parallel between the written Program of the Protocols and the actual program as followed under Jewish leadership, surely that can be shown. If it has not been shown, it is because the parallel exists, and Jewish leaders know it exists.

Preface

The following chapters take up numerous matters, chiefly the interference of the Jew with educational and religious interests of the majority of the people; the moral menace in the Jew-controlled theater and movie; the fight of the New York Stock Exchange against Jewish domination; a discussion of the question whether the Jews are a "religious denomination" or a race, only Jewish authorities being quoted; and a very slight beginning on the endless subject of Jewish influence during the Great War. Bernard M. Baruch, although secondary in the real Jewish counsels, proclaimed himself to a Congressional committee as "the most powerful man in the war," and the records show that he was.

This volume does not complete the case. It is issued to meet the demand of new readers who call for the articles from the beginning. The editions of *The Dearborn Independent* being long ago exhausted, the publication of these two volumes was undertaken to enable readers to begin with the first article. The omission of several single articles from this compilation is in the interest of compactness, and may be restored in another volume. The omitted articles are "The Jews' Complaint Against 'Americanism,'" Oct. 23; "Gentile Fall Involved in Hope of Jewish Rule," Dec. 25.

April, 1921

"The distinctive character of the Jew does not arise solely from his religion. It is true that his race and religion are indissolubly connected, ... but whatever be the cause of this junction of the race idea with the religion, it is very certain that the religion alone does not constitute the people. A believer in the Jewish faith does not by reason of that fact become a Jew. On the other hand, however, a Jew by birth remains a Jew, even though he abjures his religion." —Leo N. Levi, President of B'nai B'rith 1900 1904.

21. How Jews in the U.S. Conceal Their Strength

How many Jews are there in the United States? No Gentile knows. The figures are the exclusive property of the Jewish authorities. The government of the United States can provide statistics on almost every matter pertaining to the population of the country, but whenever it has attempted in a systematic way to get information about the Jews who are constantly entering the country and the number now resident here, the Jewish lobby at Washington steps in and stops it.

For more than 20 years the fight for the right of the United States Government to make a complete census of the people has been going on, and for the same period the Jewish lobby at the Capitol has been strong enough to win.

The alarming increase in Jewish immigration at the present time has brought the question to public attention again. For the first time in the history of the United States a national conviction is forming upon this subject. From Europe came the first news which startled this country. The reports told of vast mobilizations of Jewish people at stated rendezvous in Europe. Great barracks were built for them. Large bodies of trained men went from the United States, under orders of Jewish secret societies here, to expedite "passport work," as it is termed among those bodies. Immigration into the United States became a business—a strictly Jewish business.

Why is that statement made?—"a strictly Jewish business." For this reason: there are countries in Europe from which today no Gentile can be admitted to the United States. From Germany, from Russia, from Poland, it is with the utmost difficulty that even one person can be won permission to enter this country. But Jews from Poland, Germany, and Russia by the thousands come in most freely, in utter disregard of the laws, in open contempt of the health regulations—a strictly Jewish business of getting another million Jews into the United States. It is like moving an army, which having done duty in Europe for the subjugation of that continent, is now being transferred to America.

When the conditions overseas were made known in this country and it became apparent that Jewish societies in the United States were the principal aids in this stampede to America, the newspapers for the first time in American history began to comment on a Jewish Question in tones of alarm. This in itself is an indication that the facts are becoming too challenging to be longer ignored.

Even the ordinary immigration officials, who for years have watched the human stream as it flowed over Ellis Island, have this year been startled into attention and action by the sharp change that has come in the character of the stream. And what has startled them?

First, it is composed almost entirely of Jews. Real Ukrainians, real Russians, real Germans cannot come in. But Jews can come from anywhere, and are coming from almost everywhere. Why this special privilege?—is being asked.

Second, they do not come as refugees, as people fleeing from hunger and persecution: they come as if they own the country. They arrive as special guests. As on the other side the passport business is "arranged," so on this side the entrance business is "arranged." The laws are set aside. Health regulations are ignored. Why should they not behave as if they own the United States? They see officials of Jewish secret societies override officials of the United States Immigration Bureau. Their first glimpse of life here shows a Jewish control as potent and complete as it is in Russia. No wonder then that they literally beat down the walls and gates with all the éclat of a victorious invasion. Is not this America—"The Jews' Country," as it is called in the smaller nations of Europe?

Third, there is a perfect organization which overcomes the numerous objections which arise against admission of known revolutionary Jews. European Jews are potential revolutionists. They are the revolutionists of Italy, Germany, Russia and Poland today. They are the Red and I.W.W. leaders of the United States today. When one man whose record is known presents himself at Ellis Island—and of course he is one in a thousand whose records are not known—he is held up. Immediately there start across the country telegrams to Congressmen, editors, state and municipal officials telling them in peremptory tones to "get busy" in behalf of Mr. So-and-So who is detained at Ellis Island. And the same day there start back to Washington telegrams from Congressmen, editors and others of influence, insisting on the spotless character of Mr. So-and-So and demanding his immediate admittance into the United States. Sometimes also the Russian embassy—so-called is used in this work.

It is an invasion—nothing but an invasion; and it is helped by influences within the United States. It is thinly cloaked with sentiment—"these people are fleeing from persecution." It is cleverly assisted by photographs showing groups of forlorn looking women and children never by photographs showing the groups of husky young revolutionists who are just as ready to despoil the United States as they were to despoil Russia.

That, however, is the present situation. What this and a subsequent article propose to do for the reader is to put him in possession of some of the facts concerning the government's fight on this question during the last quarter century.

The question is not peculiar to America, and it may throw a sidelight on the American phase to note some of the facts developed at the hearings of the British Royal Commission on Alien Immigration which sat in London in 1902, a feature of whose proceedings was the testimony of Theodor Herzl, the great propagandist of Zionism.

In his initial statement to the Commission, Herzl made these statements, among others:

"The fact that there is now for the first time since Cromwell a perceptible number of our people in England is the true cause of this Commission being called together. . . . That a serious pressure exists in England, the fact of your Commission sitting is full proof."

Then the examination proceeded until the following was brought out: (the answers are Herzl's)

Q. Looking at the question of alien immigration from the standpoint of the United States for a moment, you have referred to the fact that America excludes?

A. Yes.

Q. The exclusion is a partial exclusion?

A. Exclusion, as I know, is worked in this way: the immigrant must show a certain amount of money at the moment of his landing.

Q. You are aware that the stream of immigration into the United States is twice as much as the immigration into the United Kingdom?

A. I know that. New York has now the greatest Jewish population of all the towns in the world.

Q. And the actual exclusion is the actual exclusion of a small proportion?

A. Yes; but they go, however, to America. I think it is so easy to evade such a prohibition. For instance, if they joined a small company, it would lend the necessary amount to each immigrant, and the immigrant shows it and comes in, and sends back by post the amount he has borrowed. There are no efficacious measures to prevent that.

Q. I took it that your reference to the United States was an approval of the action of that country as an act of self-preservation.

A. No.

A little later on in the examination, the question of immigration to the United States was again brought in. The answers are still Dr. Herzl's—remember that the date is still 1902:

Q. Are you aware whether it is the fact or not that the leading Jews in America have informed their correspondents here that they cannot receive and distribute any more Jewish immigrants?

A. I have heard of difficulties of emigration, and that they are overcrowded with Jews. As to that information I cannot say.

Q. In your opinion would not the stream of emigration to America have been much greater if no such law had existed?

A. I think this law did not alter it much. The prohibition could not change it.

Q. On what grounds do you believe that?

A. It is a question of coasts and harbors. They come in. How will you prevent a man from coming in?

Q. Do you mean they are smuggled in?

A. No, I do not believe that. But they always find means to come in.

Now, discussion of immigration in the United States has never been free. We have talked a great deal about it in general terms, but not in terms of specific races except the Chinese and Japanese. However, Herzl seems to have known that wherever the Jews congregate in noticeable numbers they become a trouble (his words are: ". . . America, where so soon as they form a perceptible number they become a trouble and a burden to the land") and he also knew that efforts would be made to meet that condition. But more than that, he dropped what must be construed as a warning, that such efforts would be resisted. He said:

"There exists a French proverb, 'cet animal est tres impatient; il se defend quand on l'attaque.' If the Jews are attacked, they will defend themselves, and you will get something like internal troubles."

The time apparently did come in the United States when some far-seeing official began to wonder what the Jewish invasion portended. Already it was too strong to be openly attacked. The Jewish lobby at Washington was powerful even at that time. So, apparently, this official concluded that the best way to set about so momentous a task was to collect the information.

But in order to get the information, Congress had to give its permission; and to get the permission of Congress, hearings had to be ordered. Hearings were ordered, and the records of them, though very scarce, still exist. The reader will be given important extracts from them presently, and he will see for himself how certain American statesmen reacted to the whole matter.

A remark is in order just here, namely, that the Jewish lobby eventually became more skillful in such matters. It now takes very good care that no officials shall be appointed who shall make suggestions which shall precipitate congressional hearings on the Jewish matter. The time is coming, of course, when the whole Jewish Question may be threshed out by the government of the United States, but it will not be because an official precipitated it; it will be because the people will demand it.

Officials are now much too wary to meddle with this Question. They know too well the consequences. During the war many a secret trail of danger led into Jewish quarters, and the secret service man who loyally made his reports was often surprised to find himself lifted completely off that trail. Why? All Jewish trails in this country were powerfully protected by hidden influences during the war.

Well, the time came in the United States, when it was obviously desirable to know what elements were comprising our population; whether we were an Anglo-Saxon nation, Semitic, Latin, or what. The situation was this, and was so stated by government officials at the time:—In the '80's, and previously, it could be safely assumed that an immigrant from Ireland was Irish, an immigrant from Norway or Sweden was Scandinavian, an immigrant from Russia was Russian, an immigrant from Germany was German, and so on.

But times changed. Previous to 1880, the entry on a man's record—"born in Russia"—indicated that he was a Russian. But, says a statement made by a government official with reference to the 10 years following 1880—"So many Hebrews have come from that country to the United States, that 'born in Russia' has come in popular opinion to mean a 'Russian Jew.'" And then the same official goes on to show that during a

10-year period when 666,561 Jews came from Russia, there came also from Russia large numbers of Poles, Finns, Germans and Lithuanians.

Now, to make a census enumeration of these peoples under the heading "Russian" was plainly misleading, and not only misleading but valueless for census purposes.

The racial identity would be lost, and our knowledge of the racial make-up of the nation very incomplete. Therefore, the census authorities asked Congress for permission to classify people by "race" as well as by "country of birth." It seemed perfectly reasonable. Of what possible use is it to classify 3,000,000 Jews as "Russians" when there are very few real Russians in the country, and when the Russian and Jew are so deeply different one from another?

Senator Simon Guggenheim arose in the committee to object. He used the common formula in such cases. He said:

"Personally I object to it, not because I am a Hebrew, but because it is not in place."

That is the common Jewish formula of objection. The B'nai B'rith says the same thing when it forces Shakespeare's "Merchant of Venice" out of the public schools. That society's "anti-defamation circular" always includes the thought:—"We do not base our request on the embarrassment which may be caused to the Jewish students in class, nor is our attitude in this regard based on thin-skinned sensitiveness. Our objection is made because of the effect upon the non-Jewish children who subconsciously will associate in their minds the Jew as Shakespeare portrayed him with the Jew of today." So Senator Guggenheim, therefore, was playing the game according to the rules made and established in such cases.

At this hearing, Senator LaFollette was chairman. Senator Guggenheim's contention was that "Jew" was the name of a member of a religious denomination, and not of a race.

Chairman LaFollette—"I can see broad ethnological reasons why some time it would be important to know from what blood and race the man came."

Senator Guggenheim—"Why not ask his religion?"

Senators McCumber and Bailey came to the support of Senator Guggenheim's contention, that "Jew" is a religious and not a racial term.

Chairman LaFollette—"I do not just get your objection to this, Senator Guggenheim. What objection can one have to having the race to which he belongs correctly entered?"

Senator Guggenheim—"Because it is not correct when stated that way. The Jews are not a race. . . . "

Later on in the hearing, Senator Cummins entered the discussion in response to a pro-Jewish remark made by Senator Bailey:

Senator Bailey—"If I were a Hebrew and I had been born here and they wanted me to say I was anything but an American, I would have a difference with the enumerator. I perhaps would refuse to answer their questions."

Senator Cummins—"I would not have any hesitancy in stating from what blood I was."

Senator Bailey—"No; but in the case that I refer to, it would be a matter of religion."

Senator Guggenheim—"That is the point; it is a question of religion."

That was in April, 1909. In December, 1909, Simon Wolf was the chief witness for the pro-Jewish contention. Simon Wolf is a very interesting character. From before the days of President Lincoln, he has been lobbyist for the Jews at the National Capitol, and has been in contact with every President from Lincoln to Wilson. At the hearing where Mr. Wolf testified, Senator Dillingham acted as chairman, and the whole proceeding was enlivened and clarified by the vigorous part which Senator Lodge took in it. Certain extracts, which entirely reproduce the spirit and argument of the hearing, follow:

Mr. Wolf—"The point we make is this: A Jew coming from Russia is a Russian; from Rumania, a Rumanian; from France, a Frenchman; from England, an Englishman; and from Germany, a German; that Hebrew or Jewish is simply a religion."

Senator Lodge—"Do I understand you to deny that the Jews are a race?"

Mr. Wolf—"How?"

Senator Lodge—"Do you deny that the word 'Jew' is used to express a race?"

Mr. Wolf—"As the representative of the Union of American Hebrew Congregations—which I have been for nearly 30 years—I took up the matter and propounded a series of interrogations to some of the leading Jews of the United States, among others . . . Dr. Cyrus Adler, who was librarian of the Smithsonian . . . and every one of them states that the Jews are not a race."

Senator Lodge—"That, I think, is an important point. I have always supposed they were. I find in the preface of The *Jewish Encyclopedia*, which is signed by Cyrus Adler, among others this statement: 'An even more delicate problem that presented itself at the very outset was the attitude to be observed by the encyclopedia in regard to those Jews who, while born within the Jewish community, have, for one reason or another, abandoned it. As the present work deals with the Jews as a race, it was found impossible to exclude those who were of that race, whatever their religious affiliations might have been.'

"In the same encyclopedia is a statement by Joseph Jacobs, B.A., formerly president of the Jewish Historical Society of England:

'Anthropologically considered, the Jews are a race of markedly uniform type, due either to unity of race or to similarity of environment.'

"Do you mean to deny—I want to understand your position— that the word 'Jew' is a racial term?"

Mr. Wolf—"I have made my statement, and my opinions are in this pamphlet."

Senator Lodge—"Let me get at it. How would you classify Benjamin Disraeli? Was he a Jew?"

Mr. Wolf—"He was born a Jew."

Senator Lodge—"He was baptized as a Christian. He then ceased to be a Jew?"

Mr. Wolf—"Yes; religiously he ceased to be a Jew."

Senator Lodge—"Ah! Religiously. He was very proud of the fact that he was a Jew, and always spoke of himself in that way. Did the fact that he changed his religion alter his race?"

Mr. Wolf—"It did not change the fact that he was born a Jew; not at all; and I know the Jewish people throughout the world have claimed him, Heine, and Borne, and others who were born of their blood, as being Jews, when they speak of persons who have accomplished something wonderful in the world. But they ceased to be Jews from the standpoint of religion—"

Senator Lodge—"Undoubtedly. What I want to get at is whether the word 'Jew' or 'Hebrew' is not a correct racial term?"

Mr. Wolf—"If you will pardon me, you will find a letter from Dr. Cyrus Adler right at the close of the pamphlet, which perhaps you might read for the benefit of the committee."

Senator Lodge—(after reading the letter referred to) "I do not think that answers anything."

Senator Lodge—"It never occurred to me until I heard you were coming here that the classification as made by the immigration authorities had anything to do with religion. I supposed it was a race classification. It is important, very important, to get the race classification as nearly as we can."

Mr. Wolf—"You are aware that the Census Bureau some time ago attempted to classify in the same manner and it was prohibited from doing so."

Senator Lodge—"The word 'race' was stricken out of the census bill. I think it was a great mistake. It makes the returns almost valueless."

Mr. Wolf—"I can simply repeat what I have said—that I am voicing the opinions of those whom I represent—the Union of American Hebrew Congregations, and the Order of B'nai B'rith. They are opposed to the classification as made in the last few years and as contemplated, so far as I am informed, in the report of the commission."

The hearings continued, Julian W. Mack later appearing for the Jewish contention.

From the extracts given in this article, four matters become very clear:

First, the Jew is opposed to any restrictive legislation against his entrance into a country.

Second, the Jew is opposed to any racial classification of himself after he has entered a country.

Third, the Jewish argument to the Gentile authorities is that the Jew represents religion and not race.

Fourth, that at least one indication has appeared in which the Jew has one view to present to the Gentiles, and another which he cherishes among his own people, on this question of Race.

Another point might be made, as this: when the authorities disregard as untenable the argument of "religion, not race," the Jewish spokesmen fall back on the fact that their organizations don't want certain things and won't have certain things—argument or no argument, commission or no commission.

The Jewish lobbyists had their way. There is no enumeration of Jews in the United States. There are 46 other classifications, but none for the Jew. The Northern Italians are distinguished in the records from the Southern Italians; the Moravians are distinguished from the Bohemians; the Scotch from the English; the Spanish-American from the Spanish-European; the West Indians from the Mexicans—but the Jew is not distinguished at all.

None of the other races made objection. On this point the report of the commission reads:

"As far as ascertained by the commission, the practice of classifying the foreign-born by race or people, rather than by country of birth, is acceptable to the people of the United States with one exception.

The officials, who were endeavoring to have the Census Report show with scientific accuracy the actual racial components of the population of the United States, were compelled to see their recommendation eliminated.

What is the result? If you ask the government of the United States how many Frenchmen there are in the country, it can give you the figures. If you ask for the number of Poles, it is there. If you ask for the number of Africans, it is known. On down a long list you may make your inquiries, and you will find that the government knows.

But ask the government of the United States how many Jews are in the country—and it cannot tell; there are no records. If you want information upon that point, you will have to go to the officials or representatives of the Jewish Government in the United States.

Of course, if "Jew" is a religious term, like Baptist, Catholic, Christian Scientist or Quaker, then there is merit in the argument that religious questions are not proper for the government to ask unless the religion comes in conflict with, or is a menace to, the ideals of the Republic. But if "Jew" is a racial term, or a national term, then the government is properly interested in making record of all the inhabitants of this land who bear it.

Like all questions pertaining to the Jews, this can be settled by their own words. What the Jews teach the Jews on this matter should be the determining point. In the next article we shall see what Jews themselves have to say about "race or religion?"

The Dearborn Independent, October 9, 1920

"I will give you my definition of a nation, and you can add the adjective 'Jewish.' A Nation is, in my mind, an historical group of men of a recognizable cohesion held together by a common enemy. Then, if you add to that the word 'Jewish' you have what I understand to be the Jewish nation." —THEODOR HERZL.

"Let us all recognize that we Jews are a distinct nationality of which every Jew, whatever his country, his station, or shade of belief, is necessarily a member." —LOUIS D. BRANDEIS Justice of the United States Supreme Court.

22. Jewish Testimony on "Are Jews a Nation?"

This article is designed to put the reader in possession of information regarding the Jew's own thought of himself, as regards race, religion and citizenship. In the last article we saw the thought which Jewish representatives wish to plant in Gentile minds concerning this matter. The Senate committee which was to be convinced was made up of Gentiles. The witnesses who were to do the convincing were Jews.

Senator Simon Guggenheim said: "There is no such thing as a Jewish race, because it is the Jewish religion."

Simon Wolf said: "The point we make is this . . . that Hebrew or Jewish is simply a religion."

Julian W. Mack said: "Of what possible value is it to anybody to classify them as Jews simply because they adhere to the Jewish religion?"

The object of this testimony was to have the Jews classified under various national names, such as Polish, English, German, Russian, or whatever it might be.

Now, when the inquirer turns to the authoritative Jewish spokesmen who speak not to Gentiles but to Jews about this matter, he finds an entirely different kind of testimony. Some of this testimony will now be presented.

The reader will bear in mind that, as the series is not written for entertainment, but for instruction in the facts of a very vital Question, the present article will be of value only to those who desire to know for themselves what are the basic elements of the matter.

It should also be observed during the reading of the following testimony that sometimes the term "race" is used, sometimes the term "nation." In every case, it is recognized that the Jew is a member of a separate people, quite aside from the consideration of his religion.

Jewish Testimony on "Are Jews a Nation?"

First, let us consider the testimony which forbids us to consider the term "Jew" as merely the name of a member of a religious body only.

Louis D. Brandeis, Justice of the Supreme Court of the United States and world leader of the Zionist movement, says:

"Councils of Rabbis and others have undertaken at times to prescribe by definition that only those shall be deemed Jews who professedly adhere to the orthodox or reformed faith. But in the connection in which we are considering the term, it is not in the power of any single body of Jews—or indeed of all Jews collectively—to establish the effective definition. The meaning of the word 'Jewish' in the term 'Jewish Problem' must be accepted as co-extensive with the disabilities which it is our problem to remove ... Those disabilities extend substantially to all of Jewish blood. The disabilities do not end with a renunciation of faith, however sincere ... Despite the meditations of pundits or decrees of councils, our own instincts and acts, and those of others, have defined for us the term 'Jew.'" (*"Zionism and the American Jews."*)

The Rev. Mr. Morris Joseph, West London Synagogue of British Jews: "Israel is assuredly a great nation ... The very word 'Israel' proves it. No mere sect or religious community could appropriately bear such a name. Israel is recognized as a nation by those who see it; no one can possibly mistake it for a mere sect. To deny Jewish nationality you must deny the existence of the Jew." (*"Israel a Nation."*)

Arthur D. Lewis, West London Zionist Association: "When some Jews say they consider the Jews a religious sect, like the Roman Catholics or Protestants, they are usually not correctly analyzing and describing their own feelings and attitude.... If a Jew is baptized, or, what is not necessarily the same thing, sincerely converted to Christianity, few people think of him as no longer being a Jew. His blood, temperament and spiritual peculiarities are unaltered." (*"The Jews a Nation."*)

Bertram B. Benas, barrister-at-law: "The Jewish entity is essentially the entity of a People. 'Israelites,' 'Jews,' 'Hebrews'—all the terms used to denote the Jewish people bear a specifically historical meaning, and none of these terms has been convincingly superseded by one of purely sectarian nature. The external world has never completely subscribed to the view that the Jewish people constitute merely an ecclesiastical denomination...." (*"Zionism—The National Jewish Movement."*)

Leon Simon, a brilliant and impressive Jewish scholar and writer, makes an important study of the question of "Religion and Nationality" in his volume, "Studies in Jewish Nationalism." He makes out a case for the proposition that the Religion of the Jews is Nationalism, and that Nationalism is an integral part of their Religion.

"It is often said, indeed, that Judaism has no dogmas. That statement is not true as it stands." He then states some of the dogmas, and continues—"And the Messianic Age means for the Jew not merely the establishment of peace on earth and good will to men, but the universal recognition of the Jew and his God.

It is another assertion of the eternity of the nation. Dogmas such as these are not simply the articles of faith of a church, to which anybody may gain admittance by accepting them; they are the beliefs of a nation about its own past and its own future." (p. 14.)

"For Judaism has no message of salvation for the individual soul, as Christianity has; all its ideas are bound up with the existence of the Jewish nation." (p. 20.)

"The idea that Jews are a religious sect, precisely parallel to Catholics and Protestants, is nonsense." (p. 34.)

Graetz, the great historian of the Jews, whose monumental work is one of the standard authorities, says that the history of the Jews, even since they lost the Jewish State, "still possesses a national character; it is by no means merely a creed or church history. . . . Our history is far from being a mere chronicle of literary events or church history."

Moses Hess, one of the historic figures through whom the whole Jewish Program has flowed down from its ancient sources to its modern agents, wrote a book entitled "Rome and Jerusalem" in which he stated the whole matter with clearness and force.

"Jewish religion," he says, "is, above all, Jewish patriotism." (p. 61.)

"Were the Jews only followers of a certain religious denomination, like the others, then it were really inconceivable that Europe, and especially Germany, where the Jews have participated in every cultural activity, 'should spare the followers of the Israelitish confession neither pains, nor tears, nor bitterness.' The solution of the problem, however, consists in the fact that the Jews are something more than mere 'followers of a religion,' namely, they are a race brotherhood, a nation . . . " (p. 71.)

Hess, like other authoritative Jewish spokesmen, denies that forsaking the faith constitutes a Jew a non-Jew.

". . . Judaism has never excluded anyone. The apostates severed themselves from the bond of Jewry. 'And not even them has Judaism forsaken,' added a learned rabbi in whose presence I expressed the above-quoted opinion."

Jewish Testimony on "Are Jews a Nation?"

"In reality, Judaism as a nationality has a natural basis which cannot be set aside by mere conversion to another faith, as is the case with other religions. A Jew belongs to his race and consequently also to Judaism, in spite of the fact that he or his ancestors have become apostates." (pp. 97 98.)

Every Jew is, whether he wishes it or not, solidly united with the entire nation." (p. 163.)

Simply to indicate that we have not been quoting outworn opinions, but the actual beliefs of the most active and influential part of Jewry, we close this section of the testimony with excerpts from a work published in 1920 by the Zionist Organization of America, from the pen of Jessie E. Sampter:

"The name of their national religion, Judaism, is derived from their national designation. An unreligious Jew is still a Jew, and he can with difficulty escape his allegiance only by repudiating the name of Jew." ("*Guide to Zionism,*" p. 5.)

It will be seen that none of these writers—and their number might be multiplied among both ancients and moderns—can deny that the Jew is exclusively a member of a religion without at the same time asserting that he is, whether he will or not, the member of a nation. Some go so far as to insist that his allegiance is racial in addition to being national. The term "race" is used by important Jewish scholars without reserve, while some, who hold the German-originated view that the Jews are an offshoot of the Semitic race and do not comprise that race, are satisfied with the term "nation."

Biblically, in both the Old Testament and the New, the term "nation" or "people" is employed. But the consensus of Jewish opinion is this: the Jews are a separate people, marked off from other races by very distinctive characteristics, both physical and spiritual, and they have both a national history and a national aspiration.

It will be noticed how the testimony on the point of "race" combines the thought of race and nationality, just as the previous section combined the thought of nationality with religion.

Supreme Justice Brandeis, previously quoted, appears to give a racial basis to the fact of nationality.

He says: "It is no answer to this evidence of nationality to declare that the Jews are not an absolutely pure race. There has, of course, been some intermixture of foreign blood in the three thousand years which constitute our historic period. But, owing to persecution and prejudice, the intermarriages with non-Jews which have occurred have resulted merely in taking away many from the Jewish community. Intermarriage has brought few additions. Therefore the percentage of foreign blood in the Jews of today is very low. Probably no important European race is as pure. But common race is only one of the elements which determine nationality."

Arthur D. Lewis, a Jewish writer, in his "*The Jews a Nation*," also bases nationality on the racial element:

"The Jews were originally a nation, and have retained more than most nations one of the elements of nationality—namely, the race element; this may be proved, of course, by the common sense test of their distinguishability. You can more easily see that a Jew is a Jew than that an Englishman is English."

Moses Hess is also quite clear on this point. He writes of the impossibility of Jews denying "their racial descent," and says: "Jewish noses cannot be reformed, and the black, wavy hair of the Jews will not turn through conversion into blond, nor can its curves be straightened out by constant combing. The Jewish race is one of the primary races of mankind that has retained its integrity, in spite of the continual change of its climatic environment, and the Jewish type has conserved its purity through the centuries."

Jessie E. Sampter, in the "*Guide to Zionism*," recounting the history of the work done for Zionism in the United States, says: "And this burden was nobly borne, due partly to the commanding leadership of such men as Justice Louis D. Brandeis, Judge Julian W. Mack, and Rabbi Stephen S. Wise, partly to the devoted and huge labors of the old-time faithful Zionists on the Committee, such as Jacob de Haas, Louis Lipsky, and Henrietta Szold, and partly to the aroused race consciousness of the mass of American Jews."

Four times in the brief preface to the fifth edition of "*Coningsby*," Disraeli uses the term "race" in referring to the Jews, and Disraeli was proud of being racially a Jew, though religiously he was a Christian.

In The *Jewish Encyclopedia*, "the Jewish race" is spoken of. In the preface, which is signed by Dr. Cyrus Adler as chief editor, these words occur:

"An even more delicate problem that presented itself at the very outset was the attitude to be observed by the Encyclopedia in regard to those Jews who, while born within the Jewish community, have, for one reason or another, abandoned it. As the present work deals with the Jews as a race, it was found impossible to exclude those who were of that race, whatever their religious affiliations might have been."

But as we are not interested in ethnology, the inquiry need not be contained further along this line. The point toward which all this trends is that the Jew is conscious of himself as being more than the member of a religious body. That is, Jewry nowhere subscribes in the persons of its greatest teachers and its most authoritative representatives, to the theory that a Jew is only "a brother of the faith."

Often he is not of the faith at all, but he is still a Jew. The fact is insisted upon here, not to discredit him, but to expose the double minds of those political leaders who, instead of straightforwardly meeting the Jewish Question, endeavor to turn all inquiry aside by an impressive confusion of the Gentile mind.

It may be argued by the small body of so-called "Reformed Jews" that the authorities quoted here are mostly Zionists. The reply is: there may be, and quite possible are, two Jewish programs in the world—one which it is intended the Gentiles should see, and one which is exclusively for the Jews. In determining which is the real Program, it is a safe course to adopt the one that is made to succeed. It is the Program sponsored by the so-called Zionists which is succeeding. It was made to succeed through the Allied Governments, through the Peace Conference, and now through the League of Nations. That, then, must be the true Jewish program, because it is hardly possible that the Gentile governments could have been led as they are being led, were they not convinced that they are obeying the behests of the real Princes of the Jews. It is all well enough to engage the plain Gentile people with one set of interesting things; the real thing is the one that has been put over. And that is the program whose sponsors also stand for the racial and national separateness of the Jews.

The idea that the Jews comprise a nation is the most common idea of all—among the Jews. Not only a nation with a past, but a nation with a future. More than that—not only a nation, but a Super-Nation.

We can go still further on the authority of Jewish statements: we can say that the future form of the Jewish Nation will be a kingdom.

And as to the present problems of the Jewish Nation, there is plenty of Jewish testimony to the fact that the influence of American life is harmful to Jewish life; that is, they are in antagonism, like two opposite ideas. This point, however, must await development in the succeeding article.

Israel Friedlaender traces the racial and national exclusiveness of the Jews from the earliest times, giving as illustrations two Biblical incidents—the Samaritans, "who were half-Jews by race and who were eager to become full Jews by religion," and their repulse by the Jews, "who were eager to safeguard the racial integrity of the Jews"; also, the demand for genealogical records and for the dissolution of mixed marriages, as recorded in the Book of Ezra. Dr. Friedlaender says that in post-Biblical times "this racial exclusiveness of the Jews became even more accentuated." Entry into Judaism "never was, as in other religious communities, purely a question of faith. Proselytes were seldom solicited, and even when ultimately admitted into the Jewish fold they were so on the express condition that they surrender their racial individuality."

"For the purposes of the present inquiry," says Dr. Friedlaender, "it is enough for us to know that the Jews have always felt themselves as a separate race, sharply marked off from the rest of mankind. Anyone who denies the racial conception of Judaism on the part of the Jews in the past is either ignorant of the facts of Jewish history, or intentionally misrepresents them."

Elkan N. Adler says: "No serious politician today doubts that our people have a political future." This future of political definiteness and power was in the mind of Moses Hess when he wrote in 1862—mark the date!—in the preface of his "*Rome and Jerusalem*," these words:

"No nation can be indifferent to the fact that in the coming European struggle for liberty, it may have another people as its friend or foe."

Hess had just been complaining of the inequalities visited upon the Jews. He was saying that what the individual Jew could not get because he was a Jew, the Jewish Nation would be able to get because it would be a Nation. Evidently he expected that nationhood might arrive before the "coming European struggle," and he was warning the Gentile nations to be careful, because in that coming struggle there might be another nation in the list, namely, the Jewish Nation, which could be either friend or foe to any nation it chose.

Dr. J. Abelson, of Portsea College, in discussing the status of "small nations" as a result of the Great War, says: "The Jew is one of these 'smaller nations,'" and claims for the Jew what is claimed for the Pole, the Rumanian, and the Serbian, and on the same ground—that of nationality.

Justice Brandeis voices the same thought. He says:

Jewish Testimony on "Are Jews a Nation?"

"While every other people is striving for development by asserting its nationality, and a great war is making clear the value of small nations . . . Let us make clear to the world that we too are a nationality clamoring for equal rights . . . "

Again says Justice Brandeis: "Let us all recognize that we Jews are a distinct nationality, of which every Jew, whatever his country, his station, or shade of belief, is necessarily a member."

And he concludes his article, from which these quotations are made, with these words:

"Organize, organize, organize, until every Jew must stand up and be counted—counted with us, or prove himself, wittingly or unwittingly, of the few who are against their own people."

Sir Samuel Montagu, the British Jew who has been appointed governor of Palestine under the British mandate, habitually speaks of the Jewish Kingdom, usually employing the expression "the restoration of the Jewish Kingdom." It may be of significance that the native population already refer to Sir Samuel as "The King of the Jews."

Achad ha-Am, who must be regarded as the one who has most conclusively stated the Jewish Idea as it has always existed, and whose influence is not as obscure as his lack of fame among the Gentiles might indicate, is strong for the separate identity of the Jews as a super-nation. Leon Simon succinctly states the great teacher's views when he says:

"While Hebraic thought is familiar with the conception of a Superman (distinguished, of course, from Nietzsche's conception by having a very different standard of excellence), yet its most familiar and characteristic application of that conception is not to the individual but to the nation—to Israel as the Super-Nation or 'chosen people.' In fact, the Jewish nation is presupposed in all characteristically Jewish thinking, just as it is presupposed in the teaching of the Prophets."

"In those countries," says Moses Hess, "which form a dividing line between the Occident and the Orient, namely, Russia, Poland, Prussia and Austria, there live millions of our brethren who earnestly believe in the restoration of the Jewish Kingdom and pray for it fervently in their daily services."

This article, therefore, at the risk of appearing tedious, has sought to summon from many sides and from many periods the testimony which should be taken whenever the subject of Jewish nationalism comes under discussion. Regardless of what may be said to Gentile authorities for the purpose of hindering or modifying their action, there can be no question as to what the Jew thinks of himself: He thinks of himself as belonging to a People, united to that People by ties of blood which no amount of creedal change can weaken, heir of that People's past, agent of that People's political future. He belongs to a race; he belongs to a nation; he seeks a kingdom to come on this earth, a kingdom which shall be over all kingdoms, with Jerusalem the ruling city of the world. That desire of the Jewish Nation may be fulfilled; it is the contention of these articles that it will not come by way of the Program of the Protocols nor by any of the other devious ways through which powerful Jews have chosen to work.

The charge of religious prejudice has always touched the people of civilized countries in a tender spot. Sensing this, the Jewish spokesmen chosen to deal with non-Jews have emphasized the point of religious prejudice. It is therefore a relief to tender and uninstructed minds to learn that Jewish spokesmen themselves have said that the troubles of the Jew have never arisen out of his religion, the Jew is not questioned on account of his religion, but on account of other things which his religion ought to modify. Gentiles know the truth that the Jew is not persecuted on account of his religion. All honest investigators know it. The attempt to shield the Jews under cover of their religion is, therefore, in face of the facts and of their own statements, an unworthy one.

If there were no other evidence, the very evidence which many Jewish writers cite, namely, the instant siding of the Jews one with another upon any and every occasion, would constitute evidence of racial and national solidarity. Whenever these articles have touched the International Jew Financier, hundreds of Jews in the lower walks of life have protested. Touch a Rothschild, and the revolutionary Jew from the ghetto utters his protest, and accepts the remark as a personal affront to himself. Touch a regular old-line Jewish politician who is using a government office exclusively for the benefit of his fellow Jews as against the best interests of the nation, and the Socialist and anti-government Jew comes out in his defense. Most of these Jews, it may be said, have lost a vital touch with the teachings and ceremonials of their religion, but they indicate what their real religion is by their national solidarity.

This in itself would be interesting, but it becomes important in view of another fact, with which the next article will deal, namely, the relation between this Jewish nationalism and the nationalism of the peoples among whom the Jews dwell.

The Dearborn Independent, October 16, 1920

(Special Dispatch to the Evening Telegram.)
A CHANGE IN THE THANKSGIVING PROCLAMATION.
HARRISBURG, Nov. 10th—An important change has been made in the Thanksgiving proclamation. In the last paragraph the words "Christian Commonwealth" have been altered to read: "A Commonwealth of freemen." This change has been made because of animadversions made by prominent Israelites. Gov. Hoyt says he used the word "Christian" in the sense of "civilized" and not particularly in a religious sense. —Vol. 20, American Jewish Historical Society "Documents regarding the Thanksgiving Proclamation of Gov. Hoyt, of Pennsylvania (1880)"

23. Jew Versus Non-Jew in New York Finance

The Jewish problem in the United States is essentially a city problem. It is characteristic of the Jew to gather in numbers, not where land is open nor where raw materials are found, but where the greatest number of people abide. This is a noteworthy fact when considered alongside the Jews' claim that the Gentiles have ostracized them; the Jews congregate in their greatest numbers in those places and among those people where they complain they are least wanted.

The explanation most frequently given is this; the genius of the Jew is to live off people; not off land, nor off the production of commodities from raw material, but off people. Let other people till the soil; the Jew, if he can, will live off the tiller. Let other people toil at trades and manufacture; the Jew will exploit the fruits of their work. That is his peculiar genius. If this genius be described as parasitic, the term would seem to be justified by a certain fitness.

In no other city of the United States can the Jewish Problem be studied with greater profit than in the city of New York. There are more Jews in New York than in all Palestine. The communal register of the Jewish Kehillah (or Kahal) of New York sets the population at about 1,527,778. "The next largest Jewish community in the world, that of the city of Warsaw, is estimated to have been between 300,000 and 330,000 Jews, about one-fifth as many as we estimate for New York." (Communal Register, 1917-1918.)

"If we accept the estimate of the number of Jews in the world as about 14,000,000, one Jew out of every ten resides in New York." As a population, the Jews exert more power in New York than they have ever exerted during the Christian Era in any place, with the exception of the present Russia. The Jewish Revolution in Russia was manned from New York. The present government of Russia was transported almost as a unit from the lower East Side of New York. The New York Ghetto has long since overflowed the lower East Side. Brownsville, Brooklyn, is a Jewish town, with its own language, theaters and press. The upper East Side of New York is practically in large sections a Jewish Ghetto. The prosperous West Side and the middle class section of the city north of Central Park are practically Jewish.

With the exception of one great department store and a few lesser ones, all the large department stores in New York are Jewish. Men and women's ready-to-wear apparel, laundries, furriers, the general run of shopkeeping is practically monopolized by Jews. The legal profession is predominantly Jewish. It is estimated that of the 27,000 news stands that control the distribution of New York's reading matter, 25,000 are in the hands of Jews. There are 360 synagogues on the East Side of New York alone.

The New York Kehillah is a very powerful organization, whose membership strength is not accurately known. It may be described as the Jewish government of that city. It was organized in 1908 as the result of a statement by General Bingham, then police commissioner of New York, that the Jewish population, which then amounted to 600,000, contributed 50 per cent of the criminals of the city. The Kehillah is the bar before which the authorities must answer for statements or acts touching the Jewish community. Its power is very great and its methods far reaching.

Politically, while the rest of the country is entertained with the fiction that Tammany Hall rules the politics of New York, the fact is rarely published that the Jews rule Tammany.

But it is not the possession of power that constitutes an indictment of any people, it is their use or misuse of it. And if the fact of power is established, no misuse of it being found, the fact has a commendatory side. If the Jews who flock to New York become American, and if they do not work ceaselessly to twist Americanism into something else; if they strengthen the principles and traditions of America, and do not cease to vitiate the one and abolish the other, the judgement upon them must be one of friendship.

However, to establish the fact of Jewish power, one need not remain in the ghetto, nor in the mercantile districts. There are higher fields

Jew Versus Non-Jew in New York Finance

awaiting survey. In Wall Street, the Jewish element is both numerous and powerful, as might be expected of a race which from early days has played an important part in the financial operations of the world.

This is not to say, however, that Jewish influence in American financial affairs is paramount.

At one time it threatened to be, but American financiers have always been silently aware of the International Jewish Financier, and have endeavored quietly to block his game. Time and again the contest seemed to turn in favor of the Jew, but when the widespread secret wrestlings of the two powers have been suspended for a moment, it has been found that American finance has maintained its superiority, if only in a slight degree.

The Rothschilds were the first to be beaten on American soil; the story of their hidden hand in American finance, politics and diplomacy is a voluminous one; but even their finesse did not avail against the sterling worth of American Business—not "American business" as it has come to be known, now that thousands of Jews are scattered about the world, representing themselves to be "American business men" although they can scarcely speak English!—but American Business as represented by the combination of American ability and American conscience. If the reputation of American business has suffered, it is because something other than American methods have been used under the American name.

In the New York financial district, Jewish finance makes itself felt through its private banking institutions. As distinct from the great trust companies and banks of deposit, the private banker utilizes his own capital and that of his partners and associates.

Jewish finance differs radically from non-Jewish finance in the fact that Jewish bankers are essentially money-lenders. They may underwrite great flotations of bond and stock issues for railroad and industrial companies, governments and municipalities, but these securities are immediately sold to the public. There is a quick money turnover. The public carries the bonds; the Jewish financier gets his money. The Jewish banker himself rarely has a permanent interest in the corporations he finances.

Non-Jewish bankers usually feel obligated to retain a connection with the enterprises they have financed, in order to assure the investors a proper administration of funds; they feel obligated to contribute to the success of the investments which they handle for other people.

The Jewish banker keeps his capital liquid. The cash is always in his coffers. This is essential to his position as one who deals in money. And when the inevitable day of financial stress arrives, he profits greatly by the higher value then placed on liquid capital.

Far and away the leading Jewish banking house in Wall Street is that of Kuhn, Loeb & Company. The head of this great firm was the late Jacob Schiff, whose associates were his son Mortimer, Otto H. Kahn, Paul M. Warburg, and others, who have taken prominent parts both in public life and giant financial operations.

Other private Jewish banking houses may be named as follows: Speyer & Company; J. and W. Seligman & Company; Lazard Freres; Ladenburg, Thalmann & Company; Hallgarten & Company; Knauth, Nachod & Kuhne; Goldman, Sachs & Company, as well as others of relatively less prominence. These firms enjoy a high reputation for financial integrity. They are cautious bankers, skillful in their operations, and sometimes brilliant in their financial strategy.

There is much control of industry, from the financial side, represented by Jewish power in Wall Street, and they have gained a monopoly of many metal markets. Large, prosperous Jewish brokerage houses are on every hand. The further one goes down the line of speculative operations, the more of the Jewish race one finds to be active in the work of company promotions and the marketing of oil and mining stocks.

Yet one amazing fact stands out from the mass: there is not, at this writing, a Jewish bank president on Wall Street; that is, a president of a bank of public deposit. Of all the great banks of public deposit and corporation finance, the enormous trust companies whose individual resources often run up to $400,000,000 and whose combined resources approximate many billions, not one of them has Jewish management or Jewish officers.

Why is this so? Why have the powerful banking families of Wall Street surrounded themselves so carefully with non-Jewish associates? Why has this great dividing line been drawn between members of the Jewish and non-Jewish races in the financial district that manages the financial resources of the nation?

Why? The answer to the question is in the custody of the stronger and sounder financial heads of Wall Street.

Only here and there will one discover a Jewish director in the boards of some of the lesser banking institutions. The situation may be due merely to a shrewd analysis of the public mind. Rightly or wrongly the

Jew Versus Non-Jew in New York Finance

public prefers not to confide its money to an institution under Jewish control. It is true that in certain uptown sections of New York there are a few banks of a local character which are completely under Jewish management. But even the Jews prefer to deposit their money in banks which are free of Jewish control.

The situation may also be the effect of the unfortunate experience which the public has had with Jewish management of banks in the past. Several large failures have served to impress upon the public mind a certain peculiarity which attached to the Jewish element in those failures. The public has not forgotten, among others, the failure of Joseph G. Robin, whose real name was Robonovitch. He was an Odessa Jew. In an incredibly short space of time he built up four large banking institutions in which public money was deposited. He wrecked them all. His failure was most sensational and caused untold suffering. Robonovitch's career illustrated very vividly the extent of the gifts and energies of the Jew from Russia, his wonderful faculty for building up large concerns through chicanery, and his cowardice and duplicity in the hour of defeat. This banking career ended in a felon's cell.

However, one fact of importance, a fact that should be reassuring to the general public, is that the men to whom is entrusted the crucial task of putting to work and keeping at work the financial resources of the United States have hedged themselves about with a non-Jewish wall of great and long standing.

The effort of Jewish interests to gain control of the Stock Exchange is also an interesting story, and although the record shows a steady Jewish gain toward the end they desire, it is slow; but there are indications that the relentless persistence for which the Jew is noted, will prevail in the end—that is, if stock gambling continues to prove an alluring source of wealth.

When the Jews gain control of the Stock Exchange they will, for the first time, possess the power to wrest public banking control from the non-Jewish group.

There is a silent resistance to Jews on the Stock Exchange also, in virtue of an unwritten law, just as there is in the banking world of Wall Street, and the story of the counter-resistance calls for an historian.

It is related by Sereno S. Pratt that in 1792 there was a little office at No. 22 Wall Street for the public sale of stocks. A number of men, engaged in the business of buying and selling, were accustomed to meet near a large buttonwood tree which stood near 68 Wall Street. In 1817, the

New York Stock Exchange, about as present constituted, was organized.

The Stock Exchange is private institution. It is practically a commission club in private hands. It is not incorporated.

Its membership is strictly limited to 1,100 men.

There are only two ways by which an outsider can become owner of seat on the Exchange—by obtaining it from the executor of a deceased member, or by purchasing from a retiring or bankrupt member.

These memberships or seats cost at present more than $100,000. About ten years ago a seat could be bought for $77,000.

The Stock Exchange is ruled by a Governing Committee of 40 members. For many years no Jew was elected to this Committee. Of recent years, an occasional Jewish broker has succeeded in being admitted to this upper group, but not often. This position, however, has not been the main objective of Jewish traders. When they secure a sufficient number of seats on the Exchange, they will take care of the matter of control in their own well-known way.

The two barriers which at present operate to prevent a large inroad of Jews are these: first, a silent resistance on the part of the other members against the admission of Jews, a resistance which is said to date from the earliest formation of this famous trading institution. And, second, the restrictions which are placed by the constitution of the Stock Exchange itself on all applications for membership.

The Governing Committee of 40 has a Committee on Admissions which comprises 15 members and which considers all applications for membership. As the membership is fixed at 1,100 and as no new seats are ever sold, a new member can gain entrance only through the transfer of an existing seat. But even such a transfer is under the strict control of the Committee of Admissions, to whose scrutiny the name of the applicant must be submitted, and whose two-thirds approval is necessary to his being seated.

But one outstanding characteristic of the Jewish race is its persistence. What it cannot attain this generation, it will attain next. Defeat it today, it does not remain defeated; its conquerors die, but Jewry goes on, never forgiving, never forgetting, never deviating from its ancient aim of world control in one form or another. So, though it would seem impossible that Jewish membership in the Stock Exchange could increase under these conditions, the plain fact is that it has increased. Slowly but surely the Jews are gaining numerical power on the floor of the Exchange. And they are doing it with a subtlety that is amazing.

Jew Versus Non-Jew in New York Finance

How do they do it? In the first place, no Jewish member ever transfers his seat to a non-Jew. In times of market dullness, when the prices of seats drop and the demand is not so keen as usual, Jewish bidders offer, invariably, the highest sums to the seller. Then, in the case of the bankruptcy of a non-Jewish member, the receiver is almost compelled by the demand of creditors to accept the highest bid for the transfer of his membership; and, of course, a Jew is always at hand to make the bid as high as necessary. These are the two principal methods by which Jewish membership in the Exchange is being increased.

Another method, however, is more insidious than all the others combined. It is based on the rather common practice of adopting non-Jewish names or professing some phase of the Christian faith. The "changed name," or, as Jews know it, "the cover name," is a very potent part of the policy of concealment. In an advertisement, on business stationery, at the head of a magazine or newspaper article, such names as Smith, Adams, Robin, serve as a "blind."

The stage is flooded with Jewish actors and actresses, but their names are very distinguished Anglo-Saxon. Jewish papers often print jokes based on this habit of changing names. For long-distance dealing, or any business that is carried on "unsight and unseen," the name-veil is very useful. On this account, many Gentiles would be surprised to learn the extent to which they are involved with Jews, whose names give no indication of Jewishness. And this very system, an old American name, coupled with membership in some Christian sect (preferably one of the newer sects), has accounted for some memberships in the Stock Exchange which probably would not otherwise exist.

It is interesting to tabulate the growth of Jewish membership as shown by the old directories of the Exchange.

In the year 1872, with a total of 1,009 members there were 60 Jews. In 1873, with a total of 1,006 members, the Jewish membership decreased to 49. In 1890, with membership limited to 1,100 there were 87 Jews. In 1893, with the same limit of membership, there were 106 Jews. At the present time, still with the same rigid limitation of membership, there are 276 Jewish members.

It is said that the Jewish membership is really somewhat larger than the last figures indicate, owing to the fact that some of the Jewish members bear non-Jewish names and have adopted some phase of the Christian faith and have cut themselves off, outwardly at least, from the Jewish community.

The figures show, therefore, that Jewish membership increased from 5 7/8 per cent of the total in 1872 to 25 per cent in 1919.

In its reference to the Stock Exchange under the head of "Finance," the *Jewish Encyclopedia* states that Jewish membership is "only 128," "a little more than 10 per cent." The date of these Jewish statistics is not given. The article quoted has, however, an argumentative as well as informative purpose. The statement concerning the 10 per cent membership on the Exchange is made to call attention to the fact that "Jews form at least 20 per cent of the whole population of New York, and much more than that percentage of the business section." The Jewish population of New York City has since increased to 25 per cent of the whole, and the membership on the Stock Exchange has increased to the same point.

But it has taken 47 years for the Jews to gain that 25 per cent membership. Their control of the Exchange, at the given rate of progress, is only a question of time.

In spite of these details, it is probably a fact that the Jewish speculators in the New York financial district greatly outnumber the non-Jewish speculators. Speculation and gambling are known historically as special propensities of the Jewish race. While many Jews patronize non-Jewish firms, the great mass of them follow in the speculative path of the leaders of their race.

In Europe, where their financial control is more firmly fixed and of longer standing than here, it is rarely that the Jews are caught in speculative failure. They are sometimes found in speculative scandals, but seldom in any scandal involving losses to themselves. As a rule they dabble in "Jewish" securities, and in Wall Street one hears many stories concerning the victories or defeats of "the Jewish following."

Some of the biggest Jewish sensations which ever occurred in the United States, sensations which disclosed by their lurid light the interlocking of Jewish finance, politics and racial objectives, have been brought to light by occurrences in Wall Street. It is probably the nature of these disclosures which accounts for the strong and silent anti-Jewish resistance which characterizes straight American finance.

Meanwhile, to leave the exalted sphere of Wall Street, banking and brokerage activities, let us descend to the street level of the Curb Market in Broad Street. Here the Jewish brokers flourish in their oil, mining and stock promotion offices. They are so numerous as to give a Semitic cast to the vicinity, as if it were a quarter in a foreign city. It is true that these concerns are frequently operated under non-Jewish names, but that is merely part of the Jew's consciousness that, in financial matters, whether rightly or wrongly, he is under suspicion. Gentile names carry with them no such handicap.

Going still further down the line, in shadier lanes, in semi-hidden offices, may be seen numerous members of the Jewish race who are identified with no established market which deals with securities. These are the true parasites of the Wall Street environment, they are the camp followers without status. Their work is that of fraudulent stock promotion, and they enter upon it with a zeal and an energy which nothing can dismay.

Their purpose is to make money without labor, to get money without giving value, and in this they are immensely successful. It is amazing the number of these men who make immense fortunes; it is equally amazing the continuous crop of unwary, poorly informed, and unsuspecting Gentiles who send their money from all parts of the United States for the worthless bits of paper in which these Jewish parasites deal. It is a most heartless business; it has not even brilliance in its deviltry.

It is the old-time shell game in other terms. The operations of these men are mostly conducted by mail or telephone. They deal in "sucker lists," and they circulate "market letters" by which, under the pretense of giving disinterested advice to investors, they seek to boom their own shady game. These "market letters" are, of course, innocuous to those who are informed and who can read their fraudulent import between the lines, but they are dangerous to the honest but uninformed minds of tens of thousands of thrifty people.

Pursued by detective agencies, watched constantly by the government secret service, exposed by the newspapers, placed on trial in the courts, convicted and sentenced to terms in prison, this type of Jewish swindler is undeterred. Where other men would regard exposure as a lifelong shame, this type regards it simply as a trifling interruption, as a sailor would regard an accidental tumble overboard.

There are lower depths still, where bald theft and violence prevail. The persons most found there are the henchmen of the lower type of speculators. The stories of criminality in Wall Street, a numerous and startling list, involving sometimes the high, but mostly the low, and all marked with a peculiar racial and groupal cast, have at times challenged the attention of the whole world, but as is usually the case with the general publication of such stories, the fundamental explanatory facts are omitted.

But it will be seen, as the story of actual conditions in Wall Street and its financial environs is unrolled, that there are always the two elements—Jewish and non-Jewish. It is perhaps the only non-Jewish coalition in America, this silent resistance which American finance is making to Semitic control.

It is, in a sense, unnatural to the American mind, but has been forced as a defensive against the strong offensive operations of the Semitic coalition. If there is ever in the United States a strong non-Jewish combination, it will be the direct result of the ancient Jewish coalition against non-Jews. The condition in the United States at this moment, with regard to the financial question, is this: The Jewish coalition goes lower, but it does not yet go higher than non-Jewish control. It is struggling to go higher, but has thus far been estopped. It is believed that when the people are made aware of what is transpiring, it will be forever estopped.

As readers of former articles will remember, the attack upon Capital represented by the disorderly forces who operate under the forged banner of "Progress," is an attack against Gentile capital only. The only financial managers attacked in the United States are Gentile managers. In England also, the same attack is made. Readers of the newspapers know what strenuous efforts are being made in that country to wreck railroad and coal mine administration by a constant series of strikes. But what readers of newspapers are not told is that the railroad and coal mines are still in Gentile hands, and that the Bolshevist-led strike is a Jewish financial weapon to wreck these forms of Gentile business, that they may easily fall into Jewish hands.

The Dearborn Independent, November 13, 1920

"Economic crises were created by us for the Gentiles only by the withdrawal of money from circulation .... The present issue of money does not coincide with the need per capita, and consequently it cannot satisfy all the needs of the working classes. . . . . You know that gold currency was detrimental to the governments that accepted it, for it could not satisfy the requirements for money, since we took as much gold as possible out of circulation." —Protocol 20.

24. The High and Low of Jewish Money Power

Jewish high finance first touched the United States through the Rothschilds. Indeed it may be said that the United States founded the Rothschild fortune. And, as so often occurs in the tale of Jewish riches, the fortune was founded in war. The first twenty million dollars the Rothschilds ever had to speculate with was money paid for Hessian troops to fight against the American colonies.

Since that first indirect connection with American affairs, the Rothschilds have often invaded the money affairs of the country, though always by agents. None of the Rothschild sons thought it necessary to establish himself in the United States. Anselm remained in Frankfort, Solomon chose Vienna, Nathan Mayer went to London, Charles established himself in Naples, and James represented the family in Paris. These were the five war-lords of Europe for more than a generation, and their dynasty was continued by their successors.

The first Jewish agent of the Rothschilds in the United States was August Belmont, who came to the United States in 1837, and was made chairman of the Democratic National Committee at the outbreak of the Civil War. The Belmonts professed Christianity and there is today a Belmont memorial, called the Oriental Chapel, in the new Cathedral of St. John the Divine on Morningside Heights.

Rothschild power, as it was once known, has been so broadened by the entry of other banking families into governmental finance, that it must now be known not by the name of one family of Jews, but by the name of the race. Thus it is spoken of as International Jewish Finance, and its principal figures are described as International Jewish Financiers. Much of the veil of secrecy which contributed so greatly to the Rothschild power has been stripped away; war finance has been labeled for all time as "blood money"; and the mysterious magic surrounding large transactions between governments and individuals, by which individual controllers of large wealth were made the real rulers of the people, has been largely stripped away and the plain facts disclosed.

The Rothschild method still holds good, however, in that Jewish institutions are affiliated with their racial institutions in all foreign countries. There are Jewish banking firms in New York whose connections with firms in Frankfort, Hamburg and Dresden, as well as in London and Paris, can be traced by the mere matter of the signs over the doors. They are one.

As a leading student of financial affairs puts it, the world of high finance is largely a Jewish world because of the Jewish financier's "absence from national or patriotic illusions."

To the International Jewish Financier the ups and downs of war and peace between nations are but the changes of the world's financial market; and, as frequently the movement of stocks is manipulated for purposes of market strategy, so sometimes international relations are effected for mere financial gain.

It is known that the recent Great War was postponed several times at the behest of international financiers. If it broke out too soon, it would not involve the states which the international financiers wished to involve. Therefore, the masters of gold, that is, the international masters, were compelled several times to check the martial enthusiasm which their own propaganda had aroused. It is probably quite true, as the Jewish press alleges, that there has been discovered a Rothschild letter dated 1911 and urging the kaiser against war. The year 1911 was too early. There was no such insistence in 1914.

Not only do these foreign financial affiliations cast a different light on purely national matters affecting the peace and prestige of the peoples, but they tend toward an extra- or super-nationality. When these foreign affiliations enable Jewish bankers to excel in the more highly specialized forms of finance, such as foreign exchange, they also enable them to exercise almost complete control over international money movements.

There is no question whatever of International Jewish Finance being deeply concerned in the matters of war and revolution. This is never denied as to the past; but it is just as true of the present. The league against Napoleon, for example, was Jewish. Its headquarters were in Holland. When Napoleon invaded Holland, the headquarters were moved to Frankfort-on-the-Main. It is remarkable how many of the International Jewish Financiers have come out of Frankfort—the Rothschilds, the Schiffs, the Speyers, to name but a few. The racial affiliations running all through the world of international finance are readily recognized. These associations produce in Jewish banking circles a constant tendency toward control or monopoly of certain lines of industry which are identified with the fields of finance. The rule is, once control is gained, all non-Jewish interests must be driven out. "Jewish financial interests have rarely been connected with industrials," says the *Jewish Encyclopedia*, "except as regards some of the precious stones and metals, the Rothschilds, controlling mercury, Barnato Brothers and Werner, Beit & Company diamonds, and the firms of Lewisohn Brothers and Guggenheim Sons controlling copper, and to some extent silver." To this, of course, may be added whiskey, wireless, theaters, the European press and part of the American, and a number of other fields. The list will be made complete in this series of articles before they are finished.

The *Jewish Encyclopedia* continues:

"It is, however, mainly in the direction of foreign loans that there has been any definite predominance of Jewish financiers, this being due, as before stated, to the international relations of the larger Jewish firms."

In order that the senseless denials of certain portions of the Jewish press may be checked, it may be said that Jewish authorities do not deny such statements as are made about Jewish international financial control, although they declare it is not as strong as it once was. "Of more recent years," says The *Jewish Encyclopedia*, "non-Jewish financiers have learned the same cosmopolitan method, and, on the whole, the control is now rather less than more in Jewish hands than formerly."

This is true, at least so far as the United States is concerned. Previous to the war, the status of many of the Jewish financial concerns in Wall Street was stronger than it is now. The war brought about a condition which threw a new light on the internationalism of Jewish finance. During the years of American neutrality there was opportunity to observe the extent of the foreign affiliations of certain men, and also the extent to which ordinary national loyalty was subordinated to the business of international finance. The war really forced a coalition of Gentile capital on one side of the struggle, as against certain blocks of Jewish capital which were willing to play both sides. The old Rothschild maxim, "Do not put all your eggs in one basket," becomes perfectly plain when transposed into national and international terms. Jewish finance treats political parties the same—bets on them both, and so never loses. In the same way, Jewish finance never loses a war. Being on both sides, it cannot miss the winning side, and its terms of peace are sufficient to cover all advances to the side that lost. This was the significance of the great swarming of Jews at the Peace Conference.

Many of the Jewish houses on Wall Street were originally the American branches of long established houses in Germany and Austria.

These international firms were accustomed to support one another with capital, and maintained other intimate associations. Some of them are linked by intermarriage. But the bond above all is the Jewish racial bond. Most of these houses received a severe setback during the war, because their over-sea associations were not of the right kind. But this setback is expected to be only temporary, and the Jewish financiers will again be ready to give battle for the entire financial control of the United States.

Whether they will be successful, the future will decide. But a strange fatality seems to follow all forms of Jewish supremacy. Just as the capstone is ready to be placed upon the edifice of Jewish triumphs, something occurs and the structure shrinks. It occurs so often in Jewish history that the Jews themselves have been exercised to find an explanation. In many cases "anti-Semitism" offers the readiest excuse, but not always. Just at the present time, when the light which was shed by the fires of war has revealed so many matters formerly hidden in shadow, the awakening of world attention is called "anti-Semitism," and the explanation is given that "after every war the Jew becomes the scapegoat"—a curious admission which would lead a less self-centered people to inquire, Why?

But so handy and so untrustworthy an explanation as "anti-Semitism" does not account for the failure of Jewish financial interests to become absolutely dominant in a country like the United States. Anti-Semitism among the people does not surge high enough to injure those securely entrenched behind great financial influence. The silent resistance of the Wall Street financial group or of the New York Stock Exchange, for example, is not anti-Semitism. It is not a hindrance to the Jews in doing business; it is opposition to an apparent program for total control which is sought not for the general good, but for a racial benefit.

It was only a few years ago that the banking house of Kuhn, Loeb & Company was commonly regarded as being destined in the near future to win complete financial supremacy in Wall Street as an underwriting and money-lending institution. There were many reasons for this belief, among them the fact that Kuhn, Loeb & Company were the financial backers of Harriman in his terrific railroad duel with James J. Hill. But the prophecy regarding this financial institution was never realized. Untoward events intervened, in no way affecting the financial integrity of the firm, but bringing it into the light of undesirable publicity not of a financial character.

In the firm of Kuhn, Loeb & Company, Jewish finance in the United States reached its high-water mark. The head of this firm was the late Jacob Schiff, who was born in Frankfort-on-the-Main and whose father was one of the Rothschilds' brokers. One of Jacob Schiff's associates, Otto Kahn, was born in Mannheim, and was early associated with the Speyers, who also originated in Frankfort-on-the-Main. Another associate, Felix Warburg, married into Jacob Schiff's family. Jewish finance has spread, but it has not risen higher than in this firm.

A flank movement, however, has been attempted which may bring Jewish ambitions nearer the goal of their desire. Checked in Wall Street, Jewish financiers have sought out other American centers, and even foreign centers whose future influence on American affairs promises to be considerable. The first flank movement is toward Central and South America. It may be said that the financial assistance, practical and advisory, offered to Mexico during the most unsatisfactory period of her relations with the United States, was given by Jewish financial groups. The attempt to gain influence with Japan seems to have come off rather badly. It is known, of course, that Jacob Schiff gave material assistance to Japan in the war with Russia. This was explainable on the ground of good business and also of a desire to revenge Russia's treatment of the Jews. Mr. Schiff used the opportunity also to instill the principles, which have since grown up into Bolshevism, into the minds of Russian prisoners in Japanese war camps.

But more than that, the idea appears to have been to add the newly rising Japanese power to the string of Jewish financial conquests. Jewish finance already has a foothold in Japan, but it appears that Mr. Schiff's hopes in this respect were not fully realized. The Japanese are credited with knowing much more about "the Jewish peril" than even the United States does, and they were exceedingly wary. They kept the business deal strictly a business deal, and Mr. Schiff was said to have been displeased with Japan generally. This is well worth knowing at this time, especially in view of the propaganda which seeks constantly to cause misunderstandings to arise between the United States and the Empire of Japan.

But South America appears to be the latest objective. It must be remembered that the Jews exercise world control in two departments: in movements of men, and in movements of money. No government, no church, no school of thought could order the movement of 250,000, half a million, or even a million people, from one part of the world to another, shifting them as a general shifts his army, but the Jews can do that. They are doing it now. It is only a matter of ships. From Poland, where Jewish special privileges have been written into the law of the land by the all-powerful Peace Conference, and where it would seem that the Jews have every reason to remain, there is a great movement westward. It is not a stampede, as the American Commissioner of Immigration says, although it may look so from this side.

It is an orderly movement, as can be seen when the American Jewish directors on the other side are observed. And part of it is being directed to South America. It is said that after a period of training in the United States, some of the immigrants who are now landing here will be shipped south again.

The other mastery which the Jews exert in a world degree is that over the movement of gold. Without giving expression to what the purpose may be, there is this to be said: a large movement of Jewish men and Jewish gold proceeds toward South America these days. And there is said to be a large movement of other materials, which when interpreted by the Protocols can mean but one thing.

The next attempt for control of the Americas may come from the South, where the Jews are already stronger than their numbers would indicate, and where their revolutionary proclivities have already come into play as between the various states.

These rebuffs and these strategic flank movements do not, however, complete the record. We are now speaking of American finance only. The Jews have not been restrained elsewhere as they have been in Wall Street. They exercise a very ominous control in a number of other fields, each of which will be taken up in detail in due time. For the present, our attention is being directed to New York and its financial district.

We have just shown the high-water mark of Jewish control as it has been reached up to date in the Street. There is another aspect of Jewish influence on the financial affairs of America which is not so flattering to that race. If Jewish financial activity does not go higher, it goes lower and finds its way into darker channels than does any other form of financial activity in the country.

The High and Low of Jewish Money Power

It would make a sordid tale, the operations of the Robins, the Lamars, the Arnsteins and the others who have contributed to the long roll of criminality produced within the shadow of Wall Street and the only point that could be served by its retelling is that such criminality is predominantly Jewish. This is not to say that it has the approval of the Jewish community, but it is very significant that while whole volumes of abuse have been heaped upon *The Dearborn Independent*'s very modest effort to state the status of the Jewish Question in America, the leaders of Jewry have been silent about the criminal financial operations of those who could be made to feel the displeasure of their race. The Jewish passion for the defense of the race, regardless of the degree of guilt, is well known to every prosecuting attorney, although it must be said that during the investigation made some years ago which revealed the business of commercialized vice to be under Jewish control, certain public-spirited Jews commendably aided the work. This aid, however, did not prevent the severest opposition to certain publications which gave notice of the facts that the investigators were finding.

This country was lately astounded by the revelation that stocks and Liberty bonds to the value of $12,000,000 had been lost through a systematic series of thefts in Wall Street.

Beginning with the spring of 1918, messengers sent out by New York Stock Exchange firms to make deliveries of stocks and bonds to other houses, in the course of ordinary business, began to disappear as if the earth had swallowed them up. For a time these disappearances were without explanation.

Wall Street is really a small district. Most of its business is done within the space of a city block. Messengers on their trips sometimes went only to another floor in the same building, or to an office across the street. Yet in those short trips they would disappear with all their securities, seldom to be heard of again.

Up to the summer of 1918 the absconding messenger boy was a rarity. The type was regarded with good-humored indulgence on the Street. They were generally happy-go-lucky youngsters, and the steadier heads among them graduated into clerks in the commission houses.

The labor shortage struck Wall Street, along with other sections of the country, and messenger boys were difficult to find. During this period there was also a great expansion in business. Nearly everyone in the country possessed bonds of some kind, and these changed hands in unparalelled quantities. On the floor of the Stock Exchange, daily transactions in bonds up to $20,000,000, and in stocks up to one or two million shares, were common. Following the sales, the stocks and bonds were transferred from seller to buyer by messenger boy. It was not unusual for irresponsible lads to be running from office to office in Wall Street with $250,000 each under the arms.

Then, with the shortage of boys, another type of messenger began to appear, and with this type trouble began. Disappearances and losses became more frequent and costly. The indemnities paid by the insurance companies reached such staggering figures that the custom of issuing blanket insurance was withdrawn. Various expedients were adopted to solve the mystery; boys were required to travel in pairs, guards were posted throughout Wall Street, the best detectives in the land were assigned to the matter, but without avail.

There was a strong disinclination in Wall Street toward publishing the figures of the losses, for fear the publication might be destructive of public confidence in the Street's financial condition. But the news was known in the underworld and drew to New York criminals from all parts of the country. For a time all efforts were fruitless; the losses continued and the mystery deepened.

Then, suddenly, in the early part of 1920, certain arrests were made and confessions obtained, which disclosed one of the most amazing criminal conspiracies in the history of the United States.

There was proved the existence of a vast Jewish conspiracy to loot Wall Street. It was found that a band of astute Jewish criminals, many of them wealthy men, some of them ex-convicts, had created an organization by which Wall Street financial houses were to be plundered.

Bands of young Jews, mostly of Russian origin and living on the East Side, had been shaped into being. These lads, instructed by clever Jewish principals, applied to Wall Street messenger agencies for employment in brokerage houses. It was part of the plan for them to assume good, honest-sounding Anglo-Saxon names. The "cover name"— how often we meet it!

These lads turned over their stolen stocks and bonds to the heads of their organizations, who in turn passed the securities on to the Jewish principals, who were for the most part members of the criminal band of "confidence men" in the White Light district—the "bank-roll men," whose immunity from punishment has always been one of the standing puzzles of Gentiles residing in New York.

These Jewish criminals were aided by Jewish lawyers in their transactions. The stolen stocks and bonds were taken to Cleveland,

Boston, Washington, Philadelphia and parts of Canada, where they were pledged as collateral for loans in an apparently legitimate course of business. One of the messenger boys refused to deliver his stolen securities for the small sum he was offered for them, and ran away to enjoy alone his ill-gotten wealth. His hiding place was discovered and members of a band of Harlem assassins were sent for him, with instructions to find where the securities were. If they were on the boy's person, he was to be killed at once.

This band entertained the boy with drinks and women for several days until they learned that the securities were sewed inside the lining of his coat. They took him for a "joy-ride" into the country, and his dead body was afterward found, typically slain, with about two dozen dagger wounds in his body.

In one instance a non-Jew was inveigled into the nefarious scheme, and the method was also typical. The Jewish principals wished for another clearing-house through which to dispose of their securities, and were "tipped off" that a young non-Jewish broker was on the verge of bankruptcy. He was "helped out" and given what appeared to him to be a very profitable piece of business. Once in the power of his "friends," and deeply entangled in their game, he tried to get out of it. He was threatened with death. The Jewish principal said to him: "I don't want any double-crossing here, or I'll kill you in a minute. If I can't do it—if I am locked up—there are plenty of my gang who will do it."

Upon the arrest and confession of this non-Jew, many of the Jewish principals fled New York, traveling, as usual, under their assumed Christian names. But their identity had at last become known, and although many of their messenger-boy dupes have been made to suffer the penalty for their crimes, the leaders are at this writing yet free, and the most powerful influences seem to be invoked to protect them from the ordinary operations of the law. A few have been captured, but although their accusers are the most powerful banking, brokerage and surety companies on Wall Street, a power greater still seems to defend them from the treatment usually accorded known criminals.

One of the ringleaders has defied the courts with impunity and still walks the streets. Jewish theatrical managers in New York have headlined his actress wife, a Jewess, presumably because of the added prestige it gave her to be the wife of the world-defying bond thief.

That is the element which strikes something like consternation to the heart of the ordinary lover of law and order—the insolence with which these wealthy Jewish criminals regard all the agencies of the law. They are defended by clever lawyers, and the attitude of the Jewish press and Jewish population toward them is compact of sympathy and admiration. Why not?—since most of the individual victims of the thievery are Gentiles, and the general victim is Gentile capitalism itself!

There is complete silence on the Jewish side regarding this reign of crime. And yet inevitably the Jews themselves must suffer most from it. The New York Kehillah has completely ignored this outbreak and its exposure. The spokesmen of Jewry, so voluble against non-Jews, have no word to say to those whom they would probably call their "co-religionists." Yet it is well enough understood that so closely combined are all the influences in New York Jewry that a determined effort on the part of the leaders could clean up many untoward conditions now existing. But there seems to be a distinct aversion to anything that will indicate a division of one class of Jews against another. It is a racial instinct, evidently, to protect the threatened one no matter how richly he may deserve punishment.

It is this fact which puts the finishing Jewish touch on the whole matter. It may, of course, be an accident that all the criminals and their tools, with an occasional exception, are Jews. That of itself might not be a reason, in the extreme sense, for labeling the condition with a racial name. But the silence, the approbation in some quarters, the very active sympathy in others, all combining as a racial protectorate around the wrongdoers, is the more regrettable manifestation of the two.

The Dearborn Independent, November 20, 1920

25. "Disraeli of America"— A Jew of Super-Power

Although the war had the effect of decreasing Jewish power in Wall Street by temporarily hindering, but perhaps not altogether breaking off, the communication between Jewish financial houses in the United States and their associates overseas, it also had the effect of greatly increasing Jewish wealth in this country. It is stated upon the authority of a well-informed Jewish source that in New York City alone fully 73 per cent of the "war millionaires" are Jews.

The mistake should not be made of assuming that because of the temporary setback in Wall Street, the war meant a total setback for the Jewish program. It did not. Jewry emerged from the war more strongly entrenched in power, even in the United States, than it was before. And in the world at large the ascendancy of the Jew, even where he was in control before, is very marked.

A Jew is now President of the League of Nations.

A Zionist is President of the Council of the League of Nations.

A Jew is President of France.

A Jew was President of the committee to investigate the responsibility for the war, and one incident of his service was the disappearance of vital documents.

In France, Germany and England, the financial power of the Jews, as well as the filtration of their dangerous ideas of social disorder, have greatly increased.

It is a most remarkable fact that in those countries which can justly be called anti-Semitic, the rule of the Jew is stronger than anywhere else. The more they are opposed, the more they show their power. Germany is today an anti-Semitic nation. Yet, in spite of all the German people have done to rid themselves of the visible show of Jewish power, it has entrenched itself more firmly than before, above and beyond the reach of the German popular will. France becomes increasingly anti-Semitic, and as the anti-Jewish wave rises, a Jewish President appears. Russia itself is anti-Semitic to the core, and the Jew is Russia's new tyrant. And at a moment when, as all Jewish spokesmen inform us, there is a world wave of anti-Semitism—which is their name for a new awakening of the nations to what has been going on—what should occur but that at the head of the League of Nations, in a position which but for the absence of the United States would constitute the Chief Magistracy of the World, a Jew appears. Nobody seems to know why. Nobody can explain it. Neither previous fitness nor public demand pointed him out—yet there he is!

In our own country we have just had a four-year term of Jewish rule, almost as absolute as that which exists in Russia. This appears to be a very strong statement, but it is somewhat milder than the facts warrant. And the facts themselves are not of hearsay origin, nor the product of a biased point of view; they are the fruits of an inquiry by the lawful officials of the United States who were set aside in favor of a ready-made Jewish Government, and they are forever spread upon the official records of the United States.

The Jews have proved for all time that the control of Wall Street is not necessary to the control of the American people, and the person by whom they proved this was a Wall Street Jew.

This man has been called "the pro-consul of Judah in America." It is said that once, referring to himself, he exclaimed: "Behold the Disraeli of the United States!"

To a select committee of the Congress of the United States he said:

"I probably had more power than perhaps any other man did in the war; doubtless that is true."

And in saying so he did not overstate the case. He did have more power. It was not all legal power, this much he admitted. It reached into every home and store and factory and bank and railway and mine. It touched armies and governments.

It touched the recruiting boards. It made and unmade men without a word. It was power without responsibility and without limit. It was such a power as compelled the Gentile population to lay bare every secret before this man and his Jewish associates, giving them a knowledge and an advantage that billions of gold could not buy.

Doubtless not one in every 50,000 of the readers of this paper ever heard of this man before 1917, and doubtless the same number have clear knowledge of him now. He glided out of a certain obscurity unlighted by public service of fame, into the high rulership of the nation at war. The constituted government had little to do with him save vote the money and do his bidding. He said that men could have appealed over his head to the President of the United States, but, knowing the situation, men never did.

Who is this figure, colossal in his way, and most instructive of the readiness of Judah to take the rule whenever he desires?

His name is Bernard M. Baruch. He was born in South Carolina 50 years ago, the son of Dr. Simon Baruch, who was a medical man of some consequence. "I went to college with the idea of becoming a doctor, but I did not become a doctor," he told the Congressional Committee. He was graduated at the College of the City of New York when he was just under 19 years of age.

This college is one of the favorite educational institutions with the Jews, its president being Dr. S. E. Mezes, a brother-in-law of Colonel E. M. House, the colonel whose influence and disfavor at the White House has for a long time been a favorite subject of wondering speculation on the part of the American people, though it scarcely need be so any longer.

Apparently young Baruch knew exactly what he wanted to do, and set out to do it. He says he spent "many years" after his graduation in certain studies, "particularly economics" as related to railroads and industrial propositions. "I tried to make Poor's Manual and the financial supplement of the *Financial Chronicle* my bible for a number of years."

He could not have spent very "many years" in these pursuits, for after going down to Wall Street as a clerk and a runner, and when he was "about 26 or 27" he became a member of the firm of A. A. Housman & Company. "In about 1900 or 1902" he left the firm, but he had meanwhile gained a seat on the Stock Exchange.

He then went into business for himself, a statement which must be taken literally in view of his testimony that he "did not do any business for anybody but himself. I made a study of the corporations engaged in the production and manufacture of different things, and a study of the men engaged in them."

In answer to questions intended to disclose the exact nature of his operations before he suddenly appeared as the man who "had more power than perhaps any other man did in the war," he stood off from any intimations that he perhaps engaged in mere buying and selling of stock. "My business then became the organization of various enterprises," he said, "and in connection with that, I, of course, did buy and sell stocks ... If I organized any concern, I naturally took a large interest in it, or I would not organize it if I did not believe in it, and I stayed with the development of that concern; and then if I cared later on to sell it, I would sell it."

Pressed by the examiners for a still more detailed account of his activities in business, he said:

"Well, I was instrumental in the purchase of the Liggett & Myers Tobacco Company; in the purchase of Selby Smelter, Tacoma Smelter, and various copper, tungsten, rubber—I was instrumental in building up one of the great industries in rubber in Mexico, which was the establishment of the source of supply of rubber, and developed a large concern there for the production of raw material, which is still going on

"I became interested in the new process of concentration of low-grade ores in the Mesaba Range, but the interest I had particularly in steel was in the study of the present-day organization, in order to get myself posted so that I could intelligently buy or sell their securities . . . "

It is an important point, one not made very clear in the testimony, what interests Mr. Baruch held at the beginning of the war. His previous activities in various fields, principally perhaps in the field of metals, had been important and numerous.

In any case, as a young man, he is found to be master of large sums of money, and there is no indication that he inherited it. He is very wealthy. What change the war made in his wealth, if it made any change at all, is a matter on which nothing may be said now. Certainly many of his friends and closest associates reaped great quantities of money from their activities during the war.

Now, as to the point of his business connections just prior to the war, this testimony appears:

Mr. Graham—"You continued in the operation of these various businesses, in the formation of companies and the flotation of their stocks, and in your business in the Stock Exchange and elsewhere up until the time of the beginning of the war?"

Mr. Baruch—"I was gradually getting myself away from business, because I had made up my mind to retire, and I had been getting less active with that end in view, and I was not very much in sympathy with the organization of companies. I am not criticizing other men who engage in business that resulted in profits even before we had gotten into war. I had made up my mind to leave and do some other things that I hope to be able to do now; but that process was interrupted by my appointment as member of the advisory commission without any suggestion or without any knowledge or idea it was coming."

Does he mean that the process of getting out of business was interrupted by his appointment on the advisory commission, which appointment led straight to his complete rulership of the United States at war?

Mr. Jefferis—"Had any of the members of the advisory commission been engaged in the production of raw materials or in manufactured products, or not?"

Mr. Baruch—"I had."

Mr. Jefferis—"In what way?"

Mr. Baruch—"I had made a rather deep study of the production and the distribution and manufacture of many of these raw materials. I had to make an intensive study of these things in order to do the things I was engaged in."

Mr. Jefferis—"You were not running any raw material production?"

Mr. Baruch—"I was interested in concerns—I was interested in the study and production of a great many of these things, because I developed and organized concerns which did it."

Does he mean that he was interested in concerns at the time of his appointment?

This would be an interesting point to clear up.

Another matter which would be not only of interest, but of great usefulness in explaining the gathering of a Jewish government around the President during the war, is the question of Bernard M. Baruch's acquaintance with Woodrow Wilson.

When did it begin? What circumstances or what persons brought them together?

There are stories, of course, and one of them may be true, but the story ought not to be told unless accompanied by the fullest confirmation. Why should it occur that a Jew should be the one man ready and selected for a position of greatest power during the war?

Mr. Baruch, in his testimony, sheds no light on this question.

He had opportunity to do so, had he wished.

Mr. Graham—"I assume that you were personally acquainted with the President prior to the outbreak of the war?"

Mr. Baruch—"Yes, sir."

Mr. Graham—"Up to the time that you were appointed as a member of the advisory commission, had you ever had any personal conferences with the President about these matters?"

Mr. Baruch—"Yes, sir."

Mr. Graham—"Had he called you in consultation or had he talked to you about these matters and about the matter of your appointment before you were appointed?"

Mr. Baruch—"Never suggested anything about the appointment, because I would have told him that I would prefer not to be appointed."

Mr. Graham—"Do you now recall, Mr. Baruch, how long before you were actually appointed as a member of that advisory commission you had your last conference with the President?"

Mr. Baruch—"No . . . "

That is not all of Mr. Baruch's answer, but it is his reply to the question. Having said "No," Mr. Baruch became very communicative on another matter. His complete reply is—

"No; but I can tell you something that may be of interest, and that is probably what you want to know. I had been very much disturbed by the unprepared condition of this country, so much so that I was one of the first men to support General Wood in the Plattsburg encampment, and I think he will admit I gave him the first money and told him whatever he did I would guarantee to stand behind that movement, which happily only took a few thousand dollars so far as I was concerned, having caught the public approval and it went ahead, and in that relation naturally one had to think about the mobilization of the industries of the country, because people do not fight alone with their hands; they have got to fight with things."

It is thus shown that Mr. Baruch was a forehanded gentleman. It was only the year 1915. The European war had then not become more than an amazing spectacle to the mass of the American people. But still Mr. Baruch was convinced we were going to have war, and he spent money on his guess. The government which was then "keeping us out of war" was also consulting with Mr. Baruch who was already ahead of the government in creating the atmosphere of war in this country. If the reader, by a mental effort, can reconstruct the year of 1915, and then put into his picture of that year the element of which he was not then possessed, namely, the activity of Mr. Bernard M. Baruch and other Jews, he will see that he did not know much about what was going on, even if he did read the newspapers with attention!

To proceed with the examination, following the place where Mr. Baruch made his interesting disclosure of his part in the Plattsburg experiment:

Mr. Graham—"That was about 1915, was it not?"

Mr. Baruch—"Yes, 1915; and I had been thinking about it very seriously, and I thought we would be drawn into the war. I went off on a

"Disraeli of America"—A Jew of Super-Power

long trip, and it was while on this trip that I felt there ought to be some mobilization of the industries, and I was thinking about the scheme that practically was put into effect and was working when I was chairman of the board. When I came back from that trip I asked for an interview with the President. It was the first time I had seen the President since his election, so far as I can remember now."

Mr. Graham—"You mean his first election?"

Mr. Baruch—"His first election, yes."

So it is probable that Mr. Baruch, if any stress may be placed on the manner of his words, had known the President before. Ordinary men, who meet the President seldom, usually have a very clear recollection of those meetings. The fact probably is that Mr. Baruch saw the President so frequently that he found it difficult to distinguish the meetings in his memory. He describes the visit referred to:

"I explained to him as earnestly as I could that I was very deeply concerned about the necessity of the mobilization of the industries of the country. The President listened very attentively and graciously, as he always does . . . and the next thing I heard—some months afterward . . . my attention was brought to this Council of National Defense. Secretary Baker brought it to my attention. This was the first time I had met the Secretary of War. He asked me what I thought of it."

Mr. Graham—"That was before the bill was passed; before it became a law?"

Mr. Baruch—"I think it was. I am not certain about that. I said I would like to have something different."

This is rather important. A council is a council. Mr. Baruch wanted something different. Eventually he did get something different. He got the President so to change matters as to make Mr. Baruch the most powerful man in the war.

The Council of National Defense eventually became the merest side show. It was not a council of Americans that ran the war, it was an autocracy headed by a Jew, with Jews at every strategic point down the line.

What Mr. Baruch did was very masterly, but it was not in the American manner. He did what he set out to do, but it is seriously to be questioned whether any man ought to have done what he did, and probably no one but a member of his race would have wanted to do it.

Mr. Graham—"Did the President express any opinion about the advisability of adopting the scheme you proposed?"

Mr. Baruch—"I think I did most of the talking. I do not remember what the President said on that subject, but I think it can be best seen as expressed in the bill."

Mr. Graham—"Did you impress him with your belief that we were going to get into the war?"

Mr. Baruch—"I probably did. I would like to tell you exactly, but I do not want to guess at it."

Mr. Graham—"That was your opinion at the time?"

Mr. Baruch—"Yes; I thought we were going to get into the war. I thought a war was coming long before it did."

The examination then reverted to Mr. Baruch's conference with the Secretary of War, in which the former had said he "would like to have something different."

Mr. Graham—"Mr. Baker said he thought that was the best that could be gotten at that time?"

Mr. Baruch—"I got that impression. Whether he said so or not, I do not know, but I got that impression that that was the best that could be gotten at that time."

If the event had not turned out exactly as Mr. Baruch planned it, a great deal of his testimony might be discounted on the principle of the natural boastfulness of the Jew after a scheme has succeeded; but there is no discounting anything that he says. The President did exactly what Baruch wanted in a thousand matters, and what Baruch apparently wanted most of all was a ruling hand upon productive America. And that he got. He got it in a larger measure than even Lenin ever got in Russia; for here in the United States the people saw nothing but the patriotic element; they did not see the Jewish Government looming above them. Yet it was there.

The Council of National Defense, as originally constituted— "the best that could be gotten at that time," though Mr. Baruch "would like something different"—was headed by six secretaries of the Cabinet, the secretaries of War, Navy, Interior, Agriculture, Commerce and Labor. Beneath this official group was an advisory commission, of seven men, three of whom were Jews; one of these Jews was Mr. Baruch. Beneath this advisory commission were scores and hundreds of men, and many committees. One of the groups subordinate to the two groups just mentioned was the War Industries Board, of which Mr. Baruch was originally merely a member, Daniel Willard being the chairman. Now, it was this War Industries Board which become the "whole thing" later

"Disraeli of America"—A Jew of Super-Power

on, and it was Mr. Baruch who became the "whole thing" in that board. The place where he was put became the corner stone; he became the chief pillar of the war administration. The records show it; he himself admits it.

What influence reached into this Council of hundreds of Americans and chose a single Jew to be their undoubted lord and master for the duration of the war? Was it Baruch's brains that elevated him? Or was it the suggestion of Jewish finance already well forward in its work of mobilization?

There is no desire to minimize the Baruch brain. Brains and money are the Jews' two greatest weapons. No Jew is picked for a key place who has not brains. Baruch has brains. He is a ceaseless wonder among men who know him. He can do six things at once and control the most colossal operations without fuss or fever. He has both brains and money.

But there is something for Jewry to learn: brains and money are not enough. There is another element which even brains cannot cope with, and which renders money cheap. The chess-playing expert may mystify and compel admiration; but the chess-player does not rule the world.

So, Baruch did things. But Trotsky also has done things. The point is this: Are people to be carried away by an appeal deliberately made to their imagination, or are they to scrutinize what has been done, and weigh its consequences?

The Jews could do greater things in the United States than even Barauch has done, if the opportunity offered, acts of superb ease and mastery—but what would it signify? The ideal of a dictator of the United States has never been absent from the group in which Baruch is found witness the work, "Philip Dru, Administrator," commonly attributed to Colonel E. M. House, and never denied by him.

As a matter of fact, Baruch could probably do a better job than Trotsky did. Certainly, the recent experience which he had in governing the country during the war was a very valuable education in the art of autocracy. Not that it is by any means Mr. Baruch's possession alone; it is also the possession of scores of Jewish leaders who flitted about from department to department, from field to field, receiving a post-graduate course in the art of autocracy, not to mention other things.

Before Mr. Bernard M. Baruch got through, he was the head and center of a system of control such as the United States Government itself never possessed and never will possess until it changes its character as a free government.

Mr. Jefferis—"In other words, you determined what everybody could have?"

Mr. Baruch—"Exactly; there is no question about that. I assumed that responsibility, sir, and that final determination rested within me." Mr. Jefferis—"What?"

Mr. Baruch—"That final determination, as the President said, rested within me; the determination of whether the Army or Navy should have it rested with me; the determination of whether the Railroad Administration could have it, or the Allies, or whether General Allenby should have locomotives, or whether they should be used in Russia, or used in France."

Mr. Jefferis—"You had considerable power?"

Mr. Baruch—"Indeed I did, sir. . . . "

Mr. Jefferis—"And all those different lines, really, ultimately, centered in you, so far as power was concerned?"

Mr. Baruch—"Yes, sir, it did. I probably had more power than perhaps any other man did in the war; doubtless that is true."

What preceded Mr. Baruch's attainment of this power, how far his power reached and how it was used will be our next inquiry.

The Dearborn Independent, November 27, 1920

"The King of Israel must not be influenced by his passions, especially by sensuality. No particular element of his nature must have the upper hand and rule over his mind. Sensuality, more than anything else, upsets mental ability and clearness of vision by deflecting thought to the worst and most bestial side of human nature. "The Pillar of the Universe in the Person of the World Ruler, sprung from the seed of David, must sacrifice all personal desires for the benefit of his people."
—Protocol 24.

26. The Scope of Jewish Dictatorship in the U.S.

The common criticism made against President Wilson that "he played a lone hand" and would not avail himself of advice, can be made only by those are in ignorance of the Jewish government which continually advised the President on all matters.

While the President is supposed to have been extremely jealous of his authority, this view of him can be maintained only by remaining blind to the immense authority he conferred on the members of the Jewish War Government. It is true he did not take Congress into his confidence; it is true that he made little of the members of his Cabinet; it also true that he ignored the constitutional place of the United States Senate in the advisory work of making treaties; but it is not true that he acted without advice; it is not true that he depended on his own mind in the conduct of the war and the negotiations at Versailles.

Just when Bernard M. Baruch, the Jewish high governor of the United States in war affairs, came to know Mr. Wilson is yet to be told; but just when he got into and out of the war are matters about which he himself has told us. He got into the war at Plattsburg, two years before there was a war; and he got out of the war when the business at Paris was ended.

"I came back on the George Washington," he testified, which means that he remained in Paris until the last detail was arranged.

It is said that Mr. Baruch was normally a Republican until Woodrow Wilson began to loom up as a Presidential possibility. The Jews made much of Woodrow Wilson, far too much for his own good. They formed a solid ring around him. There was a time when he communicated to the country through no one but a Jew.

The best political writers in the country were sidetracked for two years because the President chose the Jewish journalist, David Lawrence, as his unofficial mouthpiece. Lawrence had the run of the White House offices, with frequent access to the President, and for a time he was the high cockalorum of national newspaperdom, but neither that privilege nor the assiduous boosting of the Jewish ring availed to make him a favorite with the American public.

American Jewry was Democratic until it had secured the last favor that Woodrow Wilson could give, and then it left the Democratic party as with the indecent haste of rats leaving a sinking ship. Baruch stayed, rather ostentatiously spending his money for motion picture appeals in favor of the League of Nations, but it is entirely probable that he has a genuine interest in the new administration.

For one thing, there may be investigations. It remains to be seen whether the investigations which the Republican majority in the House began to make with regard to war expenditures will be continued. There are those who profess to believe that they will not be continued, the explanation being that such investigation as was made before election was solely for the purpose of securing campaign data, or creating a political atmosphere unfavorable to the Democrats.

It is sincerely to be hoped that the Republicans will not rest under that imputation, but that they will rigorously pursue the investigations that have been begun. There are two reasons why this should be done; first, that the country may know, with a view to future contingencies, what was "put over" on the government during the war; second, that the full sweep of Jewish influence in this country may be exposed. The second reason is not expected to appear very weighty to practical politicians, and that is no matter, for if the first reason is deemed sufficient, and if the investigations are honestly made, then inevitably the Jewish power will be further exposed. It is linked up at every stage of the business.

This may have had something to do with the sudden desertion of the Democratic party by the Jews. They may have swung over in order to have something to say about the pursuit of further investigations. Already the counsel is being heard, "Let bygones be bygones," "The people are tired of investigations, and don't want any more"; already attempts are being made to introduce fresher issues to deflect the public mind from war affairs, and the attempts are doubtless Jewish in their origin.

That portion of the public who are awake to the Jewish Question will do well to observe with care the attitude of the new administration toward completing the investigations. The Jews did not flock to the Republicans for nothing. The country is entitled to know what was done

The Scope of Jewish Dictatorship in the U.S.

with the fabulous amounts of money spent during the war. The people are entitled to know who were their masters, and who were responsible for certain strange situations which were created.

Members of the House, Senators, and other officials should, at the very least, pay particular attention to the directions from which influences against further inquiry come.

Now, as to Mr. Bernard M. Baruch, who for some as yet undefined reason was made head and front of the United States at war, we have his own word on several occasions that he was the most important man in the war.

"I probably had more power than perhaps any other man did in the war; doubtless that is true," he told Representative Jefferis.

And again: "We had the power of priority, which was the greatest power in the war ... Exactly; there is no question about that. I assumed that responsibility, sir, and that final determination rested within me."

And when Representative Jefferis said "What?" to that startling statement, Mr. Baruch repeated it:

"That final determination, as the President said, rested within me."

Representative Graham said to him: "In other words, I am right about this, Mr. Baruch, that yours was the guiding mind ... "

And Mr. Baruch replied: "That is partly correct—I think you are entirely correct ... "

Now, in what did Baruch's power consist? Briefly, in this—in the dictatorship of the United States. He once expressed the opinion that the United States could have been managed that way in time of peace, but he explained that it was easier in war time, was made easy because of the patriotic mood of the people.

It is not sufficient, however, to say that Mr. Baruch's rule constituted a dictatorship of the United States; it remains to be shown just how rigid and far-reaching that dictatorship was. The reader may recognize at what point the Jewish rule touched his affairs also.

Mr. Baruch, who had the "final determination" of everything, says that his power extended to the needs of the Army and Navy, the Shipping Board, the Railroad Administration, touched also the Food and Fuel Administrations, and besides all that had a vital control of the Allies' purchases not only in the United States, but also in other countries with reference to certain materials.

There were $30,000,000,000 (Thirty Billions of dollars) spent by the United States Government during the war, all of it raised by taxation and bonds. Of this sum, $10,000,000,000 (Ten Billions) was loaned to the Allies and spent here—all of the purchases being viséed under Mr. Baruch's authority.

As told by himself, his power consisted in the following authorities:

1. Authority over the use of capital in the private business of Americans.

This authority was nominally under the Capital Issues Committee, the controlling factor of which was another Jew, Eugene Meyer, Jr. Here is another inexplicable circumstance. Was he the only banker in the United States capable of exercising a dominant influence? Why did it happen that a Jew should be found in this important position, too? Is it only accident? Was there no design involved?

Well, it was necessary during the war for anyone wishing to use capital in business enterprise, to lay all his cards on the table. He was required to reveal his plans, his ground for expecting success—in brief, tell the Jewish rulers and their Jewish representatives all that he would tell in confidence to his banker in negotiating a loan. The organization which a few Jews perfected was the most complete business inquisition ever set up in any country. And that the knowledge thus gained should always be sacredly guarded, or always honestly used, would be expecting too much of human nature.

Mr. Baruch gave some instances of this, though they were not the instances that are calculated to throw the most light on the inner workings of the organization. He said:

"The Capital Issues Committee (where Mr. Meyer reigned), in the Treasury Department, had a man who sat with the War Industries Board (where Mr. Baruch reigned), and who always came to the War Industries Board to find out whether the individual or the corporation who wanted this money was going to use it for the purpose to win the war. To cite a case that happened at Philadelphia, that city wanted to make extensive public improvements; New York City wanted to spend $8,000,000 for schools, which would take an enormous amount of steel, labor, materials and transportation. We said, 'No, that won't help win the war. You can postpone that until later on. We cannot spare the steel on all these various things.'"

Very well. Does Mr. Baruch know of an enormous theater which a Jewish theatrical owner was permitted to build in an eastern city during the war?

Did he ever hear of non-Jews being refused permission to go ahead in a legitimate business which would have helped produce war materials,

The Scope of Jewish Dictatorship in the U.S.

and that afterward—afterward—on almost identically the same plans, and in the same locality, a Jewish concern was given permission to do that very thing?

This was a terrible power, and far too great to be vested in one man; certainly it was such a power as should never have been vested in a coterie of Jews. The puzzle of it becomes greater the deeper it is probed. How did it occur? How could it occur—that always, at the most critical and delicate points in these matters, there sat a Jew enthroned with autocratic power?

Well could Mr. Baruch say—"I had more power than any man in the war." He could even have said, "We Jews had more power than you Americans did in the war"—and it would have been true.

2. Authority over all materials.

This, of course, included everything. Mr. Baruch was an expert in many of these lines of material involved, and had held interests in many of them. What the investigators endeavored to learn was in how many lines he was interested during the war.

In lines where Mr. Baruch was not expert he, of course, had experts in charge. There was Mr. Julius Rosenwald, another Jew, who was in charge of "supplies (including clothing)" and who had a Mr. Eisenman to represent him. Mr. Eisenman was on the stand for a considerable period with regard to uniforms, the change made in their quality, the price paid to the manufacturers (mostly Jewish) and other interesting questions.

The great Guggenheim copper interests, who sold most of the copper used during the war, were represented by a former employe; but undoubtedly Mr. Baruch himself, who was much interested in copper during his business career, was the principal expert in that line.

It is impossible to escape the names of Jews all down the line in these most important departments. But, for the present, attention is called to the scope of Mr. Baruch's control in the country at large. It is best stated in his own words: "No building costing more than $2,500 could be erected in the United States without approval of the War Industries Board. Nobody could get a barrel of cement without its approval. You could not get a piece of zinc for your kitchen table without the approval of the War Industries Board."

3. Authority over industries.

He determined where coal might be shipped, where steel might be sold, where industries might be operated and where not. With control over capital needed in business, went also control of the materials needed in industry. This control over industry was exercised through the device called priorities, which Mr. Baruch rightly described as "the greatest power in the war." He was the most powerful man in the war, because he exercised this power.

Mr. Baruch said there were 351 or 357 lines of industry under his control in the United States, including "practically every raw material in the world."

"I had the final authority," he said. Whether it was sugars or silk, coal or cannon, Mr. Baruch ruled its movements.

Mr. Jefferis—"For instance, this priority that you had would decide whether civilians should have any commodities for building?"

Mr. Baruch—"Yes; if we had not had that priority committee the civilians would have had nothing."

Mr. Jefferis—"Did they get anything?"

Mr. Baruch—"They got all there was."

Mr. Jefferis—"Did you sit with these priority boards at any time, or not?"

Mr. Baruch—"Sometimes; not very frequently. I was ex-officio of every one of the committees, and made it my business to go around as far as I could and keep in touch with everything."

Mr. Jefferis—"And all these different lines, really, ultimately, centered in you, so far as power was concerned?"

Mr. Baruch—"Yes, sir, it did. I probably had more power than perhaps any other man did in the war; doubtless that is true."

That, however, was not the full extent of Mr. Baruch's control over industry. The heart of industry is Power. Mr. Baruch controlled the Power of the United States. The dream of the Power Trust, an evil dream for this country, was realized for the first time under the organization which this single individual formed. He says:

"Not only did we endeavor to control the raw materials, but as well the manufacturing facilities of the country. We established priority uses also for power . . . "

4. Authority over the classes of men to be called to military service.

Baruch pointed out, virtually pointed out to the Provost Marshal of the United States, the classes of men to be taken into the army. "We had to decide virtually the necessity of such things," he said. "We decided that the less-essential industries would have to be curbed, and it was from them that man power would have to be taken for the army." In this

The Scope of Jewish Dictatorship in the U.S.

way he ruled chauffeurs, traveling salesmen, and similar classes into military service. It was, of course, necessary that some such ruling be made, but why one man, why always this one man?

5. Authority over the personnel of labor in this country. "We decided upon a dilution of men with women labor, which was a thing that had always been fought by the labor unions."

6. And now behold as complete an illustration of one part of the Protocols as ever could be found in any Gentile government. Readers of previous articles will remember the passage:

"We will force up wages which, however, will be of no benefit to the workers, for we will at the same time cause a rise in the prices of necessities."

Mr. Baruch at one time was inclined to sidestep the matter of fixing wages; he did not like the expression. But that the reader himself may decide, we quote the testimony in full:

Mr. Jefferis—"Did the War Industries Board fix the price of labor?"

Mr. Baruch—"If you can call it that way, but I would not say so; no, sir."

Mr. Jefferis—"I am trying to get at what you did."

Mr. Baruch—"No, sir; we did not fix the price of wages."

Mr. Jefferis—"What did you do?"

Mr. Baruch—"Just what I told you."

Mr. Jefferis—"Probably I am a little dense, but I did not catch it if you told me."

Mr. Baruch—"When the price-fixing committee fixed the price of steel, we will say, they said 'This price is agreed upon, and you shall keep wages where they are'—and those were the wages that were prevailing at the price we fixed. At the time prices were fixed at first they were very much higher than the prices that we fixed."

Mr. Jefferis—"When you got the price of any of these low materials you would fix the price of labor that was to be employed in producing them?"

Mr. Baruch—"To the extent that it should remain at the maximum of what it was when we fixed the price."

Considering the weight of Mr. Baruch's authority, and the stipulations he made, this was to all intents and purposes a fixing of the rate of wages.

Now, as to the fixing of prices, Mr. Baruch is much more positive. In answer to a question by Mr. Garrett, Mr. Baruch said: "We fixed the prices in co-operation with the industries, but when we fixed a price we fixed it for the total production, not alone for the army and the navy, but for the Allies and the civilian population."

The minutes of one of the meetings of Mr. Baruch's board show this:

"Commissioner Baruch directed that the minutes show that the commission had consumed the entire afternoon in a discussion of price fixing, particularly with reference to the control of the food supply, grain, cotton, wool, and raw materials generally."

Mr. Graham—"Tell me something else: How much personal attention did you give to the matter of price-fixing?"

Mr. Baruch—"In the beginning, considerable . . . "

At another time, Mr. Baruch said—"There was no law at all in the land to fix prices."

Mr. Jefferis—"We grant that, but you did it."

Mr. Baruch—"Yes, we did it, and we did a great many things in the stress of the times."

Here was one man, having supreme dictatorial power, at both ends of the common people's affairs.

He admits that of the 351 or 357 lines of essential industry which he controlled, he fixed the prices at which the commodities should be sold to the government and to civilians. In fixing the prices, however, he made wage stipulations.

The matter of wages came first—it entered into Mr. Baruch's computation of the cost, on which, to a certain extent, he based the price. Then, having decided what the producer was to receive in wages, he decided next what the producer should pay for living. The producer himself may answer the question as to how it all turned out! Wages were "high," but not quite so high as "living"; and the answer to both is in the testimony of Barney Baruch.

That is not the whole story by any means. It is inserted here merely to find its place in the list of authorities conferred on Mr. Baruch.

How completely Baruch felt himself to be the "power" is shown by a passage which occurred when he was trying to explain the very large profits made by some concerns with which he did business.

Mr. Jefferis—"Then the system which you did adopt did not give the Lukens Steel & Iron Company the amount of profit that the low-producing companies had?"

Mr. Baruch—"No, but we took 80 per cent away from the others." Mr. Jefferis—"The law did that, didn't it?"

Mr. Baruch—"Yes; the law did that."

Mr. Jefferis—"What did you mean by the use of the word 'we'?"

Mr. Baruch—"The government did that. Excuse me, but I meant we, the Congress."

Mr. Jefferis—"You meant that the Congress passed a law covering that?"

Mr. Baruch—"Yes, sir."

Mr. Jefferis—"Did you have anything to do with that?"

Mr. Baruch—"Not a thing."

Mr. Jefferis—"Then I would not use the word 'we' if I were you."

Whether Mr. Baruch slipped up there, he best knows. Just as he had power to give the workers wages, and take it away again by price-fixing, so he had power to allow the raw material corporations to make fabulous profits—and it would not be at all unthinkable that he also had something to do with taking part of it away again. He said once, "We took away 80 per cent"; then he confessed it was a slip. Of the tongue, or of his prudence?

Certainly, the profits he allowed were so large that even where the 80 per cent was paid back—where it was paid back (there were all kinds of evasions and frauds)—the profits were still enormous.

And 73 per cent of the "war millionaires" of New York, in spite of the 80 per cent, are Jews.

The Dearborn Independent, December 4, 1920

27. Jewish Copper Kings Reap Rich War-Profits

With this article we shall dismiss Mr. Bernard M. Baruch for the present. His activities are not by any means to be construed as the main effort of Judah in the United States, nor is he himself to be regarded as an important factor in the Jewish World Program. Indeed, it is to be doubted that he has been entrusted with many of the secrets of the Elders.

But he has been found to be a useful man, willing to play the Jewish game with Jews, and consciously bound as all Jews are by an obligation to see that Jewish interests get the better of the balance wherever possible.

Mr. Baruch, of course, is much pleased with the role he was permitted to play in the government of the United States during the war; but he probably has sense enough to know that he was chosen for other than mere personal reasons.

Indeed, one of the keys to the controlling part which a few Jews were permitted to play in American affairs during the war is to be found just here in the question, Why was Mr. Baruch chosen? What had he been, what had he done, that he should have been chosen as head and front of governmental power in the war? His antecedents do not account for it. Neither his personal nor commercial attainments account for it. What does?

There was no elected member of the United States Government who was closer, or even as close, to the President during the war as was this Jew out of Wall Street. No one whom the people sent to represent them at Washington ever came within leagues of the privileges accorded to Mr. Baruch. Plainly this is an unusual situation, not explainable by the emergency at all, certainly not explainable by anything that is as yet a matter of public knowledge.

As one man out of many, all together serving the country, Mr. Baruch, of course, would be perfectly explainable. But as the man, the man whose single committee was run up through the fabric of the Council of National Defense until it formed the focus of the war government, he is not explainable. It was not only during the war, but also after the armistice, that these tokens of signal choice were showered upon Mr.

Baruch. He went to the Peace Conference. Resigning as chairman of the War Industries Board on December 31, 1918—

"I went down to my place in South Carolina, and there received a wireless message from the President to come to Paris. I then went to Paris. I think I sailed about the first or second of January. I know one vessel broke down and I had to transfer from one to the other. But I had no further activities in connection with the government; that is, the War Industries Board.

Mr. Graham—"How long were you in Paris?"

Mr. Baruch—"I sailed, returning June 28 or 29. I came back on the George Washington." (This means that he was a part of the President's entourage.)

Mr. Graham—"What were you doing there, Mr. Baruch?"

Mr. Baruch—"I was economic advisor connected with the peace mission."

Mr. Graham—"You stayed until the Peace Treaty was concluded?" Mr. Baruch—"Yes, sir."

Mr. Graham—"Did you frequently advise with the President while there?"

Mr. Baruch—"Whenever he asked my advice I gave it. I had something to do with the reparation clauses. I was the American Commissioner in charge of what they called the 'Economic Section.' I was a member of the Supreme Economic Council in charge of raw materials."

Mr. Graham—"Did you sit in the council with the gentlemen who were negotiating the treaty?"

Mr. Baruch—"Yes, sir; sometimes."

Mr. Graham—"All except the meetings that were participated in by the Five?" (Meaning the Big Five premiers.)

Mr. Baruch—"And frequently those also."

This, then, is a sidelight on what has been called the "Kosher Conference," a name given to the Peace Conference by Frenchmen who were astounded to see thousands of Jews from all parts of the world appear in Paris as the chosen counsellors of the rulers of the nations. Jews were so conspicuous in the American mission as to excite comment everywhere. A Persian representative left on record this protest: "When the United States delegation accepted a brief for the Jews and imposed a Jewish semi-state on Rumania and Poland, they were firm as the granite rock, and no amount of opposition, no future deterrents, made any impression on their will. Accordingly, they had their own way. But in the case of Persia they lost the fight, although logic, humanity, justice, and the Ordinances solemnly accepted by the Great Powers were all on their side."

The comment is rather humiliating. But it is true. The Jewish World Program was the only program that passed through the Peace Conference without hindrance or revision.

So numerous and ubiquitous were the International Jews in Paris, so firmly established in the inner councils, that the keen observer, Dr. E. J. Dillon, whose book, "The Inside Story of the Peace Conference" (Harper's), is the best that has appeared, was constrained to say this:

"It may seem amazing to some readers, but it is none the less a fact, that a considerable number of delegates believed that the real influences behind the Anglo-Saxon peoples were Semitic." (p. 496.)

And again:

"They confronted the President's proposal on the subject of religious inequality, and, in particular, the odd motive alleged for it, with the measures for the protection of minorities which he subsequently imposed on the lesser states, and which had for their keynote to satisfy the Jewish elements in Eastern Europe. And they concluded that the sequence of expedients framed and enforced in this direction were inspired by the Jews, assembled in Paris for the purpose of realizing their carefully thought-out program, which they succeeded in having substantially executed.

However right or wrong these delegates may have been, it would be a dangerous mistake to ignore their views, seeing that they have since become one of the permanent elements of the situation. The formula into which this policy was thrown by the members of the Conference, whose countries it affected, and who regarded it as fatal to the peace of Eastern Europe, was this: 'Henceforth the world will be governed by the Anglo-Saxon peoples, who, in turn, are swayed by their Jewish elements.'" (p. 497. The italics are ours.)

There are other matters pertaining to Mr. Baruch which must await the development of this study, but it is worth while just now to possess ourselves of the information at hand regarding his peculiar handling of the copper situation during the war.

Mr. Baruch is known as a copper man. Copper is Jewish. That metal, throughout the world, is under Jewish domination. The Guggenheims and the Lewisohns, two Jewish families, are the copper kings of the planet—not that they confine themselves to copper; for example,

Jewish Copper Kings Reap Rich War-Profits

their output of silver throughout the world is one-fourth more than is produced in the entire United States. By his own testimony, Mr. Baruch was interested in copper concerns. What his holdings were during the war he did not disclose. But what his actions were has been very clearly set forth bit by bit in various inquiries.

Before the United States entered the war, Mr. Baruch rounded up the copper kings.

"I went to New York and saw there Mr. John D. Ryan and Mr. Daniel Guggenheim," he said in his testimony. This was in February or March, 1917, he wasn't sure which, but he said it was "before we went into the war."

Now, who were these gentlemen? Mr. Ryan was apparently in charge of the reorganized Lewisohn properties, while Mr. Guggenheim was chief of the seven Guggenheims who form "a business family and a family business." They divided business during the war.

The United Metals Selling Company, which sold the United States Government its copper during the war, was the Lewisohn business reorganized, of which Tobias Wolfson was vice president; and the American Smelting and Refining Company was, apparently, the Guggenheim interests.

There was no competition between these two during the war!

How did it come about that these two worked together? Their case is clear on paper: their answer is that Mr. Baruch asked them to! And Mr. Baruch is clear, too; was he not a government official? And did they not show patriotism in doing as the government official bade them?

It came to this: the "Government" made a rule that it would do business only through the American Metals Selling Company as the representative of the copper producers of the United States. This meant, of course, that if the few competitors of this Jewish copper combine were to do business with the government, they too had to make arrangements with the American Metals Selling Company.

Mr. Graham—"But how did it happen that you were representing the other companies who were your competitors?"

Mr. Wolfson—"Well, at the request of the War Industries Board, we offered a copper producers' committee."

Mr. Graham—"Who requested that?"

Mr. Wolfson—"Mr. Eugene Meyer, Jr., representing Mr. B. M. Baruch."

Mr. Graham—"Now let us find out who Mr. Eugene Meyer, Jr. was. Do you know him?"

It develops that Mr. Eugene Meyer, Jr., is another Wall Street man who "had large investments in copper," though whether he retained them during the war, Mr. Wolfson did not know.

Mr. Graham—"Then Eugene Meyer, Jr., went into the War Industries Board and took up with the copper producers the question of furnishing copper, did he?"

Mr. Wolfson—"Yes, sir."

As a result of that request a meeting was held at 120 Broadway, at which were present, among a few others, S. S. Rosenstamm, L. Vogelstein, Julius Loeb, T. Wolfson, G. W. Drucker and Eugene Meyer, Jr.

Mr. Graham—"Any army officers there?"

Mr. Wolfson—"No."

The witness here quoted, Tobias Wolfson, was one of the most active instruments in the actual passage of business, but the Washington representative was a Mr. Mosehauer. The interesting thing about Mr. Mosehauer is that he represented both the American Metals Selling Company and the American Smelting and Refining Company—the Lewisohns and the Guggenheims—and by order of Baruch, with the approval of the government, the business was done with these two corporations.

How did they divide? It was very simple. Mr. Wolfson euphoniously describes it as a division of labor: the Lewisohn group took the trade with the United States; the Guggenheim group took over the foreign business with the Allies.

Now, the next interesting point is the special committee through which Baruch's board dealt with the copper producers. This committee, representing the government, consisted of three persons: Pope Yeatman, chief; E. C. Thurston, assistant; Andrew Walz, assistant.

Pope Yeatman was a mining engineer employed by the Guggenheims at $100,000 a year.

E. C. Thurston was Pope Yeatman's assistant in that private employment.

Andrew Walz was consulting mining engineer for the Guggenheims.

Everything was all set. The Jewish metal monopoly was assured of control on both sides of the Atlantic.

It was perhaps thought desirable, in view of the bad political odor which had accompanied the copper power in several states, mostly in connection with the "copper Senators," like Clarke, of Nevada (readers of this series will remember, in connection with the name of Guggenheim,

Jewish Copper Kings Reap Rich War-Profits

that it was Senator Simon Guggenheim who fought against the census enumeration of Jews as once proposed by the census officials), that something be done to gild the arrangement.

It was apparently necessary to do something to disarm the protest that might arise against this thorough Judaizing of the war metals, therefore a very fine show of patriotism was made. This is worthy of notice in view of the "show institutions" mentioned in the Protocols. The American public is becoming accustomed to these "show institutions"—proposals which promise everything and then fade away into nothingness. It is one of the most effective methods of destroying the morale of a people.

When Mr. Baruch saw the heads of the two copper families, he says he found them willing to think of nothing but giving copper to the government—money was of no consideration whatever.

Mr. Baruch—"They said that so far as the United States Government itself was concerned they would give Uncle Sam all the copper he wanted for his preparedness campaign at any price that was decided upon. In order to arrive at some price we took the average price for 10 years which was about 16 2-3 cents; and that is how the price happened to be arrived at. At the time that they said this, copper was selling somewhere around 32 and 35 cents a pound."

There, then, was a magnanimous thing! The government was to be given copper at half the market price. But did the government get it at this price?

Wait—the story is a good one.

This unheard-of sacrifice of profits for pariotism was extensively advertised. The secretary of the Council of National Defense wrote a stirring story for one of the best magazines, in which he said:

"Mr. Baruch first announced his presence in the tremendous task of mobilizing American industry by procuring 45,000,000 pounds of copper for the army and navy at about half the current market price, saving the government in the neighborhood of $10,000,000."

Mr. Baruch himself, in his testimony, expanded with the generosity of it all. In an apparent mood of "help yourself to all you want" he said:

"On inquiry we found that the army and navy wanted only 45,000,000 pounds, which used to be a lot of copper before we got to dealing in astronomical figures; and they were given all the opportunity to consider what they wanted. They could just as well have had 450,000,000 pounds as 45,000,000 pounds, because there was an open offer."

Now for the effect which this produced on the country at large:

"The effect of that offer of the copper producers was electrical," said Mr. Baruch. "It showed that there was in this country a desire to set aside selfishness, so far as our government was concerned in its need. 'Make us any price you want.' So that was practically the attitude that the producers took."

But the government did not get copper at that much-advertised patriotic price.

Mr. Graham—"They did not pay 16 2-3 cents for the 45,000,000 pounds?"

Mr. Baruch—"Oh, no; not these other large quantities of materials."

He said that the copper was furnished to the government without receiving money for it; price-fixing was yet in the future. "Then we came to the point, 'Well, what about the civilian population?' So we made a rule that became a policy, that whatever price was fixed it should be for everybody; that what was fair for the army and navy was fair for the civilian population."

There seems to have been a rapid cooling of generosity under the prospect of colossal sales. And the upshot of it was that, after all the hurrah, the government really paid about 27 cents.

What these figures mean, can be deduced from the fact that during the war the government bought 592,258,674 pounds of copper.

If the reader is not already staggered by the import of these facts, there remains one more for him to consider—After the armistice the surplus copper was sold back to the copper producers. In April and May, 1919, the American Metals Selling Company received from the United States Government over 16,500,000 pounds of copper at a fraction over 15 cents.

This was less than the boasted patriotic price of 16 2-3 cents at the beginning. Not counting what they had received from the government for the copper in the first place, their profits on the difference between the price they paid for the surplus copper and the price for which they sold it again, were beyond counting.

This is what occurred under the triple copper monarchy of the Baruchs, the Lewisohns and the Guggenheims, and their Jewish assistants and Gentile fronts. However, "Gentile fronts" were boldly dispensed with to a very large degree during the war. The real powers behind the throne themselves stood out, and did not hesitate to set their own people at every crossroads along the line of war business. It is not to be supposed that the Baruch influence began or ceased with copper, nor with any

Jewish Copper Kings Reap Rich War-Profits

of the multitudinous industrial powers which he possessed. A man like Baruch makes the most of such opportunities as were then his. In matters political, personal and even military, there were many openings for the use of his influence, and well-informed people about Washington did not doubt his facility in these things.

Once, however, Mr. Baruch felt he was skating on thin ice with regard to the law. He had gone ahead on his own plan, but in such a way that he would exercise the power without taking the responsibility. That seems to have been a very clear ideal with him—power without responsibility. Everything was fixed, all the conditions within which every contract would have to be made were carefully determined, but Mr. Baruch never permitted himself or his board to make a contract. After having consulted with numbers of his associates in business, an agreement was reached, and only then were the responsible officers of the government told, "Go ahead and make contracts." The officials took the responsibility, but the Baruch coterie made the conditions and then remained aloof.

Even this plan, however, had a questionable aspect which came to trouble Mr. Baruch, and the manner in which he manipulated the matter shows either a very shrewd mind or else very shrewd advice. The latter undoubtedly went with the former: there were plenty of Jewish advisors about.

To begin with, Mr. Baruch says: "The members of that committee were picked out by myself; the industries did not pick them out." Which means, in fact, that Mr. Baruch picked out a group from a group that had previously been chosen by the producers, although plainly Mr. Baruch was desirous of modifying this impression. And again: "It is true that these great copper producers were on the committee, and I selected them because they were great men."

Now, these men, as members of a government committee, were to all appearances selling to themselves as members of the government committee, and, apparently, buying from themselves as owners and controllers of the great producing combinations. Not necessarily in any discreditable way, but in a very unusual way.

In the face of this condition, Mr. Baruch had the coolness to say, "So you can see that the government was as much in the saddle as it was possible to be." The producer-members of the committee, headed by Baruch, were the government, so far as this statement is concerned. Time and again it was shown that the responsible officials of the government

263

were not even visible until this extra-government had determined all the conditions.

Mr. Garrett—"Did any troubles arise with the committees growing out of the legal situation, that you remember of?"

Mr. Baruch—"The committees of the trade, especially some of those that I had asked to serve, were very much disturbed about their standing in reference to the Sherman Anti-Trust Law. Is that what you refer to?"

Mr. Garrett—"Yes."

Mr. Baruch—"And also in regard to the Lever Act, on the point that 'no man could serve two masters.' There was no basis for it because these men were not serving two masters. They did not make trades with themselves, but, with the instrumentality provided, carried out the government's wishes or orders or suggestions with reference to the particular industry which they represented."

The "instrumentality" with which the copper men dealt, for example, was the American Metals Selling Company, which, together with the American Smelting and Refining Company, was represented at Washington by Mr. Mosehauer. The special copper committee, composed of Guggenheim employes, did business pertaining to the "instrumentality" which carried on the business of the combined copper companies.

It was dangerous. Some of the members seem to have felt it before Mr. Baruch did. Mr. Baruch never seems to have questioned anything that he did. Why should he? He "had more power than any other man in the war" and he had the most powerful and autocratic backing that a man ever had. But the others, the non-Jewish members, were thinking of the law.

So Mr. Baruch solved it very nicely. He took the committees, comprising the same men, and had them named as committees of the United States Chamber of Commerce for their various industries, and although the process was not changed in the least, the legal aspect of it was changed. It was rather clever. It was more, it was typical.

And after that, Mr. Baruch who had previously insisted that he himself had picked those men and that the industries had not, thus clearly encouraging the inference that these men did not represent the industries' side, but the government side of the matter, he now insists that they represented the industry.

Mr. Graham—"You changed and took these advisory committes and had the National Chamber of Commerce reappoint them, so that they then were direct representatives of the Chamber of Commerce and not of the officials of the United States or connected with any governmental machinery?"

Mr. Baruch—"I never considered them officials of the government, Mr. Graham."

Mr. Graham—"They were as much officials of the government as the rest of you, were they not?"

Mr. Baruch—"I do not think so. (after several questions). I asked them to serve so that when the government wanted anything they could go to one small, compact body, rather than to send out to I do not know how many people. You see?"

Mr. Graham—"Let us see about that. They were serving under you, were they not? You were the head?"

Mr. Baruch—"I appointed them and asked them to do this so that I could have a compact body to deal with."

Mr. Graham—"You did not think for a minute that they were representing the government, but did you not think you were?"

Mr. Baruch—"I was doing the best I knew how."

Mr. Graham—"But you had authority to bring these men in, Mr. Baruch, and appoint them as committeemen under you, and you did so. Surely, if they were representing anybody it was the government, was it not?"

Mr. Baruch—"I do not think so."

Mr. Graham—"Am I right in assuming that you thought they represented the industries?"

Mr. Baruch—"Yes."

A great deal, of course, can be overlooked in men who were working under stress and endeavoring to do things the best way. It does not follow that because a business man serves the government in matters pertaining to his own business, he is necessarily dishonest.

But so frequent is dishonesty under such conditions, or, if not dishonesty, then a loss to the government because of a divided interest, that laws have been framed to regulate such matters. These laws were on the books at the time.

This is a fact, whatever else may be true, that "copper" made tens and hundreds of millions out of the war and it is not at all inconceivable that if "copper" had not been so completely in control of the government operations of purchase, the profits might not have been so great, and the burdens which the people bore through taxation, high prices and

Liberty bonds might not have been so heavy. Mr. Baruch is but one illustration of the clustering of Jewry about the war machinery of the United States. If the Jews were the only people left in the United States who were able enough to be put in the important places of power, well and good; but if they were not, why were they there in such uniform and systematized control? It is a definite situation that is discussed. The thing is there and is unchangeably a matter of history. How can it be explained?

The Dearborn Independent, December 11, 1920

28. Jewish Control of the American Theater

The Theater has long been a part of the Jewish program for guidance of public taste and the influencing of the public mind. Not only is the Theater given a special place in the program of the Protocols, but it is the instant ally night by night and week by week of any idea which the "power behind the scenes" wishes to put forth. It is not by accident that in Russia, where they now have scarcely anything else, they still have the Theater, specially revived, stimulated and supported by Jewish-Bolshevists because they believe in the Theater just as they believe in the Press; it is one of the two great means of molding popular opinion.

Everybody has assumed offhand that the Theater is Jew-controlled. Few, if put to the test, could prove it, but all believe it. The reason they believe it is not so much what they see as what they feel; the American feel has gone out of the Theater; a dark, Oriental atmosphere has come instead.

Not only the "legitimate" stage, so-called, but the motion picture industry—the fifth greatest of all the great industries—is also Jew-controlled, not in spots only, not 50 per cent merely, but entirely; with the natural consequence that now the world is in arms against the trivializing and demoralizing influences of that form of entertainment as at present managed. As soon as the Jew gained control of American liquor, we had a liquor problem with drastic consequences. As soon as the Jew gained control of the "movies," we had a movie problem, the consequences of which are not yet visible. It is the genius of that race to create problems of a moral character in whatever business they achieve a majority.

Every night hundreds of thousands of people give from two to three hours to the Theater, every day literal millions of people give up from 30 minutes to two hours to the Movies; and this simply means that millions of Americans every day place themselves voluntarily within range of Jewish ideas of life, love and labor; within range of Jewish propaganda, sometimes cleverly, sometimes clumsily concealed. This gives the Jewish masseur of the public mind all the opportunity he desires; and his only protest now is that exposure may make his game a trifle difficult.

The Theater is Jewish not only on its managerial side, but also on its literary and professional side. More and more plays are appearing whose author, producer, star and cast are entirely Jewish. They are not great plays, they do not remain long. This is natural enough, since the Jewish theatrical interests are not seeking artistic triumphs, they are not seeking the glory of the American stage, nor are they striving to develop great actors to take the place of the old line of worthies. Not at all. Their interest is financial and racial—getting the Gentiles' money and Judaizing the Theater. There is a tremendous Judaizing movement on; the work is almost complete. Boastful articles are beginning to appear in the Jewish press, which is always a sign.

Gentile attendants on the Theater are frequently insulted to their faces, and never know it. Recently one of the best known Jewish entertainers on the stage indulged in vulgar and sacrilegious references to Jesus Christ, whereat the Semitic portions of his audience went into loud laughter, while the Gentiles sat blank-faced—because the remarks were in Yiddish asides!

Time after time the Jewish entertainer did that thing, and it was very plain to one who knew that the Jewish portion of the audience was enjoying the insult to the Gentiles much more than they were enjoying the well-worn humor of the entertainer's remarks. It was a great thing for them that in several important American cities they could see and hear being done under cover, and to American Gentiles, what is being done openly to Russian Gentiles.

In the audience referred to there was probably $4,500 to $5,000 in gate money represented. Of this the Jews present, at the very highest estimate, could not have contributed more than $500. Yet the Jewish star several times slapped the religious sensibilities of the major portion of his audience under cover of Yiddish. The Theater is felt by him and his ilk to be a Jewish institution.

Down to 1885 the American Theater was still in the hands of the Gentiles. From 1885 dates the first invasion of Jewish influence. It meant the parting of the ways, and the future historian of the American Stage will describe that year with the word "Ichabod." That year marks not only the beginning of the Jewish wedge of control, but something far more important.

It is not important that managers are now Jews whereas managers were formerly Gentiles. That is not important. The importance begins with the fact that with the change of managers there came also a decline

Jewish Control of the American Theater

in the art and morals of the stage, and that this decline has become accelerated as the Jewish control became widened. What Jewish control means is this: that everything has been deliberately and systematically squeezed out of the American Theater except its most undesirable elements, and these undesirable elements have been exalted to the highest place of all.

The Great Age of the American Theater is past. About the time that Jewish control appeared, Sheridan, Sothern, McCullough, Madame Janauschek, Mary Anderson, Frank Mayo, John T. Raymond, began to pass off the stage. It was natural that, life being brief, they should pass at last, but the appalling fact began to be apparent that they had left no successors! Why? Because a Hebrew hand was on the stage, and the natural genius of the stage was no longer welcomed. A new form of worship was to be established.

"Shakespeare spells ruin," was the utterance of a Jewish manager. "High-brow stuff" is also a Jewish expression. These two sayings, one appealing to the managerial end, the other to the public end of the Theater, have formed the epitaph of the classic era. All that remained after the Hebrew hand fell across the stage were a few artists who had received their training under the Gentile school—Julia Marlowe, Tyrone Power, R. D. McLean, and, a little later, Richard Mansfield, Robert Mantell, E. H. Sothern. Two of this group remain, and with Maude Adams they constitute the last flashings of an era that has gone—an era that apparently leaves no great exemplars to perpetuate it.

The present-day average of intelligence appealed to in the American Theater does not rise above 13 to 18 years. "The tired business man" stuff (another Jewish expression) has treated the theatergoing public as if it were composed of morons. The appeal is frankly to a juvenile type of mind which can be easily molded to the ideals of the Hebraic theatrical monopoly. Clean, wholesome plays—the few that remain— are supported mainly by the rapidly vanishing race of theatergoers who survive from an earlier day; the present generation has been educated by the narrowed compass of modern dramatic themes to support plays of an entirely different type. Tragedy is taboo; the play of character, with a deeper significance than would delight the mind of a child, is out of favor; the comic opera has degenerated into a flash of color and movement—a combination of salacious farce and jazz music, usually supplied by a Jewish song-writer (the great purveyors of jazz!) and the rage is for extravaganza and burlesque.

The bedroom farce has been exalted into the first place. With the exception of "Ben Hur," which is favored by Jewish producers apparently because it holds before the public a romantic picture of a Jew (a very un-Jewish Jew, by the way), the historical drama has given way to fleshly spectacles set off with overpowering scenic effects, the principal component of which is an army of girls (mostly Gentiles!) whose investment of drapery does not exceed five ounces in weight.

Frivolity, sensuality, indecency, appalling illiteracy and endless platitude are the marks of the American Stage as it approaches its degeneracy under Jewish control.

That, of course, is the real meaning of all the "Little Theater" movements which have begun in so many cities and towns in the United States. The art of the drama, having been driven out of the Theater by the Jews, is finding a home in thousands of study circles throughout the United States. The people cannot see the real plays; therefore they read them.

The plays that are acted could not be read at all, for the most part, any more than the words of jazz songs can be read; they don't mean anything. The people who want to see the real plays and cannot, because Jewish producers won't produce them, are forming little dramatic clubs of their own, in barns and churches, in schools and neighborhood halls. The drama fled from its exploiters and has found a home with its friends.

The changes which the Jews have made in the theater, and which any half-observant theatergoer can verify with his own eyes, are four in number.

First, they have elaborated the mechanical side, making human talent and genius less necessary. They have made the stage "realistic" instead of interpretative. The great actors needed very little machinery; the men and women on the pay rolls of the Jewish managers are helpless without the machinery. The outstanding fact about the vast majority of present-day performances of any pretension is that the mechanical part dwarfs and obscures the acting, however good.

And this is the reason: knowing that good actors are growing scarce, knowing that the Jewish policy is death to talent, knowing perhaps most keenly of all that good actors constitute a running charge on his revenue, the Jewish producer prefers to put his faith and his money in wood, canvas, paint, cloth and tinsel of which scenery and costumes are made. Wood and paint never show contempt for his sordid ideals and his betrayal of his trust. And thus we have, when we go to the theater today, bursts of color, ruffles of lace and linen, waving lines and dazzling effects of light and motion—but no ideas, a great many stage employees, but very few actors. There are drills and dances without end, but no drama.

That is one influence on the American Theater which the Jew claims, and the credit for which can be given him in full. He has put in the iridescence, but he has taken out the profounder ideas. He has placed the American public in the position of being able to remember the names of plays without being able to recall what composed them. Like the "Floradora Girls," a Jewish creation, we remember the name of the group, but not of any individual in it. The Jew has done this to perfection, but no one will contend that it represents a forward step; taken by and large, it is part of a very serious and harmful retrogression.

Second, the Jews may be credited with having introduced Oriental sensuality to the American stage. Not even the most ardent Jewish defender will deny this, for the thing is there, before the eyes of all who will see. Little by little the mark of the filthy tide has risen against the walls of the American Theater until now it is all but engulfed. It is a truism that there is more unrefined indecency in the higher class theaters today than was ever permitted by the police in the burlesque houses. The lower classes must be restrained in the vicarious exercise of their lower natures, apparently, but the wealthier classes may go the limit. The price of the ticket and the "class" of the playhouse seems to make all the difference in the world between prohibited and permissible evil.

In New York, where Jewish managers are thicker than they ever will be in Jerusalem, the limit of theatrical adventuresomeness into the realm of the forbidden is being pushed further and further. Last season's spectacle of "Aphrodite" seemed to be deliberately designed as a frontal attack on the last entrenched scruple of moral conservatism. The scenes are most Oriental in their voluptuous abandonment. Men in breech-clouts, leopard skins and buckskins, women in flimsy gowns of gossamer texture, slashed to the hips, with very little besides, made a bewildering pageant whose capstone was the unveiling of a perfectly nude girl whose body had been painted to resemble marble. Save that it was all designed, and all put through on schedule, it was almost the "limit" to which such exhibitions could go in real life. Its promoter, of course, was a Jew. As an entertainment it was infantile; the splendor of its insinuations, the daring of its situations, were the fruitage of long study of the art of seducing the popular mind.

It was said when "Aphrodite" first appeared that the police had moved against it, but some held that this was a clever press-agent stunt to excite public interest in the promised pruriency. It was also said that even had the police interference been the genuine result of outraged official minds, the fact that the Jews of New York are represented in the judiciary out of all proportions to their numbers, would have rendered the Jewish producer free from interference. In any event, the piece was not molested. The sale of narcotics is illegal, but the instilling of insidious moral poison is not.

The whole loose atmosphere of "cabaret" and "midnight frolic" entertainment is of Jewish origin and importation. Mention the best known and the worst known, they are all Jewish. The runway down which less than half-dressed girls cavort, fluttering their loose finery in the faces of the spectators, is an importation from Vienna, but a Jewish creation. The abuses of the runway will not bear description here. The Paris boulevards and Montmartre have nothing at all in the nature of lascivious entertainment that New York cannot duplicate. *But* neither New York nor any other American city has that *Comedie Francaise* that strives to counterbalance the evil of Paris.

Where have the writers for the Stage a single chance in this welter of sensuousness? Where have the actors of tragic or comic talent a chance in such productions? It is the age of the chorus girl, a creature whose mental caliber has nothing to do with the matter, and whose stage life cannot in the very nature of things be a career.

It is only occasionally that a great writer for the stage, a Shaw, a Masefield, a Barrie, an Ibsen, or any Gentile writer of merit, is permitted to get as far as actual production, and then only for a short period; the stream of colored electric lighting effects, of women and tinsel closes in behind them and they are washed away, to survive in printed books among those who still know what the Theater ought to be.

A third consequence of Jewish domination of the American stage has been the appearance of "the New York star" system, with its advertising appliances. The last few years of the Theater have been marked by numerous "stars" that really never rose and certainly never shone, but which were hoisted high on the advertising walls of the Jewish theatrical syndicates in order to give the public the impression that these feeble lantern-lights were in the highest heaven of dramatic achievement.

The trick is a department store trick. It is sheer advertising strategy. The "stars" of yesterday, who did not even survive yesterday were either the personal favorites of managers, or goods taken off the shelf and heaped into the window for the sake of giving the appearance of a new stock. In brief, whereas in normal times the public made the "star" by their acclaim, nowadays the Jewish managers determine by their advertisements who the star shall be. The "New York stamp," which frequently means nothing at all, is the one imperial sign of favor, according to the Jewish theatrical hierarchy. It is just this "New York stamp" that the rest of the country protests against; and the "little theater" movement throughout the West and Central West is a significant protest.

A Mary Anderson or a Julia Marlowe would be impossible under the Jewish system. They were disciples of art, who later became artists, and then were rightfully acclaimed as stars. But their development was a tedious process. Their fame was based on the rising approval of the people, year after year. These actresses put in season after season traveling the same circuit, learning little by little, rounding out their work. They did not have nor did they seek the "New York stamp"; they worked first for the approval of the people of "the provinces," which is the contemptuous Jewish term for the rest of the United States. There was, however, no Jewish dictatorship of the Theater when Mary Anderson and Julia Marlowe were building their art and careers; which throws a light on the reason for there being no Mary Andersons or Julia Marlowes coming up to the succession.

The Jew seeks immediate success in all but racial affairs. In this breakdown of the Gentile theater, the process cannot be too swift for him. The training of artists takes time. It is far simpler to have the advertising bills serve as a substitute and, as the itinerant faker-dentist had a brass band blare loud enough to drown the anguished cries of his victims, so the Jewish manager seeks to divert attention from the dramatic poverty of the Theater by throwing confetti, limbs, lingerie and spangles dazzlingly into the eyes of his audience.

These three results of Jewish control in the Theater are all explainable by a fourth; the secret of the serious change which has occurred since 1885 is found in the Jewish tendency to commercialize everything it touches. The focus of attention has been shifted from the Stage to the box office.

The banal policy of "give the public what they want" is the policy of the panderer, and it entered the American Theater with the first Jewish invasion.

About 1885 two alert Jews established in New York a so-called booking agency and offered to take over the somewhat cumbersome system by which managers of theaters in St. Louis, Detroit or Omaha arranged engagements of attractions for their houses for the ensuing season. The old process involved extensive correspondence with producing managers in the East and many local managers were obliged to spend several months in New York to make up a season's bookings. The advantages were that the booking agency, supplied with a list of the "open dates" of the houses they represented, were able to lay out a complete season's itinerary, or "route," for a traveling company and enabled the producer of a play to spend his vacation at the seashore instead of passing the sultry mid-season in New York, while the local manager was saved the trouble of much writing or even a trip East, and was content to let the booking concern attend to all details and send him his next season's bookings when completed.

In this manner was laid the foundation of the later-day Theatrical Trust. The booking firm was that of Klaw & Erlanger, the former a young Jew from Kentucky who had studied law, but drifted into theatrical life as an agent; the latter a young Jew from Cleveland with little education but with experience as an advance agent.

The booking system was not of their devising. They borrowed the idea from Harry C. Taylor who established a sort of theatrical exchange where producers and local managers could meet, desks being provided them at a small rental, and who took over the booking in the smaller cities, without foreseeing—but probably scorning—the opportunity thus placed in his hands to club the whole theatrical world into submission to his dictates.

With characteristic shrewdness Klaw & Erlanger elaborated the idea they had borrowed from Taylor, opened competition against the latter and enlisted the support of a number of young Jewish advance agents who were beginning to recognize the lucrative opportunities which the theatrical profession afforded.

Prominent among their earliest supporters was Charles Frohman, employed by J. H. Haverley. His brother, Daniel, had been business manager for the Mallorys at the Madison Square Theater since 1881, and though the Frohmans stand out in relief from the background of the Polish Jewish influence on the theater, they found it to their advantage to co-operate with the booking firm and subsequently became prominent members of the Trust.

The establishment of the Jewish booking agency system is the key to the whole problem of the decline of the American stage. The old booking system had the enormous advantage of the personal touch in the relationship between manager and company, and made possible the development of genius in accordance with the organic laws which determine nurture, growth and fruition. Except in its highest form, acting is not an art; but heaven-born genius is no more vocal in an Edwin Booth without long training than a Bonaparte is necessarily a world conqueror without the technique of the artillery school. These two thoughts have the utmost bearing on giving the Jews the control of the theater.

There being no "syndicate," no pooling, among the Gentile managers of the 80's, they presented their stars or other attractions at rival theaters in competition as individual offerings, and at the end of a reasonable New York run, not forced for "road consumption," took their companies on a tour of the country. The manager's whole investment was probably tied up in his enterprise. He thus became a part of his group of artists, sharing their hardships of travel, their joys and sorrows. If business was good they shared the satisfaction; if otherwise, it was sink or swim for one as well as the other. In those days much was heard about troupes traveling "on their trunks." The stories were not exaggerated, but life had its better side, too. The manager and the actor were daily companions; there was a mutual absorption of ideas; the manager learned to know and appraise the "artistic temperament"—which is a tangible asset when not a form of artificial grouch or congenital ill-nature—and to respect the actor's point of view, while, reciprocally, the actor was able to place himself in the manager's position and to get his point of view from close personal affiliation.

The Dearborn Independent, January 1. 1921

29. The Rise of the First Jewish Theatrical Trust

It has long been known among dramatic critics that the reason for the maintenance of "Ben Hur" in the theater for nineteen years is this: it is the most successful of all the vehicles for pro-Semitism now on the stage. That will appear to be a prejudicial statement in the minds of the thousands who have seen and enjoyed "Ben Hur," but there is truth in it.

The point which should not be overlooked, however, is that if "Ben Hur" is useful in framing the public mind favorably toward the Jews, it is not because of a pro-Semitic intention in the story. That may be the intention of the producers, Messrs. Klaw and Erlanger, but it was not the intention of General Lew Wallace.

It would seem that art and fate conspire against the propagandist play, for in no other way can the failure of avowedly pro-Semitic drama be explained. Perhaps there was never such a serious and even strenuous attempt made to force the Jewish controlled theater into the service of pro-Semitism as has been made in recent months. And the attempts, with one possible exception, have been failures. Lavishly produced, heralded by an unbroken clacque of press announcement, swathed in an initial chorus of praise, sponsored by officialdom which had been dragged out to stand godfather to the productions, they nevertheless have failed.

Be it said to the credit of the American Jew that he has been one of the causes of the failure. A most significant and hopeful sign was the reaction of the intelligent Jewish community against the attempt to utilize the stage as a hustings to boost the Jew into an unreal eminence and desirability. Certain competent Jews wrote their opinions about this with much freedom and wisdom.

And they evinced a spirit, which, if it could be made to permeate all Jewish activities, would quickly dispose of the Jewish Question under whatever phase it may be considered.

It is this spirit of judging Jewish interests in the light of the whole which promises a helpful and lasting solution of all the differences which unfortunately have been permitted to arise between the people of Judah and the others.

The Rise of the First Jewish Theatrical Trust

The fact of Jewish control of the theater is not of itself a ground for complaint. If certain Jews, working separately or in groups, have succeeded in wrenching this rich business from its former Gentile control, that is purely a matter of commercial interest.

It is precisely on the same footing as if one group of Gentiles won the control from another group of Gentiles. It may be regarded as a business matter. In this, as in other business matters, however, there is the ethical test of how the control was gained and how it is used. Society is usually willing to receive the fact of control with equanimity, providing the control is not used for anti-social purposes.

The fact that old-time Gentile producing managers usually died poor—Augustin Daly being about the only exception—while Jewish producing managers wax immensely wealthy (there being on this side the exception of the late Charles Frohman), would indicate that the Gentile managers were better artists and poorer business men than the Jewish managers. At least poorer business men, perhaps; and in any case working on a system whose chief object was to produce plays and not profits.

The advent of Jewish control put the theater on a more commercialized basis than it had previously known. It really represented applying the Trust Idea to the theater before it had been largely applied to industry. As early as the year 1896 the Theatrical Trust controlled 37 theaters in strategic cities. The men composing this alliance were Klaw and Erlanger, Nixon and Zimmerman, and Hayman and Frohman. All but Zimmerman were Jews, and his racial origin was a subject of dispute. This group was later joined by Rich and Harris, of Boston, and Joseph Brookes, all known as Jews.

Controlling these theaters, the Trust was able to assure a long season to both managers and playing companies. Outside the Trust, the managers and companies were left to make arrangements between each other, which resembled a species of barnstorming.

The effect on the independent theaters and managers was disastrous. The Trust boosted royalties on plays from $50 to $450 and eventually to $1,000 a week. This of itself cut off the material of the stock companies with which the independent managers endeavored to keep open their houses.

The running out of the stock companies by excessive charges for the use of plays that had already been used in the regular theaters of the Trust, really served Jewish interests in another way. The motion picture industry was coming to the front. It was a Jewish enterprise from the first. There never was any need to drive Gentiles out of that, because the Gentiles never had a chance to get in. Thus, the driving out of the stock companies threw the empty theaters over to the "movies," and the benefit was again confined to a particular racial group.

This will answer the question so frequently asked by people who wonder why the theaters they formerly saw offering plays at all seasons, are now devoting the larger part of the year to "movies."

It was not to be expected that this sort of thing could be put through without a struggle. There was a struggle and a severe one, but it is ended with what the public can see today.

The opposition offered by the artists was prolonged and dignified. Francis Wilson, Nat C. Goodwin, James A. Herne, James O'Neil, Richard Mansfield, Mrs. Fiske and James K. Hackett stood out for a time, all of them with the exception of Goodwin bound by a forfeit of $1,000 if they deserted the cause of a free theater.

Joseph Jefferson was always with the actors in this opposition and continued of the same mind to the end, playing in both Trust and anti-Trust houses.

It is a matter of record that Nat Goodwin was the first to give in. He was the head and front of the opposition, but he had his weaknesses which were well known to the Trust, and upon these they played. One of his weaknesses was for New York engagements, and he was offered a long engagement at the Knickerbocker Theater. He was also given the promise of dates wherever and whenever he wanted them. Goodwin thereupon deserted the alliance of stars and became the henchman of the Trust. (The "Trust" was the name by which the new control was known in these days. The racial name was not given although the racial nature was plainly discerned.)

Nat Goodwin's star began to decline from that day. He made a final essay as Shylock, and with that he was practically ushered out as a headliner of the serious stage.

Richard Mansfield and Francis Wilson were delivering nightly curtain speeches against the Trust wherever they appeared, and although the public was sympathetic it was very much like the present state of affairs—what could the public do? What can an unorganized public ever do against a small organized, determined minority? The public hardly ever appears as a party in any of the movements that concern itself; the public is the prize for which the parties strive.

The Trust dealt strongly with Wilson. His dates were canceled. Neither his status nor his ability was of any avail to him. One of the Trust made an open statement: "Mr. Wilson is a shining mark, and we determined to make an example of him for the benefit of the lesser offenders."

Wilson's strong spirit was finally subdued to see "reason." In 1898 the Philadelphia members of the Trust offered him $50,000 for his business, and he took it.

In due time Richard Mansfield also surrendered, and Mrs. Fiske was left alone to carry on the fight.

The Theatrical Trust, which must be described as Jewish, because it was that, was at the beginning of the new century in full control of the field. It had reduced what was essentially an art to a time-clock, cash-register system, working with the mechanical precision of a well-managed factory. It suppressed individuality and initiative, killed off competition, drove out the independent manager and star, excluded all but foreign playwrights of established reputation, fostered the popularity of inferior talent which was predominantly Jewish, sought to debase the service of the dramatic critics of the public press, foisted countless "stars" of mushroom growth upon a helpless public while driving real stars into obscurity; it handled plays, theaters and actors like factory products, and not began a process of vulgarizing and commercializing everything connected with the theater.

If space permitted, a number of opinions could be presented here from men like William Dean Howells, Norman Hapgood and Thomas Bailey Aldrich, whose concern was for the theater, but who voiced no other observation as to the racial influences at work.

Their concern was justified. It is quite possible that many who read this article are not interested in the theater, and are, in fact, convinced that the theater is a menace. Very well. What principally makes it a menace? This—that the stage today represents the principal cultural element of 50 per cent of the people. What the average young person absorbs as to good form, proper deportment, refinement as contrasted with coarseness, correctness of speech or choice of words, customs and feelings of other nations, even fashions of clothes, as well as ideas of religion and law, are derived from what he sees and hears at the theater. The masses' sole idea of the homes and the life of the rich is derived from the stage and the movies. More wrong notions are given, more prejudices created by the Jewish controlled theater in one week, than can be charged against a serious study of the Jewish Question in a century.

People sometimes wonder where the ideas of the younger generation come from. This is the answer.

As was just said, all the original opposers of this new control of the theater surrendered and left Mrs. Fiske to fight alone. She had, however, an ally in her husband, Harrison Grey Fiske, who was editor of the New York Dramatic Mirror.

Mrs. Fiske herself had said: "The incompetent men who have seized upon the affairs of the stage in this country have all but killed art, ambition and decency."

Her husband wrote in his paper: "What then should be expected of a band of adventurers of infamous origin, of no breeding and utterly without artistic taste? . . . Let it be kept in mind that the ruling number of these men who compose the Theatrical Trust are absolutely unfit to serve in any but the most subordinate places in the economy of the stage and that they ought not to be tolerated even in these places except under a discipline, active, vigorous and uncompromising. Their records are disreputable and in some cases criminal, and their methods are in keeping with their records." (First printed in the *Dramatic Mirror*, December 25, 1897; reprinted March 19, 1898.)

This attack was regarded, foolishly and wrongfully of course, as an attack on the whole House of Israel and, as is always the case when one Jew is censured for wrongdoing, all the Jews in the United States came to the rescue.

Pressure was brought to bear on a famous news company which handled the circulation of the most important magazines in the United States. Leading hotels were induced to withdraw the Dramatic Mirror from their news stands. Mirror correspondents were refused admittance to theaters controlled by the Trust. Any number of underground influences were set in operation to "get" Fiske and his business.

Suit was brought against Fiske for $10,000 damages for the strictures he had printed upon the personal character of certain members of the Trust. Fiske replied in his answer, setting up various facts against specific members of the Trust, their records, actions, and so on. One he accused of carrying on business under a fictitious name ("cover name," as it is known in Jewish circles).

Another he accused of charging managers for advertising expenses that were never incurred. Another he accused of issuing "complimentary" tickets in which he did a private speculative business of his own, selling them and pocketing the proceeds. Another he accused of specific crime for which he had been arrested and convicted. He charged that the Trust as a whole advertised in various cities that "the original New York company" would play, charging exorbitant admission fees on the strength of this advertisement, when in truth these were secondary companies and not the one advertised.

A strange court hearing was held in which the magistrate did not wish to hear any of Fiske's testimony, even forbidding him to enter official records of the criminal proceedings had against a certain member of the Trust. The magistrate did not seem to want to hear what Fiske based his statements upon. There was a serious shooting scrape involving a woman, but the magistrate did not want to hear about it. There was even considerable difficulty on the part of Fiske's lawyer in procuring the attendance of Abraham L. Erlanger at court, although he was one of the complainants.

All the important questions asked of Klaw were overruled.

As to Al Hayman, the court overruled all questions relating to his real name and the circumstances under which he left Australia. The facts were not brought out in this hearing, but the whole character of the hearing was made known to the public. Fiske was bound over to the Grand Jury, with $300 bail in every allegation of libel.

The Grand Jury lost no time in dismissing all the complaints against Fiske. The Trust members had come off badly because of their evident unwillingness to meet the case. They were revealed to be a much lower type of men than the American public had supposed was in charge of the American theater. They were shown to be a type that would not even stop at demanding the discharge of a local newspaper reporter whose critique of their plays did not please them.

The fight of the dramatic critics first against the bribery and then against the bludgeoning of the Theatrical Trust makes a story of which echoes have frequently come to the American public through the press. Conciliatory at first, with managers, actors, playwrights and critics, the Trust, as soon as it gained power, showed the claws beneath the velvet. It had the millions of dollars of the public coming its way, why should it care?

Whenever a critic opposed its methods or pointed out the inferior, coarse and degrading character of the Trust productions, he was ordered barred from the Trust's theaters, and local managers were instructed to demand his discharge from his newspaper. It is with mingled feelings that an American is compelled to relate that in many, many cases the demand was complied with, the papers being threatened with the loss of Sunday advertising! But here and there courageous writers on the Stage held to the honor of their profession and refused to be bribed or intimidated.

Writers like James S. Metcalfe, of *Life*; Hillery Bell, of the *New York Press*; Frederick F. Schrader, of the *Washington Post*; Norman Hapgood, on the *New York Evening Globe*; James O'Donnell Bennett, of the *Chicago Record-Herald*, stood out against the Trust and made their fight. Metcalfe went so far as to bring suit against the Trust for unlawful exclusion from a place of public amusement. The courts were kind to the Trust. They decided that a theater may pick its patrons. Even in very recent years the Trust has followed blacklisted dramatic critics in an effort to prevent their employment by newspapers.

The Theatrical Trust does not exist in the form it did ten years ago. It grew arrogant and bred secret enemies among its own people. A new force arose, but it also was Jewish, as it originated in the Shubert brothers with David Belasco. Instead of one, the American have now a dual dictatorship of the stage. The rage of the day is not plays, but playhouses. With not three plays of any character to distinguish them from the dregs of the stage, there are now building in New York alone a dozen new playhouses. The theatrical business has entered upon its real estate phase. There is money in renting chairs at the rate of $1 to $3 an hour. The renting of the chairs is a reality. The Stage is rapidly becoming an illusion.

The Dearborn Independent, January 8, 1921

30. How Jews Capitalized a Protest against Jews

The American stage is under the influence and control of a group of former bootblacks, newsboys, ticket speculators, prize ring habitués, and Bowery characters. At the present writing the most advertised man in the world of theatrical production is Morris Gest, a Russian Jew, who has produced the most salacious spectacles ever shown in America—"Aphrodite" and "Mecca." It is reported that the scent of nastiness has been so strongly circulated among theatergoers that tickets are sold a year ahead for the Chicago exhibition of one of these shows, the patrons being, of course, mostly Gentiles.

Now, it is a fair question, who is this Morris Gest who stalks before his fellow Jews as the most successful producer of the year? It is nothing against him to say that he came from Russia. It is nothing against him to say that he is a Jew. It is nothing against him to say that although success has favored him, his father and mother are still in Odessa, or were until recently. Yet, in a recent interview, in which the professional note of pathos was obtrusively present, he lamented that he was not able to bring his parents to America.

The story of Morris Gest is the last one in the world to use as a "success story" of the type of "the poor immigrant boy who became a great theatrical producer." He is not a great producer, of course, although he is a great panderer to the least creditable tastes of the public whose taste he has been no mean factor in debasing. Gest sold newspapers in Boston and became property boy in a Boston theater. In 1906 he was a member of a notorious gang of ticket speculators who were the bane of the public until ticket peddling on the sidewalks in front of theaters was suppressed by the police. There are still other stories told about him that link his name with another sort of traffic, but whether these stories are true or not, there is nothing in Gest's career to indicate that he would ever contribute anything to the theater's best interest. He is the son-in-law of David Belasco.

Then there is Sam Harris, long the junior partner of the firm of Cohan & Harris, who began his career in the arts by managing Dixon, the colored champion featherweight pugilist, and the redoubtable Terry

McGovern, champion lightweight prize fighter. With tastes formed at the ringside, he launched into theatrical ventures, allying himself with Al Woods. He catered to the lower classes and made a fortune by producing atrocious melodramas in second and third class houses.

And yet this is the Sam Harris who commands the patronage of hundreds of thousands, yes, millions of theatergoers, some of whom go on innocently believing that when they invade the theater they also enter, by some mystical process, "the realms of art."

Al H. Woods has but one good eye. It is not this personal loss that matters, but the history of the misfortune which goes back to the time when Al was a member of an East side gang. The common report was that he used to play the piano in a downtown place, east of Fifth Avenue. Mr. Woods is also a distinguished patron of dramatic art—he presented "The Girl from Rector's" and "The Girl in the Taxi," two of the most immoral and pointless shows of recent years. Several times he has secured the rights to certain Viennese operas, which were bad enough in themselves from a moral point of view, but which were at least constructed with true artistry; but even these he marred by an inept infusion of vulgarity and blague.

The public, of course, does not see and does not know these gods before whom they pour their millions yearly, nor does the public know from what source theatric vileness comes. It is amusing to listen to the fledgling philosophers discuss the "tendencies of the stage," or expatiate learnedly on the "divine right of Art" to be as flippant and as filthy as it pleases, when all the time the "tendency" is started and the "art" is determined by men whose antecedents would make Art scream!

The American Theater is a small group of Jewish promoters and a large group of Gentile gullibles, and it is only the latter, who "kid themselves" that there is anything real about the matter.

It is perfectly natural, therefore, that the complete Judaization of the theater should result in its being transformed into "the show business," a mere matter of trade and barter. The real producers are often not culturally equipped for anything more than the baldest business. They can hire what they want, mechanicians, costumers, painters, writers, musicians. With their gauge of public taste and their models of action formed upon the race track and the prize ring; with their whole ideal modeled upon the ambition to pander to depravity, instead of serving legitimate needs, it is not surprising that the standards of the Theater should now be at their lowest mark.

As theatergoers are noticing more and more, the Jewish manager whenever possible employs Jewish actors and actresses. Gentile playwrights and actors are steadily diminishing in number for want of a market. At times the employment of Jewish actors has been so obtrusive as to endanger the success of the play.

This was notably the case when the part of a young Christian girl of the early Christian Era was given to a Jewess of pronounced racial features. The selection was so glaringly inept, ethnically and historically, that it militated strongly against the impression the play was intended to produce.

The "cover-name" conceals from the thearter-going public the fact that the actors and actresses who purvey entertainment are, in large and growing proportion, Jewish.

Some of the more prominent Jewish actors, many of them prime favorites, are Al Jolson, Charlie Chaplin, Louis Mann, Sam Bernard, David Warfield, Joe Weber, Barney Bernard, "Ed Wynne, or to mention his real name, Israel Leopold," Lou Fields, Eddie Cantor, Robert Warwick.

Among the prominent Jewish actresses are: Theda Bara, Nora Bayes, Olga Nethersole, Irene Franklin, Gertrude Hoffman, Mizi Hajos, Fanny Brice (wife of Nicky Arnstein), Bertha Kalisch, Jose Collins, Ethel Levy, Belle Baker, Constance Collier. The late Anna Held was a Jewess.

In addition to these there are others whose racial identity is not revealed by their names or any public knowledge about them.

The Jewish press claims for the Jews, aside from the commercial control of the stage, the control of the fun-making business. "The greatest entertainers, vaudevillians and fun-makers are Jews," says an article in the Chicago Jewish Sentinel, commenting on the extent to which Jewish actors monopolized the Chicago stage that week.

Among the composers we once beheld Victor Herbert and Gustav Kerker in honorable places; but now the Irving Berlins have forced themselves into places hewn out and established by Gentiles who had a regard for art.

There are no great Jewish playwrights. Charles Klein wrote "The Lion and the Mouse," but never repeated. There is, of course, much commonplace work turned out for the stage; a commercialized stage needs a certain amount of "product."

Among those engaged in such work are Jack Lait, Montague Glass, Samuel Shipman, Jules Eckert Goodman, Aaron Hoffman, and others.

The Jewish claim to exceptional genius is not borne out by the theater, although the Jewish will to power is therein amply illustrated.

Belasco's name comes to mind, perhaps, oftener than any; and Belasco is the most consummate actor off any stage. To understand Mr. Belasco is to understand the method by which the "Independents" fought the Jewish Theater Trust, and still retained the monopoly of the Theater for the Jews.

The old Trust was bowling along merrily, smashing everything in its way, thrusting honored "stars" into obscurity, blocking the path of promising playwrights, putting out of business all actors who would not prostitute art to commercialism, and there occurred what always occurs for even the Jews are not superior to natural law—a bad case of "big head" was developed.

Klaw, Erlanger and their immediate associates felt themselves to be kings and began to exhibit a few supposedly royal idiosyncrasies.

There were some protests, of course, against the arrogance of the Czars of the Theater. The Vanderbilts and other New York millionaires embodied their protest in a movement toward a national theater which was erected at Grand Central Park, and for which $1,000,000 was spent. One of the members of the Trust proved his birth and breeding by saying that this attempt to cleanse the theater was really only a plan to provide a place of vice for the benefit of the millionaire backers.

The remark inspired deep rancor, but was more revelatory of the Jewish Trust's essential conception of the theater, than anything else. Belasco came from San Francisco, where he had done various stunts, including those of an itinerant recitationist, illusionist and actor. James E. Herne took an interest in him as a youth and discovered him to be adept at helping himself to dialogues out of printed plays. Under Herne, Belasco learned much about stage effects, and soon became very successful in touching up defective plays. Coming to New York, Belasco fell in with DeMille, a Jewish writer for the stage, who only needed Belasco's "sense of the theater" to make his qualities effective.

Belasco became a factor in enlarging the Jewish control of the stage, in this way: he was connected with the Frohmans, but was unable to persuade them that Mrs. Leslie Carter, who had been the center of a sensational divorce suit and who had placed herself under Mr. Belasco's professional direction, was a great actress. The making of a star out of Mrs. Carter, and the gaining of public recognition for her, proved a long task. The Frohmans were unsympathetic.

Then, among the managers there was dissension too. The Shuberts had been compelled to take the leavings of the other Jewish magnates, especially the leavings of Charles Frohman, and the Shuberts revolted. The Shuberts were natives of Syracuse, and their preparation for the theater was not promising of their devotion to art. They were program boys and ushers. Then the haberdashery business claimed them as possibly a speedier course to wealth. Samuel Shubert eventually became a ticket seller in the box office. In due time, having learned a few marketable secrets of the theater, he launched a frivolous burlesque and comedy show. With this he floated into New York, and continued with his musical shows of a shallow kind, until the name Shubert has come to be descriptive of the productions. The Shuberts, of course, booked in Trust theaters.

About the year 1900, the Shuberts quarreled with the Trust and Belasco quarreled with the Frohmans, and the two hailed each other as fellow belligerents and proceeded to see what could be made of their belligerency. The public was showing signs of disgust with the Trust. That was the cue!—the Shuberts and Belasco would appeal to the public to help in the fight against the Trust. Belasco and the Shuberts would play the part of injured independents; public sympathy would be aroused, and public patronage would boost the "Independents" into the strength of a new Trust. That is exactly what occurred

Belasco's theatricalism helped to this end. He is an actor off, as well as on the stage. He affects the pose of a benevolent priest, and dresses the part, wearing a priestly collar, with clerical vest and coat. Although of Portuguese-Hebraic origin, Belasco dresses after this manner to honor, as he says, a tutor of his early days. Anyway, the costume is very effective, especially with the ladies. He has a tremulous, shy way about him, and he sits in his sanctum with the lights so arranged that his priestly face and splendid shock of silver hair seem to rise out of an encompassing and shadowy mystery. It is very effective—very effective. One woman declared, after being admitted to the presence and gazing on the face that rose out of the shadows into the light—"I have a better understanding of the divine humility of Jesus Christ since I have been privileged to meet Mr. Belasco."

Thus, "the master," as he is called, was well equipped to appeal to public sympathy. And he did appeal. There was no end to his appeal. He told stories of personal attacks made on him. He wrung his hands in desperate grief against the Trust's menace to the stage. His own productions, however, were not all immaculate. There was one, "Naughty Anthony," which brought the police censor down upon him. But there was a very clear conception in the public mind as to what the Trust had done to the stage; Belasco said he was against the Trust, and the rest was snap judgement.

The Shuberts and Belasco thus found themselves in a very favorable combination of circumstances. Their first financial aid came, strangely enough, through ex-Congressman Reinach, a Jew, "Boss" Cox, of Ohio, and others who were interested. These supplied the first money; the Shuberts supplied the management; Belasco supplied the wonderful impersonation of a Daniel come to call the Jewish Theater Trust to judgement. The campaign succeeded and the wealth rolled in. For a time Belasco did prove to the public that he could produce better plays than the old Trust had given to the public, and to that extent he justified public confidence in him.

The end of the old Trust came in a natural way. The Shuberts became rich and powerful, and the Trust was then willing to do business with them. Some of the Trust members died, and about 1910 the old Trust ceased to exist as the dominant factor in American theatrical affairs. But the rise of the "Independents" did not bring relief; it only captured for Jewish enterprise that part of the theater which might have become the prize of a legitimate body of protesters against the old cheapness and vulgarity. The pretended protest won. The theater was saved to Jewish control.

Jewish managers had created the public disgust in the first place. They knew what the public reaction would be, so they prepared to capitalize the reaction, and thus control the theatergoing public both going and coming. This they did with admirable strategy.

During the outbreak there was some genuine feeling of independence on the part of a few non-Jewish managers. John Cort organized a western theater circuit. Colonel Henry W. Savage swung loose from Klaw and Erlanger, as did also William A. Brady. But independence of the Jewish control has never flourished. Wherever it did keep up an independent front, it stood for the theater in its best sense, and served as the only channel of expression for the remaining few stage artists. The coming of the motion picture, however, gave true independence its quietus. The motion picture "industry"—and it is rightly named an "industry"— is entirely Jewish controlled, and as it is pushing its way into the legitimate theaters and crowding out human players for long periods every year, theater managers have to bow to it more and more. It remained for the Shuberts, however, to give the theatrical business a most original twist. They made it a real estate speculation. Readers of this article may recall that recently they have read that in their own or a neighboring city the Shuberts are going to build one or two theaters. In one city, the announcement was made that two theaters were to be built. That particular city happens to need almost everything else but theaters. However it cannot get anything else it needs, and there is no doubt it will get the theaters.

The Shuberts learned this trick when they were supposed to be "bucking the Trust." They went after any building they could get, and because of the public enmity to the Trust, they got better terms than otherwise could have been possible. An old riding school in New York became the Winter Garden.

The great Hippodrome, the materialized dream of a non-Jew, Frederick Thompson, was taken over by the Shuberts. It soon dawned on the Shuberts that there was more money in theatrical real estate than in theatrical art.

Today, the Shuberts, while nominally theatrical managers, are really dealers in theatrical leases and buildings where theatrical productions are made. A theater, as a real estate proposition, pays amazingly well. Figure up the amount of space you occupy as a show, the length of time you occupy it, and the price you pay for it. It is rent raised to the nth degree; then the offices which make the bulk of the structure, and the stores in front. Really, "the show business" is the minor consideration.

What does it cost the Shuberts? Very little but the use of their name. When it is the matter of a new theater, outside capital supplies three-fourths of the money, but the lease and the control are vested in the Shuberts. That is a rather handsome arrangement.

In the matter of producing plays, the same arrangement is often followed—the author, the star, or their backers supplying the larger part, sometimes all of the capital, while the Shuberts lend their name to the management and take their share of the booking fees and the rental of the theaters where the show is produced.

In October of last year (1920) a serious slump hit the theatrical business. Even in New York the theaters were experiencing the worst depression of years. More than 3,000 actors were idle and managers were compelled to resort to the cut-rate ticket agents to sell their seats. And yet, in the midst of it, Shubert announced six new theaters for

New York alone. At the same time they announced the production of forty plays. Forty plays! If a man announced that he was going to build six new art museums in one city and fit them up with the requisite number of oil paintings produced under his own direction, he would be considered crazy, especially if it were a matter of common repute that he knew nothing of art and was having the pictures painted merely to give value to his real estate!

It indicates how thoroughly accustomed the public has become to "the show business" and the "motion picture industry," that the announcement of these former haberdashers is taken so complacently. Forty plays!—when anyone can count on the fingers of both hands all the present-day American and English playwrights even remotely deserving of notice!

It is said that the Shuberts do not expect more than three out of forty plays to succeed. The success of a play, in the artistic sense, is not their business. To maintain enough plays on the road to keep alive their real estate investments is really the thing.

Thus it is now not strange where theatrical slang comes from. An actor who wins success is said to have "delivered the goods." An approved actress is "all wool and a yard wide." An author "puts it over" his audience. A girl of no particular class is a "skirt." A young chorus girl is a "broiler" or a "chicken." An actress who plays the part of an adventuress is a "vamp." A very successful play is a "knockout." Taken all together, it is "the show business." This is the effect of Jewish control of any profession—as any American lawyer will tell you.

The only protest now being offered is by the small dramatic clubs which, whether or not they know it, are the strongest "anti-Semitic" influence on the theatrical horizon.

The Dearborn Independent, January 22, 1921

31. The Jewish Aspect of the "Movie" Problem

There was once a man named Anthony Comstock who was the enemy of public lewdness. Of course he was never popular. No newspaper ever spoke of him without a jeer. He became the stock joke of his time—and it was not very long ago. He died in 1915. It is very noticeable that the men who mocked his life with banal jesting were non-Jews. It is also worth recording that the men who profited from the commercializing of much of the vice which he fought, were Jews. It was a very familiar triangle—the morally indignant non-Jew fighting against public lechery, and the Jewish instigators of it hiding behind ribald Gentiles and Gentile newspapers.

Well, the fight is still going on. If you will subscribe to a clipping bureau, or if you will look over the press of the country, you will see that the problem of the immoral show has been neither settled nor silenced. In every part of the country it is intensely alive just now. In almost every state there are movie censorship bills pending, with the old "wet" and gambling elements against them, and the awakened part of the decent population in favor of them; always, the Jewish producing firms constituting the silent pressure behind the opposition.

This is a grave fact. Standing alone it would seem to charge a certain Jewish element with intentional gross immorality. But that hardly states the condition. There are two standards in the United States, one ruling very largely in the production of plays, the other reigning, when it does reign, in the general public. One is an Oriental ideal—"If you can't go as far as you like, go as far as you can." It gravitates naturally to the flesh and its exposure, its natural psychic habitat is among the more sensual emotions.

This Oriental view is essentially different from the Anglo-Saxon, the American view. And it knows this. Thus is the opposition to censorship accounted for. It is not that producers of Semitic origin have deliberately set out to be bad according to their own standards, but they know that their whole taste and temper are different from the prevailing standards of the American people; and if censorship were established, there would be danger of American standards being officially recognized, and that is what they would prevent. Many of these producers don't know how filthy their stuff is—it is so natural to them.

Scarcely an American home has not voiced its complaint against the movies. Perhaps no single method of entertainment has ever received such widespread and unanimous criticism as the movies, for the reason that everywhere their lure and their lasciviousness have been felt. There are good pictures, of course; it were a pity if that much could not be said; we cling to that statement as if it might prove a ladder to lift us above the cesspool which the most popular form of public entertainment has become.

The case has been stated so often that repetition is needless. Responsible men and organizations have made their protests, without results. The moral appeal meets no response in those to whom it is made, because they are able to understand only appeals that touch their material interests. As the matter now stands, the American Public is as helpless against the films as it is against any other exaggerated expression of Jewish power. And the American Public will continue helpless until it receives such an impression of its helplessness as to shock it into protective action.

In a powerful indictment of the movie tendency and the National Board of Review of Motion Pictures, Frederick Boyd Stevenson writes in the *Brooklyn Eagle:*

"On the other hand the reels are reeking with filth. They are slimy with sex plays. They are overlapping one another with crime.

"From bad to worse these conditions have been growing. The plea is set up that the motion picture industry is the fourth or fifth in the United States, and we must be careful not to disrupt it. A decent photoplay, it is argued, brings gross returns of, say, $100,000, while a successful sex play brings from $250,000 to $2,500,000."

Dr. James Empringham was recently quoted in the *New York World* as saying: "I attended a meeting of motion picture owners in New York, and I was the only Christian present. The remainder of the company consisted of 500 unChristian Jews."

Now, there is little wisdom in discoursing against evil in the movies and deliberately closing our eyes to the forces behind the evil.

The method of reform must change. In earlier years, when the United States presented a more general Aryan complexion of mind and conscience, it was only necessary to expose the evil to cure it. The evils we suffered from were lapses, they were the fruits of moral inertia or

The Jewish Aspect of the "Movie" Problem

drifting; the sharp word of recall stiffened the moral fiber of the guilty parties and cleared up the untoward condition. That is, evil doers of our own general racial type could be shamed into decency, or at least respectability.

That method is no longer possible. The basic conscience is no longer present to touch. The men now mostly concerned with the production of scenic and dramatic filth are not to be reached that way. They do not believe, in the first place, that it is filth. They cannot understand, in the second place, that they are really pandering to and increasing human depravity. When there does reach their mentalities the force of protest, it strikes them as being very funny; they cannot understand it; they explain it as due to morbidity, jealousy or—as we hear now anti-Semitism.

Reader, beware! if you so much as resent the filth of the mass of the movies, you will fall under the judgement of anti-Semitism. The movies are of Jewish production. If you fight filth, the fight carries you straight into the Jewish camp because the majority of the producers are there. And then you are "attacking the Jews."

If the Jews would throw out of their camp the men and methods that so continuously bring shame upon the Jewish name, this fight for decency could be conducted without so much racial reference.

An analysis of the motion picture industry in the United States will show:

That 90 per cent of the production of pictures is in the hands of 10 large concerns located in New York City and Los Angeles.

That each of these has under it a number of complete units, making up the large aggregate of companies seen in photoplays all over the world.

That these parent concerns control the market.

That 85 per cent of these parent concerns are in the hands of Jews.

That they constitute an invincible centralized organization which distributes its produces to tens of thousands of exhibitors, the majority of whom are Jews of an inferior type.

That the independent motion pictures have no distributing center but sell in the open market.

It may come as a surprise to many people that there is no dearth of good pictures. The trouble is that there is no means by which good pictures can reach the public. One of the notable libraries of beautiful pictures, containing the cream of dramatic and educational films, has been rendered absolutely useless because of the impossibility of getting them before the public. The owners of these pictures achieved a little advance by engaging Jewish salesmen to push the pictures, but against them has always been the huge and silent force of that concentrated opposition which is apparently against the introduction of decency and delight into the screen world.

Once in a while an independent producer like David Wark Griffith or Charles Ray gives the world a screen production that is not only without offense or propaganda, but is a veritable delight and joy. These pictures, with their attendant success, are the strongest answers that can be made to the cry of some producers that the only profitable plays are the nasty ones.

That cry, of course, is based on fact. Without doubt, as things now go, the nasty pictures are the more profitable, because they are the most elaborately made and the most gorgeously advertised. The very lewdest of them have secured their patronage by advertising that they deal with "moral problems."

But all public taste is cultivated. Every city which can boast of public spirit has citizens who spend tens of thousands of dollars annually in an attempt to create a community taste for good music. They succeed to a certain extent, but very rarely do they make it pay. It appears that the work of demoralizing the public taste is far more profitable. And as our whole range of public entertainment, outside of the higher musical field, has fallen into the hands of groups who do not know what the term "art" means, it is evident how overwhelming the appeal of the dollar must be.

If the public taste is now so fixedly demoralized that the moving picture producers can confidently claim that "the public demands what we are giving it," the case is more damning than otherwise. For it is recognized by all detached observers that such a public taste is a most urgent reason why immediate and heroic remedies should be adopted.

Cocaine peddlers can easily establish a "public demand" for their drugs, and they do. But that demand is never considered to be an extenuation for the peddling of "coke." So with the psychic poison and visual filth of the ordinary movie—the demand it has created is morally lawless, and the further satisfaction of the demand is morally lawless too.

Carl Laemmle, one of the leading producers in America and head of the Universal Film Company, testified before a congressional committee that he had sent a circular entitled "What Do You Want?" to the exhibitors who bought his pictures. At that time his company was in

The Jewish Aspect of the "Movie" Problem

communication with about 22,000 exhibitors. Mr. Laemmle says that he expected 95 per cent of the answers to favor clean, wholesome pictures, but "instead of finding 95 per cent favoring clean pictures, I discovered that at least one-half, or possibly 60 per cent, want pictures to be risque, the French for smutty."

Laemmle himself is a German-born Jew, and did not state what percentage of the replies were from people of what is euphemistically termed his "faith."

It is a very noticeable fact that whenever any attempt is made to control the tumultuous indecency and triviality which the movies ceaselessly pour out day and night upon the American public, the opposition thereto is Jewish. Take, for example, the attempt to arouse the sober spirit of America to a proper appreciation of what is happening to Sunday, the Day of Rest. The opponents for the whole movement—a movement for the awakening of conscience, not for the passage of laws—are Jews, and they justify their opposition on Jewish grounds.

Whenever the movies are before the bar of public opinion, their defenders as they are, are Jews. In the Congressional hearing before referred to, the lawyers who appeared for the companies were all Jews, distinguished by the names Meyers, Ludvigh, Kolm, Friend and Rosenthal.

There was even a Jewish Rabbi involved, who gave a most ingenuous explanation both of Jewish control of the movies and also of Jewish opposition to control of the character of the movies.

"I am a Jew," he said. "You know as well as I do that we have been the unfortunate victims of the nasty, biting tongue, and you know as well as I do that the movie first held us up to ridicule, and we have not only been disgraced in these movies, but we have had our religion traduced, and disgracefully traduced."

If this is true, it is chargeable to the Jews themselves, for Jews have always controlled the business. That it is true is probable, for the most zealous lampooners of the Jews have been Jewish comedians. Non-Jews fail abjectly in endeavoring to portray the character.

"We felt very much hurt," he continued, "and we felt there was a remedy, and that remedy was public opinion; and what did we do? We did not come to Congress. We organized a society—the Independent Order of B'nai B'rith, which is the largest Jewish fraternal order in the world. It organized what is called the Anti-Defamation League with headquarters in Chicago; and the league for the defense of the

Jewish name united with other people—in the Catholic Church, the Truth Society and Holy Name Society—and it wrote to all the movie manufacturers of the country asking them that they do not traduce the Jewish character and the Jewish religion, and that they do not hold us up to ridicule; that we did not object to the depiction of Jewish character, but we did object to the caricature of Jewish character and the caricature of our name and religion; and after thus having explained to the manufacturers our position, we appointed a committee of men in every city in the country, asking them that they appeal to the municipal authorities that they permit not the presentation of pictures that were calculated to offend the Jewish character and the Jewish sensitiveness.

"What has been the result? There has been necessary not a protest, because movies in this country are not producing that class of movies any longer."

Of course! there are excellent reasons why the Jewish protests, if any really were necessary, should be instantly obeyed. But why has not the continued and clamorous protest of decent America been equally heeded? Why not? Because the protest has come largely from non-Jews.

If the Jews can control the movies to the extent the rabbi claimed, why cannot they control them for decency—why do not they control them for decency?

The one weakness of the rabbi's statement is the charge that the Jewish religion was traduced. It would be most interesting to learn how this was done, and by whom. It is a religion which does not easily lend itself to that sort of treatment, picturesque as some of its forms may appear to alien eyes.

There is, however, a meaning hidden in this statement of the rabbi. The Jew considers any public expression of Christian character as being derogatory to his religion. For example: if the President of the United States or the governor of your state should make a specifically Christian allusion in his Thanksgiving Proclamation, or mention the name of Christ, that act would be protested as offensive to Jewish sensitiveness. Not only would be done, but has been done.

In the same hearing referred to, quotation was made from a letter written by Carl H. Pierce, special representative of the Oliver Morosco Photoplay Company, to the executive secretary of the Motion Picture Board of Trade, in which the following statement appeared:

"You and I have seen boards turn down such plays as the 'Life of the Savior' because they thought it might offend the Hebrews."

The Jewish Aspect of the "Movie" Problem

It is apparent that "Jewish sensitiveness" is a spoiled child which has been unduly coddled and that it has interfered to such an extent that the real question becomes one of non-Jewish rights.

The Jewish defenders have been asking, Why should a nation of 110,000,000 people be considered in danger from 3,000,000 Jews? And "Gentile fronts," with all the zest of a new idea, have shouted the same challenging question.

It might be advantageous to answer thus: Why should a country of 110,000,000 people, mostly of Christian faith and practice, be prevented from seeing the "Life of the Savior" portrayed on the screen because it is feared to offend the Jews?

The answer in both cases is not a comparison of numbers, but a recognition of the fact that, as in the motion picture world the Jews are at the neck of the bottle where they can absolutely control what goes to the public, so they are in other fields at corresponding places of control.

But whether the Jewish producer is qualified to do better than he is doing is a question. When you consider the conditions from which many of them sprang, you will be rendered rather hopeless of voluntary reform.

Why were not "Way Down East" and "The Shepherd of the Hills" put on the screen by Jews? Because the Jews in control of the movies have no knowledge of American rural life, and therefore no feeling for it. The Jew is a product of city life, and that peculiar phase of city life which is found in the ghetto. He sees in a farmer only a "hick" and a "rube." You may rest entirely assured that it was not the Yankee, himself a product of the farms, who turned the agriculturist into a joke, until today the joke has emptied our farms of men. The theatrical "hick" and "rube" of the gold-brick story and the hayseed play, were of Jewish origin. The Jew is a product of city life, and of that phase of city life where the "wits" play a large part.

The America of the average Jew who caters to the entertainment of Americans is comprehended in a beaten path from the box-office, to back-stage, and thence to an eating place. He doesn't know America as yet, except as a huge aphis which he may milk.

It follows, therefore, that in all probability he is equally ignorant of American home life. He has not yet been able to understand what American domesticity means. The American home is an almost unknown quantity to foreigners of the Eastern races. An Armenian woman who has lived in America for five years says that she knows nothing of an American home save what she can see through the windows as she passes.

This, of course, is a lack not easily to be bridged over. It may not be strictly true that the majority of movie producers do not know the interiors of American homes, but there is certainly every indication that they have not caught its spirit, and that their misrepresentation of it is more than a false picture, it is also a most dangerous influence.

It is dangerous to foreigners who gain their most impressive ideas of American life from the stage. It is dangerous to Americans who fancy that the life of the screen is the life that is lived by "the better classes." If we could map the community mind of whole sections of our cities and trace the impressions of American people, American habits and American standards which those mind-groups hold, we should then see the dangerous misrepresentation which movie producers have given to things American. Falsity, artificiality, criminality and jazz are the keynotes of the mass of screen productions.

American life is bare and meager to the Eastern mind. It is not sensuous enough. It is devoid of intrigue. Its women of the homes do not play continuously and hysterically on the sex motif. It is a life made good and durable by interior qualities of faith and quietness—and these, of course, are ennui and death to the Orientally minded.

There lies the whole secret of the movies' moral failure: they are not American and their producers are racially unqualified to reproduce the American atmosphere. An influence which is racially, morally and idealistically foreign to America, has been given the powerful projecting force of the motion picture business, and the consequences are what we see.

The purpose of this and succeeding articles is not to lift hands in horror and point out how rotten the movies are. Everybody is doing that.

The case against the movies is not contested at all. It is unanimous. Women's clubs, teachers, newspaper editors, police officers, judges of the courts, ministers or religion, physicians, mothers and fathers—everybody knows just what the movies are.

What all these disgusted groups evidently do not know is this: their protests will be entirely useless until they realize that behind the movies there is another group of definite moral and racial complexion to whom the protest of non-Jews amounts to next to nothing at all, if they can possibly circumvent it. As the rabbi previously quoted showed, the Jews got what they wanted from the producers as soon as they made their request.

What have the non-Jewish teachers, women's clubs, newspaper editors, police officers and judges, ministers of religion, physicians, and just plain parents of the rising generation—what have they obtained for all their complaints and protests?

Nothing!

And they can go on beating the air for a lifetime and still obtain no improvement, unless they face the unpleasant racial fact that the movies are Jewish. It is not a question of morals—that question has been settled; it is a question of management.

When the people know who and what is this intangible influence we call the "movies," the problem may not appear so baffling.

The Dearborn Independent, February 12, 1921

32. Jewish Supremacy in Motion Picture World

A little "Who's Who in the Motion Picture Industry" would make a valuable department in the movie theaters' printed programs, but it is not pleasant to think of what would happen to the manager who should print one. There is a strange confusion in the Jewish mind, a struggle between a desire to remain unidentified and a desire to be known. Sometimes they measure friendship by the depth of the silence about their being Jews; sometimes by the amount of open laudation. To say a man is a Jew is sometimes to be vilified as an "anti-Semite," and sometimes to be honored as "a friend of our nation."

In what is said now, the only purpose is to inform "movie fans" of the source of the entertainment which they crave and the destination of the millions of dollars which they spend. When you see millions of people crowding through the doors of the movie houses at all hours of the day and night, literally an unending line of human beings in every habitable corner of the land, it is worth knowing who draws them there, who acts upon their minds while they quiescently wait in the darkened theater, and who really controls this massive bulk of human force and ideas generated and directed by the suggestions of the screen.

Who stands at the apex of this mountain of control? It is stated in the sentence: The motion picture influence of the United States—and Canada—is exclusively under the control, moral and financial, of the Jewish manipulators of the public mind.

Jews did not invent the art of motion photography; they have contributed next to nothing to its mechanical or technical improvement; they have not produced any of the great artists, either writers or actors, which have furnished the screen with its material. Motion photography, like most other useful things in the world, is of non-Jewish origin. But by the singular destiny which has made the Jews the great cream-skimmers of the world, the benefit of it has gone not to the originators, but to the usurpers, the exploiters.

Who is who in the motion picture world? The names of the leading producing companies are widely known: The Famous Players; Selznick; Selwyn; Goldwyn; Fox Film Company; The Jesse L. Lasky Feature Play

Jewish Supremacy in Motion Picture World

Company; United Artists' Corporation; The Universal Film Company; The Metro; Vitagraph; Seligs; Thomas H. Ince Studios; Artcraft; Paramount, and so on.

The Famous Players is headed by Adolph Zukor. Mr. Zukor is a Hungarian Jew. He was a fur dealer in Hester street, and is said to have gone from house to house selling his goods. With his first savings he went into the "nickel" theater business with Marcus Loew. He is still in his forties and immensely wealthy. He is conceded to be the leader of the fifth largest industry in the world—an industry which is really the greatest educational and propagandist device ever discovered.

The reader will not be deceived by the use of the word "educational" in this connection. Movies are educational, but so are schools of crime. It is just because the movies are educational in a menacing way that they come in for scrutiny.

Zukor's control extends over such well-known names as Famous Players-Lasky Corporation, The Oliver Morosco Photoplay Company, Paramount Pictures Corporation, Artcraft Pictures, all of which have been absorbed within the past five years.

It is commonly supposed that the United Artists' Corporation is a non-Jewish concern, but according to an article in the American Hebrew, the head of this photoplay aggregation is Hiram Abrams. The United Artists' Corporation was formed several years ago by the Big Four among the actors—Mary Pickford, Douglas Fairbanks, Charlie Chaplin and David Wark Griffith, and notwithstanding the fact that Charlie Chaplin is a Jew, the company was regarded by the public as being non-Jewish. Hiram Abrams is a former Portland, Oregon, newsboy and graduated from that wholesome occupation into the position of manager of a "penny arcade." He was one of the founders of the Paramount Pictures Corporation, and became its president.

The Fox Film Corporation and the Fox circuit of theaters are under control of another Hungarian Jew who is known to the American public as William Fox. His original name is said to have been Fuchs. He also began his artistic and managerial career by running a "penny arcade." The penny arcade of 15 and 20 years ago, as most city-bred men will remember, was a "peep show" whose lure was lithographed lewdness but which never yielded quite as much pornography as it promised.

Fifteen years ago William Fox was in the clothes sponging business. He also is still in his early forties, is immensely wealthy, and one of the men who can pretty nearly determine what millions of movie fans shall think about certain fundamental things, what ideas and visions they shall entertain.

Marcus Loew also reached fame via the penny arcade and cheap variety vaudeville routes. He went into pictures and is now said to be the active head of 68 companies in various parts of the world. He is in the neighborhood of 50 years old. Loew controls the Metro Pictures Corporation. The names of Marcus Loew and Adolph Zukor are closely linked in the history of the movies. Both were in the fur business, and both were partners in the first penny arcade venture. Zukor went the way of pictures exclusively, although he later made investments in Loew's enterprises, but Loew went into variety and vaudeville of the type which is now to be found in the less desirable burlesque houses. From this he developed great entertainment enterprises which have made him a name and a fortune. The theaters he personally controls now number 105.

At the head of the Goldwyn Film Corporation is Samuel Goldwyn who is described as having been engaged "along mercantile lines" until motion pictures won his attention. In company with Jesse Lasky and Cecil DeMille he organized a $20,000 corporation in 1912. In 1916 he had prospered so greatly that he organized a $20,000,000 corporation with the Shuberts, A. H. Woods and the Selwyns, the purpose of this latter company being to screen the works of prominent non-Jewish writers—a matter of which more will be said presently.

The Universal Film Company, known everywhere through the name of Universal City, its studio headquarters, is under the control of Carl Laemmle. It would seem, from a reading of Who's Who, that Laemmle was his mother's name. His father's name is given as Julius Baruch. He is a Jew of German birth. He was manager of the Continental Clothing Company of Oshkosh until 1906, in which year he branched out into pictures, taking his first stand in a small Chicago motion picture theater. Laemmle conceived the idea of fighting the "trust." He bought an enormous tract of land near Los Angeles and built Universal City as the headquarters of his production work.

The Select Pictures Corporation is headed by Lewis J. Selznick, who is also head of Selznick Pictures, Incorporated. He was at one time vice-president of the World Film Corporation. With him are associated a number of members of his race.

This is but to name a few. These are the official heads. Penetrate down through the entire organizations, until you come to the last exhibition of the cracked and faded film in some cut-price theater in an obscure part of a great city, and you will find that the picture business, on its commercial side, is Jewish through and through.

In the above notes, reference has been made to the occupations out of which the present arbiters of photo-dramatic art have come to their present eminence. They are former newsboys, peddlers, clerks, variety hall managers and ghetto products. It is not urged against any successful business man that he formerly sold newspapers on the streets, or peddled goods from door to door, or stood in front of a clothing store hailing passers-by to inspect his stock. That is not the point at all. The point is here: men who come from such employments, with no gradations between, with nothing but a commercial vision of "the show business," can hardly be expected to understand, or, if they understand, to be sympathetic with a view of the picture drama which includes both art and morality.

Mr. Laemmle, it will be remembered from a former article, said of his company, "The Universal does not pose as a guardian of public morals or of public taste." This is probably the attitude of other producers, too. But though they avoid any responsibility for taste or morals, they consistently fight all attempts of the state to set up a public guardianship in those regions. A business that frankly brutalizes taste and demoralizes morals should not be permitted to be a law unto itself.

It is very difficult to see how the Jewish leaders of the United States can evade the point that Motion Pictures are Jewish. And with this being true, there is the question of responsibility upon which they cannot very well be either impersonal or silent.

The moral side of the movies' influence need not be discussed here because it is being discussed everywhere else. Everybody who has an active moral sense is convinced as to what is being done and as to what ought to be done. But the propaganda side of the movies does not so directly declare itself to the public. That the movies are recognized as a tremendous propagandist institution is proved by the eagerness of all sorts of causes to enlist them. It is also proved by the recent threat of a New York "Gentile front," that the movies themselves could prevent any progress being made in the attempt to save Sunday to the American people.

But who is the propagandist? Not the individual motion picture exhibitor on your street. He doesn't make the films. He buys his stuff as your grocer buys his canned goods—and has a far narrower margin of choice. He has hardly any choice in the kind of pictures he shall show. In order to get any good pictures that may be distributed, he must take all of the other kind that may be distributed. He is the "market" of the film producers and he must take the good with the bad, or be cut off from getting any.

As a matter of fact, with the "movie bug" so rampant in the country, it is next to impossible to supply enough good pictures for the stimulated and artificial demand. Some people's appetite calls for two or more pictures a day. If working people, they see a show at noon, and several at night. If shallow-pated wives, they see several in the afternoon and several at night. With all the brains and the skill of the country engaged on the task it would be impossible to supply a fresh drama of quality, hot out of the studios every hour, like bread.

Where the Jewish controllers have overstepped themselves is here: they have overstimulated a demand which they are not able to supply, except with such material as is bound to destroy the demand. Nothing is more dangerous to the motion picture business than the exaggerated appetite for them, and this appetite is whetted and encouraged until it becomes a mania.

Like the saloon business, the movie business is killing itself by killing that quality in its customers on which it was built.

Now, as to propaganda, there is evidence that the Jewish promoters have not overlooked that end of it. This propaganda as at present observed may be described under the following heads:

It consists in silence about the Jew as an ordinary human being. Jews are not shown upon the stage except in unusually favorable situations. Among the scenes offered the public you never see Hester Street or lower Fifth Avenue at noontime. Recall if you have ever seen a large Jewish group scene on general exhibition. After a terrible fire in a clothing factory, the mayor of New York asked a certain motion picture company to prepare a film to be entitled, "The Locked Door," to show how buildings are turned into firetraps by ignorance and greed. The scenario was written by a fire official who knew the circumstances of many holocausts. As most of the fire victims had been sweatshop girls, the scenario included a sweatshop. The picture was made as true to life as possible, so the head of the sweatshop was depicted as a Hebrew.

The gentleman who told this incident to a committee of Congress said: "It was no discredit to the Hebrew race. We all know they have been the fathers of the clothing industry; in fact, they made the first clothes."

Jewish Supremacy in Motion Picture World

But all the same, the picture was declared taboo by Jewish leaders. It broke the cardinal rule of silence about the Jew except when he can be depicted under exceptionally favorable circumstances.

This ill-concealed propaganda of the Jewish movie picture control is also directed against non-Jewish religions. You never saw a Jewish rabbi depicted on the screen in any but a most honorable attitude. He is clothed with all the dignity of his office and he is made as impressive as can be. Christian clergymen, as any movie fan will readily recall, were subjected to all sorts of misrepresentation, from the comic to the criminal. Now, this attitude is distinctly Jewish. Like many unlabeled influences in our life, whose sources lead back to Jewish groups, the object is to break down as far as possible all respectful or considerate thought about the clergy.

The Catholic clergy very soon made themselves felt in opposition to this abuse of their priestly dignity. You never see a priest made light of on the screen. But the Protestant clergyman is still the elongated, sniveling, bilious hypocrite of anti-Christian caricature. More and more the "free love" clergyman is appearing on the screen. He is made to justify his deeds by appeals to "broad" principles—which really kills two birds with one stone: it degrades the representative of religion in the eyes of the audience, and at the same time it insidiously inoculates the audience with the same dangerous ideas.

In the February *Pictorial Review,* Benjamin B. Hampton, a successful picture producer, throws a sidelight on this. He quotes a poster outside a movie show. The text says: "'I refuse to live with you any longer. I denounce you as my wife—I will go the HER—my free-lover.' Thus speaks the Rev. Frank Gordon in the greatest of all Free-Love dramas."

You may not depict a Hebrew as owner of a sweatshop—though all sweatshop owners are Hebrews; but you may make a Christian clergyman everything from a seducer to a safe-cracker and get away with it.

There may be no connection whatever, but beholding what is done, and remembering what is written in the Protocols, a question arises. It is written:

"We have misled, stupefied and demoralized the youth of the Gentiles by means of education in principles and theories, patently false to us, but which we have inspired."—Protocol 9.

"We have taken good care long ago to discredit the Gentile clergy."—Protocol 17.

"It is for this reason that we must undermine faith, eradicate from the minds of the Gentiles the very principles of God and Soul, and replace these conceptions by mathematical calculations and material desires."—Protocol 4.

Two possible views are open to choice: one, that this constant caricature of representatives of religion is simply the natural expression of a worldly state of mind; the other, that it is part of a traditional campaign of subversion. The former is the natural view among uninformed people. It would be the preferable view, if peace of mind were the object sought. But there are far too many indications that the second view is justified, to permit of its being cast aside.

The screen, whether consciously or just carelessly, is serving as a rehearsal stage for scenes of anti-social menace. There are no uprisings of revolutions except those that are planned and rehearsed. That is the most modern fruit of the study of history: that revolutions are not spontaneous uprisings, but carefully planned minority actions. Revolution is not natural to the people, and is always a failure. There have been no popular revolutions. Civilization and liberty have been set back by those revolutions which subversive elements have succeeded in starting.

But if you are to have your revolution, you must have a rehearsal. In England, the whole process of sovietizing the country has been set forth on the stage, as in vivid object lessons. In this country they have rehearsals by parades, by starting marches through factories and up to the offices, by importing lecturers who tell just how it was done in Russia, Hungary and elsewhere. But it can be done better in the motion pictures than anywhere else: this is "visual education" such as even the lowest brow can understand, and the lower the better.

Indeed, there is a distinct disadvantage in being "high-brow" in such matters. Normal people shake their heads and pucker their brows and wring their hands and say "we cannot understand it; we simply cannot understand it!" Of course they cannot. But if they understood the lowbrow, they would understand it, and very clearly. There are two families in this world, and on one the darkness dwells.

Reformers, of course, heartily agree with this as far as criminal portrayals are concerned. Police protest against the technique of killing a policeman being shown with careful detail on the screen. Business men object to daily object lessons in safe-cracking being given in the pictures. Moralists object to the art of seduction being made the stock motif no matter what the subject. They object because they recognize it as evil schooling which bears bitter fruits in society.

Well, this other kind of education is going on too. There is now nothing connected with violent outbreaks which has not been put into the minds of millions by the agency of the motion picture. It may, of course, be a mere coincidence. But coincidences also are realities.

There are several developments proceeding in screendom which are worthy of notice. One is the increasing use of non-Jewish authors to produce Jewish propaganda. Without using names, it will be easy for each reader to recall for himself the more popular non-Jewish authors whose books have been screened by Jewish producers, and who are soon after announced to have a new photoplay in preparation. In several cases these new photoplays have been sheer Jewish propaganda. They are the more effective because they are backed by non-Jewish names famous in the literary world. Just how this state of affairs comes about it is not possible now to say. How much of it is due to the authors' desire to enter the field of pro-Semitic propaganda, and how much of it is due to their reluctance to refuse amiable suggestions from movie magnates who have already paid them liberal sums and are likely to pay them more is a question. It is not difficult to bring oneself to believe that "anti-Semitism" is wrong. Everybody knows it is. It is not difficult to bring oneself to an admiration of Israel. Every writer is happy in idealizing an individual or a nation; it is a pleasure to write about an altogether admirable Jewish hero or heroine. And so the non-Jews are writing Jewish propaganda ere they are aware.

The flaw, of course, is here: in avoiding anti-Semitism, they fall into the snare of pro-Semitism. And one is as inconclusive as the other.

Another development is one which movie fans have doubtless noticed: it is the abolition of the "star" system. Readers of this series will recall that it was this same sort of thing which marked Jewish ascendancy in the control of the legitimate stage. Not long ago the full glare of movie publicity was thrown upon names and personalities—the Marys and Charlies and Lulus and Fatties of screen fame. The name was headlined; the star was featured; it did not matter what the theme of the play was suffice it that it was "a Chaplin film," or a "Pickford film," or whatever it might be.

The motion picture "industry" has reached its present importance because of the exaltation of the "star." But it has its inconveniences, too. Educate the public to demand a star, and that demand will eventually rule the business. Jewish control will not permit that. The way to break the control which the public may exercise through such a demand, is to eliminate the stars. Then all pictures will be on the same plane.

This is occurring now in filmdom. Some of the stars have taken the hint and set up their own studios. But steadily the doctrine is preached throughout fandom that "the play's the thing," not the star. You don't see so many star names before the theaters; you see more and more lurid names of plays. The star is being sidetracked.

There is a triple advantage in this. The bloated salaries of the stars can be eliminated. The public can be deprived of a point on which to focus a demand. Exhibitors can no longer say, "I want this or that," even within the narrow margin they recently had; they will have no choice because there will be no choice; the business will be a standardized "industry."

These, then, are some of the facts of the American motion picture world. They are not all the facts, but each of them is important. Not one can be overlooked by students of the influence of the theater. Many a perplexed observer of everyday affairs will find in these facts a key which explains many things.

The Dearborn Independent, February 19, 1921

33. Rule of the Jewish Kehillah Grips New York

Are the Jews organized? Do they consciously pursue a program which on one side is pro-Semitic and on the other anti-Gentile? How can a group so numerically inferior wield so large an influence upon the majority of the world?

These are questions which have been asked and which can be answered. The clan solidarity of the Jew, the ramifications of his organizations, the specific purpose which he has in view, are themes upon which there is any amount of "say so," but very little authoritative statement. It may therefore be useful and informing to study one or two of the more important Jewish organizations in the United States.

There are Jewish lodges, unions and societies whose names are well known to the public, and which seem to be the counterpart of similar groups among the non-Jewish population, but those are not the groups upon which to focus attention. Within and behind them is the central group, the inner government, whose ruling is law, and whose act is the official expression of Jewish purpose.

Two organizations, both of which are as notable for their concealment as for their power, are the New York Kehillah and the American Jewish Committee. By concealment is meant the fact that they exist in such important numbers and touch vitally so many points of American life, without their presence being suspected.

If a vote of New York could be taken today it is doubtful if one per cent of the non-Jewish population could say that it had ever heard of the New York Kehillah, yet the Kehillah is the most potent factor in the political life of New York today. It has managed to exist and mold and remold the life of New York, and very few people are the wiser. If the Kehillah is mentioned in the press, it is most vaguely, and the impression is, when there is any impression at all, that it is a Jewish social organization like all the rest.

The Kehillah of New York is of importance to Americans everywhere because of two facts: it not only offers a real and complete instance of a government within a government in the midst of America's largest city, but it also constitutes through its executive committee District XII of the American Jewish Committee, through which pro-Jewish and anti-Gentile propaganda is operated and Jewish pressure brought to bear against certain American ideas. That is to say, the Jewish government of New York constitutes the essential part of the Jewish government of the United States.

Both of these societies began at about the same time. The records of the Kehillah state that the immediate occasion of its organization was to make a protest against the statement by General Bingham, then police commissioner of the City of New York, that 50 per cent of the crime of the metropolis was committed by Jews.

There had been a government investigation into the "White Slave Traffic," the result of which was a direct set of public opinion into channels uncomplimentary to the Jewish name, and a defensive movement was begun. There is no intention to rake up past scandals, unless it shall become necessary; it is enough to say here that, very soon afterward, General Bingham disappeared from public life, and a national magazine of power and influence which had embarked on a series of articles setting forth the government's findings in the White Slave investigation was forced to discontinue after the printing of the first article. This was in the year 1908. The American Jewish Committee, to whose influence the Kehillah really owes its existence, came into being in 1906.

The word "Kehillah" has the same meaning as "Kahal," which signifies "community," "assembly" or government. It represents the Jewish form of government in the dispersion. That is to say, since destiny has made the Jews wanderers of the earth, they have organized their own government so that it might function regardless of the governments which the so-called "Gentiles" have set up. In the Babylonian captivity, in Eastern Europe today, the Kahal is the power and protectorate to which the faithful Jew looks for government and justice. The Peace Conference established the Kahal in Poland and Rumania. The Kahal itself is establishing its courts in the city of New York. The Kahal issues laws, judges legal cases, issues divorces—the Jews who appeal thereto preferring Jewish justice to the justice of the courts of the land. It is, of course, an agreement among themselves to be so governed; just as citizenship in the United States assumes an agreement to be governed by institutions provided for that purpose.

The New York Kehillah is the largest and most powerful union of Jews in the world. The center of Jewish world power has been transferred to

Rule of the Jewish Kehillah Grips New York

that city. That is the meaning of the heavy migration of Jews all over the world toward New York. It is to them what Rome is to the devout Catholic and what Mecca is to the Mohammedan. And by that same token, immigrant Jews are more freely admitted to the United States than they are to Palestine.

The Kehillah is a perfect answer to the statement that the Jews are so divided among themselves as to render a concert of action impossible. That is one of the statements made for Gentile consumption, that the Jews are hopelessly divided among themselves. Hundreds of thousands of Americans have had opportunity during recent weeks to see and hear for themselves that when an anti-Gentile purpose is in view, Jews of all classes make the same threats and the same boasts. They are either going to "get" somebody, or they have "got" somebody.

A recent Jewish writer attempted to raise a laugh about the very idea of the members of the Jewish needle-workers' unions of New York having anything in common with the needle-work bosses. He made his attempt in confidence that the public knew little or nothing about the Kehillah. But the public can find all groups and all interests in that body, for there they meet as Jews. The capitalist and the Bolshevik, the rabbi and the union leader, the strikers and the employers struck against, are all united under the flag of Judah. Touch the conservative capitalist who is a Jew, and the red anarchist who is also a Jew will spring to his defense. It may be that sometimes they love each other less, but altogether they hate the non-Jew more, and that is their common bond.

The Kehillah is an alliance, more offensive than defensive, against the "Gentiles." The majority of the membership of the New York Kehillah is of an extremely radical character, those seething hundreds of thousands who carefully organized on the East Side the government which was to take over the Russian Empire, even choosing in the Jewish Quarter of New York the Jew who was to succeed the Czar—and yet, in spite of this character of membership, it is officered by Jews whose names stand high in government, judiciary, the law and banking.

It is a strange and really magnificent spectacle which the Kehillah presents, of a people of one racial origin, with a vivid belief in itself and its future, disregarding its open differences, to combine privately in a powerful organization for the racial, material and religious advancement of its own race to the exclusion of all others.

The Kehillah has mapped New York just as the American Jewish Committee has mapped the United States. The city of New York is divided into 18 Kehillah districts which comprise a total of 100 Kehillah neighborhoods, in accordance with the population. The Kehillah District Boards administer Kehillah affairs in their respective districts in accordance with the policy and rules laid down by the central governing body.

Practically every Jew in New York belongs to one or more lodges, secret societies, unions, orders, committees or federations. The list is a prodigious one. The purposes interlace and the methods dovetail in such a manner as to bring every phase of New York life not only under the watchful eye, but under the swift and powerful action of experienced compulsion upon public affairs.

At the meeting which organized the Kehillah a number of sentiments were expressed which are worthy of consideration today. Judah L. Magnes, then rabbi of Temple Emanu-El, chairman of the meeting, set forth the plan.

"A central organization like that of the Jewish Community of New York City is necessary to create a Jewish public opinion," he said. Rabbi Asher was loudly applauded when he said:

"American interests are one, Jewish interests are another thing."

The delegates at this meeting represented 222 Jewish societies, as follows: 74 synagogues, 18 charitable societies, 42 mutual benefit societies, 40 lodges, 12 educational societies, 9 communal federations, 9 literary and musical societies, 9 Zionist societies and 9 religious societies.

At a meeting somewhat more than a year later the number of organizations under the jurisdiction of the Kehillah aggregated 688. These included 238 constituent organizations, 133 congregations, 58 lodges, 44 educational and benevolent societies, and 3 federations. These three federations were made up of 450 societies.

The affiliation now numbers more than 1,000 organizations.

The Kehillah has produced a map of New York City on which the varying densities of the Jewish population are represented by varying densities of shade.

In order to comprehend the power of the Kehillah, the Jewish population of New York must be considered. Three years ago, according to Jewish figures (there are no others) there were 1,500,000 Jews in the city alone. Since that time the number has considerably increased—even the Government of the United States cannot say how much. In 1917–18 the Jews resident in the five boroughs of New York City were

Rule of the Jewish Kehillah Grips New York

estimated—again by Jewish officials—as follows: Manhattan, 696,000; Brooklyn, 568,000; Bronx, 211,000; Queens, 23,000; Richmond, 5,000; making a total of 1,503,000.

The Kehillah districts form distinct and segregated parts of the City's population, and are 18 in number. These 18 in turn comprise 100 neighborhoods, or little ghettos. The districts, with the number of neighborhoods in each, are represented in the following table:

Neighborhoods
No. 1. North Bronx District 7
No. 2. South Bronx District   7
No. 3. West Side and Harlem District 7
No. 4. East Harlem District   7
No. 5. Yorkville District   5
No. 6. Central Manhattan District   4
No. 7. Tompkins Square District   6
No. 8. Delancey District   8
No. 9. East Broadway District 8 No. 10. Williamsburg District 7
No. 11. Bushwick District   6
No. 12. Central Brooklyn District   6
No. 13. Brownsville District 6
No. 14. East New York District 7 No. 15. Borough Park District 6
No. 16. West Queens District 1
No. 17. East Queens District 1
No. 18. Richmond District   1

Districts such as the Delancey Street and East Broadway sections cover the Great Ghetto of the East Side, while the West Side and Harlem Districts represent the neighborhoods which are the residential goals of the prosperous Jews of New York.

It has been stated that there are districts in which the density of Jewish population is more than 300,000 per square mile, which is more than 2,150 to the usual square city block. There are 19 neighborhoods in which the density is more than 200,000 to the square mile (1,430 to the square block); and 36 neighborhoods in which the density is more than 100,000 to the square mile (715 to the square block).

The average density of the general population for New York City both Jewish and non-Jewish, in 1915, was about 16,000 to the square mile, or 107 to the square block. More than one-third of the Jews, about 38 per cent, that is, 570,000 Jews, live on one per cent of the area of New York. If all New York's population were as dense as is the Jewish population of the congested districts, the City would have almost as many inhabitants as the whole United States, or about 95,000,000.

These figures dimly portray the overcrowding which has resulted from the terrific influx of Russian-Polish Jews of the ghetto type, who have settled in the Metropolis and steadfastly refused to go any farther, resulting in problems which are probably unparalleled in the history of civilization.

Yet it is out of such conditions that the far-reaching power of the Kehillah is derived.

When the aggressive program of the Kehillah to make New York a Jewish city, and through New York the United States a Jewish country, was announced, some of the more conservative Jews of New York were timorous. They did not expect that the American people would stand for it. They thought the American people would immediately understand what was afoot and oppose it. There were others who doubted whether the same Kehillah authority could here be wielded over the Jews as was wielded in the old country ghettos. As an official of the Kehillah wrote:

"There were those who doubted the ultimate success of this new venture in Jewish organization. They based their lack of belief on the fact that no governmental authority could possibly be secured; in other words, that the Kehillah of New York could not hope to wield the same power, based on governmental coercion, as the Kehillahs of the Old World."

There is much in that paragraph to indicate the status of the Kehillah in Jewish life. Add to this the fact that the vast majority of adult Jews in New York lived under the Kehillahs of the Old World, whose power was based on coercion, and you have an interesting situation.

What the doubt consisted in, however, is not as stated there. No doubt existed as to what it would be possible to do with the Jews. The entire doubt consisted in how far the Americans would let the thing go on. The program of the Kehillah was ostensibly "to assert Jewish rights." No Jewish rights have ever been interfered with in America. The expression is a euphemism for a campaign to interfere with non-Jewish rights.

Just how the free exercise of American rights by an American may be construed and is construed by the Jew to be an interference with his rights, will be shown in a separate article.

The doubters felt that when the Jews began to make such demands as that Christmas carols should be suppressed in the schools, as "offensive to the Jews"; and that Christmas trees should be banished from police

Rule of the Jewish Kehillah Grips New York

stations in poor neighborhoods as "offensive to the Jews"; and that the Easter holidays should be abolished as "offensive to the Jews"; and that the phrase, "a Christian gentleman" should be protested everywhere, as "offensive to the Jews";—the business class of Jews felt that the American would not stand for it.

The American has never interfered with any man's religious observances; would he stand to have his own prohibited in his own institutions and in his own country?

However, the Jews' misgivings were not justified. The Americans made no protest. The Kehillah went ahead with its campaign and the native population submitted. New York is Jewish. From the City Hall to the Bowery, from Fifth Avenue to Hester street, in board of education, newspaper row, and courts of justice, New York is Jewish. It is actually an offense, an offense speedily though unofficially punished, to intimate in any public way that New York may possibly be other than Jewish. New York is the answer to those who ask, "How can a numerically inferior group dictate the terms of life for all the rest?" Go into a New York school, and see. Go into a New York court, and see. Go into a New York newspaper office, and see. Stand anywhere in New York, and see.

But with it all one gets a sense of the insecurity of this usurpation of power. It doesn't belong to those who have seized it; it doesn't belong either by right of numbers, or by right of superior ability, or yet by right of a better use made of the power thus taken. They have taken it by audacity; they have taken it in such a way as to make resentment of it seem like an anti-racial movement—and that is why they have held it as long as they have.

That is the only way to explain the meekness of the American in this matter, and it also accounts for the sense of insecurity which even the Jews feel in the position they hold. The American is the slowest person in the world to act on any line that savors of racial or religious prejudice. Even when his justifiable act is taken without the slightest prejudice, he is extremely sensitive even to the charge that he is prejudiced. This makes for a seeming aloofness from matters like the Jewish Question. This also leads men to sign protests against "anti-Semitism" which are really designed to be protests against the publication of Jewish facts.

But it would be a serious mistake to believe that the Americans have accepted within their minds the fact of Jewish supremacy in any field, for they have not. And the Jews know that they have not. Present Jewish importance in American affairs threatens to become as precarious as Bolshevik rule in Russia; it may fall at any time. The Jews have overplayed their hand. They have threatened too wildly and boasted too loudly. The very weight of the importance of the Kehillah and the American Jewish Committee is to be one of the factors in the fall. The Jews may live among us, but they may not live upon us.

These things are better known to the Jew than to the non-Jew, for the Jew knows the Jewish Question better than anyone else, and he knows better than any Gentile when a statement hits the bull's-eye of the truth. The American Jews are not now protesting against lies; they would welcome lies against themselves; they are roused to protest by the power of the truth, and they are the best judges of the truth with reference to themselves.

The situation is not one that calls for expulsion, or resistance, but simply exposure to the light—for to vanquish darkness, what is better than light?

The Jews had a great opportunity in the New York Kehillah. They had an opportunity to say to the world, "This is what the Jew can do for a city when he is given freedom to work." They have the city government, the police department, the health department, the school board, the newspapers, the judiciary, financiers—every element of power. And what have they to show for all this? The answer is,—New York.

New York is an object lesson set in the sight of the whole world, as to what the Jew can do and will do when he exalts himself to the seat of rule. It is inconceivable that even the Jewish spokesmen will defend Jewish New York. Lest the New York Kehillah—in view of statements yet to be made concerning it—should be disregarded, or its importance minimized, by the feeling that, after all, it only represents the more radical elements, "the apostate Jews" which seems to be a recent favorite designation for them, a partial view is here given of its leaders.

Present at the 1918 convention were Jacob H. Schiff, banker; Louis Marshall, lawyer, president of the American Jewish Committee and frequent visitor to Washington; Otto A. Rosalsky, judge of the General Sessions Court, who has taken part in several affairs of interest both to Jews and Gentiles; Adolph S. Ochs, proprietor of the *New York Times*; Otto H. Kahn, of the banking firm of Kuhn, Loeb & Company—AND Benjamin Schlesinger, who is lately returned from Moscow where he had a conference with Lenin; Joseph Schlossberg, general secretary of the Amalgamated Clothing Workers of America, with 177,000 members; Max Pine, also recently a consultant with the Bolshevik rulers of Russia;

Rule of the Jewish Kehillah Grips New York

David Pinski; Joseph Barondess, labor leader. The high and the low are here; Judge Mack, who headed the War Risk Insurance Bureau of the United States Government, and the little leader of the reddest group in the East End—they all meet in the Kehillah, as Jews.

As to the Kehillah being officially representative, it may be added that the Kehillah has in it representatives of the Central Conference of American rabbis, Eastern Council of Reform rabbis, Independent Order of B'nai B'rith, Independent Order of B'rith Sholom, Independent Order Free Sons of Israel, Independent Order B'rith Abraham, Federation of American Zionists—othodox Jews, reform Jews, "apostate Jews," Zionist Jews, Americanized Jews, rich Jews, poor Jews, law-abiding Jews and red revolutionary Jews—Adolph Ochs of the great *New York Times*, together with the most feverish scribbler on a Yiddish weekly that calls for blood and violence—Jacob Schiff who was a devoutly religious Jew of strong faith and obedience, and Otto H. Kahn, of the same banking house, who professes another religion—all of them, of all classes, bound together in that solidarity which has been achieved by no other people so perfectly as by Judah.

And these are banded together for the purpose of "protecting Jewish rights." From what? If Americans were not large in their liberal-mindedness the very statement of purpose would be an offense. Who in this country is interfering with anyone's rights? The American wants to know, for that is the kind of thing he wants to put down, and always has put down, and will put down again wherever or from whatever quarter it arises. Therefore it will occur to him sooner or later to demand particulars of these rights that need protection, and from what they need to be protected.

What rights have Americans that Jews in America do not possess? Against whom are the Jews organized, and against what?

What basis is there for the cry of "persecution"? None whatever, except the Jews' own consciousness that the course they are pursuing is due for a check. The Jews always know that. They are not in the stream of the world, and every little while the world finds out what Judah always knows.

Rabbi Elias L. Solomon has been quoted as saying:

"There is no thinking Jew outside of America whose eyes are not turned toward this country. The freedom enjoyed by the Jews in America is not the outcome of emancipation purchased at the cost of national suicide, but the natural product of American civilization."

Of course. Then where is the "protection" needed? What are the "rights" which the Kehillahs of this country are organized to "defend"? What are the meanings of these committees in every city and town of the land, spying upon American activities and bringing protests to bear to keep those activities within well-defined channels acceptable to the Jews?

These questions have never been answered by the Jewish spokesmen. Let them prepare a Bill of Rights, as they conceive their rights to be. Let them name every right they desire and claim. They have never done so. Why? Because the rights they dare name in public are such as they already possess in abundance, and further, because the rights that in their hearts they most desire are such that they cannot state to the American public.

A Jewish Bill of Rights, such as could be published, would be met by the American people thus: "Why, you have all these things already. What more do you want?" And that is the question which lies at the core of the entire Jewish Problem—What more do they want?

A further penetration of Kehillah activities may help to answer that question.

The Dearborn Independent, February 26, 1921

34. The Jewish Demand for "Rights" in America

During the twelve years of its existence the New York Kehillah has grown in power and influence until today it includes practically the entire Jewish population in its operations. Among its direct or affiliated leaders and supporters are the owners of powerful newspapers, officials in the state, Federal and city administration; influential officeholders on public boards, such as the department of health, the board of education and the police department; members of the judiciary; financiers and heads of banking houses, mercantile and manufacturing establishments, many of which exert a controlling influence in certain industries and financial combinations.

But the New York Kehillah is more than a local organization. It is the pattern and parent Jewish community in the United States, the visible entourage of the Jewish government, the dynamo which motivates those "protests" and "mass meetings" which are frequently heralded throughout the country, and the arsenal of that kind of dark power which the Jewish leaders know so well how to use. Incidentally, it is also the "whispering gallery," where the famous whispering drives are originated and set in motion and made to break in lying publicity over the country.

The people of the United States have a deeper interest than they realize in the New York Kehillah.

The liaison between this center of Jewish power and the affairs of the people of the United States is made by the American Jewish Committee. The Committee and the Kehillah are practically identical as far as the national Jewish program is concerned. It may be added that through their foreign associations they are also identical as far as the world program is concerned.

The United States is divided into 12 parts by the American Jewish Committee. The remark that this division is after the Twelve Tribes of Israel may be disregarded. Suffice it to say that every state belongs to a district, and that District No. XII includes New York, and that the District Committee of District No. XII is chosen by the New York Kehillah, and is by weight of wealth, authority and continuous effort in behalf of Judah justly recognized as the center of Jewish power in America, and it may be in the world also. This committee, some of the names of whose members are impressive, represents the focusing point of the religious, racial, financial and political will of Jewry. This committee, it should be remembered, is also the executive committee of the New York Kehillah.

New York Jewry is the dynamo of the national Jewish machinery. Its national instrument is the American Jewish Committee.

There are certain announced purposes of these associations, and there are certain purposes which are not announced. The announced purposes may be read in printed pages; the purposes not announced may be read in the records of attempted acts and achieved results. To keep the record straight let us look first at the announced purposes of the American Jewish Committee, then of the Kehillah; next at the line which binds the two together; and then at the real purposes as they are construed from a long list of attempts and achievements.

The American Jewish Committee, organized in 1906, announced itself as incorporated for the following purposes:

1. To prevent the infraction of the civil and religious rights of the Jews in any part of the world.

2. To render all lawful assistance and to take appropriate remedial action in event of threatened or actual invasion or restriction of such rights, or of unfavorable discrimination with respect thereto.

3. To secure for the Jews equality of economic, social and educational opportunities.

4. To alleviate the consequences of persecution wherever they may occur, and to afford relief from calamities affecting Jews.

It will thus be seen to be an exclusively Jewish program. There is nothing reprehensible about it. If it meant only what it said, and was observed only as to its ostensible purpose, it would be not only unobjectionable but commendable.

The charter of the Kehillah empowers it, among other things, to establish an educational bureau, to adjust differences between Jewish residents or organizations by arbitration or by means of boards of mediation or conciliation; while the Constitution announces the purpose to be: "to further the cause of Judaism in New York City and to represent the Jews in this city with respect to all local matters of Jewish interest." Where the American Committee and the Kehillah join forces is shown as follows: "Furthermore, inasmuch as the American

The Jewish Demand for "Rights" in America

Jewish Committee was a national organization, the Jewish Community (Kehillah) of New York City, if combined with it, would have a voice in shaping the policy of Jewry throughout the land.

1. It is expressly understood that the American Jewish Committee shall have exclusive jurisdiction over all questions of a national or international character affecting the Jews generally.

2. The membership of the American Jewish Committee is to be increased, so that the Twelfth District shall have allotted to it 25 members.

3. These 25 members are to be elected by the Jewish Committee (Kehillah) of New York City.

4. These 25 men shall at the same time constitute the Executive Committee of the Community (Kehillah).

It will be seen, therefore, that the Kehillah and the principal body of the American Jewish Committee are one. The capital of the United States, in Jewish affairs, is New York. Perhaps that may throw a sidelight on the desperate efforts which are being continually made to exalt New York as the spring and source of all the thoughts worth while today. New York, the Jewish capital of the United States, has also been sought to be made the financial center, the art center, the political center of the country. But its art is Aphrodite, Mecca and Afgar; its politics are those of a Judaized Tammany. Tell it not to the American Jewish Committee, nor yet to the Kehillah, but let all Americans know that most of the United States lies west of New York. The country has come to view that strip of Eastern coast as a miasmatic place whence rises the fetid drivel of all that is subversive in public thought. It is the home of anti-American propaganda, of pro-Jewish hysteria, a mad confusion of mind that passes in some quarters as a picture of America. But America is west of the "metropolis"; New York is an unassimilated province on the outskirts of the nation.

As nine-tenths of all the Jews in the United States live in allegiance to organizations which look to the American Jewish Committee as their overlord, the influence of the New York Kehillah on the nation is not hard to measure.

In every town, large and small, even where the Jewish community consists of a few, 30 or 75 souls, there is a leading Jew, be he rabbi, merchant or public officeholder, who is in constant touch with headquarters. What is done in New Orleans or Los Angeles or Kansas City is known in New York with surprising dispatch.

Incidentally, it would interest some clergymen to know that their names are listed among those who can be depended on to play the Jewish hand whenever required.

Now, the public statement of purpose on the part of these Jewish bodies has just been shown. It is seen that the protection of Jewish rights is the ostensible program—against which no one can say a word. Perhaps the term "Jewish rights" is unfortunately chosen. If Jewish rights coincide with American rights, then more than the Jews are protecting them— the whole American nation is engaged in that work.

But it is not true that "Jewish rights" are the same as "American rights." Unfortunately the Jews have adopted an attitude which could only have sprung from the belief that it is a "Jewish right" to Judaize the United States.

This is one of the dangerous doctrines being preached today, and most assiduously by Jews and those who have been influenced by Jewish thought, namely, that the United States is not any definite thing as yet, but that it is yet to be made, and it is still the prey of whatever power can seize it and mold it to its liking. It is a favorite Jewish view that the United States is a great unshapen mass of potentiality, of no particular character which is yet to be given its definite form. It is in the light of this view that Jewish activity must be interpreted.

That doctrine with which so large a mass of Americans are inoculated is making havoc with the whole Americanization program today. It is "broadening" America out of all semblance to its distinctive self and blurring those determining ideals and ideas on which American institutions are based. The attempt, first to give the people to understand that the United States is "nothing particular" as yet, and second to make it something different spiritually from what it has always been, is peculiarly agreeable to the philosophy which sways the internationally-minded Hebrew. We are not making Americans; we are permitting foreigners to be educated in the theory that America is a free-for-all, the prize of whatever fantastic foreign political theory may seize it.

There you have the secret of the great refusal of the foreign population to change themselves into conformity with America; why should they, when they are taught that America may be changed into conformity with them?

It is time to limit our "broad-mindedness" until it will fit within the limits of the Constitution and the traditions which made America what it is—the desired haven, even in preference to Palestine, of all the Jews

The Jewish Demand for "Rights" in America

and every other race. So, then, what is the conception of "Jewish rights" which the Kehillah and the American Jewish Committee are organized to defend? It is only by deductions from the acts of these bodies that the answer can be formulated.

In the Jewish records for the year 5668 (1907-1908) we read:

"Perhaps the most noticeable feature of the year in America has been the demand in certain quarters for the complete secularization of the public institutions of the country, what may be deemed the demand of the Jews for their full constitutional rights."

Let the reader notice that the only time he finds the religious note struck in this series of studies of International Jewish activity, it is struck by the Jews. Honest non-Jews have been nonplussed by the Jewish charge that any scrutiny of Jewish action is "religious persecution," even when religion has never been thought of or mentioned. The explanation is not far to seek. In the above quotation the religious note is struck at once: the "full constitutional rights" of Jews demands that we effect "the complete secularization of the public institutions of the country."

That is worth thinking of. But to continue the quotation:

"Justice Brewer's article asserting that this is a Christian country has been challenged more than once, and the idea was formally combated in papers by Dr. Herbert Friedenwald, of New York, Isaac Hassler, of Philadelphia, and Rabbi Ephraim Frisch, of Little Rock, Arkansas.

"The legal and theoretical argument was supplemented in a practical way by widespread opposition to Bible readings and Christmas carols in public schools, an opposition specifically decided upon by the Central Conference of American Rabbis.

"In New York the agitation against the carols produced a counter-demonstration in their favor, and the matter seems to have been left to the discretion of the individual teacher.

"In Philadelphia, Cincinnati, St. Paul and maybe elsewhere, there were similar movements and counter-movements, and the question may yet return to plague us."

There you have, in officially authorized Jewish statement, what the Jews conceive to be a part of their Jewish rights.

A careful examination of the intensive propaganda conducted by the Kehillah and the American Jewish Committee will not only reveal that the whole United States is considered to be the legitimate field for Jewish interference, but also that a very wide diversity of "rights" is insisted upon by them.

In dozens of states and hundreds of towns and cities this program has been plied, but always with too little publicity to appraise the people what is going on. In any number of cases the Jews win their contentions because of the local pressure they are able to produce, usually by their very forehanded way of selecting and obligating public officials. In other instances they have lost, but every loss they credit to a beginning of their "educational" campaign. A loss enables them to "teach a lesson" to somebody by means of a boycott or a changed attitude on the part of the local bank, or in some other way equally effective in creating "the fear of the Jews."

The Jews have evidently convinced themselves that the Constitution of the United States entitles them to change the character of many of the time-honored practices obtaining here, and if this is true, American citizens should take cognizance of these things and prepare to adjust themselves to further changes. If they do not take kindly to further changes at the behest of Jewry, they owe it to themselves to know what the Jewish program is, that they may meet it with a higher type of weapon than that to which the Jew naturally resorts.

It is intended in this and the following article to indicate, by the actual program, what the real objective of Jewry is in the United States. When you collect and summarize all the demands that have been made by the New York Kehillah alone, you gain an idea of what is afoot. A few of these demands are referred to now, subject to further illustration in another article.

1. The unrestricted admission of Jewish immigration to this country from any part of the world.

Heads of Kehillah labor unions in New York demand that the Jews in Europe be exempted from the operation of whatever American immigration law may be passed. The Kehillah is many times on record to this effect. No matter where the Jews may come from—Russia, Poland, Syria, Arabia or Morocco—they are to be let in no matter who may be kept out.

Note: As one pursues the study of "Jewish rights," the quality of "exemption" seems to appear in most of them. Nowhere do the Jews proclaim their separateness as a people more than in their unceasing demands that they be treated differently than any other people and given privileges that no other people would dream of asking.

2. The official recognition by City, State and Federal governments of the Jewish Religion.

The Jewish Demand for "Rights" in America

The Kehillah in its reports describes its efforts to obtain special recognition of Jewish holidays, in some cases going so far as to demand the continuance of pay to public employees who absent themselves at Yom Kippur, at the same time, opposing the continuance of pay to Catholic public employees who desired to observe the chief Lenten days. This is a peculiarly inconsistent form of the demand for "exemption" which has led to some interesting situations, to be dealt with later.

3. The suppression of all references to Christ by City, State and Federal authorities, in public documents or at public gatherings.

Kehillah records show that the Jews of Oklahoma addressed a petition to the convention which formulated the first state constitution, protesting that the acknowledgement of Christ in the instrument would be repugnant to the Constitution of the United States.

The record also shows that a Jewish rabbi protested against a governor of Arkansas using "a Christological expression" in his Thanksgiving Day proclamation.

4. Official recognition of the Jewish Sabbath.

The educational, cultural, business and industrial life of the United States is regulated with reference to Sunday as the legal day of rest. For over ten years the Kehillah has sought legislative recognition for Saturday. In the absence of official recognition, however, much public business is held up on account of jurors and others refusing to serve on Saturday. Jewish lawyers in the trial of cases are frequently "ill" on Saturdays.

There is, of course, no objections to Jews recognizing their own Sabbath. This is their American privilege. But to make their Sabbath the Sabbath of all the people is another question. The Jews' chief objection to the observance of Sunday is that it is "a Christological manifestation."

5. The right of the Jews in this country to keep open their stores, factories and theatres, and to trade and work on the Christian Sunday.

The Kehillah, through the Jewish Sabbath Alliance (Rabbi Bernard Drachman, president), is "promoting the observance of the Holy Sabbath in every possible way," through propaganda made to promote Sabbath sentiment, and the distribution of circulars and pamphlets to the Yiddish populations of New York City. Sabbath sentiment is unobjectionable, but it becomes anti-Sunday sentiment.

The Sunday laws of the city are, therefore, often broken. Much agitation and ill feeling result. Kehillah records are full of the disagreeable conditions which this demand promotes.

6. Elimination of Christmas celebrations in public schools and public places, police stations, and so on, public displays of Christmas trees, singing of Christmas carols and Christian hymns.

Kehillah compelled the Council of University Settlement in New York City to adopt a resolution that in holiday celebrations held annually by the Kindergarten Association, Christmas trees, a Christmas program for celebration and the singing of Christmas songs be eliminated.

Kehillah records show that Jews petitioned the Chicago School Board, demanding that sectarian teachings in public schools and the singing of Christian hymns be discontinued.

Also that at the demand of a Jewish rabbi, three public school principals were compelled to omit all Christmas celebrations and the use of the Christmas tree in public schools.

7. The removal from office or prosecution of all public persons who criticize the Jewish race, even where such action is in the public interest.

Judge Otto A. Rosalsky, member of the Kehillah, announces that he will try to put through a bill for the prosecution of all persons who criticize the Jewish race.

Kehillah leaders at public meeting condemn City Magistrate Cornell for criticizing the East Side Yiddish Community because of the increase in criminality of Jewish youth, and demand his impeachment.

Leaders of New York Jewry succeed in having Police Commissioner Bingham removed from office by the Mayor because of his criticism of criminality among Russian-Polish Jews of New York City.

8. The establishment of Bet Dins, or Jewish courts, in public courthouses.

The Kehillah has succeeded in the establishment of a Bet Din in the Criminal Courts Building, New York, at which there presides the Rev. Dr. Aaron A. Yudelovitch, Chief Rabbi of the United States.

Kehillah records show that prominent Jews of Jersey City, Paterson, Newark, Bayonne and Hoboken have organized to establish Bet Dins in New Jersey.

9. The right to eliminate from all schools and colleges all literature that is objected to by Jews.

Kehillah records show that Jews have prohibited the reading of the "Merchant of Venice" and Lamb's "Tales from Shakespeare" from schools throughout the country, including those in Galveston and El Paso, Texas; Cleveland, Ohio, and Youngstown, Ohio. At the present time a cleaning of public library shelves is proceeding in a number of cities to prevent the public securing books which public money has bought—the objection to the books being that they discuss Jews as they are. All books in praise of Jews are spared.

10. Prohibition of the term "Christian" or the use of the phrase "state, religion and nationality" in any public advertisement, as being an invasion of Jewish rights and a discrimination against Jews.

Louis Marshall, as president of the American Jewish Committee, obtained apologies from Charles M. Schwab, as director of the United States Shipping Board; Benjamin Strong, governor of the Federal Reserve Bank and head of the Liberty Loan Committee; Secretary McAdoo and Secretary of War Baker, because of the use of the term "Christian" in help wanted advertisements inserted in newspapers by their subordinates.

The Jews succeeded in obtaining the withdrawal of the Junior Plattsburg Manual, used by students in officers' training camps, because it contained the phrase "the ideal officer is a Christian gentleman," which the Jews construed to be an infringement of their rights.

The Kehillah in its report for 1920 stated that several important New York newspapers, having been informed by it that the term "Christian" had appeared in the help wanted advertisements of mercantile firms, the owners of the newspapers sent in their apologies, and promised stricter censorship in the future.

The Jews do not consider the use of the term "Jews" in help wanted advertisements as discrimination against non-Jews, and Jewish mercantile houses continue its use in their advertisements in the *New York Times* and other Jewish-owned dailies.

These are "Jewish rights" as they are indicated by Jewish demands. But they are by no means all; they are merely typical of all the so-called "rights" and all the insistent demands.

To go still further: the Kehillah condemned the use of the term "Americanization," because of the implication that there is no distinction between "Americanization" and "Christianization." "Americanization" is claimed by Jews to be a mere cloak for proselytizing.

The Kehillah is behind demands on public funds for the support of Jewish educational, charitable, correctional and other institutions. One important point about the great influx of Jewish immigration is that tens of thousands of these people come from lands where Jewish government has been established by order of the Peace Conference, and where public funds supported Jewish activities. Their attitude toward

America in this respect may therefore be accurately gauged. It is a common practice in New York for the Jews to force themselves into juries which try Jewish cases. Jewish law students, with which the city swarms, "work their way through college" partly or wholly by jury duty.

Another "Jewish right" is that the Associated Press shall print what the Jews want printed and in exactly the tone the Jews desire. This is perhaps one of the factors in the loss of luster on the part of the Associated Press of late years, the feeling that it is too much under the influence of certain groups, which are not non-Jewish groups. Newspapermen all sense this; A.P. men throughout the country sense it; but they express it in newspaper terms; they say "The A.P. gives a New York coloring to everything." But the ingredients of the New York coloring are 85 per cent Jewish.

From a survey of the demands, these appear to be some of the "Jewish rights" which the Kehillah and the American Jewish Committee are organized to secure. And how far they say they have succeeded, we shall next see.

The Dearborn Independent, March 5, 1921

35. "Jewish Rights" Clash With American Rights

It is well that the public should understand that the present study of the Jewish Question in the United States is not based upon religious differences. The religious element does not enter except when it is injected by the Jews themselves. And it is injected in three ways: First, in their allegation that any study of the Jews is "religious persecution"; second, by their own records of what their activities in the United States consist of; third, by the impression which is very misleading if not corrected, that the Jews are the Old Testament people of the Old Testament religion which is so highly regarded in the Christian world. The Jews are not the Old Testament people, and the Old Testament, their Bible, can be found among them only with difficulty. They are a Talmudical people who have preferred the volumes of rabbinical speculation to the words of their ancient Prophets.

The note of religion does not enter this discussion until the Jews place it there. In this series of articles we have set aside every non-Jewish statement on this question, and have accepted only that which proceeds from recognized Jewish sources. It has been more than a surprise, in studying the proceedings of the New York Kehillah and the American Jewish Committee and their affiliated organizations, as represented by their activities throughout the country, to learn how large a part of these activities have a religious bearing, as being directly and combatively anti-Christian.

That is to say, when the Jews set forth in the public charters and constitutions of their organizations that their only purpose is to "protect Jewish rights," and when the public asks what are these "Jewish rights" which need protection in this free country, the answer can be found only in the actions which the Jews take to secure that "protection." The actions interpret the words.

And thus interpreted, "Jewish rights" seem to be summed up in the "right" to banish everything from their sight and hearing that even suggests Christianity or its Founder.

It is just there, from the Jewish side, that religious intolerance makes its appearance.

What follows in the course of this article is nothing less nor more than a group of citations from Jewish records covering a number of years. It is given here partly as an answer to the charge that this series of articles is "religious persecution," and partly to help interpret by official actions the official Jewish program in the United States.

An important factor is that previous to the formation of the Kehillah and the Jewish Committee, this sort of attack on the rights of Americans was sporadic, but since 1906 it has increased in number and insistence. Heretofore it has gone unheeded by the public as a whole because of our general tolerance in this country, but from this time forth the country will possess information that what it has been tolerating is intolerance itself. Under cover of the ideal of Liberty we have given certain people liberty to attack liberty. We ought at least to know when that is being done.

Look rapidly down the years and see one phase of that attack. It is the attack on Christianity.

That is rather a hard thing to set down in writing in this country, and it would not be set down did not the facts compel it. Jewish writers nowadays show a great deal of anxiety that non-Jews should follow certain Christian doctrines. "We gave you your Savior, and he told you to love your enemies; why don't you love us?" is the implication with which their statements usually come.

However, here are a few items from the record: They are recorded according to the Jewish calendar (our modern calendar is "Christian," and therefore taboo) but here both calendar dates shall be supplied.

5661 (A.D. 1899-1900) The Jews attempt to have the word "Christian" removed from the Bill of Rights of the State of Virginia.

5667 (A.D. 1906-1907) The Jews of Oklahoma petition the Constitutional Convention protesting that the acknowledgement of Christ in the new state constitution then being formulated would be repugnant to the Constitution of the United States.

5668 (A.D. 1907-1908) Widespread demand by the Jews during this year for the complete secularization of the public institutions of this country, as a part of the demand of the Jews for their constitutional rights.—Supreme Court Justice Brewer's statement that this is a Christian country widely controverted by Jewish rabbis and publications.

5669 (A.D. 1908-1909) Protests made to governor of Arkansas against "Christological expressions" employed by him in his Thanksgiving Day proclamation, 1908.—Professor Gotthard Deutsch protests against

"Jewish Rights" Clash With American Rights

"Christological prayers" at the high school graduating exercises in Cincinnati.

5673 (A.D. 1912-1913) The alarming growth of the Jewish population in New York makes it necessary for business men advertising for clerks or secretaries, or housewives advertising for help, to specify where Jewish help was not desired, otherwise the flood of Jewish applicants was overwhelming.

The expressions "Christian preferred," or "Jews please do not apply" are used. This year the New York Kehillah takes the matter in hand stating that "these advertisements indicate an alarming growth of discrimination against Jews and it is remarkable that many firms which cater to the trade of Jews display this form of prejudice."

5679 (A.D. 1918-1919) The American Jewish Committee took up the alleged discrimination against Jews by army contractors. Louis Marshall, president of the Committee, notified Newton D. Baker, Secretary of War, that advertisements had appeared calling for carpenters to work in government camps, and that the advertisements required the applicants to be Christians. Secretary Baker replied that he had made an order prohibiting contractors from making this discrimination. (On the whole, this special form of advertisement may appear rather stupid: how many Jewish carpenters are there? Not enough to discriminate against. But there were doubtless other reasons.)

Provost Marshall Crowder, in charge of the Selective Draft, had issued an order to all medical examiners, under direction of the Surgeon General, stating "The foreign-born, especially Jews, are more apt to malinger than the native born," and Louis Marshall again telegraphed both the Provost Marshall and the Surgeon General demanding that "the further use of this form shall be at once discontinued; that every copy of it that has been issued should be recalled by telegram; and that proper explanations be made, so as to expunge from the archives of the United States the unwarranted stigma upon three millions of people."

It was President Wilson, however, who eventually ordered the excision of this paragraph.

The United States Shipping Board sent an advertisement to the *New York Times* calling for a file clerk and stating that a "Christian" (by which is always meant a non-Jew) was preferred. The ad was not published as written; it was changed so that it requested applicants to state their religion and nationality. This last form would seem to be far more objectionable than the other. In the first instance the employer states fairly what he wants. In the second instance the applicant is compelled to divulge certain facts about himself in utter ignorance of the employer's preference.

In the first instance, only the two classes that can do business get together; in the second instance there is no clearness about the situation until much useless effort is undertaken. Why? Because the Kehillah demands it. And why does the Kehillah demand it? Because, while it is all right for a Jew to remember that he is a Jew, it is not all right for you to remember it.

So, Louis Marshall got into action again with the Shipping Board, this time with certain drastic demands. Strangely enough, the protest was lodged through Bainbridge Colby, who was Woodrow Wilson's last Secretary of State. Mr. Marshall demanded: "Not because of any desire for inflicting punishment, but for the sake of example and the establishment of a necessary precedent, this offense should be followed by a dismissal from the public service of the offender, and the public should be informed of the reason."

Attention is particularly called to the tone which Mr. Marshall adopts when addressing high American officials in the name of the Jewish Committee. It is not to be duplicated in the addresses of any other representatives of other nationalities or faiths.

Unfortunately for Mr. Marshall's plan of punishment, the object of his wrath was found to be a woman, and she was not discharged, although the Jewish Committee got an apology from Charles M. Schwab.

The Federal Reserve Bank and Liberty Loan Committee also got in wrong when an advertisement was printed calling for a "Stenographer for the Liberty Loan Committee (Christian)."

Protest was made to Benjamin Strong, governor of the Federal Reserve Bank and chairman of the Liberty Loan Committee, and the advertisement was withdrawn. But this was not enough. Secretary of the Treasury McAdoo was also drawn in to express his "reprobation for an unpatriotic act."

An officer in the Quartermaster's Department replied to a young woman who applied for the position of secretary to him that he preferred not to have Jews on his office staff. He was reprimanded upon the request of Mr. Marshall.

The Plattsburg Manual, published for officers in the United States officers' training camps, contained the statement that "the ideal officer is a Christian gentleman." Mr. Marshall at once made the standard protest against all "Christological manifestations," and the Manual was changed to read, "the ideal officer is a courteous gentleman."

5680 (A.D. 1919-1920) In this year the Kehillah was so successful in its New York campaign that it was possible for a Jewish advertiser in New York to say that he wanted Jewish help, but it was not possible for a non-Jewish advertiser to state his non-Jewish preference. This is a sidelight both on Jewish reasonableness and Jewish power.

One gathers that a few people are still hugging the delusion that there is no Jewish Question in the United States. But another glance down the records will show the most prejudiced person that there is such a Question.

If space permitted, the few details added below could be matched by a sufficient number to overflow all the pages of this paper.

5668 (A.D. 1907-1908) Jews agitate in many cities against Bible reading, Christmas celebrations or carols. In Philadelphia, Cincinnati, St. Paul and New York the Jewish opposition to the carols is met with strong counter-movements.

5669 (A.D. 1908-1909) Jewish Community at Tamaqua, Pennsylvania, defeats resolution providing daily Bible Reading in the schools.

—Jews attempting same compulsion in New Jersey are met with decision that pupils may absent themselves from devotional exercises.

— Jewish agitation in Louisiana stirs ministerial association to defend the right of the school to the Bible.

—Local council of Jewish Women of Baltimore petitions school board to prohibit Christmas exercises.

—On demand of Edwin Wolf, Jewish member, Philadelphia school board prohibits Christmas exercises.

—Jews present bills asking that New York Hebrews be permitted to ply trades and businesses on Sunday. Interdenominational Ministers' Conference takes official action and Rev. Dr. David J. Burrell, of the Marble Collegiate Church, states that the attempts of the Jews to undermine the sanctity of Sunday are ethically unjustified.

5670 (A.D. 1909-1910) On demand of Jews the school board of Bridgeport, Pennsylvania, votes to discontinue the recitation of The Lord's Prayer in the schools.

—In Kentucky State Senate, Jews defeat the Tichenor Bill making the Bible a book eligible for the schools.

5671 (A.D. 1910-1911) Jews oppose Bible reading and singing of hymns in Detroit schools.

—New York State Federation of Labor opposes Jewish Bill to exempt Jews from prosecution for violating Sunday laws. (The workingman knows that it means a 7-day week for the Goy!) New York Kehillah does two contradictory things; favors bill to permit Jews to do all kinds of business on Sunday, and pledges itself to cooperate in the strict enforcement of the Sunday laws.

5672 (A.D. 1911-1912) Upon the urgence of two Jews the Hartford, Connecticut, school board votes on the question of abolishing all religious exercises in the schools. The motion is lost by 5 to 4.

—Jewish pupils in a Passaic, New Jersey, school petition the board of education to eliminate the Bible and all Christian songs from the school.

—At the request of a rabbi, three principals of Roxbury, Massachusetts, public schools agree to banish the Christmas tree and omit all references to the season in their schools.

—Jewish pupils of Plainfield, New Jersey, petition the abolition of the Bible and Christian songs from the schools.

—The Council of the University Settlement, at the request of the New York Kehillah and the Federation of Rumanian Jews, adopts this resolution: "That in holiday celebrations held annually by the Kindergarten Association at the University Settlement every feature of any sectarian character, including Christmas trees, Christmas programs and Christmas songs, and so on, shall be eliminated."

—Philadelphia Kehillah demands that Jews be exempted from operation of the Sunday laws.

—In the *Outlook,* Dr. Lyman Abbott advises an inquiring schoolmaster that he is under no moral obligation to admit Jews to his private school.

—A Jewish delegate to the Ohio Constitutional Convention suggests that the constitution be made to forbid religious references in the schools

.—Jewish merchants of Paterson, New Jersey, petition for exemption from the Sunday laws.

—Board of education of Yonkers, New York, denies Jewish request to forbid singing of Christian songs in the schools.

5673 (A.D. 1912-1913) Annual Convention Independent Order of B'nai B'rith at Nashville, Tennessee, adopts resolution against reading the Bible and singing Christian songs in public schools.

—Jews at Jackson, Tennessee, seek an injunction to prevent the reading of the Bible in city schools.

"Jewish Rights" Clash With American Rights

—Jews of Nashville, Tennessee, petition board of education against Bible and Christian songs.

—Richmond, Virginia, school board restores Bible reading in the schools.

—Bill introduced into Pennsylvania legislature providing for Bible reading in schools and the discharge of teachers omitting to do so. Jewish rabbis protest against bill. Jewish Kehillah of Philadelphia sends telegram to governor urging him to veto bill. Governor approves bill.

—Chicago board of education, scene of much Jewish agitation, approves recommendation of subcommittee to remove Christmas from the list of official holidays in public schools.

—In response to demands of Jews the Revere, Massachusetts, school board consents to remove references to Jesus from Christmas exercises in public schools. This action, however, was rescinded at a special meeting.

—California Jews appeal before Senate Committee on Public Morals to protest against a proposed Sunday law.

—At Passaic, New Jersey, 29 Jewish members of the senior high school class walk out of class election, alleging "racial discrimination."

—At Atlantic City, New Jersey, during the national convention of the United States War Veterans, the proposal to restore the Cross as part of the insignia of chaplain, was defeated by Jews.

5674 (A.D. 1913-1914) This year the energies of the Jewish powers were concentrated on the task of preventing the United States from changing the immigration laws in a manner to protect the country from undesirable aliens.

5675 (A.D. 1914-1915) Jewish rabbi demands of California state superintendent of public instruction that some verses appearing in school readers be eliminated.—New York Kehillah concerns itself with attempts to secure modification of the Sunday laws.

5676 (A.D. 1915-1916) This year occupied by opposition to various movements toward making the schools free to use the Bible, and in opposition to the Gary system. The Gary system receives a great deal of attention from the Jews this year.

5677 (A.D. 1916-1917) Jews are busy carrying out an immense campaign against the "literacy clause" of the immigration bill.

And so it goes on. The incidents quoted are typical, not occasional. They represent what is transpiring all the time in the United States as the Jews pursue their "rights." There is no interference whatever with Jewish ways and manners. The Jew may use his own calendar, keep his own days, observe his own form of worship, live in his own ghetto, exist on a dietary principle all his own, slaughter his cattle in a manner of which no one who knows about it can approve—he can do all these things without molestation, without the slightest question of his right in them. But the non-Jew is now the "persecuted one." He must do everything the way the Jew wants it done; if not, he is "infringing on Jewish rights."

Americans are very sensitive about infringing on other people's rights. The Jews might have gone on for a long time had they not overplayed their hand. What the people are now coming to see is that it is American rights that have been interfered with, and the interference has been made with the assistance of their own broad-mindedness. The Jews' interference with the religion of the others, and the Jews' determination to wipe out of public life every sign of the predominant Christian character of the United States, is the only active form of religious intolerance in the country today.

But there is still another phase of the matter. Not content with the fullest liberty to follow their own faith in peace and quietness, in a country where none dares make them afraid, the Jews declare—we read it in their activities—that every sight and sound of anything Christian is an invasion of their peace and quietness, and so they stamp it out wherever they can reach it through political means. To what lengths this spirit may run is shown in the prophecies of the Talmud, and in the "reforms" undertaken by the Bolsheviki of Russia and Austria.

But even that is not all; not content with their own liberty, not content with the "secularization," which means the de-Christianization of all public institutions, the third step observable in Jewish activities is the actual exaltation of Judaism as a recognized and specially privileged system.

The program is the now familiar one wherever the Jewish Program is found: first, establishment; second, destruction of all that is non-Jewish or anti-Jewish; third, exaltation of Judaism in all its phases.

Put the Lord's Prayer and certain Shakespeare plays out of the public schools; but put Jewish courts in the public buildings—that is the way it works. Secularization is preparatory to Judaization.

The New York Kehillah is an illustration of how it is all done, and the American Jewish Committee is an illustration of the type of men who do it. Now for illustrations of the third phase of the program of "defending Jewish rights."

"Jewish Rights" Clash With American Rights

The year 5669 (A.D. 1908-1909) was marked by an effort to introduce the idea of the Jewish Sabbath into public business. Jews refused to sit as jurors in court, thus postponing cases. Boycotts were instituted in New York against merchants who opened on Saturday. That this campaign has borne fruit is known by all travelers in eastern cities who notice that even large department stores are closed on Saturday. The year 5670 (A.D. 1909-1910) was dedicated apparently to the work of introducing the idea of Jewish national holidays into public life. This question lately rose in New York in a threatening way, but was withdrawn just before the breaking point. Only temporarily withdrawn, however, The feint revealed the identity and number of those who are still on guard against the complete Judaization of their city.

—Jewish members of stock exchanges endeavored to have these institutions recognize Yom Kippur by closing; In Cleveland this was done.

—The Council of Jewish Women appealed to the Civil Service Commission at Washington for recognition of Jewish holidays.

—In Newark, New Jersey, the rabbis asked the night schools to discontinue Friday evening sessions, because the Jewish Sabbath begins at sundown on Friday.

In 1911 an attempt to have Hebrew officially recognized was frustrated by Supreme Court Judge Goff who refused incorporation of "Agudath Achim Kahal Adath Jeshurun" on the ground that the title should be in English.—Chicago Jews have election date changed because the official date fell on the last day of the Passover.

In 1912-1913 a number of special recognitions of the Saturday Sabbath were obtained, including Jersey City, Bayonne, Hoboken, Union Hill. In the Ohio legislature the Jews defeated a bill fixing a certain Saturday as the date of a primary election. In 1913-1914 the United States Bureau of Immigration granted the request of Simon Wolf, long-time Jewish lobbyist at Washington, that instructions be given the Immigration Commissioners that no Jews be deported on Jewish holidays.

—The Women's Party of Cook County, Illinois, passes resolutions against allowing Jewish teachers to draw full pay for absence during Jewish holidays.

—In this year also the question of the Jews' method of slaughtering animals—the Shehitah—was brought forward. The American Jewish Committee thought this question of sufficient importance to engage its full interest.

This series of facts could also be pursued at length. Kosher food for the children of public schools because there were Jewish children in the schools; protest against the Daylight Saving Ordinances because they were prejudicial to Jewish merchants who close their businesses on Saturday and open them after nightfall on that day. This is an illustration of the large number of small points at which Jewish life conflicts with community life. And, of course, each of these divergences is ground for an imperious "demand."

—Harvard University was severely criticized in 1917-1918 for refusing to set aside an entrance examination date that conflicted with a Jewish holiday. Since that time, however, eastern universities have become more pliable. But the whole course of the Christian year would have to be changed and all the traditional seasonal customs of the country broken up if the Jews are to be given the full measure of "liberty" which they demand.

Of course, the work of the Kehillah is claimed to be "educational." It certainly is that. The best educated members are those who come from the ghettos of Galatia where the Kehillah idea is fully understood and the Jewish community government exercises unrestricted sway.

Whatever other phase of education the Kehillah may be interested in, it certainly stresses most the education to separateness. The *New York Times* especially likes to emphasize this matter of "education." It is a convenient description and somewhat aids the effort to minimize Kehillah's importance when it is under scrutiny. Nevertheless in the *New York Times* an article appeared about the Kehillah in which Dr. S. Benderly, director of the Bureau of Education, is quoted as describing the objects of the education:

"The problem before us was to form a body of young Jews who should be on the one hand true Americans, a part of this Republic, with an intense interest in upbuilding American ideals; and yet, on the other hand, be also Jews in love with the best of their own ideals, and not anxious merely to merge with the rest and disappear among them.

"That problem confronts Orthodox and Reform Jews alike. It is not merely a religious but a civic problem."

That is separatism and exclusivism as an educational program, and its results cannot help being a cloud of difference such as this article has in part disclosed. The New York Kehillah, through its Bureau of Education, is giving "a purely religious training to 200,000 Jewish children," the religious training being, of course, not what is generally understood by

"Jewish Rights" Clash With American Rights

that term, but a training in ideas of racial superiority and separateness.

This difference is strikingly illustrated in Jewish fiction recently. To love a Christian maiden is sinful; this is the theme of all sorts of stories, sketches and editorials appearing these days. But James Gibbons Huneker, in a sketch extravagantly praised by Jewish critics, shows how deep this idea of separateness is when he makes Yaankely Ostrowicz say: "As a child I trembled at the sound of music and was taught to put my finger in my ears when profane music, Goy music, was played."

This is the root idea: All Gentile life and institutions are "profane." It is the Jews' unceasing consciousness of the Goy that constitutes the disease of Judaism, this century-long tradition of separateness.

There is no such thing as anti-Semitism. There is, however, much anti-Goyism. In England, Germany, France, America, Russia, there is no anti-Arab sentiment of which anyone knows. None of the Semite peoples have been distinguished by the special dislike of any other people. There is no reason why anyone should dislike the Semites.

It is very strange, however, that the Semitic people should be a unit in disliking the Jews. Palestine, which still has only a handful of Jews, is peopled by Semites who so thoroughly dislike the Jews that serious complications are threatening the Zionistic advances being made there. This surely is not anti-Semitism. Semites are not against Semites. But they are at odds with Jews.

When Aryan and Semite are kept conscious through many centuries that the Jew is another race, and when it is known that neither Aryan nor Semite are touchy on the race question, what is the answer? Only this, that the whole substance of such a situation must be supplied by the Jews.

There is no such thing as anti-Semitism. There is only a very little and a very mild antijewism. But a study of Jewish publications, books, pamphlets, declarations, constitutions and charters, as well as a study of organized Jewish action in this and other countries, indicates that there is a tremendous amount of anti-Goyism, or anti-Gentilism.

Not that it is anything to fear. It is, however, something to know. Knowledge is a good defense. The New York Kehillah, having as its executive committee the same committee which is also the ruling group of Jews known as District XII of the American Jewish Committee, is worth consideration, not only as an illustration of the interlaced organization which combines all classes of Jews in one group, but also as an illustration of what is meant by "Jewish rights."

The International Jew Volumes I and II

It is worth remembering that every "demand" voiced in Washington before officials and committees, that every high personage that appears there on Jewish matters—the Louis Marshalls and the Wises, the Goldfogles, the Rosalskis, besides many others, like the Kahns and the Schiffs, who keep out of the committee limelight and away from the protesting parties—are all linked up, through this Jewish interest or that, with the main interest which is based on the Kehillah and expresses itself through District XII of the American Jewish Committee.

The Dearborn Independent, March 12, 1921

36. "Jewish Rights" to Put Studies Out of Schools

The organizations of Jewry are numerous and widespread, all of them being international in tone whether so chartered or not. The Alliance Israelite Universelle is, perhaps, the world clearing house of Jewish policy, with which every national aggregation of Jewish societies has affiliation.

The Independent Order of B'nai B'rith, which is now hopeful of reaching the 1,000,000 membership mark, is frankly international. It has divided the world into 11 districts, seven of which are in the United States. Its lodges at last report numbered 426. The four members of its executive committee who do not reside in the United States, reside in Berlin, Vienna, Bucharest and Constantinople, respectively. Its lodges have been set up in the United States, Europe, Asia and Africa. Henry Morgenthau's name appears in the 1919-1920 Jewish year book as a member of this executive committee. Mr. Morgenthau will be remembered as the American Minister to Turkey, later talked of as Ambassador to Mexico, then chosen by President Wilson to mediate between the Turks and the Armenians. Mr. Morgenthau also investigated for the President the reports of Polish pogroms.

In studying the executive committees of Jewish societies it is strikingly evident that the same minds guide all the important ones. A few names recur again and again. They are the names one meets at all Senate hearings, at various strategic places in the War Government of the United States, and at every stage of Jewish interference with American foreign policy. Everything centers at last, apparently, in the American Jewish Committee and the executive committee of the New York Kehillah. Judge Mack, Judge Brandeis, the Warburgs, the Schiffs, Morgenthau, Wolf, Kraus, Elkus, Straus, Louis Marshall—these names appear over and over again, in offensive and defensive action, in all big affairs.

There are now in the United States 6,100 reported Jewish organizations. Of these, 3,637 are in New York City. This figure is offered from the 1919-1920 year book, although the statement was recently made that the New York Kehillah is the clearing house of 4,000 organizations.

Enough is shown to indicate how fully organized the Jews are, how they are linked together by every conceivable bond; the material of every bond being their racial likeness.

The organization about which the public has heard most is the Independent Order of B'nai B'rith. Its headquarters are not in New York, strange to say, but in Chicago. Its origin, however, as might be expected, was in New York.

This interesting order, without a reference to which no survey of Jewry is complete, came into existence in the back room of an Essex street saloon in 1843. Strangely enough, its most moving spirit at the beginning was a Henry Jones, although his colleagues retained their Hebraic names.

Because most of the founders were from Germany the name was given in German, *Bundes Bruder,* which is in Hebrew, B'nai B'rith (Brothers of the Covenant). The executive committee was known as The Elders. The order spread first to Cincinnati, apparently taking the course of German immigration through the country, and it is recorded that the second lodge in that city is the first where the English language was used in discussing lodge affairs. The first leap of the order abroad, was to Berlin where in 1885 Grand Lodge No. 8 was installed, followed soon after by Grand Lodges in Rumania and Austria. The order's literature lays stress on the work of inculcating patriotism, which is said to be one of B'nai B'rith's special interests. It is perhaps not meant, however, that the head office at Chicago could undertake, especially during recent years, to guide the patriotism of all the districts throughout the world. It would have been rather awkward for District No. 6, which includes Illinois, to encourage District No. 8 to loyalty, seeing that District No. 8 embraced Germany.

The Order has not avoided the political field. The diplomatic history of the United States in the last 70 years is dotted all over with indications of B'nai B'rith activities. Oscar Straus, writing from the Legation of the United States at Constantinople in 1889, tells Secretary of State Blaine that the Jerushalaim Lodge of B'nai B'rith at Jerusalem was quite satisfied with the way in which the State Department had attended to a certain matter at the lodge's request. Mr. Morgenthau in the midst of his investigation of the false pogrom rumors on Poland, goes to a B'nai B'rith lodge. In 1870 Brother Benjamin F. Piexotto was appointed "as United States consul at Bucharest for the express purpose of securing

"Jewish Rights" to Put Studies Out of Schools

an amelioration of the condition of the shockingly persecuted Jews in Rumania." The "persecution" in Rumania was the protest of the Rumanian peasantry against the two greatest menaces to the peasant farmers—the Jew-controlled liquor and mortgage traffics.

But this special appointment was made "in pursuance of suggestions made by the Order, and the negotiations were carried on chiefly by Brother Simon Wolf."

Simon Wolf has been the official Jewish lobbyist at Washington, on fixed post, for fifty years. He could write an informative story of the relation of B'nai B'rith to diplomatic appointments, if he would. It was he who suggested to William Jennings Bryan, when the latter was Secretary of State, that a Jew be appointed Minister to Spain to show Spain that the United States did not approve Spain's act of expulsion back in the fifteenth century. Jews are also suggesting to President Harding that a Jew be appointed Ambassador to Germany to rebuke the Germans' resentment against Jewish control of finance, industry and politics. This conception of the United States Diplomatic Service as a convenient agency for the transaction of Jewish world affairs has been in existence a long time, and has accounted for some of the strange appointments which have puzzled the people.

It is worth noting that while American Jews are crowding the eastern diplomatic posts with as many Jews as possible, British Jews are doing the same thing in the Judaization of the Persia, India and Palestine governments, so that the whole mid-Orient is now under Jewish control, and the Mohammedan World is given to understand that the Jews are merely coming back from their conquest of the white races. To those who have observed the Jewish attempt to seek a rapprochement between the followers of Moses and Mohammed, the situation is one of the keenest interest.

The B'nai B'rith is made up mostly of the more liberal Jews, religiously speaking, and doubtless includes a large number who are also liberal, racially speaking. The time when it stood as spokesman of Jewish ideals is now long past; it stands today the center of certain Jewish activities. It does not supersede the American Jewish Committee by any means, but it is the encircling arm, with fingers everywhere, through which the committee can get its will carried out. When there is anything to be done, the B'nai B'rith is the organization which takes the lead in putting it over. It may be described as a freemasonry exclusively for Jews. This brings up another characteristic that people have noticed and discussed:

the Jew demands as his right entrance into other Orders; into his own he admits none but Jews. This one-sided policy is found everywhere.

Chief among the B'nai B'rith's activities in so far as they directly relate to the rest of the people, is the work of the Anti-Defamation League. This inside committee in every lodge attends to the espionage work necessary to keep the Grand Lodges informed as to what is going on with reference to Jewry in the United States. In its work, the Anti-Defamation League always takes the offensive and works along pretty well defined lines.

Ordinarily the head of the Anti-Defamation League in each city is a man competent to bring pressure to bear on the public press.

Sometimes he is the head of an advertising agency which, as a rule, pools the Jewish department store advertising of that city, so that the newspapers may be controlled from that angle. Sometimes he is himself a heavy advertiser, pledged the cooperation of other advertisers in whatever he undertakes to do. The Anti-Defamation League is the instrument through which all boycotting tactics make their appearance. This league not only makes its protest from without, but directs reprisals from within. It is an exceedingly militant body and does not always depend upon "the rule of reason" in its activities.

Many quaint tales could be told of the operations of the Anti-Defamation League in various American cities, but as the present articles attempt to give no more than a bird's-eye view of widespread Jewish activities, mere story-telling will have to wait.

But perhaps the most notable accomplishment of the league has been the suppression of the word "Jew" in the public prints in any but the most laudatory connections. For a long time in the United States the people did not know how to refer to the Jews, whether as Hebrews or Israelites or what, because the fear of giving offense had been so diligently cultivated in all quarters.

The result was that other nationalities were laden with all the undesirable publicity which the Jews had evaded through the efforts of the Anti-Defamation League. Recently a Jew was on trial for the murder of his wife.

The newspapers referred to him as "a pert little Englishman." The Russians in the United States, and the Poles also, have been filled with indignation by the extent to which their national names have been used in police and newspaper reports to conceal the identity of Jews. The Russians resident in this country have several times been compelled

"Jewish Rights" to Put Studies Out of Schools

to remonstrate with the press for its misrepresentative practice in this matter.

For this state of affairs, the Anti-Defamation League receives the credit. Whenever a newspaper printed the word "Jew" as an identifying noun after the name of anyone who had been discredited, the Anti-Defamation League was instantly on the job in protest. The stock argument is, "If he had been a Baptist or an Episcopalian you would not have told it, and why should you say that he is a Jew—'Jew' being a mere religious denomination." City editors are obliging and the rule became established. In principle it is right, although it is urged on wrong grounds; but in practice it has turned out to be a great injustice to other nationalities and, more than all, it has curtailed the freedom of American speech. It has concealed the Jew where he wishes to be concealed, and it cannot be said that he has made the best use of this privilege.

It is this fixed policy of the B'nai B'rith's Anti-Defamation League which imperils the hope that the B'nai B'rith might have come to the front as one of the most useful influences in the solution of the Jewish Question. It includes a body of men sufficiently acquainted with the general point of view to be able to see where corrections and concessions are necessary as a ground, not to mere polite tolerance, but to reconciliation. There is no country more propitious for the settlement of the world's Jewish Problem than is the United States, but it cannot be settled along the old line of the Judaization of the United States, nor by its de-Christianization either. The work of the Anti-Defamation League is positive to Judaization and negative to settlement.

There is nothing that Jewry, acting through the B'nai B'rith, does so well as to hold Mass Meetings and attack "The Merchant of Venice."

Mass Meetings may be described as the Jews' great American pastime. The New York Kehillah, that is, The American Jewish Committee, can on one day's notice organize Mass Meetings in every city in the United States. They are mechanical devices, of course; they are not so much expressions of the Jewish mind as they are attempts to impress the non-Jewish mind. There is a great deal of theatrical calculation in them. This column could be filled with the dates and places of Mass Meetings held within any seven days on any question in which the Jews had decided to coerce or accelerate public or, as it usually is, official opinion. The Mass Meeting, it appears, can still be made to seem real to the political official whose vote is sought.

It was by Mass Meetings that Congress was coerced into breaking off our commercial treaty with Russia.

It was by Mass Meetings that the literacy test was defeated.

It was by Mass Meetings that every attempt to restrict immigration has been defeated.

In 100 important cities a Mass Meeting could be held tomorrow night if President Harding should attempt to remove a Jewish official, or if the census bureau should attempt to record Jews under their proper racial name.

It is a very perfect system, even if a little antiquated. Doubtless its main purpose is to let the Jewish masses believe that they too have something to say in Jewish affairs. Jewish leadership of the Jews is never quite what the Jews think it is, and its weakness was never more apparent than today. There has not been any "persecution" of the Jews in the United States and never will be any, but all that the Jews have had to carry in the way of misunderstanding has been the result of the leadership which has misled them into paths of bloated ambition, instead of substantial human achievement. At this moment there is trembling, not among the Jewish masses, but among their leaders. The Jewish people will presently take their own affairs in their own hands, and then their affairs will go better. There are too many "committees," too many "prophets," too many "wise men," who think that two minutes with a President constitutes greatness, and that a busy bustling overseas and back constitutes statesmanship. The Jews have suffered from the personal ambitions and pathetic incapacity of some of their most advertised men.

The B'nai B'rith has this much in its favor: its leadership has always been progressive. Only when it has lent itself as local agent for the "leaders" of the New York Kehillah has it set up in its neighborhoods those influences which tend toward division instead of a better understanding.

Under whose inspiration it was that the B'nai B'rith undertook to bring its great power to bear against one of Shakespeare's plays, cannot now be said; but it has been most unfortunate for Jewish influence in all directions. Successful—oh yes; but such a success as serious people could well do without.

Merely to glance over the record is interesting:

1907—Jews force "The Merchant of Venice" to be dropped from public schools in Galveston, Texas; Cleveland, Ohio; El Paso, Texas; Youngstown, Ohio.

"Jewish Rights" to Put Studies Out of Schools

1908—Jews have "The Merchant of Venice" eliminated from the English course in the high school at El Paso, Texas.

1910—Apparently the "Merchant" slipped back into Cleveland schools, for in April the superintendent of public schools issued an order that it was not to be used again.

1911—Rabbi Harry W. Ettleson and Solomon Elsner request the Hartford, Connecticut, school board to have "The Merchant of Venice" dropped from the reading list of schools. The board complies.

1912—Jewish residents of Minneapolis, Minnesota, inaugurate a movement to have "The Merchant of Venice" dropped from the public schools.—In Boston, Massachusetts, the superintendent of schools refuses to withdraw "The Merchant of Venice" as a textbook, on the demand of Rabbi Phineas Israeli.

1916—On demand of Jews the New Haven, Connecticut, board of education votes to prevent the reading of "The Merchant of Venice," and extends the prohibition to "Lamb's Tales from Shakespeare" until an edition is published which omits the play.

And so on down the list of cities. A diversion was created by the Jewish attack on Sargent's painting entitled "The Synagogue" in the art scheme of the Boston Public Library. Many denunciatory resolutions were adopted throughout the country with regard to that, but the painting is still there.

It is all part of one mistaken program, to prohibit free speech, with reference to the Jew. It is utterly at one side of all that American principles mean. Shut him up! Boycott him! Tear down his painting! Bar his words from the mails and public library!—what a waste of energy and what a self-judgment such an attitude is!

And it has become pretty general. Last Christmas most people had a hard time finding Christmas cards that indicated in any way that Christmas commemorated Someone's Birth. Easter they will have the same difficulty in finding Easter cards that contain any suggestion that Easter commemorates a certain event.

There will be rabbits and eggs and spring flowers, but a hint of the Resurrection will be hard to find. Now, all this begins with the designers of the cards. And even in this business one comes upon that same policy of declaring Anti-Semitic everything that is Christian. If Rabbi Coffey says the New Testament is the most Anti-Semitic book ever written, what must be the judgment on an Easter card that is truly an Easter card?

In November, 1919, the Anti-Defamation Committee claimed that 150 American cities had excluded "The Merchant of Venice" from the public schools. The newspapers at this writing are announcing that David Warfield, the great Jewish actor, is going to play "Shylock" in the manner which, as he believes, represents the true Shakespeare conception. The Anti-Defamation League may yet find itself to have expended much energy beating the wind, especially as the best Shakespearean critics declare that "The Merchant of Venice" is not about a Jew at all, but about Usury as a vicious practice which gripped both Jew and non-Jew and brought division.

There was, however, a certain finesse in the manner of the Anti-Defamation League in approaching the matter of the exclusion of the "Merchant." It was not an incapacity to appreciate the fine work of Shakespeare. Oh, no, anything but that. Nor was it a confession of thin-skinned sensibility on the part of Jews. Not at all. No, it was really for the benefit of the Gentile children that the Anti-Defamation League wanted them kept from that play in their reading lessons.

Here are excerpts from one of the letters sent out from the Anti-Defamation League in Chicago to the superintendent of public schools in an important city. The italics are ours:

"We have just been advised that the high schools still retain "The Merchant of Venice" in the list of required readings .We do not base our request because of the embarrassment which may be caused to the Jewish students in class, nor is our attitude in this regard based on thin-skinned sensitiveness. It is the result of mature consideration and investigation.

"Our objection is made because of its effect upon the non-Jewish children who subconsciously will associate in their own minds the Jew as Shakespeare portrayed him with the Jew of today. Children are not analysts. A character in the past vividly portrayed exists for them in the present. The Jew of Shakespeare lives in the mind of the child as the Jew of New York, or the Jew of Chicago, or the Jew of Newark. Your teachers of literature might say much in favor of Shylock's good qualities, but our experience has been that only very seldom are Shylock's good qualities brought out strongly before children. Those traits of his character which are brought out most vividly in the study of the play are Shylock's greed, hatred, revenge and cruelty.

"The fact that the College Entrance Requirements Board realized the justice of our stand and struck the play off from the list as required

"Jewish Rights" to Put Studies Out of Schools

reading for entrance to our universities and colleges indicates clearly that it is a most serious problem.

"We believe that when you realize the great harm which might be caused to hundreds and thousands of law-abiding Jewish citizens of this country, you will grant our request that the reading of 'The Merchant of Venice' be discontinued from your schools."

And in this case it was. Notwithstanding the fact that the play was used in the high school, and the argument of the letter was addressed to the effect of the play on children, it was discontinued. A study of the schedule of just what occurred showed that everything had been made ready even before the letter was written.

Does this frittering away of Jewish influence strike the Jewish leaders as a wise policy? Is there any hope whatever of doing away with "The Merchant of Venice"?

Do they not know that it is the observation of teachers of literature that even if non-Jewish children are forbidden to read the play, Jewish children are going to read it anyway, since it is the Jewish children who most heartily enjoy it because they more clearly understand it?

Do not the Jewish leaders know that non-Jews do not read the "Merchant" for Shylock, except perhaps his noble defense of the Jew as a human being? Whoever hears Shylock quoted in anything but this, which numerous Jewish writers delight to quote?—"I am a Jew. Hath not a Jew eyes? Hath not a Jew hands, organs, dimensions, senses, affections, passions?"

To effect its purpose the Anti-Defamation League will have to perform an excision on our common English tongue. The wise and witty sayings of this Shakespearean play have passed into the permanent coinage of daily speech.

"I hold the world a stage where every man must play his part; and mine a sad one."

"I am Sir Oracle, And when I ope my lips let no dog bark!"

"If to do were as easy as to know what were good to do, chapels had been churches, and poor men's cottages princes' palaces."

"The Devil can cite Scripture for his purpose."

"A goodly apple rotten at the heart: O, what a goodly outside falsehood hath!"

"Truth will come to sight; murder cannot be hid long."

"All that glitters is not gold."

"A harmless necessary cat."

"The quality of mercy is not strained, It droppeth as the gentle rain from heaven Upon the place beneath. It is twice blest: It blesseth him that gives and him that takes. It is an attribute of God himself; And earthly power doth then show likest God's, When mercy seasons justice."

This is beyond the power of the Anti-Defamation League to destroy. Shylock may be forgotten, but not these living lines. It is true, however, that in 150 American cities, according to the league's claim, school children are prevented reading and hearing these words in school.

But is it worth it? Is it a part of "Jewish Rights" that an admittedly great play, taught in all the English courses of all the universities, should be prohibited to the children of the people in the public schools?

From the prohibition of the Bible to the prohibition of Shakespeare, the whole Jewish course has been a colossal mistake, the reaction from which will be to belittle Jewish public judgment in the future.

It was all very well said by a correspondent to the *Newark Evening News,* January 13, 1920:

"To the Editor of the News:

"Sir—Protests have been made by the representatives of the Jewish, Scotch and colored races against Shakespeare's being used in the public schools, the former because of the portrayal of Shylock in 'The Merchant of Venice.' Some Scotch folk have protested, as I understand it, to the Newark Board of Education, on account of the character given Macbeth. The colored folks, judging from the letter printed in the News from Washington, do not like the character Othello, owing to his despicable treatment of Desdemona. As a descendant of the Welsh race, I enter my protest in behalf of that ancient people in regard to Shakespeare's ridicule of Henry V, of the Welshman, Captain Fluellen, who is made to look as if he did not know anything about war.

"I have no doubt that others could find fault with Shakespeare's penchant for holding up the weak side of some of his characters, so I think that Shakespeare and the Bible might well be kept out of the public schools because both books are rough on certain people whose identity is clearly shown. The board of education is to be congratulated for taking action in the matter, which promises at this late date to place the Newark educational system in a class all by itself."

The Dearborn Independent, March 19, 1921

37. Disraeli—British Premier, Portrays the Jews

The Jews have complained that they are being misrepresented. It is their usual complaint. They are always being "misrepresented" and "persecuted" except when they are being praised for what they are not. If the Jews were fully understood by the Gentiles, if the Christian churches, for example, were freed from their delusion that the Jews are Old Testament people, and if the churches really knew what Talmudic religion is, it is likely the "misrepresentation" would be still stronger.

The downfall of Russia was prepared by a long and deliberate program of misrepresentation of the Russian people, through the Jewish world press and Jewish diplomatic service. The name of Poland has been drawn in filth through the press of the United States under Jewish instigation, most of the signers of the latest Jewish protest against *The Dearborn Independent*'s articles being leaders in the vilification of Poland, whose sole crime is that she wishes to save herself from the Jews. All this real misrepresentation is regarded as the Jews' privilege.

But wherever a hand has been raised to prevent the Jews overrunning the people and secretly securing control of the major instruments of life, the Jews have raised the cry of "misrepresentation." They never meet the question outright. They are not meeting it now. They cannot meet it without confession. False denials, pleas for sympathy, and an unworthy attempt to link others with them in their fall, constitute their whole method of defense.

Freemasons may wonder how they come into this affair, as they see the name of their ancient order coupled with that of the Jews in the latest Jewish defense. It is all very easily understood by those who are acquainted with Jewish strategy during the two centuries which comprise modern Masonic history.

Twice in the history of the United States, the people have been aroused by a sense of strange influences operating in their affairs, and each time the real power behind the influences was able to divert suspicion to the Freemasons. Once in George Washington's time, once in President Adams' time this occurred. Books were written, sermons preached, newspapers took up the search, but none of the observers saw the Jewish influence there. George Washington knew that the disloyal influence was not Masonic, but he saw signs of the concealed power trying to operate under the guise of Masonry. President Adams had not so clear a view of the matter.

Masonry emerged unstained because it was guiltless of subversive purposes. A pseudo-Masonry, of French origin, given to atheistic and revolutionary purposes, strongly patronized by Jews, was the disturbing element, but all that the public was able to see was the Masonic similitude and not the Jewish hand. A recrudescence of this misrepresentation of the Masons occurred also in 1826, and from then until the other day, when the Leaders of American Jewry linked the name of Freemasonry with their own, the name of the Order has been unscathed.

This is to serve notice on the leaders of American Jewry that this time they will not be permitted to hide behind the name of Masonry, nor will they be permitted to hold up the name of Masonry as a shield to blunt the darts or as an ally to share the shafts aimed at their subversive purposes. That game has succeeded twice in the United States; it will never succeed again. Freemasonry is not and never was implicated in what the Jewish cabal has had in mind. And Freemasons everywhere are aware of the facts.

It is a curious fact that just as the Jews have sought to operate through the Masons and then leave that Order to take the brunt of the ensuing assault, so also have they at times sought to operate through the Jesuits, playing the same trick with that name and Order. If the Jesuits and the Masons would compare notes, they could both report the same thing. Jews have sought to use both, and have been frustrated, although in consequence the names of both Orders have suffered for a time.

This is one of the coincidences between the Protocols and the facts: the Protocols express themselves as against both the Masons and the Jesuits, but willing to use both to attain Jewish purposes.

Both these orders are well able to take care of themselves, once they know the key to the Jewish plan. But there is much information on these matters of which the public is not aware, and at a future date a study may be made of the historical efforts of the Jews to use and destroy Freemasonry. Such a study will be useful in showing how Jewish influence operated in a day when the people had no means of identifying it as Jewish. The people attacked the thing they saw, but what they saw was not the source of the element they opposed. Progress

Disraeli—British Premier, Portrays the Jews

has been made at least to this extent, that nowadays, more than at any previous time, the world plan of the Jews is known and recognizable.

The main purpose of the present article, however, is to show the reader that the Jews have not been misrepresented, the means of showing this being a presentation of the Jews by a notable Jew whom the Jews are delighted to honor.

Benjamin Disraeli, who was Earl of Beaconsfield and prime minister of Great Britain, was a Jew and gloried in it. He wrote many books, in a number of which he discussed his people in an effort to set them in a proper light. The British Government was not then so Jewish as it has since become, and Disraeli was easily one of the greatest figures in it.

In his book, "*Coningsby*," there appears a Jewish character named Sidonia, in whose personality and through whose utterances, Disraeli sought to present the Jew as he would like the world to see him.

Sidonia first announces his race to young *Coningsby* by saying, "I am of that faith that the Apostles professed before they followed their Master," the only place in the whole book where the "faith" is mentioned. Four times, however, in the brief preface to the fifth edition, written in 1849, the term "race" is used in reference to the Jews.

In the first conversation between these two, Sidonia reveals himself as a great lover of power, and discourses charmingly of the powerful men of history, ending in this way:

"Aquaviva was General of the Jesuits, ruled every cabinet in Europe and colonized America before he was thirty-seven. What a career!" exclaimed the stranger (Sidonia), rising from his chair and walking up and down the room; "*the secret sway of Europe!*" (p. 120. The references are to Longman's edition published in 1919. The italics are ours.)

Taking up a study of the character of Sidonia the Jew, Disraeli the Jew begins to refer to the Jews as "Mosaic Arabs." If a modern writer were to describe the Jews thus, virtually as Arabs of the Mosaic persuasion, it would be denounced as another attempt at "persecution," but Disraeli did this a number of times, his purpose evidently being to give the Jew his proper setting as to his original position among the nations. Again he refers to them as "Jewish Arabs." Both of these terms may be found on page 209.

Disraeli also gives voice to the feeling, which every Jew has, that whoever opposes the Jew is doomed. This is a feeling which is strongly entrenched in Christians also, that somehow the Jews are the "chosen people" and that it is dangerous to oppose them in anything. "The fear of the Jews" is a very real element in life. It is just as real among the Jews as among non-Jews. The Jew himself is bound in fear to his people, and he exercises the fear of the curse throughout the sphere of religion—"I will curse them that curse thee." It remains to be proved, however, that opposition to the destructive tendencies of Jewish influences along all the principal avenues of life is a "cursing" of the Jews. If the Jews were really Old Testament people, if they were really conscious of a "mission" for the blessing of all nations, the very things in which they offend would automatically disappear. If the Jew is being "attacked," it is not because he is a Jew, but because he is the source and life of certain tendencies and influences, which, if they are not checked, mean the destruction of a moral society.

The persecution of the Jew to which Disraeli refers is that of the Spanish Inquisition, which rested on religious grounds. Tracing the Sidonia family through a troubled period of European history, our Jewish author notes:

"During the disorders of the Peninsular War . . . a cadet of the younger branch of this family made a large fortune by military contracts, and supplying the commissariat of the different armies." (p. 212.) Certainly. It is a truth unassailable, applicable to any period of the Christian Era, that "persecuted" or not, "wars have been the Jews' harvests." They were the first military commissaries.

If this young Sidonia in supplying "the different armies" went so far as to supply the opposing armies, he would be following quite perfectly the Jewish method as history records it.

"And at the peace, prescient of the great financial future of Europe, confident in the fertility of his own genius, in his original views of fiscal subjects, and his knowledge of natural resources, this Sidonia . . . resolved to emigrate to England, with which he had, in the course of years, formed considerable commercial connections. He arrived here after the peace of Paris, with his large capital. He stakes all that he was worth on the Waterloo loan; and the event made him one of the greatest capitalists in Europe."

"No sooner was Sidonia established in England than he professed Judaism . . . "

"Sidonia had foreseen in Spain that, after the exhaustion of a war of twenty-five years, Europe must require capital to carry on peace. He reaped the due reward of his sagacity. Europe did require money and Sidonia was ready to lend it to Europe. France wanted some; Austria more: Prussia a little; Russia a few millions. Sidonia could furnish them all. The only country which he avoided was Spain . . . " (p. 213.)

Here the prime minister of Great Britain, from the wealth of his traditions as a Jew and the height of his observation as prime minister, describes the method of the Jew in peace and war, exactly as others have tried to describe it. He puts forward the same set of facts as others put forth, but he does it apparently for the Jews' glorification, while others do it to enable the people to see what goes on behind the scenes in war and peace. Sidonia was ready to lend money to the nations. But where did he get it, in order to lend it? He got it from the nations when they were at war! It was the same money; the financiers of war and the financiers of peace are the same, and they are The International Jews, as Benjamin Disraeli's book for the glorification of Jewry amply testifies. Indeed, he testifies on the same page just quoted:

"It is not difficult to conceive that, after having pursued the career we have intimated for about ten years, Sidonia had become one of the most considerable personages in Europe. He had established a brother, or a near relative, in whom he could confide, in most of the principal capitals. He was lord and master of the money market of the world, and of course virtually lord and master of everything else."

This comes as near being The International Jew as anything can be, but the Jews glory in the picture. It is only when a non-Jewish writer suggests that perhaps it is not good for society that a Jewish coterie should be "lord and master of the money market of the world," and as a consequence "lord and master of everything else," that the cry of "persecution" arises. Strangely enough, it is in this book of the British premier that we come upon his recognition of the fact that Jews had infiltrated into the Jesuits' order.

"Young Sidonia was fortunate in the tutor whom his father had procured for him, and who devoted to his charge all the resources of his trained intellect and vast and various erudition. A Jesuit before the revolution; since then an exiled Liberal leader; now a member of the Spanish Cortes; Rebello was always a Jew. He found in his pupil that precocity of intellectual development which is characteristic of the Arabian organization." (p. 214.)

Then followed in young Sidonia's career an intellectual mastery of the world. He traveled everywhere, sounded the secrets of everything, and returned with the world in his vest pocket, so to speak—a man without illusions of any sort.

"There was not an adventurer in Europe with whom he was not familiar. No minister of state had such communication with secret agents and political spies as Sidonia. He held relations with all the clever outcasts of the world. The catalog of his acquaintances in the shape of Greeks, Armenians, Moors, secret Jews, Tartars, Gypsies, wandering Poles and Carbonari, would throw a curious light on those subterranean agencies of which the world in general knows so little, but which exercise so great an influence on public events . . . The secret history of the world was his pastime. His great pleasure was to contrast the hidden motive, with the public pretext, of transactions." (pp. 218–219.)

Here is The International Jew, full dress; he is the Protocolist too, wrapped in mystery, a man whose fingers sweep all the strings of human motive, and who controls the chief of the brutal forces—Money. If a non-Jew had limned a Sidonia, so truthfully showing the racial history and characteristics of the Jews, he would have been subjected to that pressure which the Jews apply to every truth-teller about themselves. But Disraeli could do it, and one sometimes wonders if Disraeli was not, after all, writing more than a romance, writing indeed a warning for all who can read.

The quotation just given is not the description of Sidonia only; it is also a description—save for the high culture of it—of certain American Jews who, while they walk in the upper circles, have commerce with the "adventurers" and with "the secret agents and political spies," and with the "secret Jews," and with those "subterranean agencies of which the world in general knows so little."

This is the strength of Jewry, this commerce between the high and the low, for the Jew knows nothing disreputable within the circle of Jewishness. No Jew becomes an outcast, whatever he may do; a place and a work await him, whatever his character.

There are highly placed persons in New York who would rather not have it known what they contributed to the "adventurer" who left New York to overturn Russia; there are other Jews who would rather not have it printed how much they know of "secret agents and political spies." Disraeli did more than draw Sidonia; he portrayed The International Jew as he is found also in America.

Thus far Sidonia is described from the outside. But now he begins to speak for himself, and it is in behalf and praise of the Jews. He is discussing the discrimination practiced against his people in England. It is the old story. Everywhere, even in the United States, the same story.

Disraeli—British Premier, Portrays the Jews

Crying for pity while usurping power! "We poor Jews" wails a New York multimillionaire at whose finger legislators quail and even Presidents of the United States grow respectful. The following quotation was written in 1844: Britons must be impressed with its uncanny parallel to their affairs today: it is Sidonia speaking—

". . . yet, since your society has become agitated in England, and powerful combinations menace your institutions, you find the once loyal Hebrew invariably arrayed in the same ranks as the leveller and latitudinarian, and prepared to support the policy which may even endanger his life and property, rather than tamely continue under a system which seeks to degrade him."

Consider that. "Latitudinarianism" is the doctrine of the Protocols in a word. It is a break-up by means of a welter of so-called "liberal" ideas which construct nothing themselves, but have power to destroy the established order.

Note also Disraeli's answer to the question sometimes asked, "If the Jews suffer under Bolshevism, why do they support it?" or the Jewish spokesmen's form of it—"If we are so powerful, why do we suffer in the disorder of the world?" The disorder is always a step to a new degree of Jewish power. Jews suffer willingly for that. But even so, they do not suffer as the non-Jews do. The Soviets permit relief to enter Russia for the Jews. In Poland, the "starving war-sufferers" are able to glut all available ships in taking high-priced passage to America. They are not suffering as other people are, but, as Disraeli sees, they are willing to suffer because they see in every breakdown of Gentile society a new opportunity for the Jewish power to dig nearer the central seat of power.

Just how the Jew works to break down the established order of things, by means of ideas, as the Protocols claim, is shown in this same conversation of Sidonia:

"The Tories lose an important election at a critical moment; 'tis the Jews come forward to vote against them. The Church is alarmed at the scheme of a latitudinarian university, and learns with relief that funds are not forthcoming for its establishment; a Jew immediately advances and endows it."

If these words had been written by a non-Jew, the cry of anti-Semitism would ring through the land. They are true, neither more nor less true, because written by a Jew. And Sidonia adds:

"And every generation they must become more powerful and more dangerous to the society that is hostile to them." (These quotations from page 249.) Well, several generations have passed since these words were written. The Jew still regards every form of non-Jewish society as hostile to him. He organizes strongly against society. And, if Disraeli is to be taken as a prophet, his words remain—"they must become more powerful and more dangerous." They have become more powerful. Whoso would measure the danger, look around.

Let the charming Sidonia proceed with his revelations:

"I told you just now that I was going up to town tomorrow, because I always made it a rule to interpose when affairs of state were on the carpet. Otherwise I never interfere. I hear of peace and war in newspapers, but I am never alarmed, except when I am informed that the Sovereigns want treasure; then I know that monarchs are serious."

It will be remembered that Sidonia held no governmental position. The time had not come for that. Power was exercised behind the scenes long before the craving for the spotlight was gratified. But whether there be Jews in office or not, the power they exercise behind the scenes is always greater than the power they show in the open. It can be seen, therefore, that the more numerous they are in office, the greater their secret power. Sidonia continues:

"A few years back we were applied to by Russia. Now there has been no friendship between the Court of St. Petersburg and my family. It has Dutch connections which have generally supplied it; and our representations in favor of the Polish Hebrew, a numerous race, but the most suffering and degraded of all the tribes, have not been very agreeable to the Czar. However, circumstances drew to an approximation between the Romanoffs and the Sidonias. I resolved to go myself to St. Petersburg. I had, on my arrival, an interview with the Russian Minister of Finance, Count Cancrin; I beheld the son of a Lithuanian Jew.

"The loan was connected with the affairs of Spain; I resolved on repairing to Spain from Russia. I traveled without intermission. I had an audience immediately on my arrival with the Spanish Minister, Senor Mendizabel; I beheld one like myself, the son of a Nuevo Christiano, a Jew of Aragon.

"In consequence of what transpired at Madrid, I went straight to Paris to consult the President of the French Council; I beheld the son of a French Jew, a hero, an imperial marshal..."

If Sidonia were traveling today he would find whole groups of Jews, where, in his day, he found one, and he would find them in exalted places. Suppose Disraeli were alive today and should revise "*Coningsby*,"

Disraeli—British Premier, Portrays the Jews

including the United States in the tour of this money master of the world! What a host of Jewish names he could gather from official circles in Washington and New York—such a host, indeed, as makes the occasional Gentile look like a foreigner who had been graciously permitted to come in by the Jews!

"The consequence of our consultations was, that some northern power should be applied to in a friendly and mediative capacity. We fixed on Prussia; and the President of the Council made an application to the Prussian Minister, who attended a few days after our conference. Count Arnim entered the cabinet, and I beheld a Prussian Jew."

Sidonia's comment upon all this is offered as an address to every reader of this article:

"So, you see, my dear Coningsby, that the world is governed by very different personages from what is imagined by those who are not behind the scenes." (pp. 251-252.)

It is indeed! Why not let the world see behind the scenes for a little?

And now for the most illuminating lines Disraeli ever wrote lines which half compel the thought that maybe, after all, he was writing to warn the world of Jewish ambition for power:

"You never observe a great intellectual movement in Europe in which the Jews do not greatly participate. The first Jesuits were Jews. That mysterious Russian Diplomacy which so alarms Western Europe is organized and principally carried on by Jews. That mighty revolution which is at the moment preparing in Germany, and which will be, in fact, a second and greater Reformation, and of which so little is yet known in England, is entirely developing under the auspices of Jews." (p. 250.)

American Jews say that the Protocols are inventions. Is Benjamin Disraeli an invention? Was this Jewish Prime Minister of Great Britain misrepresenting his people? Are not his portrayals taken as true history? And what does he say?

He shows that in Russia, the very country where the Jews complained they were least free, the Jews were in control.

He shows that the Jews know the technique of revolution, foretelling in his book the revolution that later broke out in Germany. How did he foreknow it? Because that revolution was developing under the auspices of Jews, and, though it was then true that "so little is yet known in England," Disraeli the Jew knew it, and knew it to be Jewish in origin and development and purpose.

One point is sure: Disraeli told the truth. He presented his people before the world with correctness. He described Jewish power, Jewish purpose and Jewish method with a certainty of touch that betokens more than knowledge—he shows racial sympathy and understanding. He sets forth the facts which this series is setting forth. Why did he do it? Was it boastfulness, that dangerous spirit in which the Jew gives up most of his secrets? Or was it conscience, impelling him to tell the world of Judah's designs?

No matter; he told the truth. He is one man who told the truth without being accused of "misrepresenting" the Jews.

The Dearborn Independent, December 18, 1920

38. Taft Once Tried to Resist Jews—and Failed

William Howard Taft is an amiable gentleman. There is so much to agree with in the world that he seldom finds it possible to disagree with anything. It is a very comfortable attitude for one to assume, but it doesn't push the world along. Real harmony is wrung out of discord by laboring against disagreeable facts; it is not achieved by mere pit-pats on the back of untoward conditions.

There is no doubt that had one approached William Howard Taft a year ago and said: "Mr. Taft you know there are evil forces in the world which ought to be resisted," he would have replied, "Certainly, by all means."

If one had said, "Mr. Taft, some of this evil is just ignorant inclination, which can be dealt with by various means of enlightenment, but some of it represents a deliberate philosophy which has gathered about itself a definite organization for action," he would have responded: "I am afraid it is true."

And then had one said: "Mr. Taft, the people should be made aware of this, given a key to it, that they may keep their eyes open and learn the meaning of certain tendencies that have puzzled them," he would in all likelihood have replied, "I believe in enlightening the public mind that it may take care of itself."

Suppose you had added: "Mr. Taft, if you found a written program setting forth the steps to be taken to fasten a certain control on society, and if on looking about you observed a definite set of tendencies which seemed to parallel the program at every point, would it appear to you significant?"

Mr. Taft would, of course, answer, Yes. There is no other answer to make. No other answer has been made by anyone who has compared the two things. If Mr. Taft had been approached first on that side of the question, he would have uttered words very valuable to those who would attach value to his words.

But what has Mr. Taft's "testimonial" to do with either side of the case? Does his support strengthen it, or does his opposition weaken it? If it came to a battle of names, *The Dearborn Independent* could present a very imposing list of men who acknowledge the importance of the studies being made, and who agree with most of the observations presented. But such a list would add nothing to the facts in the case, and facts must stand on their own foundation regardless of the attitude of Mr. Taft, or even Mr. Arthur Brisbane.

But there is a very interesting story about Mr. Taft and the Jews. Mr. Taft knows it and can verify it. A number of American Jews also know it. And it may perhaps be useful to tell it now.

However, that we may not seem too desirous of evading Mr. Taft's latest defense of the Jews, we shall begin with that.

Unduly stirred by this series of studies, the leading Jews of the United States indicated by their perturbation that the truth in these articles made it impossible to ignore them. Perhaps as many people have been inclined toward agreement with the articles by the attitude of the Jews themselves as by the statements made in the articles. Jewish defense has been made with great formality and show of authority, but without the hoped-for effect. The Jews of the United States, evidently finding that their own statements have failed to carry, are making a wholesale conscription of Gentiles for the purposes of defense. As in Russia, the Gentiles are being pushed into the firing lines.

Mr. Taft was therefore approached with a proposition. That was some time ago, probably about November first.

Now, according to Mr. Taft's own signed statement made on November 1, he had not even read *The Dearborn Independent's* articles but was taking the Jews' word for their character and contents. And yet, on December 23, we find Mr. Taft in Chicago at the La Salle Hotel, delivering an oration before the B'nai B'rith, uttering his statements with all the finality of a man who has made a deep study of the Jewish Question and had at last attained a mature conclusion.

On November 1, Mr. Taft wrote to a New York Jew deprecating these articles as "a foolish pronouncement which I understand has been issued through *The Dearborn Independent.*"

The expression, "which I understand," is equivalent in ordinary speech to "which I have heard." He had not read them. He was taking hearsay on which to base his opinion. There are signs that he had not read them even at the time of his speech in Chicago, for he did not so much as allude to one of the startling parallels which have weighed on the minds of many important men in this country. The Jews wanted Mr. Taft's name, they wanted "a Gentile front," and they got it. The speech contributes nothing to the discussion; it proves nothing, it disproves nothing. In parts it is a rehash of a speech delivered by a New York rabbi. Indeed, one of William Howard Taft's most telling points was the almost verbal repetition of a point made by that rabbi.

Mr. Taft's business now is the delivery of addresses. Between November 1, at which time he had not read the Jewish Question at all, until December 23, when he presumed to pronounce judgment on it for all time, he had been away a great deal on the road. Indeed, he reached Chicago without having done any of his Christmas shopping. He explained that he had "been traveling over the country so fast" that his time had all been taken up. When he found time to study the Jewish Question does not appear. It is most probable that he had no time and did no studying. If he did, he carefully concealed the fruits of it when delivering his address.

Before his address was delivered, the newspapers had announced that it was to be made against "anti-Semitism," and this series of articles was specified. It was apparently foreknown, therefore, that not a judicial pronouncement was to be expected from Mr. Taft, but a partisan plea. The newspapers indicate that Mr. Taft had not even dictated his speech until he reached Chicago. The material he had at hand during his dictation was the printed propaganda with which the Jews have been flooding the country. Taft's speech reeks with it. There isn't an original idea in it. He was the human megaphone whom the Jews retained for one night through whom to voice their words. The real purpose of the speech was, of course, to secure its publication throughout the country as the voice of the people on the Question. But nothing whatever excuses the fact that the speech contains absolutely no contribution to the Question.

Mr. Taft is against religious prejudice. So is everybody else. Mr. Taft is against racial prejudice. So is everybody else. Mr. Taft wants concord and good will. So does everybody else. But what have these to do with the facts which comprise the Jewish Question?

The real story of Mr. Taft and the Jews begins back in the time when Mr. Taft lived in the White House. The Jews maintain a lobby in Washington whose business it is to know every President and every prospective President, and, of course, Mr. Taft was known to them a long while before he was made President, but whether they did not foresee his political future or whether they considered his opinions as having too little force for them to bother about, is not clear, but the fact seems to be that very little fuss was made about him. There are no indications that he ran after the Jews or the Jews after him in the days before his presidency.

As President, Mr. Taft once stood out against the Jews, was strongly denounced as unfavorable to the Jews, was soundly beaten by the Jews in a matter on which he had taken a firm stand, and has ever since shown that he has learned his lesson by accommodating the Jews in their desires.

The story involves a portion of that voluminous history which consists of the quarrels between the United States and other nations on account of the Jews. Readers interested in this phase of the history of the United States can find it fully set out by Jewish writers. There seems to be a certain pride taken in recounting the number of times the nations have been compelled to give diplomatic recognition to the Jewish Question. From 1840 until 1911, the United States had special diplomatic trouble concerning the Jews. The trouble that culminated during 1911, in an unparalleled act by the United States, involved William Howard Taft, who then was President.

For centuries, Russia has had her own troubles with the Jews and, as the world knows, has at last fallen prostrate before the Jewish power which for centuries has been working to undermine her. Even Disraeli was not blinded to the fact that Jews had a control over Russia which the rest of the world never knew. The biggest hoax in modern times was the propaganda against Russia as the persecutor of the Jews. Russia devoted to the Jews a large part of the most favored section of the land, and was always so lax in those laws which prohibited Jews from settling in other parts of the country that the Jew was able to create an underground system throughout the whole of Russia which controlled the grain trade, controlled public opinion and utterly baffled the czar's government. The cry of "persecution" arose because the Jews were not permitted to exploit the peasants as much as they desired. They have, however, gained that privilege since.

Now, when the United States appeared as "the new Jerusalem," its Jewish citizens conceived the idea of using the American Government to achieve for the Jews what other means had failed to achieve. Russian and German Jews would come to the United States, become naturalized as quickly as possible, and go back to Russia as "Americans" to engage in trade. Russia knew them as Jews and held them to be subject to the laws relating to Jews.

Protest after protest reached the State Department as more and more German or Russian Jews went back to Russia to circumvent the Russian laws. At first the matter was not serious, because it was shown in many cases that these naturalized "Americans" did not intend to return to the United States at all, but had acquired "American citizenship" solely as a business asset in Russia. In these cases, of course, the United States did not feel obligated to bestir herself.

The time came, however, when American ministers to Russia were requested to look into the situation. Their reports are accessible. John W. Foster was one of these ministers and he reported in 1880 that "Russia would be glad to give liberal treatment to bona fide American citizens, not disguised German Jews."

During all this time the "Russian Question" was being sedulously propagated in the United States. It appeared first in the aspect of the "Russian persecutions." The Jews represented that their life in Russia was a hell. John W. Foster, later Secretary of State, father-in-law of Robert Lansing, the recently resigned Secretary of State under President Wilson, was at that time representing the United States in Russia, and he reported as follows on the status of the Russian Jews:

". . . in all the cities of Russia the number of Jewish residents will be found more or less in excess of the police registry and greater than the strict interpretation of the law authorizes. For instance, persons who have given the subject close attention estimate the number of Jewish residents in St. Petersburg at 30,000, while it is stated the number registered by the police authorities is 1,500. From the same source I learn that . . . while only one Hebrew school is registered by the police, there are between three and four thousand children in unauthorized Jewish schools of this capital. As another indication of the extent of Jewish influence, it is worthy of note that one or more Jewish editors or writers are said to be employed on the leading newspapers of St. Petersburg and Moscow almost without exception . . . "

At every turn the United States Government discovered that the Jews were exaggerating their difficulties for the purpose of forcing government action.

Presently, after years of underground work and open propaganda against Russia in the daily press, until the American conception of Russia was fixed almost beyond correction, the agitation took the form of the "Russian passport question." Russia dares to flout an American passport! Russia insults the government of the United States! Russia degrades American citizens! And so forth and so on. Jews in the United States demanded nothing less than that the United States break all treaty relations with Russia. They demanded it! James G. Blaine desired one thing more than another, which was this: that something, anything, be done to block the flood of Jewish immigration then beginning to flood the country. "The hospitality of a nation should not be turned into a burden," he wrote.

There was then the strange situation of the United States itself making complaints about the Jews and at the same time being asked to question Russia's right to handle similar complaints in her own domain. The minister of foreign affairs for Russia appreciated this point, and when the American minister told him that 200,000 Jews had emigrated to the United States from Russia, he rejoined: "If such a number of people had gone to the United States as workers to aid in developing the country he supposed they would be acceptable, but if they went to exploit the American people, he could understand how objectionable it was." Of course, the whole point with Russia was that the Jews were exploiting her. They were milking Russia, not feeding her.

If space permitted, much rich material could be presented here. The attitude of the American statesmen of 25 to 40 years ago, on questions of immigration and racial propaganda, was eminently wise and sound.

So, until the days of William Howard Taft, this Jewish propaganda continued, always aimed at Russia, always planning to use the United States as the club with which to strike the blow.

It must be borne in mind at all times that the Jews maintain a lobby at Washington, a sort of embassy from the Jewish Nation to the Government of the United States, and this lobby is in the hands of a principal "ambassador." It was, of course, this ambassador's business to get hold of President Taft as firmly as possible.

But President Taft was not at that time so "easy" as the people have since been taught to regard him. There was a commercial treaty between Russia and the United States, and it had existed since 1832, and President Taft behaved as if he thought the Jewish demand that the treaty be broken was rather too much. The Jewish demand was that the United States denounce a treaty which had existed between the two countries for almost 80 years, and during the life of which Russia had repeatedly proved herself to be a reliable friend of this country.

The Jews wanted just two things from William Howard Taft: the abrogation of the Russian treaty and the veto of what Congress had

Taft Once Tried to Resist Jews—and Failed

repeatedly tried to do, namely, put a literacy test on immigrants. Jewish immigration into the United States being so important an element of Jewish plans, American Jews never cared what kind of human riffraff filled the country as long as the Jewish flood was not hindered.

Presently, President Taft had undergone the persistent nagging characteristic of such campaigns and had asked, perhaps impatiently, what they wanted him to do.

"Have a conference with some of the leaders of American Jewry" was the proposal made to him, and on February 15, 1911, there walked into the White House, Jacob H. Schiff, Jacob Furth, Louis Marshall, Adolph Kraus and Judge Henry M. Goldfogle. They had lunch with the President's family and adjourned to the library.

The President was fairly wise in the matter. There was no chance whatever for him in an argument. His guests had come prepared to talk, to "tell" him, as some of the same men lately "told" an eastern publisher, pounding the table and uttering threats. The President was to be overwhelmed, his good nature carried with a rush.

But, instead of anything like that, the President, as soon as they gathered in the library, took out a paper and began to read his conclusions! That staggered the Jewish ambassadors at once—the President was reading his conclusions! He was "telling" them!

The President's statement is really worth reading, but it is far too lengthy to present here. He called attention to the right which this country exercised to say who shall, and who shall not sojourn here, and also to the conflicting interpretations which American secretaries of State had given the Russian treaty. He contrasted with that Russia's consistent interpretation from the beginning.

He then said that the treaty was sacred because under it for more than 50 years the citizens of the United States had made their investments in Russia—resting solely on their faith in the United States' and Russia's treaty honor. He said that if it were a new treaty that was being written, the case would be different; he would then consider the Jewish argument of weight.

But he said, we had other treaties with other countries who did not always share our views as to what certain sections of the treaties meant, but we have lived and worked under them. He instanced the Italian treaty with regard to the extradition of criminals. He wished to impress on the Jewish ambassadors that they wanted to make an exception of their case, which, of course, they did.

The President then said he would be willing to consider taking some action if he did not believe that in taking action he would be endangering the status the Jews already enjoyed in Russia. If this treaty were denounced, large American interests would be jeopardized (here the President mentioned certain interests, all Gentile).

He said he liked to see Russian Jews come into the country, but added "the more we spread them out in the West, the better I like it." He ended with a plea for the Jewish ambassadors there present to consider the plight which denunciation of the treaty might involve Russian Jews, and ended with the words—"That is the way it has struck me, gentlemen. That is the conclusion I have reached."

The Jewish group was plainly taken aback. Simon Wolf, who was always on guard at Washington, said, "Please, Mr. President, do not give to the Press such conclusions," but Jacob Schiff broke in with a voice vibrant with anger—"I want it published. I want the whole world to know the President's attitude."

The discussion then opened, with the President cool and self-contained. Finally, after some useless talk, and having other business to attend to, he gave them a letter just received from the American Ambassador at St. Petersburg, Mr. Rockhill. Mr. Rockhill presented in that letter to the President the whole Russian contention about the Jews statements which have been confirmed a thousand times by the events that have since occurred.

They then renewed their expostulations and arguments, but to no avail. The President expressed regret, but said he could see no other course to pursue; he had studied the question in all its lights, and his conclusion was as stated. On leaving the White House, Jacob Schiff refused to shake the President's hand, but brushed it by with an air of offended power. "Wasn't Mr. Schiff angry yesterday!" exclaimed the President the next day.

But the President did not know what was going on. When Jacob Schiff was descending the White House steps he said, "This means war." He gave orders to draw on him for a large sum of money. He wrote a curt letter to President Taft. The President sent Mr. Schiff's letter and the reply to the Secretary of Commerce and Labor, Charles Nagel, who replied to the President with these words: "I am very much impressed with the patience which you exhibit in your answer."

Neither did the President know what was behind it all. Look at most of the names of the men who represented American Jewry in

Taft Once Tried to Resist Jews—and Failed

the White House that 15th of February, 1911. And then consider that the abrogation of the Russian treaty would throw all the vast business between the United States and Russia into Germany, into the hands of German Jews. The Frankfort bankers and their relatives in the United States knew what that meant. It meant that German Jews would be the intermediaries of trade between Russia and the United States. The business itself meant money, but the relation meant power over Russia—and Jacob H. Schiff lived to overthrow Russia. The neutrality of the United States was torn to shreds by a movement organized and financed on American soil for the overthrow of a friendly nation, and the organizers and financiers were Jews! They used their internal power to deflect the policy of the United States to assist their plans.

The game was financial and revolutionary. It was decreed. It was then part of the program to be accomplished, and the United States was to be used as the crowbar to batter down the walls.

When the Jewish ambassadors left the White House, orders flew from Washington and New York to every part of the United States, and the Jewish "nagging" drive began. It had a center in every city. It was focused on every Representative and Senator—no official, however, was too mean or unimportant to be drafted.

American editors may remember that drive; it was operated on precisely the same lines as the one which is proceeding against the press today. The Jews have furnished absolute proof in the last two months that they control the majority of the American press. There are signs, however, that their control does not mean anything, and will not last long.

Jacob Schiff had said on February 15, "This means war."

He had ordered a large sum of money used for that purpose. The American Jewish Committee, B'nai B'rith and others of the numerous organizations of Jewry (how well organized they are the signatories of the recent Jewish defense prove) went to work and on December 13 of the same year almost 10 months to a day after Jewry had declared war on President Taft's conclusions—both houses of Congress ordered President Taft to notify Russia that the treaty with Russia would be terminated.

Frankfort-on-the-Main had won!

In the meantime, of course, the Jewish press of the United States berated President Taft with characteristic Jewish unreserve. It would be an eye-opener if, at every speech which William Howard Taft makes for his Jewish clients, there could be distributed copies of the remarks printed about President Taft by those same clients nine years ago.

The methods by which the Jews set forth to force congressional action are all known, and the glee with which Jewry hailed the event is also known. Two governments had been beaten—the American and the Russian! And the American President had been reversed!

Whether this had anything to do with the fact that William Howard Taft became that unusual figure—a one-term President—this chronicle does not undertake to say.

There was quite a scurry for cover at that time. Taft had been beaten, and all the men who had stood beside him ran in out of the storm. John Hays Hammond was represented as having been sympathetic with the Russian view of the Jews—as most of the American representatives were. As late as 1917, William Howard Taft, then a private citizen, wrote to the principal Jewish lobbyist at Washington asking that Mr. Hammond be not held up in Jewish histories as one who had opposed the breaking of the Russian treaty.

The President had really done what he could to prevent the Jewish plan going through. On February 15, 1911, he withstood them face to face. On December 13, 1911, they had whipped him.

And yet in the next year, 1912, a peculiar thing occurred; the high officials of the B'nai B'rith went to the White House and there pinned on the breast of President Taft a medal which marked him as "the man who had contributed most during the year to the welfare of the Jewish cause."

There is a photograph extant of President Taft standing on the south portico of the White House, in the midst of a group of prominent Jews, and the President is wearing his medal. He is not smiling.

But even after that, the Jews were not sure of President Taft. There was a fear, expressed by private letters between prominent Jews, and also in the Jewish press, that President Taft, while officially abrogating the treaty, would consent to some working agreement which would amount to about the same thing. There were cables from Jews in Russia, stating that Taft would do that. The President was closely watched. Whenever there was an open chink in his daily program, he was approached on the matter. It was made utterly impossible for him to do anything to patch up the differences. Frankfort was to have the handling of American trade with Russia, and Jewry was to have that club over Russia. Money, more and more money, always accompanies every Jewish plan for racial or political power. They make the world pay them for subjugating it. And their first cinch-hold on Russia they won in the United States. The end of that American influence was the rise of Bolshevism, the destruction of Russia, and the murder of Nicholas Romanoff and his family.

That is the story of William Howard Taft's efforts to withstand the Jews, and how they broke him. It is probably worth knowing in view of the fact that he has become one of those "Gentile fronts" which the Jews use for their own defense.

The Dearborn Independent, January 15, 1921

39. When Editors Were Independent of the Jews

The first instinctive answer which the Jew makes to any criticism of his race coming from a non-Jew is that of violence, threatened or inflicted. This statement will be confirmed by hundreds of thousands of citizens of the United States who have heard the evidence with their own ears. Of recent months the country has been full of threats against persons who have taken cognizance of the Jewish Question, threats which have been spoken, whispered, written and passed as resolutions by Jewish organizations.

If the candid investigator of the Jewish Question happens to be in business, then "boycott" is the first "answer" of which the Jews seem to think. Whether it be a newspaper, as in the case of the old New York Herald; or a mercantile establishment, as in the case of A. T. Stewart's famous store; or a hotel, as in the case of the old Grand Union Hotel at Saratoga; or a dramatic production, as in the case of "The Merchant of Venice"; or any manufactured article whose maker has adopted the policy that "my goods are for sale, but not my principles"—if there is any manner of business connection with the student of the Jewish Question, the first "answer" is "boycott."

The technique is this: a "whispering drive" is first begun. Disquieting rumors begin to fly thick and fast. "Watch us get him," is the word that is passed along. Jews in charge of ticker news services adopt the slogan of "a rumor a day." Jews in charge of local newspapers adopt the policy of "a slurring headline a day." Jews in charge of the newsboys on the streets (all the street corners and desirable places downtown are pre-empted by Jewish "padrones" who permit only their own boys to sell) give orders to emphasize certain news in the street cries—"a new yell against him every day." The whole campaign against the critic of Jewry, whoever he may be, is keyed to the threat, "Watch us get him."

Just as Mr. Gompers and Justice Brandeis believe in "the secondary strike," as a recent Supreme Court decision reveals, so the Jews who set out to punish the students of the Jewish Question believe in a secondary boycott. Not only do they pledge themselves (they deny this, but the newspaper reports assert it, as do unpublished telegraphic dispatches to

When Editors Were Independent of the Jews

some of the newspapers) not to use the specific product in question, but they pledge themselves to boycott anyone else who uses it. If the article is a hat (it is unlikely to be a hat, however, hats being largely Jewish) not only do the Jews pledge themselves to refrain from buying that kind of hat, but also to refrain from doing business with anyone who wears such a hat.

And then, when anything seems to occur at the hat works which indicates slackness, the Jews, forgetting all about their denial of a pledged boycott, begin to boast—"See what we did to him?"

The "whispering drive," "the boycott," these are the chief Jewish answers. They constitute the bone and sinew of that state of mind in non-Jews which is known as "the fear of the Jews."

They do not always notify their victim. Recently the young sales manager of a large wholesale firm spoke at a dinner whose guests were mostly the firm's customers. He is one of those young men who have caught the vision of a new honor in business. He believes that the right thing is always practicable, and, other things being equal, profitable as well. Among the guests were probably 40 Jewish merchants, all customers of the firm. In his address the young sales agent expressed his enthusiasm for morality by saying, "What we need in business is more of the principles of Jesus Christ."

Now, as a matter of fact, the young man knows very little about Jesus Christ. He has caught fire from the Roger Babson idea of religious principle as a basis of business, but he expressed it in his own way, and everybody knew what he meant; he meant decency, not sectarianism. Yet, because he used the expression he did, he lost 40 Jewish customers for his firm, and he doesn't yet know the reason why. The agents of the firm which got the new trade know the reason. It was a silent, unannounced boycott.

This article is the story of a boycott which lasted over a number of years. It is only one of numerous stories of the same kind which can be told of New York. It concerns the New York Herald, one newspaper that dared to remain independent of Jewish influence in the metropolis.

The Herald enjoyed an existence of 90 years, which was terminated about a year ago by an amalgamation. It performed great feats in the world of news-gathering. It sent Henry M. Stanley to Africa to find Livingstone. It backed up the Jeannette expedition to the Arctic regions. It was largely instrumental in having the first Atlantic cables laid. But perhaps its greatest feat was the maintenance during many years of its journalistic independence against the combined attack of New York Jewry. Its reputation among newspapermen was that neither its news nor its editorial columns could be bought or influenced.

Its proprietor, the late James Gordon Bennett had always maintained a friendly attitude toward the Jews of his city. He apparently harbored no prejudice against them. Certainly he never deliberately antagonized them. But he was resolved upon preserving the honor of independent journalism. He never bent to the policy that the advertisers had something to say about the editorial policy of the paper, either as to influencing it for publication or suppression.

Thirty years ago the New York press was free. Today it is practically all Jewish controlled. This control is variously exercised, sometimes resting only on the owners' sense of expediency. But the control is there and, for the moment, it is absolute. One does not have to go far to be able to find the controlling factor in any case. Newspapermen do not glory in the fact, however; it is a condition, not a crusade, that confronts them, and for the moment "business is business."

Thirty years ago there were also more newspapers in New York than there are today. There were eight or nine morning newspapers; there are only five today. The *Herald*, a three-cent newspaper, enjoyed the highest prestige, and was the most desirable advertising medium due to the class of its circulation. It easily led the journalistic field.

At that time the Jewish population of New York was less than one-third of what it is today, but there was much wealth represented in it.

Now, what every newspaperman knows is this: most Jewish leaders are always interested either in getting a story published or getting it suppressed. There is no class of people who read the public press so carefully, with an eye to their own affairs, as do the Jews; and many an editor can vouch for that.

The *Herald* simply adopted the policy from the beginning of this form of harassment that it was not to be permitted to sway the *Herald* from its duty as a public informant. And that this had a reflex advantage for the other newspapers is apparent from the following statement:

If a scandal occurred in Jewish circles, influential Jews would swarm into the editorial offices to arrange for a suppression of the story. But the editors knew that not far away was the *Herald* which would not suppress for anything or anybody. What was the use of one paper suppressing, if another would not? So the editors would say, "We would be very glad to suppress this story, but the *Herald* is going to use it, so we'll have to

When Editors Were Independent of the Jews

do the same in self-protection. However, if you can get the *Herald* to suppress it, we will gladly do so, too."

But the *Herald* never succumbed. Neither pressure of influence nor promises of business nor threats of loss availed: it printed the news.

There was a certain Jewish banker who periodically demanded that Bennett discharge the *Herald's* financial editor. This banker was in the business of disposing of Mexican bonds at a time when such bonds were least secure. Once when an unusually large number of bonds were to be unloaded on unsuspecting Americans, the *Herald* published the story of an impending Mexican revolution, which presently ensued. The banker frothed at the mouth and moved every influence he could to change the *Herald's* financial staff, but was not able to effect the change even of an office boy.

Once when a shocking scandal involved a member of a prominent family, Bennett refused to suppress it, arguing that if the episode had occurred in a family of any other race it would be published regardless of the prominence of the figures involved. The Jews of Philadelphia secured suppression there, but because of Bennett's unflinching stand there was no suppression in New York.

A newspaper is a business proposition. There are some matters it cannot touch without putting itself in peril of becoming a defunct concern. This is especially true since newspapers no longer receive their support from the public but from the advertisers. The money the reader gives for the paper scarcely suffices to pay for the amount of white paper he receives. In this way, advertisers cannot be disregarded any more than the paper mills can be. And as the most extensive advertisers are the department stores, and as most department stores are owned by Jews, it comes logically that Jews often try to influence the news policies at least, of the papers with whom they deal.

In New York it has always been the burning ambition of the Jews to elect a Jewish mayor. They selected a time when the leading parties were disrupted to push forward their choice. The method which they adopted was characteristic.

They reasoned that the newspapers would not dare refuse the dictum of the combined department store owners, so they drew up a "strictly confidential" letter, which they sent to the owners of the New York newspapers, demanding support for the Jewish mayoralty candidate.

The newspaper owners were in a quandary. For several days they debated how to act. All remained silent. The editors of the *Herald* cabled the news to Bennett who was abroad. Then it was that Bennett exhibited that boldness and directness of judgment which characterized him. He cabled back, "Print the letter." It was printed in the *Herald's* editorial columns, the arrogance of the Jewish advertisers was exposed, and non-Jewish New York breathed easier and applauded the action.

The *Herald* explained frankly that it could not support a candidate of private interests, because it was devoted to the interests of the public. But the Jewish leaders vowed vengeance against the *Herald* and against the man who dared expose their game. They had not liked Bennett for along time, anyway. The *Herald* was the real "society newspaper" in New York, but Bennett had a rule that only the names of really prominent families should be printed. The stories of the efforts of newly rich Jews to break into the *Herald's* society columns are some of the best that are told by old newspapermen. But Bennett was obdurate. His policy stood.

Bennett, however, was shrewd enough not to invite open conflict with the Jews. He felt no prejudice against the race; he simply resented their efforts to intimidate him.

The whole matter culminated in a contention which began between Bennett and Nathan Straus, a German Jew whose business house is known under the name of "R. H. Macy & Company," Macy being the Scotchman who built up the business and from whose heirs Straus obtained it. Mr. Straus was something of a philanthropist in the ghetto, but the story goes that Bennett's failure to proclaim him as a philanthropist led to ill feeling between the two. A long newspaper war ensured, the subject of which was the value of the pasteurization of milk—a stupid discussion which no one took seriously, save Bennett and Straus.

The Jews, of course, took Mr. Straus' side. Jewish speakers made the welkin ring with laudation of Nathan Straus and maledictions upon James Gordon Bennett. Bennett was pictured in the most vile business of "persecuting" a noble Jew. It went so far that the Jews were able to put resolutions through the board of aldermen.

Long since, of course, Straus, a very heavy advertiser had withdrawn every dollar's worth of his business from the *Herald* and the *Evening Telegram*. And now the combined powerful elements of New York Jewry gathered together to deal a staggering blow at Bennett—as years before they had dealt a blow to another citizen of New York.

The Jewish policy of "Dominate or Destroy" was at stake, and Jewry declared war.

As one man, the Jewish advertisers withdrew their advertisements from Mr. Bennett's newspapers. Their assigned reason was that the *Herald* was showing animosity against the Jews. The real purpose of their action was to crush an American newspaper owner who dared be independent of them.

The blow they delivered was a staggering one. It meant the loss of $600,000 a year. Any other newspaper in New York would have been put out of business by it. The Jews knew that and sat back, waiting the downfall of the man they chose to consider their enemy.

But Bennett was ever a fighter. Besides he knew Jewish psychology probably better than any other non-Jew in New York. He turned the tables on his opponents in a startling and unexpected fashion. The coveted positions in his papers had always been used by the Jews. These he immediately turned over to non-Jewish merchants under exclusive contracts.

Merchants who had formerly been crowded into the back pages and obscure corners by the more opulent Jewish advertisers, now blossomed forth full page in the most popular spaces. One of the non-Jewish merchants who took advantage of the new situation was John Wanamaker, whose large advertisements from that time forward were conspicuous in the Bennett newspapers.

The Bennett papers came out with undiminished circulation and full advertising pages. The well-planned catastrophe did not occur. Instead, there was a rather comical surprise. Here were the non-Jewish merchants of New York enjoying the choicest service of a valuable advertising medium, while the Jewish merchants were unrepresented. Besides, the "punishment" that the Jews had administered showed no signs of inflicting inconvenience, let alone pain. The "boycott" had been hardest on the boycotters.

Unable to stand the spectacle of trade being diverted to non-Jewish merchants, the Jews dropped their hostile attitude and came back to Bennett, requesting the use of his columns for advertising. Bennett received all who came, displaying no rancor. They wanted back their old positions, but Bennett said, No. They argued, but Bennett said, No. They offered money, but Bennett said, No. The choice positions had been forfeited.

Then a curious circumstance transpired. A few Jews whose business sense had overcome their racial passions had continued to advertise in the Herald all through the "boycott." When they saw their rebellious brethren coming back and taking what positions they could get in the advertising pages, they suspected that Bennett had lured them back by offering a lower rate. So the wrote to Bennett, demanding to know the circumstances, and as usual Bennett published the letter and replied that his rates had not been lowered.

Bennett had triumphed, but it proved a costly victory. The Jews persistently followed the plan which they had inaugurated as early as 1877, for the ruin of another New Yorker who had refused to bow before them. All the time Bennett was fighting them, the Jews were gradually growing more powerful in New York. They were growing more powerful in journalism every year. They were obsessed by the fatuous idea that to control journalism in New York meant to control the thought of the country. They regarded New York as the metropolis of the United States, whereas all balanced minds regard it as a disease.

The number of newspapers gradually diminished through combinations of publications. Adolph S. Ochs, a Philadelphia Jew, acquired the *Times*. He soon made it into a great newspaper, but one whose bias is to serve the Jews. A tabulation of the Jewish publicity that finds its way into the *Times* reveals interesting figures. Of course, it is the quality of the *Times* as a newspaper that makes it so weighty as a Jewish organ. In this paper the Jews are persistently lauded and eulogized and defended. No such tenderness is granted other races. It is quite possible that the staff of the Times will not regard this as entirely true. Personally and individually, the majority of them are "not that kind of people." But there is the *Times* itself as evidence.

And then Hearst came into the field—a dangerous agitator because he not only agitates the wrong things, but because he agitates the wrong class of people. He surrounded himself with a coterie of Jews, pandered to them, worked hand in glove with them, even fell out with them, but never told the truth about them—"never gave them away." Naturally, he received large advertising patronage. The trend toward the Jewish-controlled press set in strongly, and has continued that way ever since. The old names, made great by great editors and American policies, slowly dimmed.

A newspaper is founded either on a great editorial mind, in which event it becomes the expression of a powerful personality, or it becomes institutionalized as to policy and becomes a commercial establishment. In the latter event, its chances for a continuing life beyond the lifetime of its founder are much stronger. The *Herald* was Bennett, and with his passing it was inevitable that a certain force and virtue should depart out of it.

Bennett, advancing in age, dreaded lest his newspaper, on his death, should fall into the hands of the Jews. He knew that they regarded it with longing eyes. He knew that they had pulled down, seized, and afterward built up many an agency that had dared speak the truth about them, and boasted about it as a conquest for Jewry; a vindication of the oft misquoted prophecy, "He that curses you I will curse."

Bennett loved the *Herald* as a man loves his child. He so arranged his will that the *Herald* should never fall into individual ownership. He devised that its revenues should flow into a fund for the benefit of the men who had worked to make the *Herald* what it was. He died in May, 1918.

The Jewish enemies of the *Herald*, eagerly watchful, more and more withdrew their advertising to force, if possible, the sale of the paper. They knew that if the *Herald* became a losing proposition, the trustees would have no course but to sell, notwithstanding Mr. Bennett's will.

But there were also strong moneyed interests in New York who were beginning to realize the peril of a Jewish press. These interests provided a large sum for the *Herald's* purchase by Frank A. Munsey. Then, to the general astonishment, Mr. Munsey discontinued the gallant old sheet and bestowed its name as part of the name of the *New York Sun*. But the actual newspaper managed by Bennett is extinct. Even the men who worked upon it are scattered abroad in the newspaper field.

Even though the Jews had not gained possession of the coveted Herald they had at least succeeded in driving another non-Jewish newspaper from the field. They set about obtaining control of several evening newspapers, which action is now complete.

But the victory was a financial victory over a dead man. The moral victory, as well as the financial victory, remained with Bennett as long as he lived; the moral victory still remains with the *Herald*. The *Herald* is immortalized as the last bulwark against Jewry in New York. Today the Jews are more completely masters of the journalistic field in New York than they are in any capital in Europe. Indeed, in every capital in Europe there is a newspaper that gives the real news of the Jews. There is none in New York. And thus the situation will remain until Americans shake themselves from their long sleep, and look with steady eyes at the national situation. That look will be enough to show them all, and their very eyes will quail the oriental usurpers.

The International Jew Volumes I and II

The moral is: whatever comes out of New York now must be doubly scrutinized, because it comes from the center of that Jewish government which desires to guide and color the thoughts of the people of the United States.

The Dearborn Independent, February 5, 1921

40. Why the Jews Dislike the Morgenthau Report

It seems a far cry from the Jewish Question in the United States to the same question in Poland, but inasmuch as the Jews of the United States are constantly referring to Poland for propaganda purposes, inasmuch as there are 250,000 Polish Jews arriving in the United States on a schedule made by their brethren here, and inasmuch as the people of Poland have had their own illuminating experience with the World Program, it would seem that Poland has something to teach the United States in this respect.

Especially is this true since it is impossible to pick up an American newspaper without finding traces of Jewish anti-Polish propaganda—a propaganda which is designed to take our eyes away from the thing that is transpiring at the Port of New York. If a reader of these articles should say, "Let us not think about Poland, let us think about the United States," the answer is that he is already thinking about Poland the way the Jews of the United States want him to think, and the fact that he is thinking according to Jewish wishes in this respect incapacitates him up to a certain point to understand the entire Jewish Question in this country.

Three chapters back in this series we presented part of a hearing before the United States Senate committee on the census question as it affected the Jew. The immigration question appeared as part of that inquiry. Then followed an article which showed that Jewish authorities adopt principles exactly opposite to those which had been defended before the United States Senators.

A third article followed showing how Jewish leaders resent the influence of the modern State upon Judaism. All these subjects are essential to a well-rounded understanding of the Jewish Question as a whole in its relation to the United States.

Today we go back to the home of that quarter of a million people who are rapidly being landed on our shores to see what they did there, and to find the basis for Jewish propaganda statements that these people are fleeing from "persecution."

We have five official witnesses whose observations have been printed under the seals of the United States and the British governments. The American document is a "Message from the President of the United States, transmitting pursuant to a State Resolution of October 28, 1919, a communication from the Secretary of State submitting a report by the Honorable Henry Morgenthau on the work of The Mission of the United States to Poland." It is Senate Document No. 177.

This document includes also a supplementary report signed by Brigadier-General Edgar Jadwin, United States Army. There is a certain mystery about this document. Though an edition was printed for public circulation, it soon became extremely rare. It seemed to disappear almost overnight. The copy from which this present examination is made was secured with the utmost difficulty. The head of that American Mission, which remained in Poland from July 13 to September 13, 1919, was Henry Morgenthau, an American Jew, who had been United States Minister to Turkey, a man of excellent public and private reputation.

It is commonly said that the Jews did not like his report, hence its scarcity. This much appears: The Jewish press has never made much of it; it is not cited in Jewish propaganda; it has not had the endorsement of American Jewry. The reason appears to be this—that it told the calm truth about the situation of the Jews in Poland and made very fair observations.

But it is indirectly that American Jews show the opinion which they hold of the Morgenthau report, and it comes about in this way: When the American Mission left Poland, the British Mission arrived, and remained until December. The chief member of the British Mission was an English Jew, Sir Stuart Samuel, whose brother Herbert is now High Commissioner of Palestine. He was accompanied by a British military officer, Captain P. Wright, who also submitted a supplementary report. The two reports were submitted with an introductory report by Sir H. Rumbold, British representative at Warsaw.

Now, of all five reports, the Morganthau, Samuel, Jadwin, Wright and Rumbold reports, the Jews of the United States have circulated only one—the Samuel report. It has been printed in full in newspapers at advertising rates; it has been circulated broadcast as an American Jewish Congress Bulletin. Any number of Samuel reports may be obtained, but none of the report which a member of the American diplomatic service made and which the President of the United States transmitted as a Message to the Senate.

Why the Jews Dislike the Morgenthau Report

Why? Because four reports examined the situation all around and reported it without bias, and if they were printed in the United States and spread broadcast before the people, it would throw an entirely different light on the Jewish propaganda in favor of Polish immigration in enormous numbers.

Even when the Jews of the United States published the Samuel report, they did not publish the Captain Wright report which accompanied it. In the American Jewish Congress Bulletin, the Wright report was condensed, mutilated, and shorn of its real meaning; while in the Maccabaean, the reports of Rumbold and Wright are treated without courtesy and the Samuel report published in full.

That the reader may form his own conclusions, the testimony of the five official witnesses (or six, if we count Homer H. Johnson, who signed the American report with General Jadwin) will be given on the principal points; the agreements and disagreements will therefore be noticeable.

1. ON THE GENERAL SUBJECT OF PERSECUTION.

SIR STUART SAMUEL says: "Poles generally are of a generous nature, and if the present incitements of the press were repressed by a strong official hand, Jews would be able to live, as they have done for the past 800 years, on good terms with their fellow citizens in Poland."

Note how easily Sir Stuart talks about repression of the press. The Polish press has at last obtained freedom of writing. It is exercising a privilege which the Jewish press of Poland always had. But now that it speaks freely of Jews, repress it with a strong hand, says Sir Stuart. He would not dare suggest that in England where the press also is finding its freedom. As to the Yiddish press in Poland, the reader will find some information in Israel Friedlaender's essay, "The Problem of Polish Jewry." Friedlaender was a Jew and his book was published by a Jewish house in Cincinnati. He says:

"The Yiddish press sprang up and became a powerful civilizing agency among the Jews of Poland. The extent of its influence may be gathered from the fact, which curiously enough is pointed out reproachfully by the Poles, that the leading Yiddish newspaper of Warsaw commanded but a few years ago a larger circulation than that of all the Polish newspapers combined."

HENRY MORGENTHAU says (par. 7)—"The soldiers had been inflamed by the charge that the Jews were Bolsheviks, while at Lemberg it was associated with the idea that the Jews were making common cause with the Ukrainians. These excesses were, therefore, political as well as anti-Semitic in character."

And again (par. 8)—"Just as the Jews would resent being condemned as a race for the action of a few of their co-religionists, so it would be correspondingly unfair to condemn the Polish nation as a whole for the violence committed by uncontrolled troops or local mobs. These excesses were apparently not premeditated, for if they had been part of a preconceived plan, the number of victims would have run into the thousands instead of amounting to about 280.

"It is believed that these excesses were the result of widespread anti-Semitic prejudice aggravated by the belief that the Jewish inhabitants were politically hostile to the Polish State."

SIR H. RUMBOLD says: "It is giving the Jews very little real assistance to single out, as is sometimes done, for reprobation and protest the country where they have perhaps suffered least."

CAPTAIN P. WRIGHT says: "It is an explanation often given of what may be called, according to the point of view, the idiosyncrasies or defects of the Jews, that they have been an oppressed and persecuted people.

"This is an idea so charitable and humane that I should like to think it, not only of the Jews, but of every other people. It has every merit as a theory, except that of being true. When one thinks of what happened to the other 'racial, religious and linguistic minorities' of Europe in modern times . . . the Jews appear not as the most persecuted but as the most favored people of Europe."

BRIGADIER GENERAL JADWIN states clearly that the "persecution" cry may be regarded as propaganda. He says:

"The disorders of November 21 to 23 in Lemberg became, like the excesses in Lithuania, a weapon of foreign anti-Polish propaganda. The press bureau of the Central Powers, in whose interest it lay to discredit the Polish Republic before the world, permitted the publication of articles . . . in which an eye-witness estimated the number of victims between 2,500 and 3,000, although the extreme number furnished by the local Jewish committee was 76." (p. 15.)

And again: "In common with all free governments of the world, Poland is faced with the danger of the political and international propaganda to which the war has given rise. The coloring, the invention, the suppression of news, the subornation of newspapers by many different methods, and the poisoning by secret influences of the instruments affecting

Why the Jews Dislike the Morgenthau Report

public opinion, in short, all the methods of malevolent propaganda are a menace from which Poland is a notable sufferer." (p. 17.)

Of course, all this propaganda has been Jewish. The methods described are typically Jewish.

Speaking about the number killed, Mr. Morgenthau estimates the total at 258; while Sir H. Rumbold says only 18 were killed "in Poland proper," the others having been killed in the disorders of the war zone. Sir Stuart Samuel estimates the total killed at 348.

2. ON THE GENERAL CAUSE OF JEWISH TROUBLE BEFORE THE WAR.

SIR STUART SAMUEL—"The Jews in Poland and Galicia number about 3,000,000 . . . Public opinion had been aroused against them by the institution of a virulent boycott. This boycott dates from shortly after the by-election for the Duma, which took place in Warsaw in 1912 . . . Business relations between Poland and Russia were very considerable in the past, and were generally in the hands of the Jews, not only in the handling of the goods exported, but also in their manufacture . . . Initiative in business matters is almost entirely the prerogative of the Jewish population . . . Nearly the whole of the estate agents who act for the Polish nobility are of the Jewish race . . . Attention must be paid to the fact that Jews form the middle class almost in its entirety. Above are the aristocracy and below are the peasants. Their relations with the peasants are not unsatisfactory. The young peasants cannot read the newspapers and are therefore but slightly contaminated by anti-Semitism until they enter the army. I was informed that it is not at all unusual for Polish peasants to avail themselves of the arbitrament of the Jewish rabbi's courts."

That shows the Jews to have occupied a very favorable position in Poland and is to be remembered in connection with the previous quotation from Sir Stuart in which he says that if the incitements of the press were repressed by a strong official hand, "the Jews would be able to live, as they have done for the past 800 years, on good terms with their fellow citizens in Poland."

Let us take the points made by Sir Stuart, and observe what the other witnesses say about them:

(a) Beginning with the point as to the Jews' monopoly of business in Poland:

SIR H. RUMBOLD—"Sir Stuart Samuel would appear to be mistaken in his appreciation of the part played by the Jews in the pre-war business relations between Poland and Russia and in the industry of the former country.

"Whereas it is true that goods exported from Poland were to a large extent handled by the Jews, only a small percentage of those goods were actually manufactured by them."

CAPTAIN P. WRIGHT—"In Poland until the last generation all business men were Jews: The Poles were peasants or landowners, and left commerce to the Jews; even now certainly much more than half, and perhaps as much as three-quarters, of business men are Jews."

"For both town and country I think it a true generalization to say that the East Jews are hardly ever producers, but nearly always middlemen."

"Economically, the Jews appear at the very outset as dealers, not as producers, nor even as artisans, and chiefly dealers in money; in course of time the whole business and commerce of Poland became theirs, and they did nothing else."

(b) With regard to the "estate agents" mentioned by Sir Stuart Samuel:

CAPTAIN P. WRIGHT—"Poland is an agricultural country, but the East Jews, unlike the West Jews, play a large part in its country life. Every estate and every village has its Jew, who holds a sort of hereditary position in them; he markets the produce of the peasants and makes their purchases for them in town; every Polish landowner or noble had his own Jew, who did all his business for him, managed the commercial part of his estate, and found him money . . . Besides this, nearly all the population of nearly all the small country towns is Jewish, corn and leather dealers, storekeepers and peddlers, and such like."

(c) Regarding Sir Stuart's assertion that "Jews form the middle class almost to its entirety," with the nobles above them and the peasants beneath them (a typical Jewish position—dividing Gentile society and standing between the parts), this illustration may help to make it clear:

CAPTAIN P. WRIGHT—"It is instructive to try and imagine what England would be like under the same conditions. Arriving in London, a stranger would find every second or third person a Jew, almost all the poorer quarters and slums Jewish, and thousands of synagogues. Arriving at Newbury he would find practically the whole town Jewish, and nearly every printed inscription in Hebrew characters.

"Penetrating into Berkshire, he would find the only storekeeper in most small villages a Jew, and small market towns mostly composed of Jewish hovels. Going on to Birmingham he would find all the factories owned by Jews, and two shops out of three with Jewish names."

Why the Jews Dislike the Morgenthau Report

Captain Wright is trying to give the people at home a picture of conditions in order that they may understand how Poland feels. The Jewish press strongly resented this. Sir Stuart Samuel's report is notable for the number of things he mentioned, and the few he explained.

3. ON THE GENERAL CAUSE OF TROUBLE ARISING DURING THE WAR.

SIR STUART SAMUEL—"The fact of their language being akin to German often led to their being employed during the German occupation in preference to other Poles. This circumstance caused the Jews to be accused of having had business relations with the Germans . . . The Government publicly declared its disapproval of boycotting, but a certain discrimination seems to have been made in the re-employment of those who served under the German occupation. I find that many Jews who thus served have been relieved of their offices and not reinstated, whereas I can find no evidence of similar procedure in regard to other Poles."

SIR H. RUMBOLD—"The fact of Yiddish being akin to German may have been the reason why the Germans employed a large number of Jews during their occupation of Poland, although a great many of the Poles with a good knowledge of German could have been found. There is this difference, however, that the Poles only served the Germans by compulsion, as they considered them to be their enemies."

BRIGADIER GENERAL JADWIN—"During the German occupation of Poland, the Germanic character of the Yiddish vernacular and the readiness of certain Jewish elements to enter into relations with the winning side, induced the enemy to employ Jews as agents for various purposes and to grant the Jewish population not only exceptional protection, but also the promise of autonomy. It is alleged that the Jews were active in speculation in foodstuffs, which was encouraged by the armies of occupation with a view to facilitating export to Germany and Austria." That is, the Jews were the means by which Poland was to be drained of its food supply.

CAPTAIN P. WRIGHT—"But the high day and triumph of the Jews was during the German occupation. The Jews in Poland are deeply Germanized, and German carries you over Poland because Jews are everywhere. So the Germans found everywhere people who knew their language and could work for them. It was with Jews that the Germans set up their organization to squeeze and drain Poland—Poles and Jews included—of everything it had; it was in concert with Jews that German officials and officers toward the end carried on business all over the country. In every department and region they were the instruments of the Germans, and poor Jews grew rich and lordly as the servants of the masters. But though Germanized, the accusation of the Poles that the Jews are devoted to Germany is unfounded . . . They have no more loyalty to Germany—the home of anti-Semitism—than to Poland. The East Jews are Jews and only Jews.

"It has seemed certain that one of two, the German or the Russian Empire, must win, and that the Jews, who had their money on both, were safe; but the despised Poland came in first. Even now the Jews can hardly believe in its resurrection, and one of them told me it still seemed to him a dream."

Mr. Morgenthau does not touch this matter in his report.

4. WITH REFERENCE TO THE BOYCOTT, THE METHOD BY WHICH THE POLES SOUGHT TO LIBERATE THEMSELVES FROM THE JEWISH STRANGLEHOLD.

SIR STUART SAMUEL—"This boycott dates from shortly after the by-election for the Duma, which took place in Warsaw in 1912 . . .

During the war, owing to the scarcity of almost everything, the boycott diminished, but with the armistice it revived with much of its original intensity . . . A severe private, social and commercial boycott of Jews, however, exists among the people generally, largely fostered by the Polish press. In Lemburg I found there was a so-called social court presided over by M. Przyluski, a former Austrian vice-president of the Court of Appeals, which goes so far as to summon persons having trade relations with Jews to give an explanation of their conduct. Below will be found a typical cutting from a Polish newspaper giving the name of a Polish countess who sold property to Jews. This was surrounded by a mourning border such as is usual in Poland in making announcements of death.

(Translation) "Countess Anna Jablonowska, resident in Galicia, has sold her two houses, Stryjska street, Nos. 18 and 20, to the Jews, Dogilewski, Hubner and Erbsen. The attorney of the countess was Dr. Dziedzic; her administrator, M. Naszkowski. Will the Polish public forever remain indifferent and passive in such cases?"

This illustration of Sir Stuart brings to mind a practice common in England. It is related on page 123 of "The Conquering Jew" by John Foster Fraser, published by Funk & Wagnalls, New York, 1916: "The housing question in the Whitechapel district has reached such a pitch that there are large blocks of buildings where 'No English Need Apply' is a common legend. Whole streets are being bought up by Hebrew syndicates, whose first act is to serve notice on all Gentile tenants."

It is also worth stating in this connection, that some of the feeling which has recently led to race riots in American cities has been engendered by the practice of small Jewish real estate syndicates purchasing a house in the middle of a desirable block, ousting the tenants and installing a Negro family, thereby using race prejudice to depreciate the property in the entire block and render it purchasable by the Jews at a low price. Thereafter, the property is lost to Gentile ownership or use.

It may be that in Poland a similar condition exists which makes the sale of property into Jewish hands a kind of disloyalty to the people generally. Apparently the Poles think so. "Racial prejudice" is not a sufficient explanation of such beliefs: there is always something pretty tangible beneath them.

The "boycott" was merely this:—an agreement among Poles to trade with Poles. The Jews were numerous, well-to-do, and in control of all the channels of business. They own practically all the real estate in Warsaw. The Jews claimed that the so-called boycott (the Polish name for it is "the co-operatives") was "persecution."

SIR H. RUMBOLD—"It must be further remembered that under the influence of economic changes and owing to the fact that since 1832 the Poles have not been allowed to hold posts in the government, they were gradually obliged to take to trade, and competition between the Jewish population and the Poles commenced. This competition became stronger when the Russian Government allowed co-operative and agricultural societies to be started in Poland. The cooperative movement is becoming very strong and will undoubtedly form an important factor in the development of economic relations in Poland, so that indirectly it will be bound to affect the position of the small Jewish trader.

"In so far as the Polish Government are able to do so by legislation or proclamations, the boycotting of the Jews should be prohibited. But I would point out that it is beyond the power of any government to force its subjects to deal with persons with whom they do not wish to deal."

HENRY MORGENTHAU, however, takes a more reasonable view than his British co-religionist, Sir Stuart Samuel. Mr. Morgenthau says:

"Furthermore, the establishment of co-operative stores is claimed by many Jewish traders to be a form of discrimination. It would seem, however, that this movement is a legitimate effort to restrict the activities and therefore the profits of the middleman. Unfortunately, when these stores were introduced into Poland, they were advertised as a means of eliminating the Jewish trader. The Jews have, therefore, been caused to feel that the establishment of co-operatives is an attack upon themselves. While the establishment and the maintenance of co-operatives may have been influenced by anti-Semitic sentiment, this is a form of economic activity which any community is perfectly entitled to pursue."

It is not difficult, therefore, to see through the eyes and minds of these five men the situation that prevailed in Poland. Eight hundred years ago, Poland opened her gates to the persecuted Jews in all Europe. They flocked there and enjoyed complete freedom; they were even allowed to form a "state within a state," governing themselves in all Jewish matters and doing business with the Polish Government only through their own chosen spokesmen and representatives. The Polish people were their friends, evincing neither religious nor racial antipathy to them. Then Europe fell upon Poland, divided her asunder, until in the roster of the nations there was no more Poland, except in the hearts of the Polish people. During this period of Poland's humiliation, the Jews grew to be a mighty power, ruling the Poles, regulating their very lives. The Great War came with its promise of liberation and the restoration of a Polish free government. The Jews were not favorable to that restoration. They were not Poland's friends. The Poles resented this and at the signing of the armistice when they were free to express their resentment, they did so. Many regrettable things occurred, but they were not unintelligible. They had explanatory backgrounds. Even the armistice was not the end. The Bolsheviks from Russia came down upon Poland, and once more, so the Poles strongly declare, the Jews were against the land that had sheltered them for 800 years.

These are a few of the facts. Another article will be required to complete the story. In the meantime enough has been said to show the utter wrong which Jewish propaganda in the United States has done to Poland. But the purpose was not altogether to injure Poland; it was also to blind the American people, and cause them to view with equanimity the great influx of those same Jews into this country.

The Dearborn Independent, October 30, 1920

41. Jews Use the Peace Conference to Bind Poland

There is one difference between the Polish report of Sir Stuart Samuel and those of the others, which illustrates a difference between the Jewish mind and the general mind. The type of mind represented by the other investigators, Captain Wright, Brigadier General Jadwin, Sir H. Rumbold and even Henry Morgenthau is the type of mind which looks behind events for causes.

Here is, for illustration, trouble between the Jews and other people. It is a continuous situation. There is always trouble between the two. We seldom hear of it, however, until the Jew begins to get the worst of it. As long as the Jew remains on top, making the Gentile serve the Jewish plan, there is no publicity whatever. The Gentiles may complain as much as they like, may protest and rebel—no international commissions arrive to investigate the matter.

Trouble between the Jews and other people is designated as trouble only when it begins to grow inconvenient for the Jew. It is then that he sends the cry of "persecution" around the earth, though the plain fact may be that he is only being nipped at his own game. The Poles saw how the Jews clung together in the most admirable teamwork, a minority absolutely controlling the majority because the minority formed a close corporation and the majority did not. So the Poles said: "We will take a leaf out of the Jews' own book. They work co-operatively among themselves; we, therefore, will work co-operatively among ourselves." Which they did, and at once the cry of "persecution" resounded loud and long; propaganda was begun against the good name of the Poles, more resentment followed, regrettable violence ensued, and the dispute still continues.

Jewish reports of these disturbances rarely go beyond the fact that Jews are suffering from certain acts of the Polish populace. Incident after incident is given with full detail, and with a very apparent journalistic appreciation of horror. Names, dates, places, circumstances are all in order. Very well. It is no part of this article to deny or minimize the suffering of Jews wherever or for whatever cause it may occur. There is nothing whatever to be said in extenuation of injustice inflicted on the humblest human being. The murder of even one person, the terrorizing of even one family, is a very terrible thing to contemplate. It is a great pity that the world has become so accustomed to the piled-up tales of horror that it no longer has any sensibilities left to feel the shame and degradation of these things. From the days of Belgium onward, all races in Europe have suffered, and by sympathy all races in America have suffered with them, though it is a fact that we hear more, far more, about the sufferings of the Jews than of any other people.

There is, however, this reaction of the practical mind: Why do these things occur? Grant that robberies, assaults and murders described in the complaint, have occurred, why should they occur?

Are the Polish people naturally given to perpetrating such acts? Have such acts marked the residence of the Jews in Poland for the last 800 years? And if the Polish people are not naturally abusive, if the story of the Jews' residence in Poland has been mostly pleasant, what causes the change now?—that is the way the practical mind works. It seeks to know the background.

Mr. Morgenthau, apparently, put in too much of this background, though at that he put in very much less than the other investigators, except Mr. Samuel. Therefore, Mr. Morgenthau's report was pigeonholed by American Jewry, because the facts make very poor material for the kind of propaganda which American Jewish leaders had in mind. Apparently they did not dare publicly to criticize or renounce his report; they simply passed it over. Captain Wright, who endeavored to put in all the background he could find to make Polish conditions comprehensible to the British people, has been handled insultingly by the Jewish press. They don't want investigation. They want sympathy for themselves and denunciation for the Poles.

In America, we are inclined to believe that every condition is explainable: it may be reprehensible, but it is intelligible; we believe that the explanation is the first step toward the remedy.

Mr. Morgenthau does not speak of "pogroms" at all. In this he sets an example that certain hysterical American Jews ought to follow. The present series of articles in *The Dearborn Independent* is a "pogrom" (some Jewish spokesmen speak as if each separate article were a "pogrom") in the hectic but uninstructive oratory of Hebrew lodge meetings. But Mr. Morgenthau exercises more precision in the use of words, He says:

Jews Use the Peace Conference to Bind Poland

"The mission has purposely avoided the use of the word 'pogrom,' as the word is applied to everything from petty outrages to premeditated and carefully organized massacres . . . "

On one point all the reports agree, namely, that the unjust killing of Jews has been on a scale so much smaller than that alleged by the propagandists that there is no comparison. In that part of Poland where war disorder was less common, 18 persons were unjustly deprived of their lives.

For the whole territory during the entire period when it was being overrun by various elements, Sir Stuart Samuel admits, apparently with reluctance, that he can count only 348.

Captain Wright says: "I estimate that not more than 200 or 300 have been unjustly killed. One would be too many, but, taking these casualties as a standard with which to measure the excesses committed against them, I am more astonished at their smallness than their greatness." Sir H. Rumbold says: "If the excesses had been encouraged or organized by the civil and military authorities, the number of victims would probably have been much greater."

That the reader may see how the various reports run with reference to specific charges of brutality, the agreements and divergences are set down. Look at the reports concerning what happened at Lemberg.

1. The excesses occurred November 21–23, 1918. The city was taken by Ukrainian troops, formerly in the Austrian service. (Samuel, Morgenthau, Wright, Jadwin.)

2. "General Monczyunski raised a Polish army, about 1,500 in number, consisting of men, women, boys, some of them criminals, and, after a severe struggle, succeeded in capturing half the city, the other half of which remained in the occupation of the Ukrainians." (Samuel.) "A few hundred Polish boys, combined with numerous volunteers of doubtful character, recaptured about half the city and held it until the arrival of Polish reinforcements on November 21." (Morgenthau.)

"When the German troops revolted all over Poland at the time of the armistice, and the whole edifice of German organization fell to the ground in a day, a few Polish officers raised a small volunteer force in Lemberg, numbering between 1,000 and 2,000, which was composed of boys, roughs and criminals, and even women in uniform. For nearly a fortnight they fought in the streets against the Ukrainians and on the arrival of a similar force . . . drove the Ukrainians out of town. This was really a splendid feat of arms." (Captain Wright.)

3. "The Jewish part of the population of Lemberg declared itself to be neutral." (Samuel.)

"The Jewish population declared themselves neutral, but the fact that the Jewish quarter lay within the section occupied by the Ukrainians, and that the Jews had organized their own militia and, further, the rumor that some of the Jewish population had fired upon the soldiery, stimulated among the Polish volunteers an anti-Semitic bias that readily communicated itself to the relieving troops." (Morgenthau.)

"During the struggle the Jews proclaimed themselves neutral; but, though I do not think they gave any armed assistance to the Ukrainians, their neutrality was highly benevolent to the Ukrainians and probably helpful. They thought the Ukrainians would win." (Captain Wright.)

4. "In the result none of the military commanders responsible for these events has been punished." (Samuel.) "As early as December 24, 1918, the Polish Government, through the ministry of justice, began a strict investigation of the events of November 21 and 23 . . . In spite of the crowded dockets of the local courts, where over 7,000 cases are now pending, 164 persons, ten of them Jews, have been tried for complicity in the November disorders, and numerous similar cases await disposal. Forty-four persons are under sentences ranging from 10 days to 18 months. Aside from the civil courts, the local court-martial has sentenced military persons to confinement for as long as three years for lawlessness during the period in question." (Morgenthau.) Speaking of the general subject of punishment, Captain Wright says: "The Government has inflicted a good deal, though an insufficient amount of punishment; these punishments it has never published, for fear of Polish public opinion." And Brigadier General Jadwin, of the United States Mission, says: "If complaints as to slowness and uncertainty of military and government punishments and relief were heard, as they were, it seemed nevertheless to indicate that orderly process of government was in operation."

5. "No compensation has been paid for the damage done." (Samuel.)

"This mission is advised that on the basis of official investigations the government has begun the payment of claims for damages resulting from these events." (Morgenthau.)

"Payments had begun to be made in Wilna, Pinsk and Lemberg before our departure from Poland." (General Jadwin.)

The occurrences in Lemberg were bad enough, to be sure. But Sir Stuart Samuel let it be understood that all the blame rested with the

Jews Use the Peace Conference to Bind Poland

Poles. The other investigators gave reports that explain the matter, although no report could excuse it. And all but Samuel agreed that the Polish Government did what it could to repair what had occurred and to prevent recurrences. This from the American report is worth considering: "General Jadwin was present at the taking of Minsk and a personal witness of the strenuous efforts of the military authorities toward preventing acts of violence." The fact seems to be that as soon as any sort of order could be brought out of the chaos of war, the disorder ceased. And yet we read, even today in our newspapers, of "thousands and tens of thousands of Jews being slaughtered in Poland."

Further, to indicate that these events did not occur without Jewish provocation to a certain extent, there is the case in Pinsk. This was on April 5, 1919.

1. Pinsk had been recaptured from the Bolsheviki a short time before. The population was overwhelmingly Jewish, only 25 per cent being Polish. (General Jadwin, Captain Wright.) The Polish officer had only a very small detachment of men, and the Bolshevist lines were quite close. The Polish officer was treated with coldness by the Jews, and he suspected them of friendly relations with the Bolsheviki; he was very anxious. He had posted notices that any unauthorized meeting would be punishable by death. (Captain Wright.)

2. The Government Organizer of Co-operative societies had given permission for the Jewish co-operatives to meet for discussion of the plan to join other co-operatives. (Samuel, Morgenthau, Wright.)

3. "It seems that two Polish soldiers . . . and another soldier . . . informed the military authorities that they had information that the Jews intended to hold a Bolshevik meeting on Saturday in what is known as the People's House, being the headquarters of the Zionists." (Samuel.) "This meeting took place in the offices of the Zionist organization, which is very anti-Polish." (Wright.)

". . . it is recognized that information of Bolshevist activities in Pinsk had been received by two Jewish soldiers . . . " (Morgenthau.)

"The town commander with judgement unbalanced by fear of the Bolshevik uprising of which he had been forewarned by two Jewish soldier informers . . . " (General Jadwin.)

"After the meeting had ended and been formally closed, a great many members of the co-operative association remained in the same room talking together; other members of the Zionist organization, including ladies, were in the room at the same time. This collection of people must have presented the appearance of a meeting, and I think the members remaining in one room were numerous enough technically to constitute a meeting. There was some insolence in this and the previous behavior of the Jews: Sir Stuart Samuel pointed out to the witnesses that their authorized meeting itself had been a breach of the Sabbath, and therefore a grave religious offense." (Captain Wright.)

All of the investigators agree in denouncing what followed. Captain Wright says the Polish officer would hardly have acted with such promptitude if the prisoners had been others than Jews.

General Jadwin sums it up thus: "The Pinsk outrage . . . was a purely military affair. The town commander with judgement unbalanced by fear of a Bolshevik uprising of which he had been forewarned by two Jewish soldier informers sought to terrorize the Jewish population (about 75 per cent of the whole) by the execution of 35 Jewish citizens without investigation or trial, by imprisoning and beating others and by wholesale threats against all Jews. No share in this action can be attributed to any military official higher up, to any of the Polish civil officials, nor to the few Poles resident in that district of White Russia."

Sir Stuart says: "Under the present local administration Pinsk is once more peaceful, and the relations between the Christian and non-Christian inhabitants have become normal."

It is sometimes forgotten here in the United States that for Poland the war is not yet over. Poland is now a free nation—on paper—but her freedom seems to be a day-by-day tenure, dependent on fighting. Bolshevism made serious inroads on her. Wherever the Bolshevik Red armies swept across Poland, the Jews met them with welcomes. This is no longer denied, even in the United States: it is explained by the statement that the Bolsheviki are more friendly to the Jews than are the Poles—a statement which readers of our recent articles on the Jewish character of Sovietism can well understand.

When the Poles beat back the Reds, they commonly found that the Jews had already set up Sovietism, as if they had long awaited it and were well prepared. It is scarcely strange, therefore, that the Poles still retain their suspicions.

The Jews do not want to become Poles. That is the root of the present difficulty between the two peoples. Sir Stuart Samuel barely touches it—"On several occasions the resentment of the soldiery and civil population was aroused by the Zionists' claim to Jewish nationality as opposed to Polish nationality." Mr. Morgenthau goes a step further—

Jews Use the Peace Conference to Bind Poland

"This had led to a conflict with the nationalist declarations of some of the Jewish organizations which desire to establish cultural autonomy financially supported by the State." Mr. Morgenthau, you will observe, gives a wider peep into conditions.

But the best description of the situation is given in the report of Captain Wright: "Their (the Jews') party program in Poland is to have all Jews on a separate register. The Jews thus registered are to elect a representative body of Jews, with extensive powers of legislation and taxation; e. g., it could tax for purposes of emigration. This body to be handed over by the Polish State a proportionate amount of money to spend on Jewish charitable and financial institutions.

Besides this separate organization, a number of seats proportionate to their numbers to be set aside in every local and in the national legislature. A sixth or seventh of the Polish Diet to be occupied only by Jews to be elected only by Jews. Some Jews also demand separate law courts, or at least the right to use Yiddish as well as Polish in legal proceedings.

This is the practical program, but the ambition of the advanced section is national personal autonomy granted in the Ukraine by one of the ephemeral governments of the Ukraine, the Ukrainian Central Rada, on January 9, 1918, and called the Statute of National Personal Autonomy, of which I have a copy. It organizes Jews as a nation with full sovereign powers; the Ukrainian bank notes were printed in Yiddish as well as in Ukrainian."

People sometimes ask, where is proof of the program of the Protocols? It is everywhere the Jewish leaders have attained power, and everywhere they are striving for power.

The Protocols can be written out of Jewish rabbinical writings; they can be written out of Jewish tendencies in the United States; they can be written out of Jewish demands in the Balkans; they can be written out of Jewish achievements in Russia. They represent the Jewish program, ideal and real, at every stage of modern history.

Do you ever hear of this Jewish program in Poland when you are invited to sympathize with 250,000 Jews who are being brought from Poland to the United States? Will these people leave their ideas outside New York harbor?

Incidentally, Captain Wright's full investigation of the Jewish program may throw some light on the refusal of the American Jews to circulate his report, although it was attached to the report of Sir Stuart Samuel, which is being so widely circulated. However, that his government at home might fully understand the situation, Captain Wright draws an illustrative parallel:

"If the Jews in England—after multiplying their numbers by twenty or thirty—demanded that the Jewish Board of Guardians should have extensive powers, including the right to tax for purposes of emigration, and that a separate number of seats should be set aside in the London County Council, the Manchester Town Council, the House of Commons, and the House of Lords, to be occupied only by Jews chosen by Jews; that the president of the board of education should hand over yearly to the Jews sums proportionate to their numbers; if some were to demand the right to have separate Jewish law courts, or at least to be allowed to use Yiddish as well as English in the King's Bench and Chancery Division; if the most advanced even looked forward to a time when the Bank of England notes were to be printed in Yiddish as well as in English, then they might well find public opinion, even in England, less well disposed to them . . . "

In view of this state of affairs, it cannot be regarded as a fact of minor significance that the Jewish investigators who must have known all this virtually concealed it, and that the other investigators brought it forth to general knowledge. Neither is it of minor significance that the Jewish press has absolutely suppressed these facts even while pretending to give the results of the British Mission's investigations. Insulting references have been made to Captain Wright's report in a Jewish publication of the better class, because he made references to certain practices which are common among the Jews in Poland. It may be said, however, that the references made by Captain Wright are in great restraint compared with the number given in the recent book by Arthur Goodhart. Whether Mr. Goodhart is a Jew or not, the present writer cannot now say. He is a Fellow of Corpus Christi College, Cambridge. He is "lately Captain, United States Army." He was transferred from the army at the suggestion of Mr. Morgenthau, to act as counsel for the Mission. And he says on page 161, "After dinner Mr. Morgenthau attended a meeting of the B'nai B'rith Lodge, the only chapter of this Jewish organization in Poland. No branches had been permitted in Russia before the war, as it was a secret society and therefore illegal in the Czar's Empire. Major Otto and I, not being members, walked round the town." Mr. Goodhart, as counsel of the American mission, makes an excellent witness as to the kind of people who are coming in such large numbers to this country. But their

Jews Use the Peace Conference to Bind Poland

sense of their own political importance and power is the principal point for Americans to consider.

The Peace Conference did not tend to bring unity in Poland; it rather established the disunity for as long a period as the treaty of Versailles remains to rule the world. The reader has just seen Captain Wright's description of what the Jews demanded. Let the reader now understand what the Peace Conference decreed.

Poland is prohibited from having an election on Saturday. Poland is prohibited from having a registration on Saturday. The Jewish Sabbath is established by law, and government and courts must govern themselves accordingly. Do what you like on Sunday—order elections on Sunday, as the Poles sometimes do—but not on Saturday; it is the Jews' Sabbath!

"Article 11—Jews shall not be compelled to perform any act which constitutes a violation of their Sabbath, nor shall they be placed under any disability by reason of their refusal to attend courts of law or to perform any legal business on their Sabbath . . . Poland declares her intention to refrain from ordering or permitting elections, whether general or local, to be held on a Saturday, nor will registration for electoral or other purposes be compelled to be performed on a Saturday."

What the Bolsheviki did in Russia, the Peace Conference did in Poland—established the Jewish Sabbath.

The people who saw this strange setting up of Jewish customs as a part of the law of the land, one of the authorities for such action being the President of the United States, are now flocking to the United States in large numbers. Is it unreasonable for them to believe that if the President of the United States could bind Poland to Jewish custom, it is all right to bind the United States too?

Moreover, the Jewish separate schools were established by law in Poland. Poland's great trouble has resulted from her lack of schools in which all the population could imbibe Polish ideals expressed in the Polish language. The Peace Conference authorizes the continuance of that source of trouble.

In Article 11, "the Jews" were mentioned. In Article 9, the term used is "Polish nationals." The reader will save himself a great deal of misunderstanding in the perusal of European news if he will translate the clause "racial, religious and linguistic minorities" to mean simply Jews. They are the "minority" that is at the bottom of most of the difficulty, and they are the minority that is most heard of. It was this minority that dominated the Peace Conference.

"Article 9—Poland will provide in the educational system in towns and districts in which a considerable proportion of Polish nationals of other than Polish speech are residents, adequate facilities for insuring that in the primary schools instruction shall be given to the children of such Polish nationals through the medium of their own language . . .

"In towns and districts where there is a considerable proportion of Polish nationals belonging to racial, linguistic or religious minorities, these minorities shall be assured an equitable share in the enjoyment and application of the sums which may be provided out of public funds under the state, municipal or other budgets for education, religious or charitable purposes."

But even that is not all. The Polish State is to hand over the money, but the Jews will distribute it:

"Educational committees appointed locally by the Jewish communities of Poland will, subject to the general control of the state, provide for the distribution of the proportional share of the funds allocated to Jewish schools in accordance with Article 9 . . . "

It is most amazing how "racial minorities" are dropped the moment money comes into view, and the definite term "Jew" is substituted.

More than all this, "the United States of America, the British Empire, France, Italy, and Japan, the principal allied and associated powers, on the one hand; and Poland, on the other hand," (so the text of the treaty begins) together make of all these special privileges, not a national agreement on the part of hard-pressed Poland, but an international demand on the part of the League of Nations. Article 12 stipulates that all the agreements affecting "racial, linguistic and religious minorities," which is mere diplomatic camouflage for "Jews," shall be placed under the guaranty of the League of Nations. This lifts the Jews in Poland completely out of Polish obligation. All they will have to do is complain to the League of Nations—and International Jewry will do the rest.

The United States was a party toward the writing of these stipulations into the treaty. The American people are not yet a party to their enforcement.

There are a quarter of a million of these Jews coming to the United States from Poland. You have read their demands in Poland. You have read their achievements in the Peace Conference.

Do you say, as an American citizen, that you are ready to take for the United States the dose of Jewish medicine, which the Peace Conference gave to Poland?

Jews Use the Peace Conference to Bind Poland

Do you say, in view of what has been said about the whole situation, that the Jews are showing anything besides a wicked and gloating spirit of revenge in the way they have propagandized against Poland after humiliating her in the Peace Conference?

The Dearborn Independent, November 6, 1920

42. The Present Status of the Jewish Question

The Jewish Question in the United States has existed for years, but until now in silence and suspicion. Everyone knew that there was such a Question; the Jew himself knew best of all; but very few possessed the courage to open the Question to the sanitary influences of sunlight and speech. The mention of courage in this connection is needful to explain the silence. A few men of insight have attempted publicly to define the Question in the United States, and they have been so effectually dealt with by an invisible power of which the public could have no knowledge, that Free Speech on the Jewish Question naturally became unpopular. The fact, it is true, reflects far more seriously on non-Jews than on Jews. But it is a fact nevertheless. He who undertakes to speak truth on this question must expect far more opposition than he could ever withstand were he not speaking the truth.

One fact that militated against Free Speech on the Jewish Question was the condition into which our American people have been trained, of expecting applause and approval to follow every act and word. There was a time in American history, and it was the most glorious period of out past, when opposition was considered an often desirable attitude. A man's weight was accounted equal, whether computed by the number of his enemies or his friends.

But a softening change has come over us. We have grown to like applause. Hisses used to stir our fathers; hisses cow their sons. Public speech has thus grown flabby; the Press has thus become neutral; we have grown pudgy and futile in our program of "helping the weak," so pudgy and futile that we no longer have gristle to attack the strong who have brought weakness upon the others.

As a people, we have passed the "bunk" around so habitually; we have enervated our judgement and moral convictions so seriously by our fake "philosophy of Boost," we have become so accustomed to measure the effectiveness of work by the applause it immediately provokes, that we have lost all stomach for courses that call for contest, unless it be those spurious contests of the political arena, which are all managed from the same Great Headquarters, or those verbal assaults against "Big

Business," which bring no reaction. We have lost all taste for tangible foes who have a ready retaliation.

Nevertheless it is true that, whereas a year ago it was not possible to speak the word "Jew" in the United States, it is now possible. The name appears on the front page of every newspaper nearly every day. It is the subject of discussion everywhere. For the time at least, speech has been liberated, although our friends of the B'nai B'rith in every state are doing their best to throttle it.

This freedom is of benefit both to Jew and non-Jew. The Jew need no longer look askance at the name of his race on the lips of the non-Jew. It only means that suppression and deceit are past, that is all; the Jew is a Jew, is recognized as a Jew, is spoken of as a Jew; and thus an honest relation between the mind and the fact is established in both the Jew and the non-Jew. The air is cleared. Concealment on the one hand is done away; on the other hand a missing fact, whose absence meant confusion, is supplied. The Jew may now say, "I am a Jew," as casually as any other man might claim his race. We may even see some noted Americans who all their lives have tried to conceal their race, come forward now and say, "We are Jews." It is freedom to the Jew; it is interpretation to the non-Jew. Half the confusion which men meet in their efforts to account for the world is due to their ignorance of just where the Jew is. He is always a key. But if the key be disguised as something else, how can it be used?

About eight months ago *The Dearborn Independent* began a series of studies on the Jewish Question. It was an attempt to state the facts on which the Question is based. It was not at its beginning, nor has it since developed into, an attack on Jews as Jews. Its purpose was enlightenment, and if it secretly indulged a hope, it was this—that the leaders of American Jewry might be wise to see that this is the country and this is the time in which the causes of distress and distrust and disrepute might be removed from Jewry and a genuine modus operandi, not of toleration, but of reconciliation, arrived at.

The proof that these articles have contained facts and only facts is found in the failure of the Jewish spokesmen to show any one of them to be false. The record stands that way—not one disproof. The reason for the record is this: when only facts are sought and are subjected to the tests, only facts are found. If, however, one embarks on a "campaign" whose purpose is to besmirch an opponent or create a prejudice, one's partisan zeal may induce him to accept as facts what is merely probability. These articles, however, do not constitute a campaign. They are the lighting of lamps here and there about the country, in this industry and that, in corners heretofore kept dark by those who should serve more faithfully on the watchtower of the Press.

What *The Dearborn Independent* has said could have had no weight at all, had not the people been able to see the same facts all about them. It is not information, but illumination, that has given these articles the importance they have found among hundreds of thousands of readers.

The Jewish response to these articles has in one way been gratifying, and in another way quite disappointing.

The Jewish response has been gratifying in that it has furnished substantial proof of all the statements made in *The Dearborn Independent*. This journal has no doubt of the truth of its statements, and is possessed of a very substantial reserve of evidence, but none the less the corroborative evidence produced by the Jewish leaders themselves in endeavoring to meet the issue is appreciated. There is no reason to believe that this was an intentional contribution on the part of Jewish leaders; it was simply impossible for them to move without revealing further evidence.

It is quite well known what is the position of Jewish leaders today: it is one of fear. For once they themselves are possessed with the fear of the unknown. Knowing how much of truth exists behind the statements made in this series, they are in fear of what may yet come forth. They do not even make any more pretense of considering it a joke; in their own conclaves they do not rave and roar like the rabbinical editors, they behave themselves like sober frightened men, who sometimes have a desire to own up to some of the things that have been charged, but who are halted by a doubt as to how far the owning-up process would lead them if once begun. They are in fear of the truth, but mostly of the whole truth.

Needless to say a responsibility rests also on those who hold the whole truth. The purpose determines everything. If the purpose is to breed hatred of the Jews, that involves one course of action. If the purpose is to excite the public mind with startling facts, that involves another course of action. There is a certain danger in certain kinds of information. If the purpose is to lay a basis for intelligent, straightforward understanding and possible solution of the question, then such information as defines the question and presents all essential material, is all that is necessary. It is within these limits that this series has endeavored to keep. If there are facts which are unfavorable to the Jews, that is a matter for the Jews. If the Jews do despite to a certain class of facts, it may be necessary to produce still another class of facts. If the leaders of the Jews had been fair, just argumentatively, oppositionally fair, they would not now be in fear of what may yet be produced.

Jews, for illustration, have proved the statement that they are the best organized people in the United States. They have proved that they are more closely grouped together in their own national interest than are the citizens of the United States whose whole nationality is defined by their citizenship. The government of the United States itself is not so well organized as American Jewry—and that fact is not due to anything American; it is the same in every country. Telegraphic speed and instantaneous mass action have marked every move organized Jewry has made in this country in the last six months.

It is not for nothing that they control the avenues of communication in this country. It is not for nothing that the wireless of the world is under ironclad Jewish control. They are not loosely organized in social lodges for occasional fellowship; they are organized as states of the Jewish people, with officials who do nothing whatever but attend to the advancement of Jewish power in this and other countries. They have proved by the mass play of their synagogues, their newspapers, their alleged "social" organizations, their conservative clubs and their Bolshevik-Socialist groups—all of them working together, under orders—that they are a separate people within the American people, a people that do not agree with the genius of the American people, and a people that constantly make distinction between Jewish and American rights.

In every state, in every city, there is a Jewish organization with a definite policy, and the first policy is to suffocate, destroy, put the "fear of the Jew" upon any man, newspaper, or institution that gives the least indication of independent thought on the Jewish Question. These organizations have special committees to do certain work. One of these works is to start "a whispering drive" against the person or institution aimed at. This "whispering drive" is a most hideous oriental device; it can be sustained only by groups of minds which bear a certain racial twist.

Without giving a full description of the devices used, it can be seen that the fact of their being centrally controlled and working simultaneously in all parts of the country, creates a considerable force. No other institution now operating in the United States can accomplish that so quickly and unitedly.

Jewish solidarity would be above criticism were it used for the benefit of the whole communal life, but it is not; it is not only Jewish, but its operations show it to be largely anti-American. This does not mean anti-American in the sense of being pro-German or pro-Mexican, but in this sense, that it opposes many things that have been conceded to constitute the American tradition. The Jew assumes that the United States is still an unformed entity which is fair prey to any who can seize it and mold it. That is his attitude today. He refuses to assume that America is here; he adopts the belief that part of his duty is to bring America into being, on Jewish lines, of course.

Now, in a sense, the United States is private property. It is the property of those who share the ideals of the founders of the government. And those ideals were ideals held by a white race of Europeans. They were fundamentally Christian ideals. And with most of these the Jews not only disagree, but hold them in contempt. Indeed, a Jewish leader recently said in New York that the United States was not a Christian land, and the context of his statement showed that he clearly intended that it should never be. He was condemning the Christian Sunday, though he is an officer of a society whose purpose is the establishment of the Mosaic Sabbath.

The Jews have also proved the charge that they exercise disproportionate influence in governmental affairs. This charge has only been stated in this series. The mass of proof has not yet been brought to bear. But it exists, fixed beyond all change. However, another important bit of evidence has been transpiring before the country's eyes. When the immigration bill was first put up to Congress, the vote was overwhelmingly in favor of restricting entry into the country. Congress voted upon the facts and its patriotic convictions. Taking the question just as it was, no other verdict could have been given.

Hardly had the vote been taken, however, than the wires were hot and the trains crowded and Jewish protests and Jewish agents began flocking to Washington. The magic name Jew was uttered. Legislators fled to cover. Learned speeches were made. Compromises were suggested. Modifications of the original law were framed. Under the magic of Jew the whole proposal simply melted like an icicle before a fire.

The only protest made against that Congressional vote was made by Jews. Their wonderful teamwork in all parts of the county gave their

The Present Status of the Jewish Question

protest the air of national importance. BUT there was one point the Jews were not able this year to deny, and that is that the majority of the immigrants are Jews. That fact, fortunately, was established beforehand. The hand of the Congress of the United States was stayed by the Jews in a matter of serious importance to national protection, just as a few years ago the hand of the Congress of the United States was forced to break the treaty with Russia when President Taft held it would be wrong to break it.

This proof of political power, based on nothing but sheer force and sheer determination to have what they want regardless of what the United States wants, has appeared broadcast as a matter of public knowledge.

And let the reader mark this: it will be found that this present immigration move is as much a part of the Jewish World Program as was the breaking of the treaty with Russia. Readers of the article of January 15 will recall how at the behest of the Jews, the United States' trade with Russia was thrown into the hands of German Jews who were using it to further their plans for the destruction of the Russian Empire, which later came to pass. The Jews "used" the United States to put across an essential part of that plan.

Well, what are they using the United States for now? We may well believe that the Jews are not without several reasons for what they are doing. The Jew excels as a chess player because he plays a game wherever he may be. The immigration matter amounts to this: Jews are streaming out of Poland as speedily as they can. It is not "pogroms" that are driving them out. "Pogroms" have been proved to be immigration propaganda for consumption outside Poland.

The Jews are leaving Poland because they know something is going to happen. And if they are leaving Poland it is a sign it is going to happen to Poland. And if the Jews have advance news of it, it is a sign that what will occur will be inflicted by Jews.

Plainly it is this: Jewish Bolshevism in Russia has made a secret decree against Poland. The Jews are getting out of the way. American Jewish agents are constantly passing into Poland. Rich American Jews are sending agents to bring back groups of "relatives." There is an exodus from Poland and there is a reason for it which spells trouble for Poland. The United States is being used as the chief means by which the Jews are to clear out. France protests against them and will not have them. England most decidedly refuses to have them. The Jews of the United

States are powerful enough to compel this country to take them. We are utilized to effect the entrance of Bolshevism into Russia; it went from our East Side thither. We are now being utilized to assist at the destruction of Poland. It is possible, however, that by the time the Jewish program reaches that point, something may have intervened.

The Jews of the United States have also given a splendid illustration of what *The Dearborn Independent* said of their control of American newspapers. Of course, the local newspaper editor is not dominated by any Jewish authority seated at Washington, New York, or Chicago, of course not; but he is very amendable to the twenty richest Jews in his community who advertise in his paper, and it is they who take orders from Washington, New York and Chicago. So the editor gets his orders from Jewish headquarters just the same, though he may not realize it.

This, however, is one instance where publicity does not count, because it represent a business favor oftener than it does an editorial conviction. The knowledge of the Jewish Question which newspaper men possess is quite complete, and a confidential council of the best informed editors of the United States would include all that the government or the people would need to know for a complete handling of the Jewish Question. The publicity demanded and received by the organized Jews has proved a roorback; it has served the cause of truth more than the cause they desired, which was suppression.

Gratifying as these proofs are to the producers of the facts, there is a very decided element of disappointment in the Jewish answers. Either Jewry is feinting, or is defenseless; certainly the present status of the defense must be humiliating to those who have any conception of the importance of the matter.

The answer signed by the Jews themselves—a list of signatures which showed as in panorama the close-locked corporational solidarity of the Jewish race in this country—was devoid of a single fact which threw light. In this, the Jewish answer was almost a confession of "no defense."

But aside from its ineptitude was the utter lack of frankness. It refuses to face the question. It will not meet a single statement, either in the substance of the Protocols or in the substance of this series. It veers off whenever it approaches a concrete theme, and loses itself in a vapor of denials. If a statement is wrong, it is provably wrong, especially a statement which deals with matters now actual in daily life.

The official Jewish answer, signed by a few, not all, of the Jewish leaders, is at least decent in its language, and that is more than can be said for most of the other Jewish answers. But it is indecent in its attempt to create the impression that anti-Semitism is abroad in the country.

Mark this: All the anti-Semitism that exists in the United States today is the deliberate creation of the Jewish leaders and is a recent creation.

The Jewish leaders want anti-Semitism here. Unable to create it among non-Jews, they are seeking the effects of it among the Jews by telling them that it exists.

The Jewish leaders of the United States have done everything possible to keep *The Dearborn Independent* away from the Jews, to prevent their reading it and learning the fact that *no attack is being made on Jews as Jews*.

From the first, after wrestling for weeks to discover a way of meeting these articles without having to confess too much, these leaders threw up their hands and took refuge in the lie of anti-Semitism.

What they ought to fear now is not the force of an anti-Semitic feeling among the non-Jews, but the force of a righteous indignation among American Jews when they discover the deceit and incompetence of their leaders.

"Anti-Semitism" has always been the last resort of scoundrelly Jewish leaders when cornered by the truth, and they have been known deliberately to incite it among the Gentile rabble in order through it to maintain their hold on their own people.

Recently there was printed in the newspapers "A Protest Against Anti-Semitism," signed by various non-Jews. The "protest" was printed twice, in fact, because it did not "go big" the first time. The newspapers were evidently growing a little weary of printing daily communiques from Jewish Great Headquarters. So, to give it more vim for a thorough circulation, the signature of Woodrow Wilson was obtained. And of course that put it on the telegraph wires again.

It was quite proper for President Wilson to sign a protest against anti-Semitism. It was quite proper for all the other signers to do so, provided that was what they meant to do.

If the protest had been sent to *The Dearborn Independent*, its responsible officials would have signed also. *The Dearborn Independent* is against anti-Semitism and protests against leading Jews using its name to foment that spirit.

The "protest," however innocent the signers may have been of this fact, was against any public discussion of the Jewish Question, and especially against this one.

The dispatches are careful to state that the Jews had nothing to do with that protest. A supposedly non-Jewish organization has been in the service of a coterie of New York Jews for a long time. The assertion that the "protest" was written by "a single citizen, a non-Jew, acting upon his own initiative and responsibility, and without consultation with anybody," is mildly amusing.

There was just enough "consultation" to make the whole "non-Jewish protest" nothing more nor less than a previously approved document, and the citizen who did the job has known for a long time where it pays to please.

As to Mr. John Spargo, whose name is beginning to appear prominently as a Gentile defender of the Jews, this much is known: he did not undertake the Jewish defense without several secret consultations with a group of New York Jews, who had to overcome several of Spargo's scruples before they could make much headway with him. Spargo's attitude was something like this: "Gentlemen, they've got it on you. It is not a matter that can be whitewashed." Spargo told a lot of truth in that New York room. The Jewish conferees knew it was truth. If Spargo should speak one-twentieth as much truth on the platform, his lecture engagements would dwindle in number.

All of the literature of the Anti-Defamation Society, all of the speech of the retained defenders, is very welcome. Open the Question up! If the Jews engage enough Gentile defenders, the time will come when Gentile logical faculties will bring about a real discussion of the Question. The Jewish spokesmen must, on pain of losing their position, limit themselves to denials, abuse and threats; but the Gentile defenders are constitutionally unable to dwell in that state of mind for long; they will probe through to the truth; in which event real discussion may be expected.

There is not a single Jewish publication, however vituperative and truthless, that we would forbid the mails or exclude from a public library. There is not a single Jewish spokesman whom we would heckle or hinder on the public platform. There is not a single Jewish enterprise that we would recommend for boycott. We believe in Free Speech and unfettered conviction. By means of these the people may yet hope to clean up the United States.

The Jews do not believe in Free Speech. They do not believe in a Free Press. In every state in the Union the B'nai B'rith is introducing into the local legislatures a bill that will prevent any publication from saying anything derogatory of the Jews. That is the Jews' answer to the facts produced in this publication.

In scores and hundreds of public libraries, the Jews are using the members of their race who happen to be on library boards, or are using committees of their race to influence library boards to clear the libraries of all books, pamphlets and papers that deal with the Jewish Question in a manner to leave any doubt that the Jews are paragons of virtue and The Chosen People.

This is occurring in the United States. It is occurring in some of those eastern American states that stood most valiantly for the cause of Free Speech and a Free Press in other days.

Let it go on! Multiply the instances! Add madness to madness! Each act of this nature simply gives a local proof, visible and intelligible to each community where it transpires, that what is written about the Jews is true.

The present status of the Jewish Question in the United States is this: A beginning has been made on the too-long accumulating facts. Jewish recognition of the truth has been expressed in soberness among the leaders. Jewish action in response has been, for themselves, denial; for others, SUPPRESSION.

The result to date is:—abject failure to meet the case.

The Dearborn Independent, January 29, 1921

CPSIA information can be obtained
at www.ICGtesting.com
Printed in the USA
BVOW08s0518201017
498039BV00001B/14/P